ADVERSARIAL LEGAL WRITING AND ORAL ARGUMENT

Michael D. Murray
University of Illinois College of Law

and

Christy Hallam DeSanctis
George Washington University Law School

FOUNDATION PRESS

2006

THOMSON

WEST

This publication was created to provide you with accurate and authoritative information concerning the subject matter covered; however, this publication was not necessarily prepared by persons licensed to practice law in a particular jurisdiction. The publisher is not engaged in rendering legal or other professional advice and this publication is not a substitute for the advice of an attorney. If you require legal or other expert advice, you should seek the services of a competent attorney or other professional.

Nothing contained herein is intended or written to be used for the purposes of 1) avoiding penalties imposed under the federal Internal Revenue Code, or 2) promoting, marketing or recommending to another party any transaction or matter addressed herein.

© 2006 By FOUNDATION PRESS
       395 Hudson Street
       New York, NY 10014
       Phone Toll Free 1–877–888–1330
       Fax (212) 367–6799
       foundation–press.com
Printed in the United States of America

ISBN–13: 978–1–58778–899–4
ISBN–10: 1–58778–899–3

TEXT IS PRINTED ON 10% POST CONSUMER RECYCLED PAPER

Acknowledgments

Many people have supported our efforts in writing this book over the last four years. The authors particularly want to thank Steve Errick at Foundation Press, for all of his efforts and for never giving up.

Several other people also are owed our gratitude for their unwavering support of our professional endeavors and participation in the process resulting in this book. Professor Murray would like to single out his research and teaching assistants: Lindsay Beyer, Brian George, Aaron Goldberg, and Maurice Holman at the University of Illinois College of Law, and Renee Auderer, Jeannie Bell, Jonathan Blitz, John Challis, and Katalin Raby at Saint Louis University School of Law; and the Saint Louis University School of Law students who allowed us to use their work as writing examples: Jeannie Bell, Kevin Etzkorn, Josh Knight, Kirsten Moder, Allison Price, Gaylin Rich, Jerrod Sharp, Katherine Weathers, and Cherie Wyatt. Special thanks also are due to Professor Murray's assistant at the University of Illinois, Deanna Shumard, whose support above and beyond the call of duty is remarkable and much appreciated.

Professor DeSanctis would like to recognize Kristen E. Murray, the Associate Director of the Legal Research and Writing program at George Washington University for her outstanding assistance running the program, friendship, unabashed humor, and superb insight on how to teach students to write well (what would I do without you?); Professor Lorri Unumb, the Director of Legal Writing at Charleston School of Law, and my predecessor at GW, for teaching me not only how to teach legal writing but also how to run a great program (and for being an inspiration); the 2004–2005 GW Law Dean's Fellows for their energy and unceasing desire to make teaching legal research and citation interesting, rewarding and fun; and the 2004–05 Writing Fellows at GW for their amazing talent as writing tutors and, in particular, their assistance with the Appendix on grammar rules.

The authors thank their legal research and writing colleagues who reviewed and commented on the text: Kenneth Chestek (University of Indiana–Indianapolis School of Law), Jane Ginsburg (Columbia Law School); Terri LeClercq (University of Texas School of Law); Pamela Lysaght (University of Detroit Mercy School of Law); Joanna Mossop (Columbia Law School); Kristen Murray (George Washington University Law School); Suzanne Rowe (University of Oregon School of Law); Ann Davis Shields (Washington University School of Law); Judith Smith (Columbia Law School); Mark Wojcik (John Marshall Law School); and Cliff Zimmerman (Northwestern University School of Law). This book is the better for their kind and generous review and input.

Professor Murray also thanks his friends and former colleagues at Saint Louis University School of Law who encouraged and supported him, especially Donald King, Alan Weinberger, Ann Cronin, Carol Needham, and Pete Salsich, and his friends and colleagues at the University of Illinois College of Law, especially Shannon Moritz, Amy Gajda, Tom Ginsburg, Heidi Hurd, Richard Kaplan, Jay Kesan, Andy Leipold, George

Mader, David Meyer, Jim Pfander, Aylon Schulte, Charles Tabb, and Michael Vogel. And Professor Murray would like to give special recognition to Professor Louis Henkin and Professor and United States District Judge Jack Weinstein, who taught him what it means to care about the law.

Professor DeSanctis also thanks the following people: Linda A. Shashoua for her unwavering support in this endeavor and all of my others, as well as her guidance, friendship, and expertise in putting thoughts into both writing and music; Michael S. Levine, my "chief of staff," for his friendship and for sharing with me his thoughts and insights from almost ten years of teaching legal writing; Dr. George D. Gopen, for teaching me everything I know about reader and listener expectations; the Honorable John W. Bissell, for the opportunity to work with a true wordsmith and master of the English language; Scott A. Sinder, for teaching me how to write anything in one hour (and a Supreme Court brief in a weekend), for demonstrating why good writing matters, and for the experience working with a fabulously creative, yet very methodical, legal mind; Pam Chamberlain for her institutional know-how and priceless advice on how the GW program operates; and to all of the past, present and future GW LRW adjunct professors, from whom I have learned and continue to learn an enormous amount about a practice-oriented approach to teaching legal writing.

Dedication

To Denise, Olivia, and Dennis, who make it fun;
To my sisters, Margaret, Mary, Jeannette, Anne, and Laura,
who proved to me that the benefits of a
teaching career outweigh all the costs.

M.D.M.
St. Louis, MO
May 2005

To Michael B. DeSanctis,
a truly phenomenal lawyer … and so much more.

C.H.D.
Washington, DC
May 2005

About the Authors

Professor Michael D. Murray teaches Art Law, Civil Procedure, First Amendment and Censorship, Introduction to Advocacy, and Legal Research and Writing at the University of Illinois College of Law. He graduated summa cum laude from Loyola College in Maryland and was a Harlan Fiske Stone Scholar at Columbia Law School. Professor Murray was a member of a national champion Jessup International Law Moot Court team at Columbia, and notes editor of the Columbia Journal of Transnational Law. After law school, he clerked for United States District Judge John F. Nangle, Eastern District of Missouri and Chair of the Judicial Panel on Multidistrict Litigation, and practiced commercial, intellectual property, and products liability litigation for seven years at Bryan Cave law firm in St. Louis. After leaving private practice, Professor Murray taught at Saint Louis University School of Law from 1998-2002. He has published several books and will publish several more in 2005, including: Adversarial Legal Writing and Oral Argument (Foundation Press, forthcoming 2005); Appellate Advocacy and Moot Court (Foundation Press, forthcoming 2005); Art Law: Cases and Materials (William S. Hein 2004); Civil Rules Practice 3d (Thomson West, forthcoming 2005); The Deskbook of Art Law (Oceana 2004, 2005); First Amendment and Censorship (Oceana 2005); Jurisdiction, Venue, and Limitations 3d (Thomson West, forthcoming 2005); Legal Research Methods (Foundation Press, forthcoming 2005); Legal Research, Writing, and Analysis (Foundation Press, forthcoming 2005); Missouri Products Liability 2d (Thomson West 2002); Objective Legal Writing and Analysis (Foundation Press, forthcoming 2005).

Professor Christy Hallam DeSanctis teaches Introduction to Advocacy and Legal Research and Writing at the George Washington University Law School, where she is the Director of the Legal Research and Writing Program and Law School Writing Center. She graduated from Duke University and New York University School of Law. Prior to joining the George Washington University Law School faculty, Professor DeSanctis practiced at the Washington, D.C., law firm of Collier Shannon Scott, PLLC, where she remains of counsel. At Collier, she focused on trial and appellate litigation at both the state and federal level, including in the U.S. Supreme Court, and worked on a variety of regulatory and legislative matters before a number of federal agencies and Congress. In addition, she published articles relating to major legislative efforts with which she was directly involved, including terrorism insurance legislation and federal health and financial privacy regulations. Professor DeSanctis began teaching as an adjunct faculty member in George Washington University Law School's legal research and writing program in 2002. She was appointed Director of the writing program in 2004. In the 2005–2006 academic year, she also will implement and direct a new series of courses focused on academic legal writing. Professor DeSanctis has also taught undergraduate English courses at the University of Maryland, including a course in argumentation developed from principles of Classical Rhetoric. She will complete a Masters in English, with a minor in Rhetoric and Composition, at Maryland in early 2006.

Contents

Chapter 1

Adversarial Legal Writing

This text deals with **advocacy** in legal writing and oral communication. The lessons to be learned involve how to satisfy your ethical duty to represent your client effectively in a contested matter. A contested matter is any legal matter in which the interests of the parties differ. This might be anything from litigation in a court, to a purchase and sale transaction, to a corporate deal, or to a license application to a governmental regulatory body. Contested matters are the most typical legal situations in which you will be representing a client. In contested matters, you often must communicate with an opponent and a third-party decision-maker, such as a court or an arbitrator, in addition to communicating with your client and your supervisors and colleagues at your law office. The examples and chapters below focus on litigation at the trial level and appellate level, but the considerations raised throughout this text apply in any contested matter.

This chapter will focus on the difference between objective legal writing and adversarial legal writing and will examine issues and considerations for writing in an adversarial context. Chapter 2 will focus on the general requirements of pretrial motions in court, and Chapters 3 and 4 will zero in on the particular requirements of motions to dismiss and motions for summary judgment. Chapter 5 will look at appellate advocacy and the general requirements for appeals and writs, and the topic of standards of review. Chapter 6 will focus on the structure and content of appellate briefs, and Chapter 7 will examine the art of oral advocacy at the pretrial, trial, and appellate levels of litigation. Chapter 8 will look beyond your first year legal writing experience to moot court and to actual practice situations in which collaborative legal writing will be the norm.

I. DIFFERENCES BETWEEN OBJECTIVE AND ADVERSARIAL LEGAL WRITING

Objectivity is required in order to render appropriate legal advice to your colleagues and clients. The office memorandum as the paradigm of objective, informative legal writing is designed to be read by people who are working for the client and are presumed to be friendly to the client or who at least owe a duty to the client to keep its confidences. Office memoranda must reflect a critical appraisal of the client's situation and not just engage in cheerleading to pump up the team. An internal office memorandum must be informative of the good and bad facts of the case and present the blemishes along with the beauty marks of the client's legal position.

Adversarial legal writing is different. It is not the opposite of objective writing—it is an honest and truthful presentation of the merits of the client's case that is crafted so that it supports the client's position and **only** the client's position in the best possible way. A good advocate does not abandon her objectivity concerning the blemishes and beauty marks of her client's legal position when she is evaluating her client's case. But the work product of an advocate emphasizes the strong points and does its best to mitigate the effects of the bad points. Adversarial writing takes sides and advocates for one outcome— the outcome favoring the client.

Adversarial legal writing does not engage in fraud or obfuscation about the facts and law concerning the matter—nothing can be gained from lying and cheating except defeat and disbarment. The briefs and memoranda that you will file with the court and serve on your opponents will not lie about the facts and misstate the law. Rather, you must use your skill to present the facts and argue the law in a way that best favors your client. The facts that support your client will be front and center, and negative facts will be explained and defused. The applicable law will not be distorted or outright misstated by you, but to the extent that the statutes, cases, and other authorities allow you to emphasize and interpret the law in a way that better supports your client's position, it is your job as an advocate to make the most of these opportunities.

Lawyers wear several hats in contested matters. They are an officer of the court, bound to uphold the law and promote justice. Attorneys who lie and cheat about the facts and the law certainly violate this duty. Lawyers also must be counselors, seeking the best pathway to the best outcome for the client, whether that means cooperation and concession or more aggressive action. Attorneys whose motto is to fight every case to the bitter end violate this obligation. Lastly, lawyers must be advocates who play a role in the adversarial legal system of the United States by promoting the interests of their client at every stage of the matter in order to allow the court to reach a just result. Proper adversarial legal writing is one of your duties as an advocate.

II. THE NATURE OF THE ADVERSARIAL SYSTEM

Anglo-American legal tradition and, in particular, the American legal system has as its fundamental underpinning the theory that a judge and jury are better able to do justice and resolve disputes when the parties to the suit each are represented by advocates who present a biased, one-sided argument in favor of their clients. The adversarial system depends on its participants approaching litigation and dispute resolution as a high stakes contest in which your client can win or lose something that is significant, and in which every player in the process expects you to promote your client's position and not promote your opponent's position. There are other models for justice and dispute resolution in the world, but this is the American way.

III. STRATEGIES AND GOALS FOR ZEALOUS REPRESENTATION IN THE ADVERSARIAL CONTEXT

A. Follow the fifteen minute rule and write clearly and concisely

Supreme Court Justice Ruth Bader Ginsburg has commented that brief writers before the United States Supreme Court make two mistakes: first, they do not write clearly and concisely, and second, they do not write with their audience—the U.S. Supreme Court, with its current composition of judges—in mind.[1] In the words of Justice Ginsburg, "Every sentence in a brief should be written so that the judge would never feel the need to read the sentence twice."[2] That is a high standard to meet.

Judges everywhere believe that they have more than enough cases to work on and too much material to read and digest in any given case. They will not tolerate complex, cumbersome, redundant, and overly verbose writing in briefs and memoranda to the court. Justice Ginsburg promised her audience that if a brief writer failed to follow her advice, and she felt bogged down in a work, she would skip back to the summary of argument and forget the rest of the brief, or hand it off to one of her law clerks to digest and encapsulate for her.[3] That kind of reception is not your goal as an advocate. If a judge on the highest court in this country with one of the smallest caseloads believes this, imagine the attitude of the typical judge with hundreds more cases pending on his docket when he receives your complex, prolix work. A judge is not going to suffer through this kind of work for very long.

In response to this judicial attitude, we advocate following the **Fifteen Minute Rule**:

FIFTEEN MINUTE RULE

Write so that you can prove your argument
to the reader in fifteen minutes.

There is nothing magical about fifteen minutes—and no guarantee that you will even get that much attention from a judge. But if you draft and edit your work so that a busy judge can capture the best parts of your entire position and argument on a given motion or appeal in fifteen minutes or less, you will have served your client and the court very well.

There are several ways to accomplish this in writing:

◆ Front load your best material. Write an introduction to your brief that tells the court enough facts, law, and argument that you can convince the judge that your client should prevail, all in roughly half a page of text;

◆ Use the statement of facts to advocate your position;

◆ Use meaningful, argumentative thesis headings throughout the discussion or argument section;

◆ Draft the discussion or argument section in as clear, concise, and direct a manner as is possible;

---

[1] Comments delivered during "A Conversation with Justice Ruth Bader Ginsburg," at the Annual Meeting of the Association of American Law Schools, Washington D.C. (Jan. 8, 2000).

[2] <u>Id.</u>

[3] <u>Id.</u>

◆ Use the conclusion solely to request your relief, not to summarize or rehash your arguments and not to make a new point in support of your case.

These topics all will be discussed at greater length in the next chapter.

B. Know your audience and write with your audience in mind

This is a general principle of legal writing, but reaching this goal is even more difficult in a litigation context. With objective writing, you will tend to know your immediate audience very well, whether they be your colleagues or your clients, because you will have worked with them for some time, or at least you will have access to people who know them well and can tell you pointers on how to draft your work to better satisfy them. With litigation, you often are writing to a judge before whom you have never appeared prior to this case, and with whom no one in your office has had much experience. At the appellate level, depending on the shuffle of panels and assignment of cases in your jurisdiction, you may never get two of the same judges on a panel more than two or three times in your career. All of this leads to uncertainty in knowing exactly who your audience is.

Simply living with the uncertainty as inevitable kismet is not good enough. You should make calls to people who have tried any number of cases (even one) before the judge. Private civil litigators may not have as much exposure as prosecutors, public defenders, and criminal defense attorneys whose case loads often give them a better chance of seeing the same judge repeatedly over the course of several years, so do not neglect them when you are gathering your information.

Use your on-line resources to read everything that your judge has written in the area of law of your case. Westlaw allows you to search the judge field (ju) for opinions written by a particular judge, and Lexis allows you to search the OPINIONBY segment for the same purpose. Justice Ginsburg is disgruntled because of all the courts and judges in the land, the sitting members of the United States Supreme Court have the most well documented track record of any court in the nation. Every opinion, concurrence, and dissent written by the members of the court is well documented, and the oral arguments before the court are recorded on audio tape and text, so that the personal style of each justice during the arguments can be reviewed. In spite of this, Justice Ginsburg bemoans that many litigants write and argue as if their client and their friends at the firm were their only audience, and that they simply are preaching to their own choir.[4]

C. Concede facts and give up arguments when it will benefit your client to do so; do not concede when it will not

Let us disabuse you of the notion that we think lawyers should never concede facts or abandon arguments. Not so. The value of a concession depends on the stage of the dispute

---

[4] Comments of Justice Ruth Bader Ginsburg, <u>supra</u> note 1.

and the nature of the dispute. Early in a contested matter, it may not benefit your client to reveal all the facts your client knows to your opponents until you discover what your opponents know and what their version of the facts is. On the other hand, early in the dispute may be a good time to reveal or stipulate to certain facts because it will save your client the time and energy in responding to discovery of those facts. Almost every relevant fact, good or bad, will be disclosed in the course of litigation, but litigation is not the only option nor is it often the best option for a client in a contested matter. Mediation or negotiation are far superior to litigation for the proper resolution of many contested matters, and management of facts is required for you properly to advocate for your client in these proceedings.

Certain concessions simply are against your client's interest no matter what the stage of the dispute. If you are representing a defendant (the accused party), be especially careful about conceding facts that have any bearing on liability or damages in a case. If you are representing a plaintiff (the aggrieved party), do not concede facts that may lead to an affirmative defense or avoidance for your opponent. Your evaluation of the facts must be long-sighted.

In litigation, give up a legal argument if it advances your cause with the court. Do not brief an argument if the chances that it will make you look foolish and obstinate are greater than the chances that any legal decision maker will agree with the argument and rule in your favor. Your best argument will look better if it is not seen in the vicinity of two other terrible arguments. Judges never make their decisions based on the number of arguments you raised.

On the other hand, do not arbitrarily limit the number of arguments you will make. Do not get stuck on one complicated argument, putting all your eggs in one basket, when you also can raise one or two less complicated arguments in addition to the complex argument. Leave your options open, as discussed below.

D. Know the facts and the law, and know your options

You cannot help your client if you do not learn the facts of your client's case. In order to know which facts are likely to be important, you have to know the law. Naturally, knowing the law and the facts is required if you are going to give advice and represent your client in any way or shape or form.

A doctor would not prescribe medicine without listening to the patient's symptoms first and determining what illnesses might be present and what side-effects might affect the patient if they take a certain medication. Similarly, a lawyer who does not know the facts and the law sooner or later will take an action that is directly against her client's interests.

Knowing the facts and the law also will enable you to know your options. If you do not know your options you will miss something important. If you do not know the facts or law, you could inadvertently close off one or more of your options and eliminate otherwise perfectly acceptable forms of relief for your client.

One of the main problems with lawyers is not that they do not know the law, but that they are too busy to be prepared. They do not take the time to figure out what they are doing or should be doing in a case. They lose sight of the big picture or never see it in the first place, and chase leads down one rabbit trail of facts or law after another without taking the time to think the case through, forming decisions on what needs to be done, planning the tactics and strategies that will get the job done, and then doing it.

The law is **not** one of the disciplines where 90% of the battle is just showing up. You must be prepared for the setting in which you are about to engage your lawyering skills. If it is the motion to dismiss stage, think about what you are doing with the motion or opposing the motion—What does it mean to bring (or defend) this motion? What are you trying to accomplish? What is the effect of this course of action as opposed to others? If it is the summary judgment stage, ask the same questions. What you can and should do at these stages differs, so think about it and make sure you are aware of what you are doing. You may not always win your motions or win the case just by being prepared, but you certainly will lose more motions and cases (and clients) if you are not prepared.

Chapter 2

Pretrial Motions

The period in litigation after a case is filed in a court and before the case actually goes to trial before a fact-finder is called the "pretrial" period. This is the time to raise defenses against claims, and investigate the facts of the case through the process of discovery. In the pretrial period, a party may make a formal request for the court to do something for it—it requests relief from the court—and these requests are called "motions" because the party is acting "to move" the court for relief. Motions cover any type of request for relief, from the relatively mundane request for an extension of time, all the way to the dramatic dispositive motions—motions to dismiss and motions for summary judgment—in which a party asks the court to throw the opponent's case out of court or to grant the party judgment in the case as a matter of law.

I. STRUCTURE OF PRETRIAL MOTIONS AND MEMORANDA IN SUPPORT

Motion practice is initiated by a party (called the "movant") when it files the motion with the court, which is then followed by the opponent's filing of a response or opposition, and often then followed by the movant's filing of a reply to the opposition. In some jurisdictions, the motion itself will be drafted so as to contain all the legal and factual support it needs. In many other jurisdictions, the document that bears the title of "motion" merely makes the specific request for relief from the court, and a separate document called a "memorandum in support of the motion"[1] contains all of the legal and factual support for the motion.

The requirements, if any, for a motion to be accompanied by a separate "memorandum in support of the motion" will be identified and defined in the local rules of the court where you are litigating. Responses or oppositions to motions[2] and replies to responses or oppositions typically include all of the factual and legal support in the same document; there is no separate document to file to accompany the memorandum in opposition or reply.

---

[1] In various jurisdictions, this document may be called "suggestions in support," "points and authorities in support," or "brief in support" of the motion. You must pay attention to the local rules and not become too attached to one particular name for this type of litigation document.

[2] Depending on the local rules, the document may be titled "response," "opposition," "memorandum in opposition," "suggestions in response," or "points and authorities in opposition" to the motion.

In the section below, we have outlined the structure of the document that will lay out the legal arguments of the movant in support of the motion, whether it is included in the motion or in a separately filed document. We will refer to this document from now on as the "**memorandum in support**." The structure outlined below for responses or oppositions to motions applies to the document that presents the opponent's legal and factual support for its opposition to the motion, and we will refer to this document as the "**memorandum in opposition**." The third structure outlined below applies to the document that presents the movant's further legal and factual support for its motion in response to the opposition to the motion; we will refer to this simply as the "**reply**."

A. The structure of the memorandum in support

A typical pretrial memorandum in support, no matter what kind of relief it seeks, will have the following sections:

Caption
Title
Pre-Introduction
Introduction
Statement of Facts
Argument
Conclusion

Each section will be discussed in detail below.

B. The structure of the memorandum in opposition

The structure of the document that opposes the motion is the same:

Caption
Title
Pre-Introduction (however, it may be unnecessary, as discussed below)
Introduction
Statement of Facts
Argument
Conclusion

C. The structure of the reply

The reply has the following format:

> **Caption**
> **Title**
> **Introduction**
> **Argument**
> **Conclusion**

You will leave out the pre-introduction because the court by now knows what the motion is, and you most often will leave out the statement of facts, unless you need to clarify or correct something your opponent put in its version of the facts.

II. THE CAPTION, TITLE, AND PRE-INTRODUCTION

The caption identifies the court, the parties, and the docket number for the case. Often the judge's name is listed, too. How this information is to be arranged varies from jurisdiction to jurisdiction, but a typical structure is shown in the examples below.

The title is straightforward—it should introduce the party filing the memorandum and the purpose of the memorandum. For example: Defendant Smith's Memorandum in Support of Motion to Dismiss Plaintiff's Complaint for Lack of Personal Jurisdiction, or Plaintiff Arch Communicator's Memorandum in Support of Motion for Summary Judgment.

The pre-introduction is our term to refer to the first one or two sentences of the motion that come right after the caption and title of the motion. This section is used solely to tell the court what the motion is and the relief that is sought. Once again, this section is straightforward—you should identify yourself (the movant) and identify the party against whom the motion is brought. Usually, you will be moving the court under the auspices of a certain rule of procedure, so cite the rule in the pre-introduction. Then state the relief sought, and move on to the introduction. Unlike the sections that follow the pre-introduction (the introduction, statement of facts, argument, and conclusion), the pre-introduction has no heading of its own.

What do all of these look like? Here is an example:

CAPTION	UNITED STATES DISTRICT COURT SOUTHERN DISTRICT OF NEW YORK

	GEORGIE BOLLING, a Minor, by)
	his father and next friend, Robert)
	Bolling,)
	         Plaintiff,)
	)
	     v.) No. 97-2345-TRW
	)
	ALDEN HALL HISTORICAL SITE,)
	and ELLIOTT STIRLING,)
	)
	      Defendants.)

TITLE	DEFENDANTS ALDEN HALL AND STIRLING'S MEMORANDUM IN SUPPORT OF MOTION TO DISMISS FOR FAILURE TO STATE A CLAIM
PRE-INTRODUCTION	Defendants Alden Hall Historical Site ("Alden Hall") and Elliott Stirling ("Stirling") move this Court pursuant to Fed. R. Civ. P. 12(b)(6) to dismiss the complaint brought by Plaintiff Georgie Bolling ("Plaintiff") for failure to state a cause of action upon which relief may be granted.

Opponents do not necessarily have to put a pre-introduction into their memorandum in opposition. Remember that the opposition follows the motion and memorandum in support, so the court has had the opportunity to become familiar with the motion and is likely to read the movant's papers before looking at the opposition papers. If the title of the opposition is sufficiently detailed to identify the party opposing the motion, the movant's name, and the nature of the motion that is opposed, then the opponent does not need to write a pre-introduction that simply would repeat the information.

➢ *Properly detailed title:* Plaintiff Van Pelt's Memorandum in Opposition to Defendant Brown's 28 U.S.C. § 1404 Motion to Transfer
➢ *But not this:* Plaintiff's Memorandum in Opposition to Motion to Transfer

The same principle applies to the reply—at this point the court should be very familiar with the motion, so a properly drafted title to the reply that identifies the movant, the opponent, and the motion will preclude the necessity of a pre-introduction.

➢ *Properly detailed title:* Defendant Brown's Reply to Plaintiff Van Pelt's Opposition to Brown's 28 U.S.C. § 1404 Motion to Transfer

III. THE INTRODUCTION

The introduction follows the pre-introduction. It has a heading ("Introduction"). It is the most important section of the motion.

A. The objective of the introduction

The introduction has a simple objective, but one that takes all of your accumulated skill and experience to accomplish. You must grab the court's attention and try to win the motion in the introduction. If you can draft an introduction that meets this end, you will be well on your way to a successful career in litigation or other adversarial contexts.

The movant and opponent obviously have different interests, but the objective to be obtained in the introduction is similar: win the motion. Therefore, the parties will state:

Movant: Why the motion at hand is necessary, and why I prevail.

Opponent: Why the motion at hand is improper (untimely, unnecessary, or scandalous), and even if it's not one of the above, why I should prevail.

B. The importance of the introduction

Remember that in the law, first things matter the most, and the attention span of your audience always will be limited. Therefore, the introduction—the first substantive section of the motion or opposition—is critical. You must place your best facts and the best points of your legal argument before the judge as soon as you can. This means that you should not be cagey in the introduction. Do everything you can to present your best points to the court and win the motion in the introduction.

C. The drafting of the introduction

1. Movant's introduction

> **Movant's introduction must include:**
>
> - Background facts (from movant's perspective)
> - Movant's theme of the case and of the motion
> - Key operative facts upon which the motion turns
> - Snapshot of the law on the motion
> - Movant's conclusions (why the client prevails)

As movant, you must present enough of the background facts to tell the court what is going on, but only facts favorable to your client's position.

➤ *Example*: This lawsuit represents Van Pelt's attempt to spread the blame for her own negligence. Van Pelt's unauthorized modification of Brown's treadmill caused it to malfunction, killing one of Van Pelt's employees. In spite of the fact that the treadmill was in perfect working order when it was delivered to Brown's shipper and when it arrived at Van Pelt's health club as acknowledged by Van Pelt on the shipping receipt, Van Pelt has sued Brown for strict liability for design defect and failure to warn.

The filing of a pretrial motion may provide the first occasion for the court to take notice of a pending lawsuit and open the court file and read about the case. Courts generally do not read complaints or answers as they are filed, and most often will wait for a reason to read up on a case before they will invest that kind of time. The filing of a motion provides that reason. The court may start with the motion papers themselves, as these papers may be sitting on top in the court file (a typical system for filing material in a court file is by reverse chronological order with the most recently filed material sitting on top in the file). Therefore, movant has a strong incentive to tell the background of the case early in its memorandum in support as this may be the court's first introduction to the case.

The next task is to tell the facts that are most important to the motion at hand, and give a snapshot of the law that applies. Remember: this is just the introduction. Only tell as much of the law as is necessary to drive home your conclusions, and only discuss the elements of the rule that turn the case in your favor. Drive home the one or two best facts that further your argument. Then plug in your conclusions. They should be obvious from what you wrote leading up to the conclusions. Your conclusion is that the client must prevail, and the client's position should appear as ironclad as a tank and as righteous as scripture.

➤ When discussing the law and your legal conclusions in the introduction, you should try to make each sentence perform two or three tasks; give a conclusion and the "because" part— the facts and the principles of the law that lead to the conclusion.

> *Example:* {**conclusion**} Personal jurisdiction over the defendant Brown is improper because the {**legal principles**} Due Process clause requires minimum contacts with the forum state and {**facts**} Brown's two visits to the state were for charity purposes unrelated to any business activity conducted by Brown. {**conclusion**} Brown did not form any substantial connection to Pennsylvania because {**facts**} his two visits to the state were volunteer appearances for fund raising, amounting to less than six hours in the state, and thus were {**legal standards, conclusion**} random and fortuitous contacts. {**conclusion**} The visits were not connected to this lawsuit because {**facts**} the suit arises from Brown's sales of exercise equipment to plaintiff Van Pelt which were {**legal principles, facts, and conclusion**} transacted in Ohio where the sales agreements were signed and the contracts were formed.

Limit your citations to authority to the barest minimum. The default rule is not to cite *any* authority in the introduction. Most of the time, you will not have anything you need to cite in the introduction, but a short reference to the one statute, rule, or regulation that governs and controls the outcome, or to the very most important and strongest controlling cases that favor your position (no more than one or two) can be appropriate. This section has to flow, and long form citations clutter it up too much.

➤ *Example:* Personal jurisdiction over defendant Brown is improper because the Due Process clause requires minimum contacts with the forum state and Brown's two visits to the state were for charity purposes unrelated to any business activity conducted by Brown.

➤ *Do not write*: Personal jurisdiction over defendant Brown is improper because the Due Process clause, U.S. Const. amend. XIV, sec. 1, requires minimum contacts with the forum state, Int'l Boot Co. v. Texas, 323 U.S. 123, 128 (1945); Hanover Trust Co. v. Blatt, 456 U.S. 678, 682 (1967), and Brown's two visits to the state were for charity purposes unrelated to any business activity conducted by Brown. See Affidavit of Derek Brown dated July 14, 2005, ¶ 4 (attached hereto as exhibit 1).

Do not apologize for bringing the motion (unless you already have brought two such motions in the case; at that point, you should explain the need for a third). There are certain conventions in legal drafting ("praying" for or "respectfully requesting" relief; "respectfully submitting" your motion) that are proper, formal writing, but they are not intended to be an apology. If you are forced to bring repetitive motions (such as in a discovery context), explain why your opponent forced you to bring the latest motion.

➤ *Example:* Defendant Brown moves this court to compel the production of the medical reports of two of plaintiff Van Pelt's doctors. This is the third such motion to compel brought by Brown to obtain Van Pelt's complete medical records because Van Pelt persists in refusing to turn over the reports. In Van Pelt's deposition, she made reference to three treating physicians who attended her at Woodstock Hospital—Doctors Linus Pauling, Ludwig Schroeder, and Patty Peppermint. Only Doctor Pauling's report has been disclosed to Brown. Brown is entitled to the reports of all physicians who treated her for the injuries at issue in this matter.

The remaining components of an introduction are the themes—a theme for the case and a theme for the motion. A properly drafted theme for the case will be a single sentence or short phrase that sums up the client's position on the merits of the case that will resonate with the court and convince it that your client's position has merit and is worthy of careful attention. Think marketing message, not dissertation.[3] Your goal is for the court

---

[3] Do marketing messages work? Try and identify the companies that are associated with these slogans: "It's the real thing." "Just do it." "You're in good hands." "The king of beers." If you identified at least two of these companies just by their slogan, the marketing agencies are doing their job.

to start to think of the case as a whole in a light that favors your client. Naturally, the sound bite you draft will resonate more completely if you back it up with background facts that support your theory of the case.

> *Example:* {**theme of the case**} This lawsuit represents Van Pelt's attempt to spread the blame for her own negligence. {**supporting facts**} Van Pelt's unauthorized modification of Brown's treadmill caused it to malfunction killing one of Van Pelt's employees. In spite of the fact that the treadmill was in perfect working order when it was delivered to Brown's shipper and when it arrived at Van Pelt's health club as acknowledged by Van Pelt on the shipping receipt, Van Pelt has sued Brown for strict liability for design defect and failure to warn.

A properly drafted theme for the motion will cause the court to be receptive to all of your arguments and to sympathize with your client's facts and circumstances.

> *Example:* {**theme of the motion**} There is no legal justification for Van Pelt to file this lawsuit in Pennsylvania. The only explanation for this choice of forum is that Van Pelt wishes to harass Brown by attempting to force him to litigate in a distant forum. {**supporting facts**} Although the sales agreement between Van Pelt and Brown were signed in Brown's place of business in Ohio and Van Pelt took delivery of the goods in Ohio through a shipping agent of her choice (Federal Express), Van Pelt sued Brown in Pennsylvania where she resides.

2. Opponent's introduction

Opponent's introduction must include:

- Background Facts (from opponent's perspective)
- Opponent's theme of the case and of the motion
- Key operative facts upon which the motion turns
- Snapshot of the law on the motion
- Opponent's conclusions (why the client prevails)

Opponents must take on the motion and the memorandum in support and turn it back on the movant. As indicated above, the requirements for the introduction are the same for the opponent as they were for the movant. Opponents must try to win the motion, and the introduction is the first step.

Opponents have more choices to make in responding to a motion. If you actually have a decent argument or even the better of the argument on the motion—the facts and the law actually support your side, not the movant's—then you can take the motion head-on, and argue point by point why the movant is erroneous on the facts, the law, or the conclusions. At the end, you argue that the client should win, and your position is ironclad scripture (not to mix metaphors or anything). This is the most satisfying option.

If, as an opponent, you have a difficult position on the merits, you should examine procedural issues regarding the timing of the motion or the propriety of movant's decision to bring this motion at this stage of the case as a whole. If laches have set in—you are in a much worse position now than if this motion had been brought a month ago—then you should argue laches in defense against the motion. If the motion is the second or third in a row by the movant, you are entitled to point out whether the second or third motion is necessary or question whether movant simply is trying to delay the case and frustrate the opponent. Courts are sensitive to tactical behavior, and if there is clear evidence that movant is being tactical, it may benefit you to raise this in your defense to the motion.

D. Themes in the introduction

Both the movant and the opponent should try to sell their theme for the case and for the motion at hand in the introduction. A theme for the case or for the motion is the summation of the strengths of the case that is designed to help the court grasp the facts and equities of the case, but in a way that favors the litigant's client. A theme should be able to be summed up in a tag line—your pitch to the court in a marketing sense. A theme that catches on with the court can help you play up your strengths and play down your weaknesses. If you make a connection with the trial judge, every time she picks up the court file of your case she will be humming your theme song ("This is the case where the woman modified the treadmill and killed her employee and now is trying to spread the blame.").

You must adopt a theme that ties in with the facts and your legal argument. Do not forget that although you may be writing an introduction to an initial procedural motion, it could be the first document the court or law clerk looks at in regard to the entire case, so you want to get them thinking about the case in the correct way (your client's way).

Themes vary from case to case. Some popular themes and variations on these themes are:

- **You've got to live by your word.** A man's word is his bond. What good is a person (or a company) if they cannot live up to their word. Holding people to their word is the foundation of contract law.
- **Misuse of power.** Big, aggressive bully of a corporation vs. smart, little, under-financed corporation (your client). Big government agency against the little guy (your client).
- **Getting what you deserve.** Getting exactly what you bargained for. Getting what is fair for a victim in your situation. Getting what is right, in spite of what a contract or a rigid legal stipulation says you should get. A case of an innovative, cutting edge competitor (your client) vs. slip-shod, rip-off upstart company.
- **Cheating, taking what you don't deserve.** Overreaching. Sponging off. Unjust enrichment. Taking unfair advantage of a fortuitous situation. Ducking important rules or regulations.

- **Placing blame on the correct party.** Innocent, diligent bystander (your client) vs. careless and highly culpable opponents.
- **Dishonesty.** Deceit. Hiding important facts. Failing to disclose material information. Your opponent lied about many things in the past. This lawsuit is just the latest example of lying.
- **Sloppiness.** Opponents are sloppy. Look how sloppy they are about the facts and authorities in the motion. Look at their own business practices. Their whole case is sloppy—you'll never get the complete, straight story from them.
- **Laches.** Opponents have brought the suit too late—we've changed our position in reliance on their acting one way, and now they sue to go the other way. This motion is the same thing—too little, too late, and we are put in a bad position by their bringing it at this stage of the case.

Be careful not to pick an offensive theme. Do not start with the American vs. foreigner theme unless you like dancing on thin ice. Do not rely on themes such as, "She was just a hysterical woman" or "He was just a typical good old boy," unless you desire to potentially offend half the jury and the judge.

Lying is a theme you have to think twice about, because it is unpopular with judges and juries. Be careful about trying to say, "The other side is bunch of liars. This latest motion is just a new pack of lies." Judges and juries do not want to assume that people lie all the time. If you are going to use this theme, you must have concrete evidence of deception on more than one occasion, and tread lightly.

This advice goes double for accusations against other lawyers in briefs and in oral argument. Do not call another lawyer a liar in front of a judge unless you have ironclad proof of the lie. Even then, be careful and only accuse as far as you need to go. Use non-confrontational language: "His statement simply was not true" instead of "He lied to me." It makes for a very tense and unpleasant situation when attorneys start pointing the finger at each other over their truthfulness. Ad hominem attacks are much more likely to turn the court against you rather than help you prevail on the motion.

E. Length of the introduction

Most introductions will be at least a half a page, and some will be as long as a full page. Filling in details of the background of the case, the facts, the theme, and the legal principles that lead up to your conclusions will take some space; nevertheless, you should limit yourself to one page of text or less because you do not want to overwhelm the reader with information. The introduction is supposed to be an introduction, not the entire memorandum.

F. Sample introductions

Here are some examples of introductions from a dog bite case. Hopefully, you will be able to see the strategies at work and the themes that each side has adopted for their side of the case.

The "objective" facts of the case are as follows:

A small boy, Georgie Bolling, was with his father, Robert Bolling, touring an outdoor historic site walking from building to building. They saw one more building farther off to the side and headed for it. No fences or rope blocked off the house. There was one sign buried halfway in a snow bank. By the time they got close enough to see what the sign said—"Private Property - Keep Out"— the two were approached by a dog, roaming loose. The dog was friendly and playful. The boy decided to surprise his father by throwing a snowball at him. The father saw it and ducked, and the snowball hit the dog, spraying it with powdery snow. The dog attacked the boy, and had to be dragged off of him. The boy received 120 stitches and multiple bruises in the altercation. The boy and his father sued the historical site and the dog's owner, Elliott Stirling, for damages for the attack. The defendant moves to dismiss the complaint for failure to state a claim.

Example 1 – Defendant's perspective

UNITED STATES DISTRICT COURT
SOUTHERN DISTRICT OF NEW YORK

GEORGIE BOLLING, a Minor, by his father and next friend, Robert Bolling,	)))	
Plaintiff,	))	
v.	))	No. 05-2345-TRW
ALDEN HALL HISTORICAL SITE, and ELLIOTT STIRLING,	)))	
Defendants.	)	

DEFENDANTS' MEMORANDUM IN SUPPORT OF MOTION TO DISMISS FOR FAILURE TO STATE A CLAIM

Defendants Alden Hall Historical Site ("Alden Hall") and Elliott Stirling ("Stirling") move this Court pursuant to Fed. R. Civ. P. 12(b)(6) to dismiss the complaint brought by Plaintiff Georgie Bolling ("Plaintiff") for failure to state a cause of action upon which relief may be granted.

INTRODUCTION

Plaintiff's action to recover for a dog bite is barred because he provoked the dog. On February 1, 2005, Plaintiff was trespassing on private property adjacent to the galleries and display areas of the Alden Hall Historical Site museum. Plaintiff admits that he provoked Stirling's dog into a defensive action by spraying the dog with snow. Complaint, ¶ 8. Although he was not trying to hit the dog with a snowball, New York law declares that inadvertent provocation of a dog precludes an action arising from the dog's bite as surely as intentional provocation. The dog acted in accordance with its training as a guard dog and reacted to Plaintiff's act by subduing Plaintiff, which in the process resulted in Plaintiff receiving lacerations on his arm. Even though Plaintiff admits that the dog was sprayed by snow and that he provoked it in this manner, Plaintiff still brings this complaint seeking damages not only from the dog's owner but also from Alden Hall, the adjacent property owner. Under controlling authority of this state, provocation of the dog is a complete bar to recovery and mandates the dismissal of this complaint as against Alden Hall and Stirling.

Example 2 – Plaintiff's Perspective:

UNITED STATES DISTRICT COURT
SOUTHERN DISTRICT OF NEW YORK

GEORGIE BOLLING, a Minor, by his father and next friend, Robert Bolling,	)))	
Plaintiff,	))	
v.	))	No. 05-2345-TRW
ALDEN HALL HISTORICAL SITE, and ELLIOTT STIRLING,	))))	
Defendants.	)	

PLAINTIFF'S RESPONSE TO DEFENDANTS ALDEN HALL AND STIRLING'S FED. R. CIV. P. 12(b)(6) MOTION TO DISMISS FOR FAILURE TO STATE A CLAIM

INTRODUCTION

Defendants Elliott Stirling ("Stirling") and Alden Hall Historical Site ("Alden Hall") have taken the position that they can give a vicious dog free rein to roam a public place where it might injure small children. Stirling's dog's attack on Plaintiff Georgie Bolling ("Georgie") on February 1, 2005, in which Georgie had his arm ripped so badly that it required 120 stitches, was not "provoked" by Georgie as that term has been defined in New York case law. The attack was vicious and disproportionate to the accidental dusting of snow that the dog experienced when it got in the middle of Georgie and his father's snowball game. The fact that the dog was loose and menacing patrons of the museum as they attempted to keep to the public walkways and go about their business touring the museum points directly to the liability of both defendants. The defendants failed to provide proper signage warning of the dog and failed to provide proper boundaries to prevent patrons such as Georgie from accidentally straying onto private property. Plaintiff's complaint states all the elements required for recovery under the New York "Dog Bite" statute, N.Y. Dog Bite Law § 516, and defendants' motion to dismiss for failure to state a claim must be denied.

IV. THE STATEMENT OF FACTS

The statement of facts is not first in order of appearance and is not first in order of importance (the introduction occupies that place in each instance), but it is an important section that many lawyers fail to use properly. The most mundane thing to be accomplished in the statement of facts is to tell a little more of the background of the case, especially if this is the first substantive motion and it is filed early in the litigation, and to tell the facts that are necessary to resolve the motion. This is where most advocates stop. But you should go further in making this section count in favor of your client.

A. Drafting the statement of facts

1. Advocacy through narrative reasoning and story telling

You should always try to advocate you client's case in every section of the motion, and the facts are no exception. Every chance that you get to write a "Background" or "Statement of Facts" section is a chance to tell your client's story—the good (your client), the bad (your opponent), and the ugly (what your opponent did).

The style of argumentation that you should employ in the facts is narrative reasoning. It is a story told through a succession of events, facts building upon other facts, that clearly adds up to the conclusion you want the reader to reach—BUT—and this is a huge "but"— you do not state the conclusion in this section if, as is most often the case, it is a legal conclusion.

The key to a successful statement of facts is being able to state the same relevant facts as your opponent ought to state, but in a manner that tends to favor your client. You will not succeed by hiding key facts; your opponent will bring them out and you will look the worse for having tried to sweep them under the rug. Instead, talk about the material facts of the case, good and bad, but emphasize the good, and put the bad in terms that mitigate their effect on your client's position.

There are various techniques for emphasizing good facts and downplaying bad facts. Facts you want to emphasize always will have a greater impact if you phrase them in the active tense. Facts you want to deemphasize sometimes can be mitigated by phrasing them in the passive tense. The passive tense also takes the focus off of the true subject of the sentence (the actor or instigator), and if your client is the actor and instigator and she did something undesirable, it will help to draw the focus off of her.

Evaluate the words you use, especially your verbs, adjectives, and adverbs. "Letting someone go" or "laying off someone" is a fairly neutral way of expressing a reduction in force (as is the term "reduction in force"); "firing" someone is not neutral at all. "Coming into contact" with something does not paint much of a mental picture; "smashing" into it paints a picture with sound effects. Consider the following examples that work from a single set of facts, but paint two widely divergent pictures:

Example 1 - Common Facts: Client Jones was going 60 m.p.h. in a 45 m.p.h. zone on his way to his therapist, a doctor of psychology. He was late. The road was wet. A poodle came out from behind a parked car and moved into the road in front of him. Jones swerved, his car slid out of control, and he hit a parked car owned by plaintiff.

Plaintiff's Version: Defendant was late for an appointment with his psycho-therapist and was speeding at 60 m.p.h. on rain slick pavement in a 45 m.p.h. zone. A poodle walked into the path of Defendant's speeding car, and Defendant swerved and sent his car spinning out of control. Defendant then smashed his car into the back of plaintiff Smith's parked car.

Defendant's Version: Mr. Jones was proceeding to an important appointment. A dog jumped out in front of him taking him completely by surprise. In an effort to avoid hitting the dog, he turned the wheel quickly but the car slid on the damp pavement and came into contact with the plaintiff's car.

> *Comment: Plaintiff's version makes us think Jones might be unbalanced, perhaps mentally ill. Plaintiff emphasizes the speed and the lateness factor. The road sounds dangerous—rain slick. The facts about Jones' reaction to the dog all are phrased in the active tense—Jones swerved, he sent the car out of control, he hit the other car. And not just hit it, he smashed into it.*

> *Defendant Jones does not ignore all of the events of that day and pretend that he was somewhere else. Jones deals with the same facts, but we hear them in terms that allow us to give Jones a little credit. Jones gives a plausible reason for his haste. Damp pavement is a much better adjective for wetness than rain-slick. The dog took Jones completely by surprise. What happened next is phrased in the passive tense, taking some of the heat off of Jones. The result is plaintiff's car was hit, but "coming into contact" certainly is not as auditory as "smashing" (with metal and glass flying).*

Example 2 - Common Facts: ABC Corp. laid off thirteen workers in a reduction in force (RIF). ABC used a business productivity formula. Six of the workers who were laid off were over the age of 40, four of these were women. Four more who were laid off were minorities, two of whom were women. Mr. Smith, a white male age 37, made the final decision of whom to lay off.

Plaintiff's Version: ABC's most recent RIF was spearheaded by Cliff Smith, a white male. Smith targeted women, minorities, and workers whose age was over 40 for ten of his thirteen cuts. When he fired six elderly workers, he made sure four of them were women, and when he singled out four minorities for firing, he made sure half of them were women. Smith used a formula that ensured that these people could be disposed of with the excuse of increasing productivity.

Defendant's Version: ABC was forced by competitive economic factors to lay off thirteen workers. A formula was used based on a worker's years of service, evaluation grades, and amount of contract revenue generated in the last five years. The thirteen lowest performing workers were laid off.

> *Comment: Isn't "spearheaded" a wonderful word for plaintiff? It is a perfectly common word in daily parlance, but in a fact pattern involving a reduction in force, it suggests that Smith carried off someone's head on a spear. Plaintiff's statement of facts is drafted entirely in the active voice, because plaintiff wants the reader to focus on a particular person (Smith) doing these things. The mention of an "excuse" is a polite and formal way of suggesting subterfuge—an artiface. Plaintiff would have liked to have used the word "pretext" or "pretextual" but these are legal conclusions, and legal conclusions do not belong in the statement of facts as discussed in the section below.*
>
> *Defendant's section is drafted in the passive voice so that the reader does not focus on who did these actions. It also is short; it suggests that this was a routine procedure, done at dozens of companies across the country each day, and there is not much more to say about it than that.*

2. Legal conclusions vs. factual conclusions

Legal conclusions do not belong in the statement of facts section. They stick out like a sore thumb. Judges get exercised about legal conclusions in the facts because when they find them, it looks like the author is trying to cheat, starting her argument too early and in the wrong section. Judges tend to think that statement of facts should be objective, not argumentative, and you only will irritate them by stating legal conclusions right under their nose in the facts section. The statement of facts can advance your argument—that is the whole point we have been trying to communicate above—but it cannot do it in a sloppy, careless manner by stating obvious legal conclusions along with the facts.

In order to carry out the objective of advancing your client's cause in the statement of facts but not stating legal conclusions, you must understand the distinction between legal and factual conclusions. Factual conclusions that are reasonable, logical inferences drawn from the facts generally are fine to insert in the statement of facts. Consider the following examples:

Factual Conclusions: The car ***was going fast*** on the wet road.

The accident happened ***when there still was enough light to see.***

The doctor had ***followed the standard procedures*** at the hospital for learning a new surgical procedure before she attempted to do it herself.

Smith used a formula that ensured that these people could be disposed of with the ***excuse*** of increasing productivity.

What you need to avoid is legal conclusions:

Legal Conclusions: The driver was ***reckless*** for driving at that speed.

The accident was ***caused*** by the defendant.

The doctor was ***not negligent*** in attempting to perform the procedure she had just learned.

Smith used a formula that ensured that these people could be disposed of under the ***pretext*** of increasing productivity.

You do not need to state legal conclusions in the statement of facts; if you tell an engaging story and emphasize the right facts and draw appropriate inferences and factual conclusions, every law trained reader will know where you are going and they will fill in the legal conclusions. Even if they do not, they are one page turn away from reading your legal conclusions in the proper place for them—the argument section.

B. Limits on drafting the facts – style and good taste

There are rules of style and decorum that clearly apply in this setting.

➤ Do not go overboard with emotion. It is unprofessional, and will turn the court against you.

Acceptable: After being fired by ABC Corp., plaintiff Smith was forced to take two jobs to support her two daughters. As a single mother living far away from all of her relations, she had no other choice. Smith became ill from stress and exhaustion, and was hospitalized for two days in May 2005 with chest pains and irregular heart beats.

> *Do not say:* Defendant ABC Corp. was not satisfied with destroying plaintiff's dreams of lifetime employment at the company; the company threw this poor, struggling single mother out into the street, abandoning her in her time of need just as her worthless lover had abandoned her seven years earlier. ABC Corp. caused Smith's heart attack and put her in the hospital just as surely as if they had injected her with adrenaline and electrified her chest. They broke her heart, plain and simple.

If you are a plaintiff, give a fair account of the injuries, using compelling terms. Do not overstate the injuries in a blatant attempt to draw sympathy or outrage. Do not give gruesome, gratuitously revolting statements of the facts.

> *Example:* If the broken machinery almost ripped your client's arm off, say so: Plaintiff's arm was caught in the machine and nearly ripped off of his body.

> *Do not say:* The machine acted with murderous efficiency to rip plaintiff from stem to stern.

A fair account of the injuries by a plaintiff is not a stump speech to inflame the listeners. If the facts are grisly—a sex crime or violent act against a child, for example—tell the story completely, but remember to write it as a professional. Think network evening news, not Jerry Springer. Write it like the New York Times would, not like a "National-Midnight-Star" rag sheet (to borrow a clever name from Second City Television) would. Be clear and compelling, but do not put on a tear-jerker or freak show:

> *Acceptable:* Plaintiff Kruger's arm was caught in the machine and nearly ripped off of his body. Kruger described the pain to a paramedic as "excruciating." In a matter of seconds, he lost complete use of his arm.

> *Do not say:* Plaintiff's screams rang out as the machine slowly, horribly tore his flesh. Blood spurted from his arm and coated the machine, dripping down to form a large puddle on the floor. Words cannot describe the sounds of a man having his arm ripped from his body and the scene of gore as the jaws of a murderous machine try to tear a limb from its shoulder.

Defendants have no incentive to dwell overly long on plaintiffs' injuries. Try to downplay them as best as possible, but move on quickly.

Example: The machine caused several lacerations to plaintiff's arm resulting in loss of its functionality. However, plaintiff experienced a quick recovery and regained nearly complete functionality of his arm within six weeks of the incident.

➤ Do not give unnecessary detail because you will wear the court out. You should not have to spend more than a page or at most two pages on the statement of facts for the average pretrial motion.

Good: Defendant Jones was late for an appointment with his psycho-therapist and was speeding at 60 m.p.h. on rain slick pavement in a 45 m.p.h. zone. A poodle walked into the path of Defendant's speeding car, and Defendant swerved and sent his car spinning out of control. Defendant then smashed his car into the back of plaintiff Smith's parked car.

Not this: Defendant Jones was running approximately eight minutes late for his appointment with his psycho-therapist, Dr. Will Shrinker. He went speeding along on his way to Dr. Shrinker's office on Mulberry Lane, a mixed business and residential street with a 45 m.p.h. speed limit. He was traveling at an average speed of 60 m.p.h. as confirmed by a passive police monitoring unit on Mulberry Lane that Jones passed by; his speed also was generally confirmed by two eye witnesses at the scene, Mrs. Vera Stigmatism and Mr. Esau Nothing. At some point soon after passing by the monitoring unit, a poodle walked out into the path of Defendant's speeding car. Defendant took action immediately. He swerved the car to the left, and sent his car spinning out of control. There is no indication that he was able to regain control of the car. Jones' car spun out of control for more than two seconds, again, as confirmed by Mrs. Stigmatism and Mr. Nothing. Defendant then smashed his car into the back of plaintiff Smith's parked car. No one witnessed the actions of the poodle after Jones swerved away from it, but the poodle was unharmed in the incident.

These details may be interesting, but it is unlikely that they will have any effect on the average pretrial motion. Remember, a motion represents only a tiny part of a much bigger case, and if these details are not relevant for the particular purpose of the motion at hand, leave them out. They will wear out your reader and squander her attention span.

➤ Do use descriptive terms for facts, verbs, adjectives, and adverbs borrowed from the case law and authorities to describe the facts (i.e., employ parallelism). For example:

Example: If the facts described in the authorities for proper conduct is "proactive measures to prevent infection," state in the facts that your client "undertook the following proactive measures to prevent infection by viral agents."

Do not say: The client undertook "safety measures," "infection control proto-col," or "strenuous action to curb infection."

➤ If the term is a legal conclusion, however, avoid stating it using the conclusory term. This would be the equivalent of writing a legal conclusion in the facts section. Simply report the action:

> *Example:* If the legal standard requires a finding of lack of provocation, do not simply state that: "Plaintiff did not provoke the dog in any way." This is a legal conclusion. Instead, say: "Plaintiff did not bother the dog, or anger, or threaten, or intimidate, or rile up the dog in any way." Even an adjective like "provoca-tive" carries a legal conclusion, so be careful of such words.

> If "immediate notification" of the injury is the operative legal standard, you can probably get away with stating that your client "immediately notified the plaintiff of the injury at 11:23 a.m." But this is a bit conclusory, and it might offend some judges. To be on the safe side, avoid the legal terms of art, but state what happened in explicit terms: "Within fourteen minutes of the inci-dent, defendant informed plaintiff of the injury."

➤ Do not be redundant, unless the point that you are making *is* the number of times your opponent did the same bad thing.

C. Do you cite authority in the statement of facts?

Cites to legal authority will be unnecessary because you are not going to be making statements about the law in the facts section. But citation to **factual authority** to back up your statements in the **statement of facts** is required. Do it whenever you cite a certain fact for the first time.

> *Example:* Brown's two visits to the state were for charity purposes unrelated to any business activity conducted by Brown. See Affidavit of Derek Brown dated July 14, 2005, ¶ 4 (attached hereto as exhibit 1) ("Brown Aff."). Van Pelt did not attend either of the visits. Complaint ¶¶ 3-5. The charity visits had nothing to do with Brown's sales of exercise equipment to Van Pelt. Brown Aff. ¶ 6. Neither visit lasted longer than three hours, putting the total time that Brown spent in Pennsylvania at less than six hours. Id.[4]

---

[4] As illustrated in the example, id. is a proper shorthand for referring back to the immediately preceding factual authority. Other shorthand phrases should be defined for the benefit of the reader, as shown in the example. Affidavit of Derek Brown dated July 14, 2005, ¶ 4 ("Brown Aff.").

Later, in the argument section, you do not need to keep citing back to the authority each time you discuss that fact.

D. In what order do you have to present the facts?

Choose whichever order is the most compelling for your argument, but with one strong piece of advice: if chronological order works, use it. It is the easiest to follow. People expect it. It makes them happy.

If a chronological presentation does nothing for your client, use a topical or thematic presentation of the facts. In a contract case, you might first talk about the contract terms, then how the parties first got together on the deal, pre-negotiation actions, then the negotiation, then the post-contracting activities, or you might talk about the three main components of the contract, and how each one was negotiated and performed. In a personal injury case, you might first talk about the accident and the injury (your client's involvement) then about the facts leading up to the injury (the causation facts).

You might use a client-oriented presentation. In a patent infringement or unfair trade practices case you might first talk about your client, its history, its business; then the development of the client's product; then the competitor and its product (which may have been earlier in time). Always tell the facts with the client's interest and client's point of view in mind.

E. Sample statement of facts

Consider the following examples:

Example 1: Introduction and Statement of Facts from Defendants' Motion to Dismiss in the Bolling v. Stirling and Alden Hall case:

UNITED STATES DISTRICT COURT
SOUTHERN DISTRICT OF NEW YORK

GEORGIE BOLLING, a Minor, by his father and next friend, Robert Bolling,	))))	
Plaintiff,	))	
v.	))	No. 05-2345-TRW
ALDEN HALL HISTORICAL SITE, and ELLIOTT STIRLING,	)))	
Defendants.	)	

DEFENDANTS' MEMORANDUM IN SUPPORT OF MOTION TO DISMISS FOR FAILURE TO STATE A CLAIM

Defendants Alden Hall Historical Site ("Alden Hall") and Elliott Stirling ("Stirling") move this Court pursuant to Fed. R. Civ. P. 12(b)(6) to dismiss the complaint brought by Plaintiff Georgie Bolling ("Plaintiff") for failure to state a cause of action upon which relief may be granted.

INTRODUCTION

Plaintiff's action to recover for a dog bite is barred because he provoked the dog. On February 1, 2005, Plaintiff was trespassing on private property adjacent to the galleries and display areas of the Alden Hall Historical Site museum. Plaintiff admits that he provoked Stirling's dog into a defensive action by spraying the dog with snow. Complaint, ¶ 8. Although he was not trying to hit the dog with a snowball, New York law declares that inadvertent provocation of a dog precludes an action arising from the dog's bite as surely as intentional provocation. The dog acted in accordance with its training as a guard dog and reacted to Plaintiff's act by subduing Plaintiff, which in the process resulted in Plaintiff receiving lacerations on his arm. Even though Plaintiff admits that the dog was sprayed by snow and that he provoked it in this manner, Plaintiff still brings this complaint seeking damages not only from the dog's owner but also from Alden Hall, the adjacent property owner. Under controlling authority of this state, provocation of the dog is a complete bar to recovery and mandates the dismissal of this complaint as against Alden Hall and Stirling.

STATEMENT OF FACTS

On February 1, 2005, Plaintiff and his father toured the grounds of Alden Hall. Complaint, ¶ 4. They did not stay on the tour route, and instead approached a building (Stirling's private residence) that was set off from the rest of the museum buildings. See Complaint, ¶¶ 4-5. Plaintiff saw a sign that indicated that he and his father were standing on private property and which advised them to "Keep Out." Id. ¶ 6. Plaintiff claims that the remaining portion of the sign, which advised them of the presence of Stirling's dog, was covered by snow and not visible. Id. Nevertheless, Plaintiff and his father ignored the sign and proceeded directly to the house that they now knew was private property. Id. ¶ 7. Shortly thereafter, Stirling's dog, Pebbles, greeted the two. Id. ¶ 8. Pebbles did not attack the two, but approached them in a friendly manner. Id. At this point, Plaintiff and his father started a snowball fight in which Plaintiff missed a throw at his father and wound up hitting the dog with a snowball, spraying the dog with snow. See Affidavit of Elliot Stirling dated June 3, 2005, ¶ 7. The dog reacted to the attack by an uninvited guest according to his training as a guard dog and engaged Plaintiff to subdue him. See id. This involves restraining the arm of the attacker with the only means available to a dog, his mouth. Id.

Plaintiff apparently struggled with the dog and received several cuts on his arm. <u>See</u> Complaint, ¶ 9.

The two most important facts in this case, which Plaintiff must concede, are that Plaintiff strayed off the public pathways and did not return to them when he and his father saw the warning sign, <u>see</u> Complaint ¶¶ 4-5, and that Plaintiff angered the dog by spraying it with snow. <u>See</u> Complaint, ¶¶ 7-8.

Example 2: same example, but from plaintiff's perspective.

UNITED STATES DISTRICT COURT
SOUTHERN DISTRICT OF NEW YORK

GEORGIE BOLLING, a Minor, by his father and next friend, Robert Bolling,	))))	
Plaintiff,	))	
v.	))	No. 05-2345-TRW
ALDEN HALL HISTORICAL SITE, and ELLIOTT STIRLING,	)))	
Defendants.	)	

PLAINTIFF'S RESPONSE TO DEFENDANTS ALDEN HALL AND STIRLING'S FED. R. CIV. P. 12(b)(6) MOTION TO DISMISS FOR FAILURE TO STATE A CLAIM

INTRODUCTION

Defendants Elliott Stirling ("Stirling") and Alden Hall Historical Site ("Alden Hall") have taken the position that they can give a vicious dog free rein to roam a public place where it might injure small children. Stirling's dog's attack on Plaintiff Georgie Bolling ("Georgie") on February 1, 2005, in which Georgie had his arm ripped so badly that it required 120 stitches, was not "provoked" by Georgie as that term has been defined in New York case law. The attack was vicious and disproportionate to the accidental dusting of snow that the dog experienced when it got in the middle of Georgie and his father's snowball game. The fact that the dog was loose and menacing patrons of the museum as they attempted to keep to the public walkways and go about their business touring the museum points directly to the liability of both defendants. The defendants failed to provide proper signage warning of the dog and failed to provide proper boundaries to prevent patrons such as Georgie from accidentally straying onto private property. Plaintiff's complaint states all the elements required for recovery under the New York "Dog Bite" statute, N.Y. Dog Bite Law § 516, and defendants' motion to dismiss for failure to state a claim must be denied.

STATEMENT OF FACTS

As stated in the Complaint, ¶¶ 4-9, the incident on February 1, 1998, involved a vicious attack by a German Shepard guard dog on a small boy, Georgie Bolling. Georgie and his father were following a tour route and keeping to the public walkways, which led them to a building which looked the same as all the other museum buildings. Id. ¶ 4. Nothing fenced in, blocked off, or otherwise demarcated this building and its surroundings from the rest of the public tour area. Id. By the time the two stumbled upon a sign partially sticking up out of the snow that informed them that they had managed to get onto someone's private property, Georgie and his father were already face to face with defendant Stirling's guard dog. Id. ¶ 5. Nothing about the dog seemed threatening at first, so the two proceeded along the public walkway to the house to ask if there was any more to see on the tour. See id. ¶ 6.

Georgie, as a typical seven year old might do, thought it would be amusing to start a friendly snowball game with his father in the yard. See Complaint, ¶ 7. Georgie never intended to involve the dog in the game and aimed his first snowball at his father. See id. The snowball somehow missed, and the dog was accidentally sprayed with the light powdery snow. See id. ¶ 8. (This accidental dusting with snow is what the defendants refer to as "direct provocation" for a vicious attack. Defendants' Memorandum in Support of Motion to Dismiss at 2, 4).

The guard dog's reaction to the snow dusting he received was completely unexpected and violent: the dog jumped on Georgie and ripped into his arm with vicious force. See Complaint, ¶ 9. The cuts he inflicted were deep and the German Shepard had to be dragged off of his victim by Georgie's father. Id. Georgie's father managed to pick Georgie up and flee from the scene, chased by the guard dog who continued to menace the two. Id. He ran several hundred feet until two museum employees could assist his escape by grabbing and restraining the dog. Id. After Georgie was rushed to the hospital emergency room, the doctors needed 120 stitches to close up the wounds inflicted by the German Shepard. See Affidavit of Walt Pacquin dated June 4, 2005, ¶ 3.

V. ARGUMENT

The argument section roughly parallels the discussion section of the office memorandum, but, as you probably already have guessed, it is not drafted in the same manner as the discussion section of an objective, informative legal memorandum. The argument must be as persuasive, well-reasoned, and credible as any office memorandum, but it must be completely one sided in favor of the client.

You may think, "The law is what it is," but that thought implies that the law always is concrete and black and white. Not so. The black letter law legal principles in any given area usually are not the rules over which you will be litigating. The law at the margins of every area of law (and they often are broad margins) is fluid, changing, painted in shades of gray, not necessarily well-defined, and sometimes even inconsistent. In many cases, it will take all of your skill as an interpreter and analyst of legal sources to take the raw material of the law and find a way to present it in such a way that the client's position looks reasonable, logical, and downright righteous under the law. But at least you often will have a good supply of paint and canvas that the authors of the legal sources have provided to you.

A. Goal for the argument

The argument has one goal: to enable the client to win the motion. It is not intended to present an in depth exposition on the general area of law presented by the motion. It is not intended to inform the court of the interesting and difficult aspects of the specific area of the law that governs the motion. It is not meant directly to educate the court about the pros and cons of a decision on the motion; the only message you should send is that the only proper outcome is ruling in your client's favor, but there are many negatives associated with not ruling in your client's favor. It is argument. It is not education.

Do not read this to mean that the goal of the argument section is to misrepresent or distort the true meaning and effect of the controlling law in your jurisdiction. Nowhere do we advocate lying and cheating about the law. Our rule for the argument section is as follows:

> ## THE RULE FOR THE ARGUMENT SECTION:
>
> **Advocacy requires a client-oriented, persuasive rendering of the correct legal standards that govern the motion.**

Every part of this rule deserves explanation and emphasis.

1. Client oriented

You are going to show why the client should prevail using controlling and persuasive legal authorities in a way that supports your arguments. It is a one-sided presentation. You will make the argument that your client should win.

2. Persuasive

No one wins an argument just by shouting the loudest. Your skills of legal exposition and creativity will be tested as never before when you have to take on a difficult assignment in a difficult area of law and present the law in such a way that any reader will be able to understand your points and be convinced that your client's position is sound. Naturally, your ultimate goal is to convince one person, the judge, that your position is not just sound, but in fact correct.

3. Correct legal standards—no cheating!

If we are being redundant, we apologize, but we want to be exceedingly clear that the proper and ethical methodology of an advocate is not to lie and cheat about the law. You must present a correct interpretation of the law, albeit not necessarily every case that has been handed down in this area, and not every sentence about the rules from the authorities in the area.

If the law does not support you, either do not make the argument (best idea) or present your argument with an explanation that it depends on a change in the law. Never misrepresent the law to the court.

4. Movant's advice

Movants should follow this advice: **Movants should never bring a motion for which there is no legal support.** If you are the Movant, you should not even wonder about stretching or distorting the law because you should not bring a motion for which there is no legal support.

5. Opponent's advice

If you are the opponent and you have a decent argument on the merits, then pursue it first and foremost. This is the best practice. But if the movant has done her job correctly, chances are that the law does not support your client's position. You still have a number of choices:

a. Be open and discuss the law as it is, but argue for a change

In every opposition, you will do you best to argue against the Movant's position, and attempt to distinguish Movant's authorities, but if the controlling law is against you, the most forthright and sometimes effective course to follow is to admit the controlling law is negative and against your client, but argue that the law should be changed or interpreted differently so that your client can win. You will not win this way very often, but you might keep the client happy because you fought the good fight, and you will impress the court a great deal with your candor. Naturally, the more effort you put into the task of finding primary and secondary persuasive authorities that are favorable to you client, and support for the policies you will assert are furthered by a change in the law, the more likely it is that you will prevail.

Note well that we only are talking about a situation where the **controlling** authority in your jurisdiction is against you, or there is no controlling authority and all of the persuasive authority you can find goes against you. If it is merely a situation where there is some good and some troublesome authority, you should not be approaching the court in a defensive posture, but rather doing your best to present the best law to the court, and trying hard to distinguish and downplay the negative authority.

b. Change the issues, and argue a legal position that you can defend

No one said you have to stick to the issues that the movant thought were important for the motion. If the substance of the motion (the merits) are bad for your client, argue procedural reasons for the denial of motion. Evaluate whether it is possible for you to argue that the motion is improper, against the rules, untimely, unnecessary, violates laches, and then, and only then, get into the merits. You might argue that the motion is described as or argues XYZ, but the movant really should be bringing PDQ motion or making a PDQ argument, and you proceed to explain that your client wins under a PDQ analysis. This is the method of the skilled litigator, to turn a sow's ear of a motion into a silk purse.

We explained this tactic more thoroughly above in the section on the introduction, and if you get the impression that we really like this option, you are right. This option turns the tables on the movant so that you can argue your own points. Not only do you increase your chances of actually winning, but the movant will have to use up his reply brief addressing your points rather than furthering hers.

B. Structure – TREAT format[5]

The TREAT format applies to the drafting of the argument section—argumentative Thesis headings, Rule section, Explanation of the positive and negative authorities, Application to the client's situation, and Thesis restated as a Conclusion. Because the argument has to further the client's cause in winning the motion, the following considerations apply that are different from or in addition to the requirements for the discussion section of the office memorandum:

1. Argumentative thesis headings

One of the reasons that we stress the importance of the introduction is that it gets the important information to the reader in the shortest possible time, so that even if she only reads the first page of your motion, she will have the chance to hear the most important parts of your entire argument on the motion. The same thing applies to the drafting of the headings that will divide up your argument section—make them useful, argumentative, and informative, so that even if your reader merely skims through your motion, she still will have the opportunity to see each point (each conclusion) of your argument.

A good thesis heading not only reveals a conclusion but provides the "because" part—the legal principles and facts that lead up to the conclusion. For example, the following are good argumentative Thesis headings:

---

[5] If you are unfamiliar with the TREAT format, please see the Appendix to this volume.

➤ **Examples of proper thesis headings in the argument**

    A. Bolling did nothing to provoke the dog prior to the attack because he did not directly attack or threaten the dog as required under New York law.

    B. Bolling was acting peacefully in a place where he had a lawful right to be because he walked on a public sidewalk at Alden Hall without causing any noisy disturbance.

    C. Provocation does not bar Bolling's recovery because the dog's attack on Bolling was vicious and disproportionate to the dusting of snow the Dog received from Bolling.

The following are **not** good headings:

    A. Lack of Provocation
    B. Bolling was acting peacefully in a place where he had a lawful right to be.
    C. The dog's attack was disproportionate.

These last three examples do not suggest enough of the facts and principles of the law to make the headings useful, and the first of these three does not even tell the author's conclusion about the topic. Do not waste a heading by writing something like these. Let your headings be a quick summary of your argument if read one right after the other.

2. Forming a favorable rule for the rule section

The law is not static, and neither does your expression of the law have to be static. There are many ways to express legal rules and to characterize how the rules work and how they ought to be interpreted and applied. This section reviews these methods.

There is one hard and fast rule for the rule section of your motion: you must cite and discuss all applicable constitutional provisions, statutes, or administrative regulations. If a constitutional, statutory, or administrative provision is on point, it is controlling and must be presented. There is no way around it. You at least must cite it, and you should go so far as to quote the pertinent, applicable language (or sections or sub-parts) from the statute or rule.

Beyond the citation and excerpting of the applicable terms of constitutional, statutory, or administrative provisions, you have many opportunities to express what the law means in a way that favors your client. Cite and discuss cases that construe (alter, modify, extend, etc.) the statute or rule, and any administrative law authorities (administrative rules and regulations) that interpret and implement the legislation.

If the rule is determined largely by case law in the absence of a statute or rule or as a progression of the law after the passage of the statute or rule, you must focus on deriving the best rule for your client using the best authorities available. This is the hardest advice to communicate tangibly, because we can describe the goal and give a few pointers, but the actual task of taking a body of undigested law and pulling from it the best authorities and the best language as to the rule and facts from each of these authorities is something that you simply will have to do for yourself. What is a good use and what is a great use of authorities will vary from assignment to assignment.

➢ *The rule reads:* Plaintiff's choice of forum is a factor in the determination of a transfer of venue motion but it is not a conclusive factor.

> *Example 1 - Favoring transfer:* Plaintiff's choice of forum never has been given conclusive weight in the venue transfer analysis. [CITES]. It merely is one of many factors for the court to consider. [CITES].

> *Example 2 - Opposing transfer:* In determining a transfer of venue motion, the court must give regard to the plaintiff's choice of forum. [CITES]. Each court is mandated to consider the effect of denying plaintiff her choice of forum, and most courts give it priority in the order of discussion of the issues. [CITES].

Both of these characterizations of the rule are accurate, but one tends to favor transfer and the other does not. "Priority" in the second example refers to the fact that in most cases, the issue of protecting plaintiff's choice of forum is discussed first, but the word has positive connotations beyond the simple expression of the order of discussion. In both examples, it may be necessary to use the prefatory word "see" in front of the citations to authority if you are drawing a direct inference supported by the authorities rather than repeating exactly what the authorities say.

➢ *The rules read:* Claimants must demonstrate a likelihood of confusion between the trademark and the allegedly infringing mark. Courts are to use a "reasonable viewer" standard.

> *Example 1 - Favoring claimant:* Plaintiff need only show that there is a likelihood of confusion by a reasonable viewer when the infringing mark is compared to the original trademark. [CITES]. Plaintiff need not prove actual confusion among a particular group of viewers, but only a "reasonable viewer." [CITES].

> *Example 2 - Opposing claimant:* Plaintiff bears the burden of proving that there is a likelihood of confusion not among a learned consumer or a devoted user of its products, but among a random group of "reasonable viewers." [CITES]. It is not enough to show that devoted users would recognize the similarity. [CITES].

The characterization of the rule in example 2 simply sounds harder to meet. It lays out the same principles of the law as the first example, but it does so in a way that expresses that the burden on the claimant is onerous. This phrasing helps to oppose the claimant.

The following chart should refresh your recollection about how to go about putting together the rule from multiple authorities, performing a "rule synthesis," and putting it into the Rule section of an objective work. Naturally, start with controlling authority.

Formulate the Rule (Rule Synthesis)

❶ Start with the highest and most recent controlling authority

- ◆ If you have a statute (or regulation), start with the statute.
- ◆ If you have a watershed case that is controlling, start with that.
- ◆ If your best authority is from the court of last resort, take the most recent opinion from that court, and start with that.
- ◆ If these first three criteria do not apply, start with the most recent actual controlling authority that is on point.
- ◆ Only if none of the above applies would you consider turning to non-controlling authority—primary or secondary.
- ◆ Don't expect to use all of your authorities.

❷ Reconcile differing statements or phrasings of the rule from controlling authorities, and attempt to synthesize the material into one coherent statement of the legal principles that govern the issue

- ◆ DON'T change the wording of or paraphrase rules from statutes, administrative rules and regs, and watershed cases.
- ◆ Unless a processed applied rule can be written smoothly and effectively in one sentence or phrase, write the rule first with modifications second.

❸ Write the rule first, interpretative rules second, and exceptions to the rule third

- ◆ Write interpretive sub-rules on elements of the rule in the section or sub-TREAT discussion that discusses that element of the rule. Write exceptions to the sub-rules after you lay out the sub-rules themselves.

❹ Do not write a rule with inherent contradictions

- ◆ Check for ambiguity in the terms you have used to formulate the rule (even if some of these terms came from the authorities).

❺ Do accept the <u>remote</u> possibility that two competing rules on the same issue might exist in the same jurisdiction

- ◆ When this happens, you may have to analyze the facts under both competing sets of rules.

Try to find a common, underlying rule of law that governs the issue at hand that can properly be derived from or traced to controlling authority. Examine the ways that the rule has been recited in the various controlling authorities. Then draft the rule section compiling the best words and standards from the authorities in the form of a rule synthesis with terms that tends to favor your client's legal position. You must be fair, but you most often will have leeway to craft the rules in a light that is more favorable to your client than a random selection of principles and interpretive rules found in cases.

The style and formatting advice for how office memoranda should be drafted generally applies, but remember that the goal in a motion is to present the law in the best possible light for your client. Explore the authorities for the best possible rendition of the legal standards that govern the issue. A rule synthesis may help you avoid a sticky wording of the rule on the issue that shows up in some but not all of the authorities. Naturally, if the rule comes from a statute or administrative rule, you are stuck with the official wording, but you still can look for later interpretive authorities that may have explained the rule in ways that are kinder to the client. Even if you refuse to do a rule synthesis, and decide to present the legal principles seriatim, start with the rules and standards that most favor your client's situation, and finish with those the client has the most problems with but still can manage to meet.

3. Use interpretive rules that support the client's case

Look for interpretive rules and sub-rules that help the client's cause. If the rule is from a statute or administrative rule, these interpretive rulings may be the only friendly rendition of the legal standards that you will find in favor of your client. Do not cite incidental interpretive rules that do not help the client's cause; leave that to your opponent, if she is on the ball. Only cite interpretive rules that support your client's facts and your theory of the case.

> *Example:* Your client combined a photograph of a famous celebrity who was on trial for murder with the famous photograph of Lee Harvey Oswald holding the mail order rifle that he allegedly used to assassinate President John F. Kennedy so that it appears that the celebrity is holding the famous rifle in the famous Oswald pose. The celebrity sued your client for violation of his right of publicity. One defense is to show that the use is a parody. In your jurisdiction, in order to prove a parody defense, you must show that the original image was transformed in such a way that it is obvious that there are two works present—an original image of the celebrity and a new image that is directly critical of the celebrity.

In your rule section that discusses this parody requirement, you have the choice of using the following interpretive rules for parody that appear in various controlling authorities of the applicable jurisdiction:

Good interpretive rule: "The creator of the new work must add value to the old work."

This is good because your client did add value to the work through her artistic additions. The new work is clever and comments on the celebrity through use of artistic symbolism.

Better interpretive rule: "It must be obvious that there are two works evident from examination of the alleged parody—an older image of the celebrity, and a new image with new content, meaning, and expression that is critical of the celebrity. It is not enough if the creator of the images intends to criticize the celebrity if the meaning of the altered image is not evident from looking at the altered image itself."

This is even better than the above example because it is closer to your client's facts. Your client's work reveals two well known original images and a third image—the combined image—and it will be obvious to anyone familiar with the two original images that the client's image has new content, meaning, and expression achieved by putting the celebrity into the position of a famous assassin. This effect needs no explanation from your client; it is obvious from looking at her work.

Not good interpretive rules: "The value of the new work may be established by showing that the application of artistic skill transformed the work into a unique new work that does not depend on the celebrity's image for its value. It also may be shown by the fact that the artist is so famous that his work is far more valuable for his having created it than any mundane image of the celebrity created by an unknown artist."

Although these interpretive rules would not necessarily be fatal to your client's situation, they are not that helpful. Remember, you have a choice in what interpretive rules to bring out, and the first rule here seems to fit the situation of a painter or sculptor—or even a cartoonist—better than an artist like your client who combines photographs for expressive effect. Would the average person viewing your client's works see the application of valuable artistic skill, or just cleverness? The second rule may not suit your client at all if your client is not a famous artist whose works are of obvious value even to a casual follower of the arts (such as most judges and some jurors). Therefore, you should avoid bringing out both of these interpretive rules in your rule section.

4. Use of explanatory synthesis[6] in the explanation section

In the explanation section, you should use explanatory synthesis to explain how the rule works in real life situations in the most compact and powerful manner. The following chart reveals the principles and methodology of drafting the explanation section and using explanatory synthesis:

---

[6] If you are unfamiliar with the process of explanatory synthesis, please see the Appendix to this volume.

Explain the Rule (Explanatory Synthesis)

Goals of the Explanation Section	
The goal is to explain how the rule is to be interpreted and applied based on how the authorities have applied it in actual concrete factual settings, and on how commentators have interpreted the rule	◆ You are going beyond what the courts already have said about the rule in interpretive rules found in cases ◆ You are presenting principles of interpretation that are supported by a careful reading of the cases ◆ You are doing the work of digesting and synthesizing the cases so the reader doesn't have to
Case-by-case presentations make the reader do most of the work and they are wasteful of space and time (<u>i.e.</u>, the reader's attention span)	◆ Avoid case-by-case presentations even though they are easy to write, and sometimes fun to write ◆ Avoid case-by-case-presentations even though courts use them ◆ The only time to resort to a case-by-case presentation is when you have one or two cases that arc so closc to the facts that you want to cover them in great detail, or if you want to distinguish one or two troublesome cases in enough detail to make your point
The Process of Explanatory Synthesis	
❶ Read cases and look for common facts and common outcomes ❷ Review the groups to find the factors or public policies that make the difference in the outcome	◆ Group cases by facts ◆ Divide groups of cases by outcome ◆ Reconcile cases that have different outcomes; what policy or theme or factor determined the outcome in these cases ◆ Reconcile cases that have the same outcome on different facts; what common policy or theme or factors brought about the same outcome on different facts
❸ Write principles of interpretation that explain your findings	◆ Phrase your principles of interpretation in language that mimics interpretive rules

❹ Cite the cases that support your principles of interpretation with parentheticals that provide facts or other information about each case ❺ When you draft the Application section, apply the principles of interpretation to your own facts; as a general rule, do not apply individual cases to your facts	◆ Often you can use interpretive rules as principles that tie together multiple authorities; there is no requirement that you always have to come up with brand new principles ◆ Parentheticals should contain enough information to illustrate how the individual case supports the general principle you have laid out ◆ Use shorthands and abbreviated phrases to save space ◆ Applying principles to facts will make your analysis more convincing; you have spelled out the connections to be made between the authorities and then followed through and showed how the principles learned from a study of the authorities determines the outcome of the case at hand ◆ The exception to this rule is when you have one or two fabulous cases that are worthy of individual attention in the Explanation section; these should be discussed individually in the Application section, whether as support or to distinguish them

You cannot waste the reader's time in an adversarial matter. Judges will not take the time to read five or more paragraphs of facts from cases that have applied the rule. You only should discuss as much of the facts from the authorities as is necessary to explain your application of the law to the client's facts. In explanatory synthesis, you can do that through the use of parentheticals and other devices that shorten the discussion (e.g., conclusory, declarative statements of the critical importance of the authorities, followed by a cite to multiple authorities, or use of the "Compare . . . with . . ." citation method). Even if you decide it is necessary to expound on the facts of one particular controlling case because it is *the* case on this topic in the applicable jurisdiction, you should limit yourself to an exposition of those facts to which you are going to draw an analogy or distinction. The necessity to provide any explanation of the authorities that discuss a rule will depend on the procedural versus substantive nature of the rule (see discussion of procedural vs. substantive arguments below), and the importance of the rule to the motion at hand.

5. Movant's anticipation and handling of negative authority

If you have a number of good **controlling** authorities, the fact that there are a number of negative **persuasive** authorities out there is of little concern to anyone. Occasionally, you, as the movant, will have a situation where nothing but favorable authority exists on the motion you are drafting— you cannot find a single authority that goes against your client's position. Enjoy that feeling as long as you can, because it is fleeting. Just as often, you will have a body of good authorities that favor your client's position and some bad authorities that go against the client in one way or the other. One of the toughest jobs of the movant is to decide how much negative authority on the law to anticipate and handle (distinguish, explain) in the opening motion. It is tough because your space always is limited, and you do not want to do such a good job raising and discussing negative authorities that you write your opponent's brief for her.

We will assume first of all that you do have some controlling authorities in favor of your position. Always cover your positive controlling authorities first in the explanation section—you do not want to start off in a defensive posture. Then, the best advice we can give is to try to save space at the end of each explanation section to discuss any significant potentially controlling negative authorities. "Significant" means they are close enough to the facts of your situation that you are given pause when you read them, and they are recent enough that you cannot easily argue (if called upon to do so, probably in the reply brief you will file) that the law has changed and moved on from these older sources. It pays to have the first word on these negative potentially controlling authorities, and it is far less likely that you will be educating the other side about cases that they would not otherwise find in their research (and even if the opponent would have missed them, the court probably will not).

If you do not have any controlling authority in favor of your position, then you **must** show why there is no controlling authority that goes directly against your position (or you should not be bringing the motion in the first place). In the explanation section, you first must discuss your positive persuasive authorities, and then distinguish any negative potentially controlling and negative persuasive authorities.

The principles of "explanatory synthesis" discussed above apply with equal force in distinguishing negative authority in the explanation section. If there are several negative cases, try to group them on the basis of common facts and common holding and discuss them as a group. Thus, you can distinguish the whole group in one fell swoop, and de-emphasize the impact of the number of cases. If there is no way to group them on the basis of facts and holding, you still should try to find a common thread of legal argument or public policy that characterizes them. If you can refute and distinguish the logical under-pinning of the cases, you can more easily convince the court that the entire group of cases should be rejected because they all rely on the same logical foundation.

If there is no negative potentially controlling authority, you have more leeway in determining how much negative persuasive authority to anticipate and distinguish. Be careful not to raise and explain too much negative persuasive authority and thus help your opponent write her brief in opposition. The scope of persuasive authority is far ranging, and if you are the kind of diligent and thorough researcher that we hope you will be after reading this book, you may be finding a lot more negative persuasive authority that your opponent and the court will not bother to look for. Remember, too, that you will have a reply brief in which to address anything that your opponent finds that she puts to good use against you.

So, what kind of persuasive authority should you incorporate? We would limit it to primary persuasive authorities (cases, primarily) that are from the proper jurisdiction.

➢ *Example:* In a case in the New York Supreme Court for New York County that is governed by New York law, your case is controlled by the decisions of the 1st Department of the Supreme Court, Appellate Division. Cases that are not from the proper hierarchy of judicial authority are not controlling (e.g., cases from the 2nd, 3rd, or 4th Departments of the Supreme Court, Appellate Division), but these may be regarded as highly persuasive

➢ *Example:* In a federal question case in the United States District Court for the District of Massachusetts, only decisions from the United States Court of Appeals for the First Circuit control. The decisions of the other United States Courts of Appeals (e.g., from the Second through the Eleventh Circuits and the D.C. and Federal Circuits in between) are not controlling, but should be regarded has highly persuasive.

These authorities are highly persuasive because of the law they apply, and even if they are not even potentially controlling, they can carry the day and deserve your attention to distinguish and explain them.

We would not go out of our way to address other kinds of primary or secondary persuasive authority unless it has an extremely high stature—for example, Wright and Miller on Federal Practice and Procedure, a restatement of the law, a judicial superstar—and the discussion is close enough to your situation to cause you to sweat.

Lastly, let us advise you that if you have nothing with which to distinguish persuasive authority or no explanation that ameliorates the effect of the authority, it is best ***not*** to raise it at all. You are drawing a lot of attention to a persuasive authority when you anticipate it in your opening brief, and if you only make a half-hearted attempt to distinguish the authority, it will stand out like a beacon for your opponent and the court to notice. Remember, we are talking about a motion and memorandum of law drafted for the adversarial system, and if you do not cover something, it is your opponent's job to raise it and cover it. Always try to distinguish an authority that is more likely than not to be controlling, but beyond that, avoid doing your opponent's work for her.

6. Opponent's handling of negative authority

The opponent has little choice in this matter—you must attempt to distinguish and explain all of the potentially controlling and strong persuasive authority that the movant has thrown at you. It is a terrible error not to address all of the potentially controlling authority in your opposition. Beyond that, we would strive to say something positive about the primary persuasive authority upon which movant relies, and do as much as you can to counteract the negative secondary persuasive authority.

C. How much of a TREAT to give – procedural vs. substantive issues and counter-arguments

1. Procedural versus substantive

The procedural-substantive distinction will often help you to make a determination about whether to draft a complete TREAT of an individual issue in your motion—especially, whether to draft a full blown explanation section to explain the rule on the issue and how it works in various factual situations. The simplest way to determine whether or not an issue is more procedural than substantive is to see if the governing rule comes from a court rule of procedure, such as the Federal Rules of Civil Procedure. For example, if you have one issue to brief in the motion that is simply "What are the standards necessary for granting summary judgment in *any* case," then you are dealing with a procedural rule, Fed. R. Civ. P. 56, and what it and the authorities that interpret it say about the award of summary judgment in any federal civil litigation.

Generally, the rules of procedure deal with topics relating to the propriety of the case being in a court (e.g., subject matter jurisdiction), a person being before the court (personal jurisdiction, service of process, and venue), the content of pleadings and papers and addition or amendment of claims and defenses, timeliness issues (timing of filings and statutory limitations periods), whether complete relief is possible between the parties (joinder of claims or parties, third-party practice), discovery matters, evidence, and whether and how a party gets to do something in the case (including motions, scheduling, stays, trials, and relief from judgment).

In contrast, a substantive issue involves the parties' rights and defenses, including claims and causes of action and the elements of same, affirmative defenses and avoidances and the elements of same, damages and remedies, and the actual substantive right to certain relief, such as the substantive law that determines whether a complaint has stated a claim upon which relief may be granted, whether the actual claims or defenses asserted in the parties' pleadings are subject to summary judgment, and whether a party is entitled to a new trial or judgment as a matter of law on one or more of its actual claims.

If you determine that an issue is purely procedural, you may consider the following when deciding how much of a TREAT and explanation to give the issue:

1. If you are citing an authority solely for a legal standard on procedure that it discusses, it is most likely unnecessary to discuss the facts of the authority. Many of the rules on procedure come from statutes and "rules," such as the Federal Rules of Civil Procedure, that have no facts. But aside from that, the facts of a case that states a useful legal standard or interpretive or explanatory rule on a procedural issue may not be important or illustrative to your argument.

2. If you are making an argument that the procedural rules should be applied in a certain way to the client's facts, then you will want to analogize to other cases where the rule was also applied to similar facts, and you will need to draft an explanation section. Often in a motion to dismiss for lack of personal jurisdiction, venue, subject matter jurisdiction, or violation of the statute of limitations, you will need to compare and analogize your client's facts to facts in similar cases in order to make a compelling argument on the procedural point.

The courts tend to be less consistent on purely procedural (who gets to do what and when and how) determinations than on substantive determinations. You will often find cases going either way. This fact may be attributed in large part to the appellate standard of review on procedural points, which generally grants a great deal of discretion to the trial court to make whatever procedural decisions it feels appropriate in the case before it. In the face of this body of potentially inconsistent authority, you still must discuss and apply or distinguish all potentially controlling authority on purely procedural points, but any persuasive authorities that go against your client's position on these points generally can be ignored. Cite the good persuasive authority on procedure and leave the rest out. Of course, if the "bad" persuasive authority is a powerhouse (some super-judge, a great treatise such as Wright & Miller, etc.), then you still might take the time to explain it away, but it is not required. Maybe wait and see if your opponent tries to make a lot of hay with it.

2. Anticipating counter-arguments

Anticipation of an opponent's defenses and counter-arguments on a motion is something a movant must worry about—movants have the choice. An opponent has to respond to the movant's arguments one way or the other. But devoting an entire TREAT section to laying out and refuting an opponent's counter-argument is a substantial investment of precious space in your motion, and you should be wary of attempting this maneuver.

In general, the same principles apply here as determine when to cite and distinguish negative authority: if the opponent's argument is fairly obvious and the negative authorities are almost certainly going to be found by your opponent, then it is a good idea to try to have the first word and set the right spin on the argument. If the opponent's argument is not particularly strong, or the authorities are fairly obscure and not easily found and interpreted, then you have much less incentive to take them up and try to refute them.

The problem is that you never want to do your opponent's work for her. Do not develop and discuss a contrary argument so well that your opponent will easily take up your discussion and do a good job briefing the counter-argument in her opposition brief. Your discussion and counter-analysis on the topic may provide more fodder for her brief than anything the opponent could develop in support of the argument on her own. Thus, if you are fairly certain that your opponent will not even think of an argument or will present it in a most unconvincing way, do not discuss the issues and points of the contrary argument ahead of time. Of course, if your opponent is a top-flight lawyer who will not miss the issues and arguments that are present in the case, then you should feel free to do as thorough a counter-analysis as you can afford to, in light of the available space for the argument.

One additional piece of advice: do not set up a straw man argument and attribute it to the opponent in one breath just so that you can tear it to pieces in the next. Do not try to reduce a rational argument to a ridiculous and frivolous position that no one would actually assert. Straw man arguments are a cheap rhetorical device that will never carry much weight with the court, and will instead make you look ridiculous for attempting this maneuver. Give fair credit to a serious counter-argument and then do the best job you can to refute it.

However, when you have decided to anticipate and refute a serious counter-argument, you should still limit your citations to negative authority in the counter-analysis. Although we are being a bit redundant, this bears repeating. When you are spinning out an argument that belongs to your opponent, you should never present it with all the cases you found in support of that argument. If there are potentially controlling authorities, discuss and distinguish only the most recent authorities. If it is an argument that will rely on persuasive authorities, discuss only a few of the weakest, most easily refuted persuasive authorities. Make the house look so shabby that even your opponent will be embarrassed to live in it.

D. How many issues do you TREAT in a given motion?

Even though we anticipate that our readers will be wondering how many TREATs are necessary in a motion, we still feel a little foolish by raising this question here—the answer is necessarily dependent on the individual problem you were assigned and the substance of the motion that relates to the problem. A single motion may present several issues to brief, some procedural and others substantive, each of which might deserve its own TREAT, and the Rule that governs each issue may have multiple elements, each of which deserves its own sub-TREAT. Your ability to identify the issues from the problem (the facts) that were told to you, and your ability to unpack these issues and add new issues based on your research into the law that applies to the problem, is the key ability that your entire law school education is attempting to develop in you.

The following example is illustrative of the process. A motion to dismiss for lack of personal jurisdiction under Fed. R. Civ. P. 12(b)(2) might assert that defendant has no minimum contacts with the jurisdiction and no "hook" or nexus with the jurisdiction under the state "Long Arm" statute. The various TREATs necessary to answer the question might be broken down as follows:

ARGUMENT

Rule Section – this **procedural** rule does not require a full TREAT. The second sentence merely is a roadmap or "umbrella" section for the rest of the motion.	Fed R. Civ. P. 12(b)(2) provides: " . . ." This action must be dismissed because plaintiff cannot obtain personal jurisdiction over defendant in this forum under either the state Long Arm statute, and any attempted exercise of jurisdiction would violate the requirements of the Due Process clause of the United States Constitution.
Thesis on first substantive Issue	**I. PLAINTIFF FAILS TO SHOW DEFENDANT'S CONNECTION TO THE FORUM UNDER THE WISCONSIN "LONG ARM" STATUTE**
Rule Section – this is a substantive rule, so a full TREAT with sub-TREATs is necessary.	A federal court sitting in diversity must evaluate the propriety of the exercise of personal jurisdiction over the defendant under both the local state "Long Arm" statute and the requirements of the Due Process clause of the United States Constitution. <u>Tough v. Easy</u>, 123 F.3d 456, 458 (7th Cir. 1998). The Wisconsin "Long Arm" statute, Wis. Stat. § 1000.01 ("Long Arm Statute"), provides for service of process and the exercise of jurisdiction over an out-of-state defendant when the defendant has performed one or more of the following acts in the State of Wisconsin: (a) made a contract in the state; (b) conducted business in the state;. . .
Sub-Thesis regarding second substantive Issue	**A. Defendant did not make a contract in Wisconsin because the sales orders between the parties were entered into in Illinois.**
Sub-Rule, Explanation, Application and Thesis-Conclusion on second Issue. This is a sub-TREAT of the first prong of the Long Arm Statute	In order to satisfy the "making of a contract" prong of the Long Arm Statute, plaintiff must show that defendant . . . Making a contract means . . . <u>Parker v. Brothers</u>, 567 N.W.2d 987, 989 (Wis. 1973) (sales order issued from Illinois so contract was made in Illinois); <u>Clifford v. Eisle</u>, . . . The instant case presents the same exact situation as in <u>Parker</u> and <u>Clifford</u> and the other sales order cases discussed above. Defendant did not . . . Therefore, plaintiff fails to satisfy the first prong of the Long Arm Statute.

Sub-Thesis regarding third substantive Issue	**B. Defendant did not transact business in Wisconsin because transaction of business requires a party's physical presence, and mere communication of business information by electronic media is insufficient.**
Sub-Rule, Explanation, Application and Thesis-Conclusion on third Issue. This is a sub-TREAT of the second prong of the Long Arm Statute	In order to satisfy the "transaction of business" prong of the Long Arm Statute, plaintiff must show that defendant . . . Transaction of business includes . . . <u>Trivial v. Pursuit Co.</u>, 897 N.W.2d 487, 488 (Wis. 1993) (yearly visits to distributors in Wisconsin was transaction of business in Wisconsin); <u>Alfred v. Wayne</u>, . . . Unlike in <u>Trivial</u> and <u>Alfred</u> and the other "doing business" cases discussed above, in the instant case, defendant never stepped foot in the jurisdiction, and only communicated over the Internet and through telephone conversations. . . . Therefore, plaintiff fails to satisfy the second prong of the Long Arm Statute. Because plaintiff cannot show defendant's nexus with the forum under either prong of the statute, this action must be dismissed.
Thesis regarding fourth substantive Issue	**II. EXERCISE OF JURISDICTION OVER THE DEFENDANT VIOLATES THE "MINIMUM CONTACTS" REQUIREMENT OF THE DUE PROCESS CLAUSE.**
Rule, Explanation, Application and Thesis-Conclusion on fourth Issue	Even if jurisdiction were proper under the Wisconsin Long Arm Statute, plaintiff still cannot show that jurisdiction would be proper under the Due Process clause of the United States Constitution . . . Due process requires a showing of minimum contacts . . . In the instant case, defendant has never stepped foot in Wisconsin, and . . . Therefore, the exercise of personal jurisdiction over defendant would violate the Due Process clause, and this action must be dismissed for lack of personal jurisdiction.

VI. THE CONCLUSION SECTION

Some lawyers mix up the introduction and the conclusion—they often confuse the benefits of a strong beginning to their argument with a strong ending. Ideally, you could do both— a reader who was entranced by your rhetoric would follow your brief to the end and receive a strong, satisfying summation that reemphasizes all points raised in the brief and caps them off with a zinger to send the happy reader on her way. However, in actuality, your reader will not necessarily get to your last page. Therefore, a strong beginning is much more important than a strong ending. Focus your efforts there.

What is left for the conclusion of a pretrial motion? You tell the court exactly what you want the court to do, and then sign your name. It is important to get this right— you really do not want the court to have to guess about what you want it to do.

Examples of perfectly good conclusions to pretrial motions:

CONCLUSION

For the reasons stated herein, this Court should dismiss plaintiff's Petition for failure to state a claim upon which relief can be granted.

CONCLUSION

For the reasons stated above, plaintiff Jones respectfully requests the Court to deny defendant Smith's motion to dismiss or in the alternative, to stay this action.

Powerful stuff, no? You might have a lot to ask the court to do, so this section might get more complicated (and interesting). Consider the following conclusion of a motion for preliminary injunction in a trademark infringement case:

CONCLUSION

WHEREFORE, for the reasons stated above, plaintiff respectfully requests the Court to:

(a) issue an order temporarily enjoining defendant and all of its agents, employees, and contractors from the creation, display, distribution, and sale of the "Bart Simpson" mark T-shirts and products described in ¶¶ 6-9 of the Complaint filed herewith this day;

(b) issue an order temporarily enjoining defendant and all of its agents, employees, and contractors from all advertising involving the "Bart Simpson" mark described and defined in ¶¶ 6-7 of the Complaint, and specifically requiring defendant to cancel, suspend, and withdraw all print ads described in ¶ 10 of the Complaint,

---

> all radio promotions described in ¶ 11 of the Complaint, and all web pages of the internet web site at http://www.gocrazyfolks.com displaying or describing "Bart Simpson" T-shirts and products described in ¶ 12 of the Complaint;
>
>   (c) issue an order temporarily enjoining defendant from the creation, display, distribution, sale, and advertising of any other and additional works (including derivative works) displaying or using the "Bart Simpson" mark described and defined in ¶¶ 6-7 of the Complaint.

VII. FORMATTING A TRIAL LEVEL BRIEF

Sometimes local rules require a certain kind of formatting. Follow the local rules. In the absence of such rules, we recommend the following:

A. The caption, title, all headings, the signature block, and all footnotes are single-spaced. Everything else is double-spaced.

B. All text should be in the same font style, e.g., Times Roman, CG Times, Courier, or other professional looking font. Footnote text should be the same size as the regular text, or no more than one point smaller than the regular text; i.e., if the regular text is 12 point, the footnote text should be 12 point or 11 point, but no smaller.

C. One inch margins on all four sides are recommended.

D. Page numbers should be at the bottom center of each page from page 2 to the end.

E. Major headings for divisions of the brief are in bold, all caps, centered, and underlined. For example:

INTRODUCTION
STATEMENT OF FACTS
ARGUMENT
CONCLUSION

F. Major headings for the Argument are in bold, all caps, and preceded by an uppercase Roman number (I, II, III, etc.), and begin at the left margin. The text of the heading is indented from the Roman number.

G. Secondary headings in the Argument are in bold, underlined, lowercase (or title case – initial letter of each significant word capitalized), preceded by an uppercase letter (A, B, C, etc.), and are indented five spaces from the left margin. The text is indented from the letter.

H. Tertiary headings are in bold, lowercase or title case, not underlined, preceded by an Arabic number (1, 2, 3, etc.), and are indented ten spaces. The text is indented from the number.

I. Quaternary headings are in lowercase, underlined, not bolded, preceded by a lowercase letter (a, b, c, etc.), and are indented fifteen spaces, with the text indented from the letter.

J. Further headings would be lowercase, not bolded or underlined, preceded alternatively by lowercase Roman numbers (i, ii, iii, etc.), or Arabic numbers in parentheses ((1), (2), (3), etc.), or other numbering of your own devising, and indented five additional spaces per level.

This looks like this:

Progression of Headings for Pretrial Motion:

<u>ARGUMENT</u>

I. **PLAINTIFF FAILS TO ALLEGE A CAUSE OF ACTION FOR FRAUDULENT MISREPRESENTATION.**

    A. <u>**Plaintiff fails to allege that the representation was material.**</u>

        1. **The representation did not impact either part of the contract implementation plan.**

            a. <u>Part I of the plan was completed.</u>

                i. The time table for Part I was met.

                    (1) Groundbreaking occurred on schedule.

If you need to go further, what you do is up to you. This many levels of headings is almost never necessary, but if you get a little crazy, you have a format to refer to.

VIII. STYLE ISSUES OF MOTIONS

A. Tone and formality

A motion must be formal in tone. Your audience usually is a judge or other legal decision maker (arbitrator, mediator, rule-making committee, etc.), and she rarely is impressed with levity or informality in writing. The same general rules regarding formality and tone that apply in the case of office memoranda also apply and with additional force in the case of court briefs. By way of review, these rules are:

1. Do not use slang.
2. Do not use colloquialisms.
3. Avoid first-person and second person references – I, my, you, your, etc. A party asserts arguments or makes motions, not the attorneys, no matter if you are referring to your own side or the opposition.

4. Avoid slash constructions (Bob was a teacher/researcher) unless that is the actual word, phrase, or address that you are quoting or referring to.

5. Do not use contractions.

6. It is fine to use shorthand words and abbreviations of parties, institutions and agencies, acts and statutes, once you have correctly identified them in your work.

> *Example:* The Securities Exchange Commission ("SEC") refused to apply the provisions of the Securities Act of 1933 ("'33 Act") to the post-sale use of the Section 14 red herring prospectus ("prospectus") by McDonnell Douglas Corporation ("MDC"). The SEC said that MDC satisfied the requirements of the '33 Act by providing an updated prospectus to each buyer.

7. Do not use symbols (&, @, #) unless the symbol is part of a rule, statute, or an email address; <u>e.g.</u>, 14 U.S.C. § 123, 13 Lab. L. Ann. ¶ 3-307, goldmanr@slu.edu.

8. Avoid the use of humor. This is not to say leave out all vivid, descriptive, and even clever language from your writing. Clever language used sparingly can be effective and is acceptable. You can turn a clever phrase, but do it to make a point, to drive something home, to make an impression that might last a bit longer; never do it just to be funny.

9. As with the statement of facts, do not show anger or other excessive emotion in your argument. No one wants to read a lawyer's vicious sniping at the other side, or a long, sorrowful recitation of the equities of the situation. It is not professional. You might lose your cool in person in the heat of argument, but you should not do it in writing. This is not to say be bland, dull, and never get assertive or forceful about your position. You can be forthright! You can be direct! You can show that you feel strongly about the equities! But not by bleeding your sympathy and sorrow all over the page or burning the very words off the paper with scorching prose.

B. Footnotes

Footnotes are a luxury in court briefs—do not abuse the privilege. Yes, they are single-spaced, and the text can be smaller in font size if you want to test your readers' eyes and irritate them, and as a result, you can fit more in them per square inch than regular text. But avoid devilish temptations and use them correctly.

Often there are local rules which force you to use footnotes in very limited ways: for example, no legal argument can be asserted in footnotes; no legal authority may be cited or discussed in footnotes; and other such rules. But even if these rules are not present, you should never try to put a significant part of your argument in footnotes for the following reasons:

1. It looks bad.

The courts (and writing instructors) create page limits for a reason: they do not want to read excessive material. If you cheat them by loading up the word count with huge footnotes, they will resent it.

2. Some people never read footnotes.

Footnotes are a distraction that some readers purposefully avoid. If you put something important in a footnote, it is lost to these people forever.

3. Footnotes are a nuisance.

Even if the judge or other reader does read footnotes, if you constantly pull her attention away from the regular text and down into footnotes she will be irritated.

So, what do you use footnotes for?

1. Side issues that deserve brief attention

If you have a minor, non-dispositive issue, not related to other issues as a stepping-stone issue or sub-issue, and you think it should be raised and discussed, but you are certain that it does not deserve its own TREAT, than you may raise it and discuss it briefly in a footnote. Again, err on the side of *not* relegating issues to footnotes until you have the confidence won from years of experience because an issue buried in a footnote may be missed completely by some of your readers.

2. Additional facts of some interest to the analysis

In the argument section, you might consider raising additional facts that have some interest value to the analysis, but which were not raised in the statement of facts. A proper citation to support for the facts is necessary.

As suggested by our warnings above, you should never relegate key facts upon which the case might turn to footnotes. We also point out that this is really only an option for the argument or Discussion section, because you should avoid using footnotes in the statement of facts.

3. Tertiary legal support for the argument

This is an area rife for abuse, so be careful. If you have a bit of persuasive primary or secondary authority that helps the cause but is not a show-stopper, and there is no critical reason for it to be discussed in the regular text, you might raise it in a footnote. In order not to appear to be violating the page limitation, you should use this option not more than two or three times in any motion.

Never use a footnote as a place to squeeze important controlling authority or any other vital part of the support for your argument. Do not use footnotes as a place to create or continue a string-cite of redundant authority—these are abuses of the page limit that will only serve to anger your reader.

C. Parentheticals

The rules on usage of parentheticals in adversarial legal writing largely are the same as with office memoranda. You can use them as a helpful way of presenting information in shorthand form, if the information is properly presented in shorthand form. The whole process of explanatory synthesis impresses on you the task of making sure you learn how to write clear, concise parentheticals to illustrate how your cases support the principles you are laying out. Parentheticals also are used in citations to indicate additional information about the authority.

> ➤ *Appropriate uses:*   Parody requires transformation. <u>Smith</u>, 12 F.3d at 34 (Johnson, J. concurring) (addition of text transformed original image into parody); <u>Jones</u>, 11 F.3d at 567 (citing <u>Hardy</u>, 123 F.2d at 45) (artistic interpretation created new meaning and message of parody).

Beyond these uses in citations and explanatory syntheses, do not attempt to use parentheticals in plain text simply as a space saving device. They do not substitute for a proper explanation of information from the facts or holding of a case when this information cannot be summarized in a few words or a short phrase. In addition, they should not be used as a way of presenting facts or other information in a brief without regard to the niceties of grammar, and thereby saving on space (<u>i.e.</u>, because in a parenthetical, you can leave out articles and connectors and "non-essential" terms). Abuse of this rule simply is another way of cheating on page limits and it is regarded with similar disdain.

> ➤ *Questionable uses:*   Parody requires transformation which creates new content, meaning or expression (parodies add: text, transforming images, commentary, ridicule, messages) so that the new work is shown to comment on the original and not supersede the objects of the original (parodies avoid drudgery of coming up with something fresh). <u>Smith</u>, 12 F.3d at 34; <u>Jones</u>, 11 F.3d at 567; <u>Hardy</u>, 123 F.2d at 45.

IX. FINISHING THE MEMORANDUM IN SUPPORT

A. Cite-checking

Cite-checking is an absolute **must** for anything you submit to a court. If you cite a case that is bad law, your opponent is afforded a great opportunity to embarrass you in front of the court, and you and your client will look very bad.

B. Proof-reading

Some of you may be allergic to proof-reading your own work. Take an antihistamine. The appearance of your work will affect what the reader thinks of your work (and you as a lawyer), whether consciously or unconsciously. Sloppy writing equals sloppy research equals sloppy lawyering equals sloppy lawyer with a sloppy case. You do not want to create such a negative perception for you, your client, and perhaps even your law firm. It is important to take the time to proof-read, and if you do not know how to, you had better learn.

Please note that using the **spell-checker** on your word processing program will not be sufficient. Your spell-checker is not going to catch "form" when you meant "from," "statue" when you meant "statute," "pubic" when you meant "public." It will not know that you meant to put "your" not "you," or "there" not "their." A spell-checker also might suggest changes to legal words that you actually spelled correctly; it may tell you to use "tortuous" when you actually mean "tortious" (in relation to a tort). Spell-checkers have their limits, and their limits require you to proof-read on your own.

There is more than one way to proof-read. The most effective way we have found is to read your writing backwards, starting at the end and reading it backwards word by word and then sentence by sentence. Reversing the reading forces you to read each word and each sentence slowly, and you will catch a lot more typographical and spelling and citation errors at this speed. This can be a painful chore, but the results are excellent.

Another method is to read the work out loud to yourself or to have someone else read it out loud to you. Not only will you or your friend catch some errors in this way, you also are likely to find awkward passages and words that do not flow easily which you can then go back and rework to improve your phrasing.

C. Editing

A much repeated adage in writing is that, "There is no such thing as good writing; only good rewriting." The first drafts of your memorandum in support will not be perfect. You must allow yourself the time to correct mistakes, clear up rough patches that destroy the flow of the work, tighten up the sentences, and improve the wording.

Editing often is needed just to get the memorandum within the page limits. Page limits are not just for legal writing classes. Every court in which we've practiced has had page limitations on motions and memoranda in support. Beyond page limits is the general rule that a pre-trial motion needs to be direct and to the point. Terse writing is more effective. Flabby writing makes the reader spend more time than she wants on your brief. This is a sin committed more often by the so called "premiere" law firms, because they allow their attorneys the time to crank out huge documents, and they have clients that can afford to pay the huge legal fees racked up when an attorney writes a massive volume of material in a brief. Do not perpetuate this trend. If you can say it very well in five or six pages, do not turn in fifteen.

The skill of what to cut out and what to leave in is the sum and substance of legal advocacy and legal writing. Naturally, the same criteria as to what to put in your brief apply when you are considering what you should take out. The practice of this skill is a lifetime devotion.

Chapter 3

Motions to Dismiss

A motion to dismiss may be brought at various stages in a litigation, but it is most commonly filed early in the pretrial proceedings, after the complaint has been filed but before defendant has filed any other motion or pleading. The motion argues that one or more or all of the claims raised by plaintiff in its complaint should be dismissed from the case.

If all of the claims asserted in the complaint are dismissed, the action is dismissed, and plaintiff can appeal the dismissal. Otherwise, plaintiff has to start over with a new complaint, or the same complaint in a new forum (if the forum was the reason for the dismissal), and plaintiff hopes the statute of limitations has not run by this point or that he might take advantage of a procedural "savings clause."

If fewer than all of the claims are dismissed, the litigation continues as to the remaining claims. Plaintiff either has to forego the dismissed claims or try to amend the complaint to reassert the claims for relief in a new and hopefully non-objectionable form, or refile the same claims in a different forum (if the forum was the problem, and if the statute of limitations has not run, and if plaintiff is willing to carry on two litigations against the same defendant at the same time). Otherwise, plaintiff has to wait for a final judgment on the remaining claims and then appeal the dismissal of these initial claims at that time.

I. INITIAL PRETRIAL MOTION FOR DEFENDANT

As mentioned above, the most typical time for a defendant to file a motion to dismiss is as the initial action by the defendant in response to the filing of the complaint. The motion is filed in lieu of answering the complaint or petition. You certainly do not need to file a motion to dismiss, and grounds for the motion will not exist in very many cases. In federal court, a motion to dismiss is governed by Rule 12(b), Fed. R. Civ. P., and its various subsections.

Plaintiff can assert a motion to dismiss a counterclaim if the plaintiff is a counterclaim defendant. It might be asserted by a cross-claim defendant (a co-defendant or co-plaintiff in the case) to dismiss a cross-claim, or by a third-party defendant to dismiss a third-party claim. Rule 12(b) governs these situations as well.

II. MOTION TO DISMISS FOR LACK OF JURISDICTION OVER THE SUBJECT MATTER - FED. R. CIV. P. 12(b)(1)

The first subsection under Rule 12(b) deals with a motion that argues that the court has no subject matter jurisdiction because:

➤ there is no diversity or not enough amount in controversy under 28 U.S.C. § 1332;
➤ there is no federal question presented by the complaint under 28 U.S.C. § 1331, or
➤ the specific subject matter of the action belongs in a different forum (e.g., a bankruptcy action that should have been brought in a United States Bankruptcy Court).

Certain allegations may overlap other subsections of Rule 12(b), such as an argument that one or more claims are not ripe, or are moot, or the complaint does not present a valid case or controversy, all of which also can be challenged under Fed. R. Civ. P. 12(b)(6).

The motion attacks some defect in the complaint itself, so the movant *might* state that the allegations of the complaint are presumed true (taken at face value) for purposes of the motion if the problem is not what plaintiff alleges to be the grounds for subject matter jurisdiction, but rather an allegation such as that claims themselves are not ripe or are moot or do not present a case or controversy. However, more often than not, the problem will be that the complaint erroneously alleges facts and makes improper factual and legal conclusions in support of subject matter jurisdiction, and movant must challenge and refute these erroneous grounds by bringing out the "correct" facts and conclusions regarding subject matter jurisdiction. In these instances, movant *cannot* assume the facts pleaded in the complaint to be true for purposes of the motion or for any other purpose—it would be a fatal error to do so.

If new operative facts regarding subject matter jurisdiction are alleged or attempted to be proved by the movant, then the opponent of the motion may request an extension of time to address the new facts, and perhaps to take discovery of the support for the new facts. There is no guaranty that movant will be afforded the time or granted the right to take discovery on subject matter jurisdiction. If the Rule 12(b)(1) motion is pled in conjunction with a Rule 12(b)(6) motion (see below), and new facts are alleged, the court has the option to convert the proceedings to a summary judgment motion under Fed. R. Civ. P. 56, and discovery more often will be afforded to the opponent of the motion to dismiss.

III. MOTION TO DISMISS FOR LACK OF JURISDICTION OVER THE PERSON - FED. R. CIV. P. 12(b)(2)

A Rule 12(b)(2) motion argues that the court has no jurisdiction over the person of the defendant(s) because:

➤ they are not present in the jurisdiction (don't reside there, aren't subject to service of process there, and cannot be found there in person or through a proper agent);
➤ they are not properly haled into the court under the applicable state Long Arm statute (the Long Arm statute of the state where the court is located); or
➤ they cannot properly or reasonably be haled into the court under the Due Process Clause of the U.S. Constitution, and the related doctrines of "minimum contacts" and "traditional notions of fair play and substantial justice."

Any facts alleged in the complaint that have any bearing on personal jurisdiction over the defendant **cannot** be presumed to be true by movant for purposes of the motion. In most cases, plaintiff will have alleged facts in support of the assertion of personal jurisdiction over the defendant, and defendant cannot buy into these erroneous allegations. The defendant movant must assert and prove the "correct" facts regarding personal jurisdiction in the motion. So, movant should strike the phrase "presume the facts alleged in the complaint to be true for purposes of the motion" from any 12(b)(2) template; you never will use this phrase.

The appropriate way to introduce new jurisdictional facts is to allege them in the motion supported by an attached affidavit or declaration under penalty of perjury from a knowledgeable person (usually your client). Not everyone does it the appropriate way, and not every judge requires you to do it the appropriate way, but we encourage you to do the right thing.

Both sides have the right to ask for discovery regarding jurisdictional facts. Neither side is guaranteed the right to such discovery, but the judge is hard-pressed not to grant it in many cases, especially if both sides ask for it. It is more likely to be granted to the opponent if the movant introduces and attempts to prove new jurisdictional facts in its motion to dismiss, and the opponent claims that it needs to explore them.

If the movant introduces new facts by affidavit or declaration, and the opponent (the plaintiff) responds by alleging still more facts by affidavit or declaration in support of personal jurisdiction, the case can degenerate into a big swearing match.[1] Judges do not like to make decisions on the basis of who swears the best or the most (this is called "trial by affidavit"), so a swearing match probably favors the opponent of the motion. In other words, the judge will probably deny the motion, perhaps without prejudice to try it again later, and leave the case as it is on the basis of the original facts alleged by plaintiff in support of jurisdiction. If this happens, defendant must be careful not to waive its argument by filing an answer or other pleading that fails to assert the same objections and challenges to personal jurisdiction—if you fail to object, defects in personal jurisdiction are deemed waived.

The judge might entertain a fact-finding hearing on personal jurisdiction, after which it will find the "true" facts and determine whether the exercise of personal jurisdiction is indeed proper. The testimony of witnesses and documents and other items that tend to prove such facts might be taken into evidence at such a hearing. Even if you wind up in a grand swearing match with your opponent or in a prolonged and expensive hearing on personal jurisdiction, the motion still is worth bringing because if you fail to assert your objections to defects in personal jurisdiction, the objections you might have had are deemed waived.

---

[1] "Swearing match" refers to the fact that the person making the affidavit (called the affiant) or the declaration (called the declarant) swears under penalty of perjury that the facts stated in the affidavit or declaration are true.

IV. MOTION TO DISMISS FOR IMPROPER VENUE - FED. R. CIV. P. 12(b)(3)

The 12(b)(3) motion argues that the venue is improper because:

➢ it fails to satisfy the requirements of 28 U.S.C. § 1391 or the applicable venue statute;
➢ there was a forum selection clause that required the case to be brought in a different venue; or
➢ plaintiff is mistaken in its facts alleged in support of its choice of venue.

If the motion to dismiss for lack of venue is granted, the plaintiff still can pick up the pieces and file the suit in an appropriate venue, as long as the statute of limitations has not run.

A 12(b)(3) motion is commonly brought in conjunction with a 28 U.S.C. § 1404 motion and a 28 U.S.C. § 1406 motion. A 1404 motion is for transfer to a more convenient venue—more convenient to the defendant, to be sure, but justified either because of a forum selection clause or under a *forum non conveniens* argument. Section 1406 provides that if the court finds that venue is improper, the court can transfer the case to an appropriate venue, rather than dismissing the suit outright.

As with a Rule 12(b)(2) motion, movant **cannot** presume the facts alleged in the complaint in support of venue to be true for purposes of the motion. It would be fatal to do so. The appropriate way to introduce new and "correct" venue facts is to allege them in the motion supported by an attached affidavit or declaration under penalty of perjury from a knowledgeable person.

Both sides have the right to ask for discovery regarding venue facts, but neither side is guaranteed the right to such discovery. Venue generally is given a back seat to personal jurisdiction issues, and judges may forego the delay simply by denying discovery or by denying the motion to dismiss.

V. MOTION TO DISMISS FOR INSUFFICIENCY OF PROCESS OR SERVICE OF PROCESS - FED. R. CIV. P. 12(b)(4),(5)

A deficiency in "the process" means something was wrong with the papers themselves—erroneous or insufficient or incomplete information in the summons, complaint, or return of service. A defect in service of process means that the way the papers were served or the person upon whom they were served is improper. Examples of this would be service by publication when personal service was required, or service on a five-year-old friend of the son of the defendant rather than on the defendant, or service on a receptionist in the building lobby and not on a proper officer or agent of a corporate defendant.

A party filing a motion to dismiss for improper process or service of process rarely succeeds in obtaining a dismissal; 90% of the time the judge is just going to grant the plaintiff additional time for service and issue an additional summons[2] so that the plaintiff perform service correctly. If delay is your primary goal, then you might go ahead and file this motion. You should be aware that modern rules often shift the costs of opposing the motion or the cost of additional service of process back onto you if your motion is found to be erroneous.

VI. MOTION TO DISMISS FOR FAILURE TO STATE A CLAIM UPON WHICH RELIEF MAY BE GRANTED - FED. R. CIV. P. 12(b)(6)

This is the granddaddy of them all—a real show-stopper. The paradigm motion argues, "Even if everything plaintiff alleges were true, under the law applicable to this case, plaintiff cannot recover under any of its claims against defendant." This is a pretrial motion you really can sink your teeth into.

Since you have waited patiently though the other five subsections of Rule 12(b), we will now tell you that **this is the motion** in which movant should assume that all facts pleaded in the complaint are true and correct for purposes of the motion. This is the best strategy, because if movant does not make this assumption, or if new operative facts regarding the claims or defenses are alleged or attempted to be proved by the movant, then the court can reject the motion, or convert the motion to a Fed. R. Civ. P. 56 summary judgment motion. In the latter case, the court generally will grant an extension of time to the party opposing the motion so as to allow it time to gather facts in opposition to the movant's new facts. Discovery may be granted to either or both sides, and delay of the proceedings will result.

Note well that the assumption should be drafted to state only "that all facts pleaded in the complaint are true and correct **for purposes of the motion**." You do not assume the complaint and its claims to be true and correct for any other purpose, and you don't want to create the impression (true or not) that you are admitting the facts. So, be careful to use the proper wording of the presumption.

---

[2] Referred to in various jurisdictions as an alias summons (the second summons issued) or pluries summons (the third and any subsequently issued summons).

VII. FORMAT OF MOTIONS TO DISMISS AND THE OPPOSITION TO THE SAME

As with most motions, motions to dismiss generally have the following sections:

[PRE-INTRODUCTION]

<u>INTRODUCTION</u>

<u>STATEMENT OF FACTS</u>

<u>ARGUMENT</u>

<u>CONCLUSION</u>

The Pre-introduction identifies the motion before the court. The Introduction, as always, is the most critical section, and you need to draft a short, persuasive summary of your argument. Discuss the facts, law, and legal conclusions that tell the court why you should win.

Unless you are writing a 12(b)(6) motion, you should draft the Statement of Facts so that your client's position looks strong. In a 12(b)(6) motion, however, you customarily presume the plaintiff's complaint to be true for purposes of the motion, so you are limited in what you can do with the facts. Reorder and reword the plaintiff's rendition of the facts, but don't change the actual facts or introduce new facts unless you are prepared to face a quick denial of the motion or conversion of the proceedings to a drawn-out, expensive summary judgment motion context.

On a motion to dismiss for lack of subject matter jurisdiction, or personal jurisdiction, or venue, you can introduce and discuss new facts supporting your position. Factual conclusions are permitted, but you should draw the necessary jurisdictional or venue-related *legal* conclusions in your discussion section, not in the Facts. Be wary of the potential creation of a swearing match on the jurisdictional facts.

The Argument (or Discussion) is drafted in the usual way as discussed in the previous chapter. The Conclusion also is the same—one sentence telling the court what you want it to do.

The opposition to a motion to dismiss follows the same format. You will attempt to refute any new facts alleged, and rebut any legal arguments raised against your complaint and your choice of forum. Dig in your heels—it's your complaint, and your choice of forum. Don't blow it.

You do not have to slavishly follow the points alleged by the movant in the order raised by the movant—raise your best points in opposition first, followed by the next best and so on. If you have additional points that support your complaint that movant did not address, be sure to throw them in. Make your opponent sweat through its reply brief.

VIII.   SAMPLE MOTIONS

Sample 1 - Memorandum in Support of Motion to Dismiss

UNITED STATES DISTRICT COURT
CENTRAL DISTRICT OF CALIFORNIA
SOUTHERN DIVISION

GLOBAL STUDIOS,	)	
	)	
Plaintiff,	)	
	)	
v.	)	No. SA CV 01-9999 AHS
	)	
KINGSTON UNIVERSITY	)	
ELECTRONIC FREEDOM	)	
FRONTIER, LARRY MULLEN,	)	
LISA ROGERS, MEGHAN MORELY,	)	
and CHRIS HANSEN,	)	
	)	
Defendants.	)	

MEMORANDUM IN SUPPORT OF DEFENDANTS' MOTION TO DISMISS FOR LACK OF PERSONAL JURISDICTION

Defendants Kingston University Electronic Freedom Frontier, Larry Mullen, Lisa Rogers, Meghan Morely, and Chris Hansen (collectively referred to as "KUEFF") move this Court pursuant to Fed. R. Civ. P. 12(b)(2), to dismiss this action for lack of personal jurisdiction.

> One of the goals of movants' introduction is to slant the reader's thinking about the case as a whole. The introduction below does a good job of this. The movant wants to communicate a theme and tell its side of the story concerning the case as a whole (the first two sentences below) as well as its points on the motion (the rest of the section). The issues of the case as a whole are covered just far enough to leave the proper taste in the reader's mouth. Then the section gets down to business laying out the facts, law, and policies relevant to the motion at hand.

INTRODUCTION

Global Studios is suing KUEFF to abolish its constitutional right to post newsworthy information concerning the CSS/DeCSS controversy. Global Studios must believe that a news organization cannot report on DVD duplication without being subject to suit in California.

KUEFF moves to dismiss the suit for lack of personal jurisdiction. None of its members have been to California since the organization was founded. Less than one percent of the hits on the web site have been from users in California. No commercial activity takes place on the web site and the level of interactivity is miniscule; therefore, the organization has not purposefully availed itself of the privilege of conducting activities in California. Also, it would be totally unreasonable to require four college students to defend themselves across the country against a corporation like Global Studios. KUEFF's contacts with California do not satisfy the "minimum contacts" and "fair and substantial justice" required by the California Long-Arm statute, Cal. Civ. Proc. Code § 410.10 (West 2001), and the state and federal constitutional "due process" standards, Cal. Const. art. 1, § 7; U.S. Const. amend. XIV.

> The statement of facts below brings out facts that are relevant to the motion, but it is too objective. It lacks the kind of advocacy we want to see in a facts section in a ligation brief that employs narrative reasoning to drive home the movants' points. This one sounds like a newspaper article, and lacks a point of view. The use of terms such as "the organization" depersonalizes the author's clients and disassociates the movants from the memo they have presented in support of their motion. The reader may wonder, "What disembodied observer wrote this?" It is better to write the facts from the clients' point of view. Compare this presentation of facts with the punchy, calculated, and effective presentation of the same facts in the Introduction of this memorandum in support: "None of its members have been to California since the organization was founded. Less than one percent of the hits on the web site have been from users in California. No commercial activity takes place on the web site and the level of interactivity is miniscule." Don't repeat yourself word for word, but maintain the same calculated selection and presentation of facts in both sections.

STATEMENT OF FACTS

DeCSS is software that can be downloaded and used to unscramble the protection program known as Content Scramble System (CSS) so DVDs can then be duplicated. Since March 2001, Kingston University in Troy, New York, has hosted a web site of a nonprofit student organization known as Kingston University Electronic Freedom Frontier (KUEFF).

> We object to authors who over-abbreviate their abbreviated short forms, such as "T.S. Dec." Give more information, such as "Sensor Dec."

See Declaration of Tracy Sensor dated Jan. 4, 2002, at ¶ 2 ("T.S. Dec."). The organization regularly posts news on its web site regarding issues of free speech on the Internet. See Declaration of Larry Mullen dated Jan. 8, 2002, at ¶ 2 ("L.M. Dec."). KUEFF's personnel and everything associated with its activities are located in New York. See L.M. Dec. at ¶ 4.

In September 2001, the organization began reporting on the CSS/DeCSS controversy. See T.S. Dec. at ¶ 3. The names and addresses of several web sites that provide DeCSS for downloading were mentioned in passing. See T.S. Dec. at ¶ 3. None of the addresses were hyperlinked. See L.M. Dec. at ¶ 3. KUEFF did nothing to encourage readers in California to visit these sites or download the software. See Complaint, Exhibit 1 ("Exhibit 1").

The organization's only contact with people in California has been through emails, the majority of which consist of information about KUEFF and news previously reported on

> Instead of simply saying, "Hey, we took two donations," the author should have undercut this negative fact by pointing out that the donations amounted to less than $100, and at least one of the donations was orchestrated by one of plaintiff's attorneys. This smacks of entrapment, and entrapment would help the movants' cause, rather than leave the court thinking, "They took money from California residents."

the web site. See L.M. Dec. at ¶ 6. There is evidence of only two donations being made via email, one by an attorney representing the plaintiff and another by the plaintiff's witness. See Declaration of Zachary Schulman dated Jan. 7, 2002, at ¶ 5; Declaration of Melanie Smead dated Jan. 12, 2002, at ¶ 5 ("M.S. Dec"). No contracts or sales have been made with anyone in California. There is no evidence that any hits from California led to installation of DeCSS. M.S. Dec. at ¶ 3.

ARGUMENT

Thesis headings can provide the reader with a useful summary of the points of your argument, but only if you make them meaningful. The heading below only presents half of the information—the conclusion. Add to this the "because" part—the facts and legal principles that support the conclusion. Then your reader has the complete picture. A better heading would be: "THE ACTION MUST BE DISMISSED FOR LACK OF PERSONAL JURISDICTION BECAUSE NONE OF THE DEFENDANTS WERE PRESENT IN CALIFORNIA AND NONE OF THEM DID BUSINESS IN CALIFORNIA."

I. THE ACTION MUST BE DISMISSED FOR LACK OF PERSONAL JURISDICTION

Observe how elegantly this rule section is drafted. There are a lot of rules to get through in the personal jurisdiction analysis, and this author is conserving space and the reader's attention span by laying them out succinctly without sacrificing the flow of the text.

Fed. R. Civ. P. 12(b)(2) provides that the defendant may make a motion to dismiss for "lack of jurisdiction over the person." This case has been brought before the United States District Court, Central District California. Therefore, the personal jurisdiction laws of California are applied.

The author needs a cite for that last proposition.

The California Long Arm provision, Cal. Civ. Proc. Code § 410.10, states, "a court of this state may exercise jurisdiction on any basis not inconsistent with the Constitution of this state or of the United States." According to Cal. Const. art. 1, § 7 and U.S. Const. amend. XIV, "a person may not be deprived of life, liberty, or property without due process of the law."

Due process requires that a defendant, if not present in the state, "have certain minimum contacts with it such that the maintenance of the suit does not offend traditional notions of fair play and substantial justice." Cybersell, Inc. v. Cybersell, Inc., 130 F.3d 414, 415 (9th Cir. 1997) (citing International Shoe Co. v. Washington, 326 U.S. 310, 316 (1945)).

Personal jurisdiction may be founded on either general jurisdiction or specific jurisdiction. <u>Panavision Int'l, L.P. v. Toeppen</u>, 141 F.3d 1316, 1320 (9th Cir. 1998). General jurisdiction exists when a defendant is domiciled in the forum state or when the defendant's activities there are "substantial" or "continuous and systematic." <u>Panavision</u>, 141 F.3d at 1320 (citing <u>Helicopteros Nacionales de Colombia, S.A. v. Hall,</u> 466 U.S. 408, 414-16 (1984)).

> Note the roadmap in the next two sentences. This direction is succinct but it keeps the reader informed as to the author's progression through this analysis.

Nothing in the complaint suggests that general jurisdiction is being asserted. Therefore, this motion will address the absence of specific jurisdiction over the defendants.

> The author created a sub-section A without writing any sub-section B. This is unnecessary, and a rookie mistake. Either set up the rule section under the main TREAT so that there does not need to be any sub-TREATs, or set it up so that there are at least two sub-TREATs. This memo was primed to have two major sections—long arm and due process, and due process is ready made for three sub-sections: purposeful availment, arising out of, and fairness. You can even break down purposeful availment into the sliding scale test and the effects test. We assume the author did not break up this memo into these parts because he felt short on space under the page limits and wanted to avoid using so many thesis headings, but some readers may become confused and alarmed if there is a subsection A and no subsection B.
>
> The heading of sub-section A lacks the "because" part. A better heading would be: "The court does not have specific jurisdiction over KUEFF because KUEFF was not present and did not do business in California and did not purposefully avail itself of California."

A. <u>The court does not have specific jurisdiction over KUEFF under the California Long-Arm statute.</u>

Courts use a three-part test to determine whether specific jurisdiction should be exercised:

(1) The nonresident defendant must do some act or consummate some transaction with the forum or perform some act by which he purposefully avails himself of the privilege of conducting activities in the forum, thereby invoking benefits and protections of its laws; (2) the claim must be one which arises out of or results from the defendant's forum-related activities; and (3) exercise of jurisdiction must be reasonable.

Panavision, 141 F.3d at 1320.

1. KUEFF did not purposefully avail itself.

Under the "sliding scale" approach, the likelihood that personal jurisdiction will be exercised is proportionate to the nature and quality of commercial activity conducted over the Internet. See Cybersell, 130 F.3d at 419 (citing Zippo Mfg. Co. v. Zippo Dot Com, Inc., 952 F. Supp. 1119, 1124 (W.D. Pa. 1997)).

At opposite ends of the scale are "passive" and "active" web sites; the middle consists of "interactive" sites where the user can exchange information with the defendant site. Callaway Golf Corp. v. Royal Canadian Golf Ass'n, 125 F. Supp. 2d 1194, 1200 (C.D. Cal. 2000).

> The author makes use of explanatory synthesis in the following explanation paragraph, but the paragraph is limited to one proposition that synthesizes two cases. The author should not have limited himself to two cases when there are dozens of cases available that illustrate these propositions. The author also should not limit the authority cited to district court cases when there are court of appeals cases that illustrate the proposition.

Specific jurisdiction primarily is exercised over "interactive" web sites when products, not advertisements or promotions, are sold. Compare S. Morantz v. Hang & Shine Ultrasonics, Inc., 79 F. Supp. 2d 537, 539 (E.D. Pa. 1999) (applying federal Due Process clause) (sale of promotional materials to forum residents via its web site too "fortuitous and random" to warrant exercise of jurisdiction); with Stomp, Inc. v. NeatO, LLC, 61 F. Supp. 2d 1074, 1077 (C.D. Cal. 1999) (specific jurisdiction appropriate over web site dedicated to sale of products on-line).

> The author commits an egregious error in the next sentence because the author states that "courts" have refused something, and then cites only one case. Do not promise multiple cases and then deliver one case. A synthesis of cases would have been better here, but at least satisfy what you promise to the reader.

Courts have refused to recognize contacts manufactured by the plaintiff. <u>Millennium Enterprises, Inc. v. Millennium Music, L.P.</u>, 33 F. Supp. 2d 907, 911 (D. Or. 1999) (no personal jurisdiction where the only sales in California motivated by the plaintiff's interest in the lawsuit).

KUEFF operates a relatively "interactive" web site that allows users to email directly to the organization. However, unlike the site in <u>Stomp</u> that was established for the purpose of transacting Internet sales, KUEFF's site does not offer products for purchase. The only commercial activity on KUEFF's site has consisted of donations that were more akin to promotional transactions than product sales. And even if deemed substantial commercial activity, the donations may be disregarded as having been manufactured by the plaintiff.

> The section that follows sounds like a new rule section. This is confusing because the last paragraph above obviously was an application section. The reader cannot tell whether this is a new rule section because the author did not start a new sub-TREAT. Flipping from an application to a new rule section within the same sub-TREAT is confusing and unwelcome. The author should have started a new sub-TREAT here.

Under the "effects test," personal jurisdiction in a tort case is predicated on (1) intentional actions that are (2) expressly aimed at the forum state, and (3) cause harm, the brunt of which is suffered—and which the defendant knows is likely to be suffered—in the forum state. <u>Callaway</u>, 125 F. Supp. 2d at 1200.

> Again, the synthesis that follows contains only two cases. There was no dearth of authority on this proposition. The purpose of the explanation is to illustrate how the rule works, and the comparison of two cases is extremely limited in its illustrative power.

Believing a corporate defendant might be located in California or "foreseeing" an article might cause harm in California does not satisfy the "effects test." <u>Compare</u> <u>Callaway</u>, 125 F. Supp. 2d at 1200 (no personal jurisdiction where defendant did not know plaintiff had its principal place of business in California and was unaware the effects would be felt in California), <u>with</u> <u>Pavlovich v. Superior Court</u>, 109 Cal. Rptr. 2d 909, 918 (Ct. App. 6th Dist. 2001), *petition for review granted*, 36 P.3d 625 (Cal. Dec. 12, 2001) ("effects test" satisfied where defendant knowingly and intentionally caused harm in California).

The "effects test" should not apply to a strict liability intellectual property case because plaintiff never will have to prove that the defendants intentionally caused harm in California. However, assuming the effects test does apply, the plaintiff fails to meet the three prongs. The only intentional action committed by KUEFF was news reporting. Unlike

Pavlovich, KUEFF had no idea their site would be used as a directory to DeCSS sites, nor did they know Global Studios would suffer in California.

> This next sub-TREAT is short because the author is willing to concede this point. We agree completely. Movants have no business arguing about this element just for the sake of argument.

2. Global Studios claim arises out of KUEFF's forum-related activities.

KUEFF does not contest the assertion that to the extent plaintiff has been injured by defendant's commercial activity on its web site, plaintiff would not have suffered the alleged injuries "but for" defendant's activity. KUEFF does not contest the assertion that the cause of action alleged by plaintiff, if valid, arises out of KUEFF's forum-related activities.

3. Exercising personal jurisdiction over KUEFF in California would be unreasonable.

> We have skipped to the conclusion of the memorandum in support.

* * *

CONCLUSION

In light of the above, KUEFF respectfully requests the court to dismiss the complaint for lack of personal jurisdiction.

Sample 2 - Memorandum in Opposition to Motion to Dismiss

UNITED STATES DISTRICT COURT
CENTRAL DISTRICT OF CALIFORNIA
SOUTHERN DIVISION

GLOBAL STUDIOS,	)	
	)	
Plaintiff,	)	
	)	No. SA CV 01-9999 AHS
v.	)	
	)	
KINGSTON UNIVERSITY	)	
ELECTRONIC FREEDOM	)	
FRONTIER, LARRY MULLEN,	)	
LISA ROGERS, MEGHAN MORELY,	)	
and CHRIS HANSEN,	)	
	)	
Defendants.	)	

**PLAINTIFF'S MEMORANDUM IN OPPOSITION TO DEFENDANTS'
FED. R. CIV. P. 12(b)(2) MOTION TO DISMISS FOR LACK OF
PERSONAL JURISDICTION**

> The opponent chose to forego a pre-introduction sentence. This is fine because she communicated all of the required information in the title of this memorandum.

INTRODUCTION

Defendants have asserted that they can enable the theft of Plaintiff's property in California, Plaintiff's home state, yet evade responsibility for the resulting damage because their contacts with that forum were directed over the Internet. Plaintiff serves the public by writing motion pictures to Digital Versatile Disks (DVDs). Defendants, through their

> This introduction is hard hitting and does a good job steering the reader to the opponent's point of view, but it does go a tiny bit overboard. No one would agree that the movie industry "serves the public" by cranking out R-rated DVDs. Otherwise, this section efficiently presents the relevant facts, issues, law, and the policies from the opponent's perspective in a section that flows well.

website, provide access to a means by which Plaintiff's copyrighted material may be stripped from those DVDs. Through maintenance of a continuously accessible website, direction of explicit emails intended to and actually causing injury to Plaintiff, and solicitation and receipt of donations to support their cause, Defendants have purposefully availed themselves of the privileges of conducting activities in California. Plaintiff's suit arises from these contacts, and reasonableness dictates that Plaintiff's and California's interests in attaining jurisdiction over Defendants be obliged. Therefore, assertion of jurisdiction meets the due process requirements of both the California and United States Constitutions and comports with the California Long-Arm statute.

> The facts section below is right on the money. The author has set the stage for his arguments by assembling and emphasizing the most crucial and beneficial facts in a crisply drafted section. This is fine work.

STATEMENT OF FACTS

The viability of Plaintiff's business hinges on the protection of its copyrighted material stored on DVDs, which is provided by a computer program known as Content Scramble System ("CSS"). See Complaint, ¶¶ 10-11. Defendants provide access to a computer program known as DeCSS, the only function of which is to decrypt CSS and allow the pirating of material stored on DVDs. See Complaint, ¶¶ 10-13. Plaintiff filed a complaint with this Court to restrain Defendants from undermining its copyrights and ruining its business. See generally Complaint.

Plaintiff operates its business in California. See Complaint, ¶ 1. Although Defendants have no physical presence in that state, their website is easily accessible to California residents through the Internet, as evidenced by the eighty-five hits the site has received from California viewers. Declaration of Tracy Sensor dated Jan. 4, 2002, at ¶ 5 ("Sensor Dec."). Bolded headings featured on Defendants' website include "Contact us," followed by an invitation to "Subscribe to the newsletter by email, [and] exchange information," and "Donations," followed by a request for credit card information and an assurance that the donations are tax-deductible. See Complaint, Exhibit 1. The first heading has resulted in seven emails from California residents and fifteen reply emails from Defendants, at least two of which accommodated requests for information regarding how DeCSS can be obtained. Declaration of Larry Mullen dated Jan. 8, 2002, at ¶ 6 ("Mullen Dec."). The second heading has induced donations from at least two California residents. Mullen Dec. at ¶ 7. Furthermore, on at least thirty occasions, California residents have downloaded usable copies of DeCSS using only the information on Defendants' website. Declaration of Melanie Smead dated Jan. 12, 2002, at ¶ 3 ("Smead Dec."); Declaration of Zachary Schulman dated Jan. 7, 2002, at ¶ 3 ("Schulman Dec.").

ARGUMENT

> Although the motion to dismiss rule is a procedural rule that can be covered in a one-sentence rule section, as this author did below, this section would be more effective if the author were to write a roadmap to guide the reader to the two major substantive arguments on long arm jurisdiction and due process that immediately follow the procedural rule.

Defendants bring a motion to dismiss Plaintiff's action for "lack of jurisdiction over the person" under Fed. R. Civ. P. 12(b)(2).

> We hope by now it will come as no surprise when we point out that the thesis headings in this memorandum in opposition lack the "because" part. The heading below and those that follow it will not summarize the opponent's points in opposition because they only present a conclusion and do not include the facts and legal principles that support the conclusion.

I. THE CALIFORNIA LONG-ARM STATUTE CONVEYS PERSONAL JURISDICTION OVER DEFENDANTS.

> There were a lot of important rules to present to the reader in this rule section, and the author really did a nice job getting them out in a concise manner. The section flows well in spite of the compacted exposition.

Cal. Civ. Proc. Code sec. 410.10 provides that "A court of this state may exercise jurisdiction on any basis not inconsistent with the Constitution of this state or of the United States." The due process clause of each constitution prohibits the state from "depriving any person of life, liberty, or property, without due process of law." Cal. Const. art. 1, sec. 7; U.S. Const. amend. XIV. Thus, the limits of the state long-arm statute are co-extensive with the limits of federal due process. See Panavision Int. L.P. v. Toeppen, 114 F.3d 1316, 1320 (9th Cir. 1998).

Federal due process permits personal jurisdiction over a defendant in any state with which the defendant has certain minimum contacts, which can be established through contacts that give rise to specific or general jurisdiction. See Helicopteros Nacionales de Columbia, S.A. v. Hall, 466 U.S. 408, 414 (1984). In the present case, Plaintiff claims only specific jurisdiction.

> In text, as opposed to citations, use "Ninth" Circuit not "9th" Circuit.

The 9th Circuit applies a three-prong test to establish specific jurisdiction:

> Specific jurisdiction exists if (1) the defendant(s) has performed some act or consummated some transaction within the forum or otherwise purposefully availed himself of the privileges of conducting activities in the forum, thereby invoking the benefits and protections of state law, (2) the claim arises out of or results from the defendant's forum-related activities, and (3) the exercise of jurisdiction is reasonable.

> The cite to <u>Bancroft</u> below should be a long form cite because this is first appearance of the case in this memorandum. Be careful that when you edit your work you don't delete the first long form cite and wind up using a short form cite the first time the case appears.

<u>See</u> <u>Bancroft</u>, 223 F.3d at 1086; <u>Cybersell, Inc. v. Cybersell, Inc</u>, 130 F.3d 414, 416 (9th Cir. 1997). This memorandum in opposition will address each basis for specific jurisdiction in the order presented above.

A. <u>Defendants purposefully availed themselves of the privileges of conducting activities in California.</u>

> This is the first sub-TREAT of the paper. The author is following the TREAT format to the letter. This makes these complicated arguments more easily understandable to the reader, even if she is not up to speed on jurisdictional issues.

When a defendant's contacts occur over the Internet, purposeful availment is established by measuring the quality and nature of the commercial activity conducted by the defendant over the Internet on a sliding scale to determine if minimum contacts exist. <u>See</u> <u>Cybersell</u>, 130 F.3d at 419; <u>Zippo Mfg. Co. v. Zippo Dot Com, Inc.</u>, 952 F. Supp. 1119, 1124 (W.D. Pa. 1997).

> The author's use of explanatory synthesis in the following explanation section is excellent. He makes his points clearly and uses a lot of authority in a small amount of space. This furthers his arguments very effectively. Our one criticism is that the author uses too many persuasive authorities early in the section when he could have used controlling authorities from the United States Court of Appeals for the Ninth Circuit.

In addition to the mere capacity for interactivity of a defendant's website, actual transactions between the defendant and residents of the forum are required to establish purposeful availment. <u>Compare</u> <u>Digital Control, Inc. v. Boretronics, Inc.</u>, 161 F. Supp. 2d 1183, 1187 (W.D. Wash. 2001) (regardless of nature of website, no purposeful availment until defendant faces and makes choice to dive into forum), <u>with</u> <u>Tech Heads, Inc. v. Desktop Serv. Ctr.</u>, 105 F. Supp. 2d 1142, 1150-51 (D. Ore. 2000) (transaction with forum resident through website was critical to establishing purposeful availment), <u>and</u> <u>Heroes, Inc. v. Heroes Found.</u>, 958 F. Supp. 1, 5 (D.D.C. 1996) (solicitation and receipt of donations through website constituted actual transactions with forum residents and was critical to finding purposeful availment).

It is the quality, not the quantity of transactions that is relevant. <u>See</u> <u>Tech Heads</u>, 105 F. Supp. 2d at 1150 (proper jurisdiction when defendant's contacts with forum included one Internet transaction); <u>Stomp, Inc. v. Neato, L.L.C.</u>, 61 F. Supp. 2d 1074, 1078 (C.D. Cal. 1999) (proper jurisdiction when defendant's contacts with forum were two sales induced by plaintiff).

Although typically reserved for tort cases, the "effects test" has been used as an alternative method to establish purposeful availment in some intellectual property actions. <u>Compare</u> <u>Panavision</u>, 141 F.3d at 1321-22 (effects test appropriate because defendant's registration of plaintiff's trademarks as domain name was akin to a tort), <u>with</u> <u>Cybersell</u>, 130 F.3d at 420 (effects test inapplicable because defendant's posting of a passive website not akin to a tort). Purposeful availment is established through the effects test by showing that a defendant's foreign act was expressly aimed at and had effect in the forum state. <u>See</u> <u>Calder v. Jones</u>, 465 U.S. 783, 791 (1984); <u>Bancroft</u>, 223 F.3d at 1087. Because jurisdiction cannot be predicated on acts with merely foreseeable consequences, the express aiming element requires that the defendant engage in wrongful conduct aimed at entities known

> The author's use of <u>id.</u> in the next citation is improper. <u>Id.</u> only can be used to refer back to a single authority. It cannot follow a citation to two authorities.

to the defendant to be forum residents. <u>Id</u>.

Plaintiffs have two opportunities to prove purposeful availment: either the effects test or the sliding scale analysis will suffice, and if one test is satisfied, the court need not consider the other. <u>See</u> <u>Cybersell</u>, 130 F.3d at 417 (effects test inapplicable, inquiry moved on to sliding scale analysis); <u>Tech Heads</u>, 105 F. Supp. 2d at 1148 (effects test applied but not met, minimum contacts shown by sliding scale test); <u>Bancroft</u>, 223 F.3d at 1088 (purposeful availment analysis ceased when effects test was met).

> Because this application section follows a synthesized explanation section, the author can apply principles of how the law is to interpreted and applied rather than applying cases.

In the present case, the motion picture industry is the exclusive major proponent of the DVD format. Thus, Defendants have expressly targeted Plaintiff, as a member of that industry, by providing access to DeCSS. Defendant's activity is tort-like, causing an injury to Plaintiff in California. Because Defendants' activity has injured Plaintiff in California by enabling at least thirty downloads of DeCSS in that forum, the effects test is both applicable and satisfied.

Even without the effects test, Defendants' minimum contacts with California are shown through the sliding scale analysis. Defendants' activity was facilitated by their website, the interactive nature of which is indicated by the invitations to subscribe to a newsletter, exchange information, and make donations. The emails regarding how to obtain DeCSS sent to known California residents, and the online receipt of donations (privileged as exemptions under California law) from residents, provide the actual transactions with the

> There is no thesis restated as a conclusion in this section, and the argument ends rather abruptly. It always is a good idea to write a thesis restated as conclusion sentence to let the reader know that you are finished with the argument and are moving on to a new point.

forum required to show purposeful availment.

B. Plaintiff's claim arises out of Defendants' forum-related activities.

> This section is amazingly short because there is little to say about this element of the rule, and Defendants conceded the point in the sample memorandum in support provided above.

As Plaintiff's suit would not have arisen but for Defendant's contacts with California, this prong is satisfied. See Bancroft, 223 F.3d at 1088; Panavision, 141 F.3d at 1322.

C. Assertion of specific jurisdiction over Defendants is reasonable.

> Once again, we are skipping the last section.

* * *

CONCLUSION

For the reasons stated above, Plaintiff respectfully requests the court to deny Defendants' motion to dismiss for lack of personal jurisdiction.

Chapter 4

Motions for Summary Judgment

A motion for summary judgment is the ultimate pretrial dispositive motion. After discovery is completed, after all the evidence is uncovered in the case, you are going to challenge your opponent's claims or defenses and state that the facts are clear and the law provides that you are entitled to judgment right here, right now, on one or more or all of your opponent's claims or defenses.

I. FEDERAL RULE OF CIVIL PROCEDURE 56(c)

Federal Rule of Civil Procedure 56(c) governs summary judgment motions in federal court. It states in relevant part:

> The judgment sought shall be rendered forthwith if the pleadings, depositions, answers to interrogatories, and admissions on file, together with the affidavits, if any, show that there is no genuine issue as to any material fact and that the moving party is entitled to a judgment as a matter of law. A summary judgment, interlocutory in character, may be rendered on the issue of liability alone although there is a genuine issue as to the amount of damages.

Many aspects of this complicated rule deserve closer attention.

A. Material facts

The key to the consideration of whether a case (or an issue in a case) is appropriate for summary judgment is an analysis of whether the issue can be resolved as a matter of law without regard to any disputed material fact. You can have disputes over facts, just not material facts. Material facts are those that affect or potentially affect the outcome of the case (or the issue at hand) on the merits.

> ➤ *Example:* In a litigation involving the performance of a contract to create a metal sculpture, in which defendant asserts that he lacked the mental capacity to understand the terms of the contract because of his intoxication on the day of the contracting, you probably could have a dispute over the metal content of the sculpture—did it contain titanium or not?—and it would not affect a motion for summary judgment on defendant's defenses to the contract.

You could not have a dispute over the number of drinks defendant had before he signed the contract or what his blood alcohol level was on that day because those facts potentially would affect the analysis of his defenses on the merits.

If the dispute over the facts does not affect the outcome (<u>e.g.</u>, no matter who is right on the facts, the outcome from those facts would be the same), then the dispute need not defeat summary judgment.

> ➤ *Example:*   If the common law marriage requirement in your state is "cohabitation for over a year," and plaintiff argues that the two lived together for seven years, while defendant argues that it was only five years, these two versions of the facts both meet the one-year requirement, so there is no need to withhold summary judgment because of this dispute.

B. Genuine dispute

The dispute over the facts must be genuine. A party's assertion of the facts (or the meaning of the facts) must be plausible and defensible. You cannot defeat summary judgment just by coming up with some outlandish version or interpretation of the facts that your client is willing to swear to in an affidavit or declaration. (Clients generally will do what you tell them to, and courts know that!) A manifestly frivolous position on the facts will not defeat summary judgment.

The party's position on the facts should not be directly inconsistent with the position it asserted before litigation was initiated or directly contrary to the position asserted earlier in the same litigation. In other words, you should not be allowed to defeat summary judgment simply by contradicting everything you said earlier in the case.

Note that the rule speaks of "pleadings, depositions, answers to interrogatories, and admissions on file, together with the affidavits," as proof of the facts that demonstrate "that there is no genuine issue as to any material fact and that the moving party is entitled to a judgment as a matter of law." Thus, the court looks to the complete record on the facts to determine if there is a genuine dispute. If your client is going to assert that there is a genuine dispute as to the facts, you had better get your story straight early, and repeat it consistently in the case, or it will appear that you are changing factual horses in midstream just for the sake of defeating the summary judgment motion and prolonging the litigation. This tactic should fail.

The affidavits and declarations offered in support of summary judgment must be asserted in good faith, and the witness must be competent (<u>e.g.</u>, the witness swearing must have first-hand information of the facts and be able to testify to the same at trial), and not be asserted solely for the purpose of delaying and prolonging the litigation by defeating a valid summary judgment motion. If the judge thinks that you and your client are cooking up affidavits just to confuse the facts and to defeat summary judgment through false factual disputes, you and your client can be sanctioned.

C. The burden shifts

Initially, the movant bears the burden to show that there is no genuine dispute as to any material fact, and that he or she is entitled to judgment as a matter of law. Once that burden is met, however, the burden shifts to the opponent to produce concrete evidence to show that there is a genuine material factual dispute or that judgment is not proper as a matter of law. In other words, if movant presents a properly supported motion with affidavits or declarations showing that there is no dispute, the opponent cannot simply rest on its pleadings and the arguments of its counsel, but must come forth with affidavits and declarations and factual support of its own to show a genuine dispute as to material facts.

D. Judgment must be appropriate as a matter of law

The court must be able to determine from the undisputed facts that judgment is appropriate as a matter of law in favor of one of the parties. Although the movant meets her burden as to the facts, the motion will be denied if the law does not support the movant's position.

Even if the parties think the undisputed facts are complete enough to determine who should win, the court must make the ultimate determination, so even cross-motions for summary judgment can both be denied. The court may disagree and find that there is a genuine dispute over one or more material facts, or the parties failed to raise and stipulate to enough facts to make a determination in the case, or the court may decide that the law is not clear enough to make a decision at this stage before trial.

II. CROSS-MOTIONS FOR SUMMARY JUDGMENT

Occasionally, the local rules require the parties to submit their dispute to the trial court on cross-motions for summary judgment,[1] or the court may request the parties to file cross-motions on some or all of the issues in the case, or the parties may agree to stipulate to a set of facts and submit the case or issues in the case on cross-motions for summary judgment (and the parties hope that they have stipulated to enough facts to determine the issues of the motion). As indicated above, the filing of cross-motions is no guarantee that one of the motions will be granted if the court thinks there are not enough facts in the record to make a determination on the issues.

---

[1] For example, the Local Rules of the U.S. District Court for the Eastern District of Missouri require all appeals from the denial of Social Security benefits to be submitted on cross-motions for summary judgment.

III. STRUCTURE AND FORMAT OF A SUMMARY JUDGMENT MOTION AND OPPOSITION

Like other pretrial motions, a summary judgment motion has the following:

[PRE-INTRODUCTION]
<u>INTRODUCTION</u>
<u>STATEMENT OF FACTS</u>
<u>ARGUMENT</u>
<u>CONCLUSION</u>

In a summary judgment motion, the movant has a strong incentive not to create the appearance of factual disputes. Therefore, if you are the movant, you should not draft the statement of facts in a way that changes the logical meaning of the stipulated facts or the facts that are established in the record. You must exercise good judgment. You have the choice of which facts to highlight by placing them prominently in the section and by phrasing them in the active voice, and which facts to downplay by placing them in obscure locations and by phrasing them in the passive voice. But you should not draw controversial inferences from the stipulated or established facts. There is no room for emotional, argumentative, conclusory rhetoric in the statement of facts of a summary judgment motion. Save that for your discussion of the law and the equities in the case. If you go too far in drafting a statement of facts section that sounds magnificently favorable to your client, you may defeat the whole purpose of summary judgment by making it sound like there is a factual dispute in the case.

The opponent of summary judgment has no incentive to follow the rules stated above. If you are the opponent, you still are bound by the rules of style and good taste, but it is in your favor to create the appearance of a factual dispute, so draft the statement of facts in a way that highlights everything that favors your client.

If you have stipulated with your opponent as to the relevant facts and submitted the same to the court, then you need not offer additional proof in form of "pleadings, depositions, answers to interrogatories, and admissions on file, together with the affidavits (and declarations), if any." If there is no stipulation, then you must support each fact you assert as material and undisputed with the type of proof listed.

An opponent may be asserting its own right to judgment as a matter of law on undisputed facts in a cross motion for summary judgment—"Plaintiff agrees that the facts are not in dispute, and there is no reason for a trial, but plaintiff prevails under the applicable law." Otherwise, the opponent either has to prove that there is a genuine material fact dispute in the case precluding summary judgment, or that movant's arguments about the law are erroneous, whether or not the opponent is also seeking summary judgment at this stage.

We have alluded to what you should ***not*** do to try to defeat summary judgment: do not try to cook up a bunch of bogus affidavits that your hapless client will no doubt endorse. Do not attempt to change factual positions 180 degrees in mid-stream. Do not go back on what you have been stating are the facts and the law since the case began. None of these tactics will do you any good. In addition, do not sit on your complaint and rest on the arguments of counsel and expect the court to give you the benefit of a doubt. If your opponent has made a credible case, then prove up a genuine material factual dispute, and refute the opponent's legal arguments. This is one motion where the court probably will not do your thinking for you.

IV. SAMPLE MOTIONS

Sample 1: Memorandum in Support of Motion for Summary Judgment

---

UNITED STATES DISTRICT COURT
CENTRAL DISTRICT OF CALIFORNIA
SOUTHERN DIVISION

GLOBAL STUDIOS,	)	
	)	
Plaintiff,	)	
	)	No. SA CV 01-9999 AHS
v.	)	
	)	
KINGSTON UNIVERSITY	)	
ELECTRONIC FREEDOM	)	
FRONTIER, LARRY MULLEN,	)	
LISA ROGERS, MEGHAN MORELY,	)	
and CHRIS HANSEN,	)	
	)	
Defendants.	)	

MEMORANDUM IN SUPPORT OF DEFENDANTS' MOTION FOR SUMMARY JUDGMENT

Defendants move this Court pursuant to Fed. R. Civ. P. 56(c) for summary judgment in favor of Defendants on Plaintiff's complaint.

> Movants seeking summary judgment need a hard-hitting introduction, and the introduction that follows gets the job done. It really grabs the reader's attention and brings the whole case into focus. The issues, the facts, the law, and the policies are all introduced in a powerful set of sentences.

INTRODUCTION

As evidenced by the filing of its original complaint, Plaintiff asserts that it is entitled to obstruct the flow of information and ideas from Defendants to the public merely because it does not condone the message of Defendants' communications. Plaintiff's attempt to suppress Defendants' First Amendment right to free speech compels this motion. Plaintiff engages in the motion picture industry by translating motion pictures to digital versatile disks (DVDs). Defendants are members of a student group that operates an informational website featuring an online student newspaper. Along with several other unrelated stories, Defendants recently reported news and information regarding the debate over the use of DeCSS, a computer program that allows users to copy DVD movies. To provide a complete report to the public, Defendants referred to, in plain text without the prefix "www.", the names of a small number of DeCSS-provider sites. Defendants did not create DeCSS, nor did they post DeCSS, or provide a hyperlink to any website containing DeCSS, on their website. Defendants' right to report news and information on their website regarding the DeCSS debate is guaranteed by the First Amendment to the United States Constitution. Although the Government has a substantial interest in protecting copyrights from unauthorized circumvention, the Digital Millennium Copyright Act ("DMCA") is not narrowly tailored to serve this interest because it imposes overbroad speech restrictions that do not withstand constitutional scrutiny. Even if the DMCA is not overbroad, it is unconstitutional as applied to Defendants to the extent that it prevents them from reporting news and information in plain text on their website.

> This statement of facts emphasizes the facts that are the most beneficial for the defendants. For example, it emphasizes that the defendants are students and they are acting as members of the press, which are good facts for the judge to be dwelling on as she reads the motion.

STATEMENT OF FACTS

Plaintiff operates in the motion picture industry by producing and selling motion pictures on the DVD format, which are encoded by a program called Content System Scramble

("CSS"). Stipulation of Facts ("Stip."), ¶ 1, 7. Defendants are members of a student organization that publishes an informational website containing an online newspaper. <u>Id</u>. ¶¶ 2, 9. In this newspaper, Defendants regularly report technology-related stories and events. <u>See</u> Complaint, Exhibit 1. One story reported by Defendants was the debate over the use of DeCSS, a program which bypasses CSS and allows users to copy DVDs. Stip. ¶¶ 8, 10.

In the process of reporting the DeCSS debate, Defendants referred, in plain text, to the names of a small number of websites where DeCSS reportedly was available. <u>See</u> Complaint, Exhibit 1. At no time was the object code or source code for DeCSS available on any part of Defendants' website. Stip. ¶ 12. Furthermore, none of the references to reported DeCSS provider sites included the prefix "www." nor were any of them hotlinked or hyperlinked to those sites. <u>Id</u>. ¶¶ 11, 12.

> We recommend that you start off your summary judgment memorandum with the summary judgment standards. We do not mind the heading chosen for this section because the section should be limited to the presentation of a procedural rule and its interpretive rules, and this heading reveals that information. The placement of this section is faithful to the TREAT format. The reader may not need the refresher, but at least it lets the reader know you are up to speed on things. The first sentence of this section is important because it establishes which jurisdiction's law applies to the case for both substantive and procedural issues.

ARGUMENT

I. LEGAL STANDARDS FOR SUMMARY JUDGMENT.

When a federal court decides a case involving a federal question, federal procedural law is applied. <u>See</u> <u>Benny v. Pipes</u>, 799 F.2d 489, 493 (9th Cir. 1986). Under Rule 56(c) of the Fed. R. Civ. P., summary judgment is permitted if there is "no genuine issue as to any material fact, and the moving party is entitled to judgment as a matter of law." <u>See</u> <u>Anderson v. Liberty Lobby, Inc.</u>, 477 U.S. 242, 247-48 (1986); <u>Fazio v. City and County of San Francisco</u>, 125 F.3d 1328, 1331 (9th Cir. 1997). The moving party bears the initial burden of demonstrating the absence of a genuine issue of material fact for trial by showing that there is a lack of evidence to support the non-moving party's case. <u>See</u> <u>Matsushita Elec. Indus. Co. v. Zenith Radio Corp.</u>, 475 U.S. 574, 587 (1986). Once the moving party has met its initial burden, the non-moving party must introduce significant probative evidence tending to support the complaint. <u>See</u> <u>Celotex Corp. v. Catrett</u>, 477 U.S. 317, 323 (1986). In the present case, Plaintiff and Defendants have stipulated to all the material facts, and Defendants are entitled to summary judgment as a matter of law.

> Here, the reader jumps into the first substantive rule section. This section really belongs under thesis heading II below. Putting part of the rule section here jumps the gun and steps out of the TREAT format, and it might cause some readers to miss some of movants' most important rules, because they might routinely skip the summary judgment standards section and head for the first substantive argument.

In 17 U.S.C. § 1201(a)(2)(A) (1998), the DMCA provides that:

> No person shall manufacture, import, offer to the public, provide, or otherwise traffic in any technology, product, service, device, component, or part thereof, that is primarily designed or produced for the purpose of circumventing a technological measure that effectively controls access to a work protected under this title.

> The author may be correct about what this next sentence says, but we would quote the second trafficking provision. Statutory rules are too important to gloss over like this.

17 U.S.C. § 1201(b)(1)(A) differs slightly from § 1201(a)(2)(A), but in the instant case the distinction is irrelevant because only the sections' shared language is at issue.

II. THE DMCA DOES NOT SURVIVE A FACIAL CHALLENGE BECAUSE IT IS UNCONSTITUTIONALLY OVERBROAD.

> When you take the trafficking provisions out of this rule section, it becomes a section on the constitutional law issues of the case. This is a nicely drafted section that weaves many explanatory and interpretive rules into the discussion. First Amendment jurisprudence is rich with such rules, and this author makes good use of favorable authorities to set the right public policy tone for the motion. Our one criticism is that the author could have used explanatory synthesis to support all of these points without making the section much longer.

The First Amendment to the United States Constitution states that "Congress shall make no law . . . abridging the freedom of speech or of the press." U.S. Const. amend. I. First Amendment protection of speech does not turn on the popularity or social utility of the ideas and beliefs which it conveys. See New York Times Co. v. Sullivan, 376 U.S. 254, 270 (1964). The freedom of the press is a fundamental personal right that extends to every medium which acts as a vehicle of information. See Branzburg v. Hayes, 408 U.S. 665,

703 (1972). The Internet is one such medium, constituting a vast public forum entitled to full First Amendment protection. See <u>Reno v. A.C.L.U.</u>, 521 U.S. 844, 868-70 (1997).

> The insertion of the next paragraph into the rule section is effective as it introduces the first step of a rule based reasoning syllogism that is separate from the syllogism developed by the other paragraphs of this rule section. The other paragraphs of this rule section are devoted to the standards and public policies of the First Amendment. This paragraph introduces a rule defining newspapers. Movants' legal strategy is to characterize its web site as a newspaper. If the internet is a big newspaper (step one), it will be easier for movants' web site to be characterized as a newspaper or part of a newspaper (step two). Movants have found a way to insert rules for two arguments into one rule section without disrupting the flow of the section. It is a shame that movants do not attempt to apply these rules to their own facts.

The Internet is rapidly evolving into a universal newspaper. See <u>Religious Tech. Ctr v. Lerma</u>, 908 F. Supp. 1353 (E.D. Va. 1995). Newspapers constitute important forums for the dissemination of information and expression of opinions and are devoted entirely to expressive activity. See <u>San Diego Comm. Against Registration and the Draft v. Governing Bd. of Grossmont Union High School Dist.</u>, 790 F.2d 1471, 1476 (9th Cir. 1985).

When speech restrictions supporting government interests and First Amendment freedoms collide, the risk of non-persuasion rests with the government and not the speaker. See <u>United States v. Playboy Ent. Group, Inc.</u>, 529 U.S. 803, 818 (2000). The appropriate level of constitutional scrutiny to be applied to a statute is determined by whether the speech restrictions it imposes are content-based or content-neutral. See <u>City of Erie v. Pap's A.M.</u>, 529 U.S. 277, 289 (2000); <u>Turner Broad. Sys., Inc. v. F.C.C.</u>, 512 U.S. 622, 642 (1994). A statute is overbroad under the First Amendment if it causes substantially impermissible applications relative to the law's legitimate sweep. See <u>New York v. Ferber</u>, 458 U.S. 747, 771 (1982).

> Movants' first substantive argument begins in sub-section A. Movant has several ways to argue this motion, and starts with the hardest argument first (proving that the DMCA is a content-based restriction on speech). This is a bold move, but it makes the most sense here because it does not sound convincing to start with the argument in subsection B (DMCA is content neutral and subject to "intermediate scrutiny" analysis) and move to a much harder point (if not content neutral, the DMCA is content based and subject to the much harder standard of "strict scrutiny").

A. The DMCA imposes content-based restrictions on speech, which are unconstitutional because they do not satisfy the strict scrutiny standard.

Content-based restrictions on speech are aimed at stifling speech on account of the message it conveys. See Turner 512 U.S. at 642. A restriction is content-neutral if it is justified without reference to the content of speech. See Hill v. Colorado, 530 U.S. 703, 720 (2000).

> This explanation section uses explanatory synthesis very well, but it appears that the author thought that she only could synthesize two cases for each point, which of course is not true. There are many First Amendment cases on point the author could have used to make broader illustrations.

In the First Amendment context, the government's purpose for regulating expressive activity is the controlling consideration in determining if the regulation is content-based or neutral. Compare Boos v. Barry, 485 U.S. 312, 321 (1988) (ban on use of signs to criticize foreign government within certain distance of embassy was attempt to regulate direct impact of message on listeners and was content based), with Renton v. Playtime Theatres, Inc., 475 U.S. 41, 48 (1986) (restriction on placement of adult theater aimed at controlling secondary effects of theater on neighborhood was justified without reference to content of theater's speech).

> Movants are using authorities well in this rule section. They prove that content based restrictions "stifle" speech (see above) and are "presumptively unconstitutional" (see below). These are points that movants want the court to be thinking about as the court evaluates this motion. Although the initial task is to convince the court to find that the DMCA is in fact content based, it doesn't hurt to set the proper tone about content based restrictions in general as movants are doing in this section.

Content-based restrictions are presumptively unconstitutional. See Free Speech Coalition v. Reno, 198 F.3d 1083, 1091 (9th Cir. 1999); Crawford v. Lungren, 96 F.3d 380, 384 (9th Cir. 1996). To defeat this presumption, content-based restrictions must meet a standard of strict scrutiny, which requires that they be narrowly tailored to serve a compelling government interest and employ the least restrictive means possible to serve that interest. See Playboy, 529 U.S. at 813; Sable Communications of California, Inc. v. F.C.C., 492 U.S. 115, 126 (1989).

Statutes placing content-based restrictions on speech conveyed through the Internet, although serving substantial government interests, have been susceptible to overbreadth defects and routinely are struck down. See Reno, 521 U.S. at 875 (content-based federal statute prohibiting communication of indecent material to minors through Internet unduly burdened protected speech of adults and was overbroad); Free Speech Coalition v. Reno, 198 F.3d 1083, 1095 (9th Cir. 1999) (statute failed strict scrutiny because it prohibited protected expression of non-minors and thus was not narrowly tailored).

If a less restrictive means of meeting the government's interest could be at least as effective in serving that interest, the restriction in question does not satisfy strict scrutiny. See Playboy, 529 U.S. at 815 (statute invalidated because targeted blocking of sexually explicit material was less restrictive means of serving government's interest); Sable, 492 U.S. at 130-31 (feasibility of technological means to control minors' access to sexually explicit phone messages provided less restrictive means of serving government's interest).

> Here is where the rubber meets the road: the Second Circuit found the DMCA to be content neutral, not content based. Movants have to convince this court to ignore that persuasive authority.

The anti-trafficking provisions of the DMCA at issue in the present case were recently analyzed in Corley v. Universal City Studios, Inc., 273 F.3d 429 (2nd Cir. 2001). In that case, the court held that the DMCA was content-neutral, and that it was not unconstitutional because it passed intermediate scrutiny. Id. at 456-58. Corley's interpretation of the DMCA was erroneous.

Like the defendants in Corley, Defendants in the present case report information to the public regarding the DeCSS debate. The right to communicate this information is ensured by the First Amendment and is not contingent upon government approval. However, the DMCA inhibits this right by restricting Defendants on account of the government's disagreement with its message. The DMCA seeks to prevent Defendants' speech solely because Defendants are talking about DeCSS as opposed to any other non-encryption related computer program. Thus, the DMCA is content-based, and Plaintiff cannot overcome the presumption against the constitutionality of content-based restrictions. As was conceded in Corley, the government has alternative means of serving its interest in preventing unauthorized access to copyrighted materials, which are less speech-restrictive than the blanket prohibitions of the DMCA. Id. at 455. Thus, similar to the statutes in Reno and Free Speech Coalition, the DMCA impermissibly hampers a substantial amount of protected speech and is overbroad.

B. Even if the DMCA is content-neutral, it does not constitute a reasonable time, place, or manner restriction and is thus unconstitutional.

> We are not thrilled with this rule section. It is not obvious that the DMCA is a time, place, manner restriction, so this rule section should have presented rules defining general content neutral restrictions first, and then explained that

> time, place, manner restrictions are a sub-set of the broader group of content neutral restrictions, and devoted its time to proving that the DMCA fits the definition. Instead, this section starts with a veiled presumption that the DMCA is a time, place, manner restriction and spends most of its time explaining the effect of its being a content neutral restriction. Movants have made it harder to persuade the court that the DMCA fits the general definition of a content neutral restriction when they start out with an erroneous presumption that its status is established.

A time, place, or manner restriction of speech is constitutional if it is content neutral, is narrowly tailored to serve a significant government interest, and leaves open ample alternative channels for communication of the information. See Ward v. Rock Against Racism, 491 U.S. 781, 799 (1989); Alameda Books, Inc. v. City of Los Angeles, 222 F.3d 719, 722 (9th Cir. 2000). This analysis of time, place, or manner restrictions varies little, if at all, from an analysis driven by the intermediate scrutiny standard announced in United States v. O'Brien, 391 U.S. 367, 376 (1968). See Clark v. Cmty. for Creative Non-Violence, 468 U.S. 288, 299 (1984).

A restriction meets the intermediate scrutiny standard if it furthers a substantial government interest unrelated to the suppression of free expression, and the incidental restriction on speech is no greater than is essential to further that interest. See O'Brien, 391 U.S. at 376. Interpreting the last element of this analysis, courts have allowed an incidental restriction on speech only to the extent that it does not burden substantially more speech than is necessary to further the relevant government interest. See Turner, 512 U.S. at 662; Ward, 491 U.S. at 799.

> Movants have shifted to explanation now. It is deceptive to start a new section with the word "However," but it is clear that the next two paragraphs employ explanatory synthesis and function as an explanation section.

However, the intermediate level of scrutiny is not satisfied if the regulation provides only ineffective or remote support for the government's purpose. See Lorillard Tobacco Co. v. Reiley, 533 U.S. 525 (2001) (statute forbidding placement of any advertisement for tobacco products lower than five feet from floor did not sufficiently serve government interest of preventing minors from using tobacco); Bolger v. Youngs Drug Products Corp., 463 U.S. 60 (1983) (statute prohibiting unsolicited mailing of contraceptive advertisements did not satisfy intermediate scrutiny test merely because such mailings were potentially offensive).

Restrictions are not narrowly tailored for purposes of intermediate scrutiny if they fail to leave open ample alternative channels of communication of the information. Compare Young v. Am. Mini Theaters, Inc. 427 U.S. 50, 54 (1976) (restriction on place where adult films could be displayed was upheld because it did not ban the form of expression altogether), with Schad v. Mount Ephraim, 452 U.S. 61, 70 (1981) (purported content-neutral restriction struck down because it imposed total ban on adult theaters).

> Proper use of explanatory synthesis makes for crisp, effective application sections, such as this one.

In the present case, the government has a substantial interest in preventing unauthorized access to copyrighted materials. However, the DMCA is not narrowly tailored to serving that interest because it leaves open no reasonable alternative means for Defendants to communicate their message. The DMCA closes off to Defendants the entire medium of expression offered by the Internet, and in so doing burdens substantially more speech than is necessary to serve the government's interest. As was mentioned above, the DMCA prohibits every means by which Defendants might communicate their message through that medium.

> The second paragraph of this application section is a little unusual, because it sounds like a new explanation section is beginning. But, in fact, the author is making clever use of Corley, the one authority that is closest on the facts to the case at hand, even though this case goes against movants' position in the instant case. Movants' use of Corley and the legislative history cited here is effective, and it is not too distracting in the application section even though it might have been included in the explanation section.

The trial court in Corley was aware of the likelihood that the DMCA burdens substantially more speech than is necessary to serve the government's interest, so the court modified the O'Brien standard to limit the DMCA's linking prohibition. See Corley, 273 F.3d at 456. The trial court's concern with the overbreadth of the DMCA also is evident in its discussion of the legislative history of the DMCA, as there was disagreement in the history over whether the House Commerce Committee's version of the statute, which was written to cure substantial overbreadth defects in the original version, adequately balanced copyright protection with First Amendment rights. See H.R. Rep. No. 105-586 (additional views of Reps. Klug and Boucher). This judicial and Congressional concern further

> There is no thesis restated as a conclusion in this section. Indeed, this section ends too abruptly. At least one sentence is missing that would conclude the thought expressed in this paragraph, such as, "Therefore, the DMCA fails intermediate scrutiny for failing to leave open ample alternate channels for Defendant's communication."

indicates demonstrates the overbreadth of the DMCA.

III. EVEN IF THE DMCA IS NOT FACIALLY OVERBROAD, IT IS UNCONSTITUTIONAL AS APPLIED TO PLAINTIFF.

> If you are keeping score, this is movants' third major argument. This one deviates from the TREAT format in that this section lacks a coherent rule section, explanation section, and application section. Rules are evident, and application is evident, but the structure is blended. Nevertheless, this section does make a positive impact on the reader in a small amount of space.

Trafficking in circumvention devices on the Internet may take the form of linking. See Corley, 273 F.3d at 456; DVD Copy Control Ass'n v. McLaughlin, No. CV 786804, 2000 WL 48512 at *4 (Cal. Super. Ct. Jan. 18, 2000). Linking is defined as the programming of a particular point on a screen to transfer the user to another web page when the point, called a hyperlink, is clicked. See Universal City Studios, Inc. v. Remeirdes, 111 F. Supp. 2d 321, 324 (S.D.N.Y. 1998), aff'd sub nom Corley, 273 F.3d at 456.

The DeCSS debate underpinning the present case has surfaced in court before, and there is disagreement on how to interpret the First Amendment rights of persons linking to DeCSS-provider sites. Compare McLaughlin, 2000 WL 48512 at *4 (links are the mainstay of the Internet, and a website owner cannot be held liable for the content of the sites to which it links), and DVD Copy Control Ass'n v. Bunner, 113 Cal. Rptr. 2d 338, 340 (Ct. App. 6th Dist. 2001) (review granted) (injunction prohibiting posting, and linking by inference, of DeCSS on website violated defendant's First Amendment rights), with Corley, 273 F.3d at 456 (linking prohibition is justified because it pertains only to non-speech component of hyperlink).

The court in Corley, analyzing this issue in the context of the DMCA, held that linking to DeCSS provider sites constituted offering DeCSS to the public or providing or otherwise trafficking in DeCSS in violation of the DMCA. See Corley, 273 F.3d at 455-58. However, Corley is distinguishable from the present case in two fundamental respects. First, the holding of Corley relied upon that court's finding that the statute was content-neutral because the DMCA regulates only the non-speech, functional component of hyperlinks. Id. at 456-58.

In contrast, the website maintained by Defendants in the present case contains only plain, non-hyperlinked textual references to the names of a small number of DeCSS-provider sites. This plain text contains no functional component. If a viewer were to click on one of these references, nothing would happen. Furthermore, Defendants chose not to attach the prefix "www." to the names of the DeCSS-provider sites. Thus, even if a visitor to Defendants' website were to "cut and paste" one of the these names into the URL text box and then instruct the computer to find the site, the viewer would be transported nowhere. It can be inferred that the lack of functionality of plain text was the source of the <u>Corley</u> court's apparent unwillingness to extend its linking prohibition to a plain text, non-hyperlinked list of DeCSS-provider sites. <u>See</u> David A. Peteys, <u>The Freedom to Link?</u>, 25 Seattle U. L. Rev. 287, 334 (2001).

The second distinction between <u>Corley</u> and the present case is that the defendants in <u>Corley</u>, by posting DeCSS on their own website and then creating several links to DeCSS-provider sites (an act of self-styled "electronic civil disobedience"), acted for the express purpose of disseminating DeCSS. <u>See Corley</u>, 273 F.3d at 442. By contrast, the Defendants in the instant case used plain text from which the prefix "www." was excluded. This confirms that Defendants' intent in using these references was merely to convey information as part of their report on the DeCSS debate, and was not to encourage the dissemination of DeCSS.

Further weakening the precedential value of <u>Corley</u> is that court's initial pronouncement that, due to the novelty of applying First Amendment law in the digital age, the court was subscribing to an evolutionary approach, favoring a narrow holding to allow the law to mature on a case-by-case basis. <u>Id</u>. at 445. These fundamental distinctions between <u>Corley</u> and the present case, along with the express admonition of that court that its holding be treated narrowly, evidence the fact that the DMCA cannot be extended to cover the activity of Defendants in the present case.

<u>CONCLUSION</u>

For the reasons stated above, Defendants respectfully request the Court to grant their motion for summary judgment on Plaintiff's complaint.

Sample 2: Memorandum in Opposition to Motion for Summary Judgment

---

UNITED STATES DISTRICT COURT
CENTRAL DISTRICT OF CALIFORNIA
SOUTHERN DIVISION

GLOBAL STUDIOS,   )
)
                   Plaintiff,   )
     v.   )
)
KINGSTON UNIVERSITY   )   No. SA CV 01-9999 AHS
ELECTRONIC FREEDOM   )
FRONTIER, an unincorporated association,)
LARRY MULLEN, LISA ROGERS   )
MEGHAN MORELY, and CHRIS   )
HANSEN,   )
                   Defendants.   )

PLAINTIFF'S MEMORANDUM IN OPPOSITION TO DEFENDANTS'
MOTION FOR SUMMARY JUDGMENT

Plaintiff Global Studios, in opposition to Defendants' Motion for Summary Judgment, states as follows:

> The introduction below is engaging and informative. It works in the applicable legal standards by its inclusion of key legal terms ("trafficking," "functional speech," "least restrictive means," "government interest"), and introduces the public policy theme of the case through terms such as "piracy" and "hackers."

INTRODUCTION

Defendants are members of an organization dedicated to circumventing technological access control measures and promoting piracy on the World Wide Web. The organization, masking its illegal activity in free speech rhetoric, wants the court to believe Internet trafficking cannot constitutionally be punished.   However, the Defendants' web site provides hackers with instantaneous access to instruments like DeCSS that are used to bypass CSS, copy the content of DVDs, and play the duplicates on unlicensed devices. By prohibiting trafficking, the Digital Millennium Copyright Act ("DMCA") is targeting the "functional" aspect of speech and is not burdening more speech than necessary. The prohibitions are the least restrictive means of advancing the government's interest in preventing DVD duplication and copyright infringement. If hacker sites are not prevented from linking users to this software, the motion picture, music, and publishing industry will be in grave danger. Defendants' Motion for Summary Judgment should not be granted as a matter of law.

> This facts section is effective because it uses loaded terms ("hackers," "instantaneously . . . access the decryption sites," and "pirates") and advances the cause of the plaintiff by telling a very pro-plaintiff story.

STATEMENT OF FACTS

Defendants operate a web site "dedicated to maintaining a free and open electronic frontier." Complaint, Exhibit 1. The organization is funded through donations by hackers and people looking to circumvent various copyright laws. Declaration of Melanie Smead dated Jan. 12, 2002, ¶ 4 ("M.S. Dec"). Defendants' site provides a directory of web addresses where DeCSS is downloadable. See Stipulation of Facts ¶ 9 ("Stip."). The addresses are listed so a user instantaneously can access the decryption sites by pasting the addresses into the locator box of an Internet browser and adding the prefix www. See Stip. ¶ 5. All references to these sites have been made with knowledge of their content. See Stip. ¶ 10. In fact, through several e-mail conversations, members of the defendants' organization directed hackers to sites where the software was located. Complaint, Exhibit 1. DeCSS allows pirates to copy the content of DVDs and to distribute the duplicates throughout the world without making payments to the lawful owners, like Global Studios. See Stip ¶ 8.

> It is a good idea to start off a summary judgment memorandum with the summary judgment standards even if you are opposing the motion. The reader will know you are up to speed on the law.

ARGUMENT

I. SUMMARY JUDGMENT STANDARDS

When federal law applies, a federal court will apply federal procedural law. New SD, Inc. v. Rockwell Int'l Corp., 79 F.3d 953, 955 (9th Cir. 1996). Under Rule 56(c), Fed. R. Civ. P., summary judgment is appropriate only if there is no genuine issue of material fact and the moving party is entitled to judgment as a matter of law. Anderson v. Liberty Lobby, Inc., 477 U.S. 242, 247 (1986). The moving party bears the burden of demonstrating the absence of a genuine issue of material fact. Celotex Corp. v. Catrett, 477 U.S.

317, 323 (1986). This burden will not be satisfied by the mere existence of a scintilla of evidence in support of the movant's position; there must be evidence on which the jury could reasonably find for the movant. Anderson, 477 U.S. at 266. All evidence must be construed in the light most favorable to the non-moving party. Gardner v. Nike, Inc., 279 F.3d 774, 777 (9th Cir. 2002). If the movant has met this burden, the non-moving party must then set forth facts showing that there is a genuine issue for trial. Fed. R. Civ. P. 56(e). A genuine issue exists when the evidence is such that a reasonable jury could find for the non-movant. K. Villiariamo v. Aloha Island Air, Inc., 281 F.3d 1054, 1060 (9th Cir. 2002).

> This next sentence is important. You should inform the court whether you are going to challenge movant's rendition of the facts and the law, or just the law.

Plaintiff and the Defendants have entered into a stipulation of facts; however, there are genuine issues of fact that remain in this matter, and Defendants are not entitled to summary judgment as a matter of law.

> This first substantive TREAT section lays out the major rules. Remember to organize your rules in the proper order of authority, stating constitutional rules first, then statutory rules, then rules created by cases, including interpretive rules.

II. DEFENDANTS' MOTION FOR SUMMARY JUDGMENT SHOULD BE DENIED BECAUSE THE DMCA IS CONSTITUTIONAL ON ITS FACE

According to U.S. Const. amend. I, "Congress shall make no law . . . abridging the freedom of speech, or of the press." One of the "trafficking" provisions of the DMCA, 17 U.S.C. § 1201(a)(2) (1998), states:

> No person shall . . . offer to the public, provide, or otherwise traffic in any technology, product, service, device, component, or part thereof, that— (A) is primarily designed or produced for the purpose of circumventing a technological measure that effectively controls access to a work protected under this title;

Another provision, 17 U.S.C. § 1201(b)(1) (1998), states:

> No person shall . . . offer to the public, provide, or otherwise traffic in any technology, product, service, device, component, or part thereof, that—(A) is primarily designed or produced for the purpose of circumventing protection afforded by a technological measure that effectively protects a right of a copyright owner under this title in a work or a portion thereof.

The courts have a duty to insulate all individuals from the "chilling effect" upon First Amendment freedoms generated by vagueness and overbreadth. <u>Walker v. City of Birmingham</u>, 388 U.S. 307, 345 (1967).

> This next section starts with a useful roadmap sentence, then succinctly disposes of several issues in reduced TREAT discussions. This was an efficient use of space because none of these issues were dispositive, but each deserves at least this much attention.

This memorandum briefly will discuss Defendants' likely claim that their web site is a newspaper, followed by an analysis of the constitutionality of the DMCA provisions. Plaintiff concedes that the Internet is a public forum. <u>Planned Parenthood of the Columbia/Williamette Inc. v. Am. Coalition of Life Activists</u>, 244 F.3d 1007, 1019 (9th Cir. 2000). A "newspaper" is a medium for the dissemination of news of passing events printed and distributed at short but regular intervals. <u>United States v. Kelly</u>, 328 F.2d 227, 234 (6th Cir. 1964). A newspaper contains a broad range of news on all subjects and activities and is not limited to any specific subject matter. 17 U.S.C.A. § 202.3 6(f)(2) (2002). Defendants' web site does not meet this definition because it reports exclusively on Internet free speech issues.

Even if considered a newspaper, Defendants' web site would not be entitled to heightened protection from the provisions of the DMCA. Laws of general application do not offend the First Amendment simply because their enforcement against the press has incidental effects on its ability to report the news. <u>Cohen v. Cowles Media Co.</u>, 501 U.S. 663, 669 (1991). The press may not publish copyrighted material without obeying the copyright laws; it has no special privilege to invade the rights and liberties of others. <u>Id</u>.

> Now, we are getting into the meat of the argument. The short, crisp initial paragraphs make this section flow very well. Remember that you need not try to cram the entire rule section into one paragraph. This memorandum in opposition breaks the rules into several paragraphs, and it works very well.

A. Sections 1201 (a)(2) and (b)(1) of the DMCA are content-neutral regulations that are constitutional on their face.

> Notice how the opponent starts with a general definition of content neutral regulations and moves on to explain the definition and apply it to the facts of this case. Compare this to movants' sub-section II(B) above that presumes that the DMCA is a time, place, manner restriction and spends

> most of its time discussing the effect of its being a content neutral regulation. Of the two, the opponent's discussion of this topic is much more effective.

Restrictions targeting the "functional" aspect of expressive activity are "content-neutral." United States v. O'Brien, 391 U.S. 367, 377 (1968). The principle inquiry in determining content-neutrality is whether the government has adopted regulation of speech because of disagreement with the message it conveys. Ward v. Rock Against Racism, 491 U.S. 781, 791 (1989). The purpose of a content-neutral restriction can be justified without reference to the content of the message; however, the mere assertion of a content-neutral purpose may not be enough to save a law which, on its face, discriminates based on content. Turner Broadcasting Sys., Inc. v. F.C.C., 512 U.S. 622, 643 (1994).

Expressive activity, whether oral or written or symbolized by conduct, may be subject to reasonable time, place, and manner restrictions. Clark v. Cmty. for Creative Non-Violence, 468 U.S. 288, 293 (1984). Such restrictions are permissible so long as they are content-neutral, are narrowly tailored to serve a significant government interest, and leave open ample alternative channels of communication. Madsen v. Women's Health Center, 512 U.S. 753, 791 (1994).

A content-neutral regulation of expressive conduct that burdens speech incidentally will be sustained if it furthers an important governmental interest that is unrelated to the suppression of free expression and the incidental restriction on alleged First Amendment freedoms is no greater than is essential to the furtherance of that interest. O'Brien, 391 U.S. at 377.

To satisfy this intermediate scrutiny standard, a regulation need not be the least speech-restrictive means of advancing the government's interests. Turner Broadcasting Sys., Inc., 512 U.S. at 642-43. The means chosen just cannot burden substantially more speech than necessary to further the government's legitimate interest. Id. at 662.

> Here, the author makes a seamless transition to the explanation section. The author's use of explanatory synthesis is natural and informative.

Courts find that a regulation is content-neutral when people can determine whether the regulation applies to them without looking at the content of the speech. Compare Sable Communications v. F.C.C., 492 U.S. 115, 119 (1989) (prohibition on indecent interstate commercial telephone messages was not content-neutral because applicability depended on the content of the speech); with Ward, 491 U.S. at 791 (1989) (sound amplification guideline is content-neutral because it has nothing to do with content of the noise); and Clark, 468 U.S. at 294 (prohibition on sleeping in Lafayette park content-neutral because it does not consider the message presented).

Whether time, place, or manner restrictions meet the requirement of narrow tailoring depends on how effectively the government interest would be achieved in their absence. See United States v. Albertini, 472 U.S. 675, 689 (1985) (legislation making it unlawful for person to reenter military base after being barred was narrowly tailored where purpose of protecting government property would be achieved less effectively in its absence); <u>Clark,</u> 468 U.S. at 297 (prohibition on sleeping in Lafayette Park no greater than necessary because park would be exposed to more harm without the restriction). However, courts will not permit regulations that prevent a person from all reasonable or effective methods of communicating a particular message. <u>See</u> <u>Frisby v. Schultz</u>, 487 U.S. 474, 483 (1988) (ordinance banning picketing in front of a residence constitutional on its face because it allowed other means of communication such as telephone or mail contact with residents); <u>Grayned v. City of Rockford</u>, 408 U.S. 104, 111-12 (1972) (provisions that forbid noisy or diversionary activity that disrupts normal school activity left open ample alternative of peaceful picketing).

A burden on speech is no greater than essential under the <u>O'Brien</u> standard so long as the provisions are proportionally related to the end the legislation was designed to serve. <u>See</u> <u>Council of Los Angeles v. Taxpayers of Vincent</u>, 466 U.S. 789, 808-810 (1984) (complete prohibition of all signs on public property was necessary because the targeted "evil," visual blight, rendered each sign "evil"); <u>Turner Broadcasting Sys.</u>, 520 U.S. at 215-16 (modest effects on free speech in the telecommunications industry permissible where burden imposed by the must-carry provisions was congruent to the benefits they afford).

The Supreme Court recognizes that the time, place, and manner test is essentially no different than the <u>O'Brien</u> test, which applies to regulations that incidentally burden speech. <u>See</u> <u>Madsen</u>, 512 U.S. at 791 (1994) (recognizing that the difference between the standards is too subtle for the Court to describe, yet acknowledging the <u>O'Brien</u> test is stricter); <u>Ward</u>, 491 U.S. at 798 (conceding that there is little, if any, difference between the tests).

> After doing a careful job synthesizing cases in the explanation section, the opponent can make the following application section short and to-the-point, which makes it all the more powerful and useful to the reader.

The DMCA "trafficking" provisions are content-neutral on their face because they can be justified without regard to the content of the trafficker's speech. Congress's purpose in enacting these provisions was to counter the threat of devices that enable pirates to reproduce and distribute DVDs at no cost. <u>See</u> H.R. Rep. No. 105-551. pt. 2, at 25 (1998). The content of the trafficker's message was irrelevant to the government's purpose. Congress has a significant interest in protecting the motion picture industry from copyright infringement. The growth of DeCSS on the Internet creates copyright problems, reduces DVD sales, and counters the utility of CSS.

Whether the regulations are assessed under the time, place, and manner test or the <u>O'Brien</u> test makes little difference. The statute is constitutional under both. Preventing copyright infringement is done most effectively by targeting people providing circumvention devices. Absent the DMCA, like the ordinance in <u>Clark</u>, the government's interest would not be effectively achieved. Also, ample alternatives for communication exist. Those who wish to promote DeCSS may speak in the print media, on the radio, or in many other contexts. They just cannot offer the DeCSS to the public. Each provision of the statute is directed at protecting the motion picture industry, which in light of developments such as the Internet and "Napster," has become such a substantial and compelling government interest that any incidental burdens on

> There is no thesis restated as a conclusion here. It would be useful to draft a summary of the many points made in this long sub-TREAT, such as, "The DMCA is content neutral because it regulates conduct, not speech, and it is narrowly tailored to further the substantial government interest of protecting the property of the DVD producing industry; therefore, it is constitution under the intermediate scrutiny analysis."

speech created by the DMCA are likely to be minimal in relation to this interest.

> This next section presents an alternative argument. The law in this area lays out several avenues movants can follow to victory, and the opponent must address and refute each one. For the opponent, the argument in sub-section A is far superior to the argument in sub-section B, so the opponent chose to defend the easier position (content neutral—intermediate scrutiny) first and the harder position (content based—strict scrutiny) second.

B. Even if the regulations are content-based, they still are constitutional.

Even if the DMCA is a content based restriction, it still passes muster under the First Amendment. Under the strict scrutiny test, content-based restrictions on speech are permissible if they serve compelling state interests by the least restrictive means available. Sable Communications, 492 U.S. at 126.

When an alternative is available that would effectively further the government's interest without being so burdensome on speech, a content-based restriction is unconstitutionally overbroad. Compare Reno v. A.C.L.U., 521 U.S. 844, 879 (1997) (legislation prohibiting "patently offensive" communications from transmission through interactive computer service to minors deemed unconstitutional because exceptions for messages with educational value could be made); and Sable Communications, 492 U.S. at 128 (prohibition of indecent dial-a-porn messages unconstitutional because credit card and scrambling rules represented a "feasible and effective" way to serve the government's compelling interest in protecting children); with Denver Area Educ. Telecomm. Consortium, Inc. v. F.C.C., 518 U.S. 727, 747 (1996) (provision permitting cable operator to prohibit patently offensive or indecent materials is constitutional because effective alternatives would require an all-out ban on such materials in order to advance the government's interest in protecting children).

The regulations proscribed by the DMCA are the least restrictive means to protect the motion picture industry from copyright infringement. The Defendants may propose exceptions for educational purposes. While a protection scheme with educational exceptions would be less restrictive, it would be ineffective in furthering the government interest in protecting the motion picture industry. The majority of people who obtain DeCSS are not going to use it for educational purposes, but many would be happy to pretend that their piracy was undertaken for these purposes. By allowing such exceptions, the courts would be opening the gates for DVD duplication, defeating the purpose of regulation.

> Once again, there is no thesis restated as conclusion at the end of this sub-TREAT. By switching the last sentence with the second-to-last sentence, and rephrasing the second-to-last sentence to read, "By allowing the exceptions proposed by Defendants, the courts would be opening the gates for DVD duplication, defeating the purpose of regulation," the opponent could have had a perfectly appropriate thesis restated as conclusion at the end of this section.

Unlike those in <u>Sable Communications</u>, the alternatives here are not feasible and effective.

III. DEFENDANTS' MOTION FOR SUMMARY JUDGMENT SHOULD BE DENIED BECAUSE THE DMCA PROVISIONS ARE CONSTITUTIONAL AS APPLIED TO THE DEFENDANTS

> The last section of the opponent's memorandum refutes yet another alternative avenue that is open to the movant. We will skip it and move to the conclusion.

* * *

<u>CONCLUSION</u>

In light of the above, Global Studios respectfully requests the court to deny Defendants' motion for summary judgment.

Chapter 5

Appellate Advocacy: Appeals, Writs, Standards of Review

This chapter discusses appeals and appellate advocacy. It examines the appellate process, types of appeals and appellate writs that exist, the timing of the various types of appeals, and the concept of standard of review. Lastly, it will discuss the procedures for the compilation and use of the record on appeal.

I. INTRODUCTION TO THE APPELLATE PROCESS

An appeal is the action taken by the non-prevailing or aggrieved litigant in a litigation or other adversarial matter. The appeal is made to a higher level court, usually a court of appeals or the court of last resort, but sometimes a trial level court can hear an appeal from an administrative agency, arbitral body, or a lower level trial court (for example, a federal bankruptcy court, federal tax court, or a state associate circuit court or magistrate court). The non-prevailing party takes an appeal when it believes that errors were committed during the course of the litigation by the judge, and sometimes by the jury. The errors assigned might involve the interpretation of the governing law, the application of the law to the facts, the finding of facts, or a procedural ruling before or during trial. The non-prevailing party will look for any way possible to reverse the outcome.

A. It is hard to win on appeal.

It is important to note that no matter what court you are in, it is very difficult to win on appeal. Most appeals fail, and in some jurisdictions, the vast majority of appeals fail. It is difficult to convince a higher court to overturn the determinations and actions of a lower court. Therefore, the first job of an advocate in a situation presenting a potential appeal is to counsel your client that most appeals fail, and that statistically there is a better than even chance (or worse) that her appeal will fail. Then you can review the potential errors that might be asserted in the appeal and see if there are grounds to reverse the lower court that make the risk worth taking.

B. Quality is much better than quantity.

When evaluating the possible errors committed by the lower court, quality is far more important than quantity. In other words, you will do much better if there is one horrible, unforgivable error you can point to, rather than a dozen somewhat troublesome errors that might be raised. Appellate courts are sensitive to the tactic of certain litigators to throw up as many assertions of error as they can think of, hoping that one will stick and cause the case to be overturned. This is a tactic of desperation, not of effective advocacy. A quantity of "also ran" errors or legal arguments on the errors also can drown out the effectiveness of any of the better allegations and arguments you may have. So, the second piece of advice we will give is to limit yourself to the most important and egregious errors and arguments in support of reversal and assert as few of these as possible.

II. TYPES OF APPEALS AND APPELLATE WRITS

A. Appeal after a final judgment

The normal channel of appeal is from a final judgment entered in the lower court. 28 U.S.C. § 1291; Fed. R. App. P. 4. Everyone has the right to take this kind of appeal, once. Timing is critical: the appeal must be made within a certain period of time after the final judgment in the case is "entered," and entered can mean "issued" (signed by the trial judge) or entered on the docket, so be sure to check and be certain what it means in your jurisdiction. If you are late, the appeals court is deprived of jurisdiction. See United States v. Robinson, 361 U.S. 220 (1960); Fed. R. App. P. 3, Advisory Committee Notes to 1967 adoption. The court cannot simply excuse your mistake.

The "notice of appeal" required to be filed by Fed. R. App. P. 3 and 4 is important. It triggers the appeal and identifies what exactly it is that you are appealing from—a summary judgment or other order disposing of some issues and claims earlier in the case, a verdict and judgment after trial, the granting or denial of a post-trial motion, or all or some of the above. It is not necessarily sufficient or accurate simply to state that you appeal from the final judgment in the case.

Although each litigant is entitled to one appeal as of right, it still must be noted that few of these appeals succeed. You may get in the door easily enough, but you may soon be walking out that same door empty-handed. There are ways to try to improve your odds: pick your appeals carefully, only challenge the most important errors, and only raise the strongest legal arguments in support of reversal. Beyond that, follow the advice on the drafting of briefs and the planning, preparation for, and execution of oral argument that will be discussed in the next two chapters.

B. Interlocutory appeals

The next type of appeal in order of frequency (going down the scale to remedies that are less frequently available) is the interlocutory appeal, which in federal court is governed by 28 U.S.C. § 1292. "Interlocutory" means that the appeal happens prior to a final judgment in the case. A final judgment is one that disposes of *all* claims of *all* the parties in the case, damages and all. That can take a while, especially in a multi-party, multi-claim case, and litigants do not necessarily want to go that far and spend that much money just to have someone take an appeal from the final judgment and show that certain interlocutory decisions were wrong, and then the case has to be done over. So, if a legal issue is resolved by the trial court in the middle of a case, not as part of the final disposition of all of the claims and defenses, and that determination of the issue will or may have a tremendous effect on one party's or both parties' prosecution of the case from that point forward, one or more parties might ask the trial court, "May we please find out what the appellate court thinks about this issue before we go further in this case?"

Both sides may have an interest in taking the interlocutory appeal. While the side that lost the point might feel totally handcuffed or crippled by the decision, the other side might think they got a good ruling but are not sure it will hold up on the appeal from a final judgment in the case, thus creating the potential that any judgment in the case will be overturned later on. A reversed judgment and a new trial would not be a good use of the client's litigation budget. So, although it is unusual for the party that prevailed on the point to join in the request for an interlocutory appeal, it is not unheard of, or the prevailing party might simply fail to oppose the request very strenuously.

All the party or parties can do is ask; no one has a right to an interlocutory appeal. Whether you get an interlocutory appeal may depend as much on the personality and background experiences of the trial judge (both in private practice and on the bench) as it does on your authority supporting the request. Some trial judges are neutral to the request, or they at least respect the argument that a lot of time and money could be wasted if the appeal is not granted. Other trial judges hate delay, or have been disappointed in the past by an interlocutory appeal that dragged one of the judge's case out for years and years, making the judge decidedly unfriendly to the request.

In any event, even if the trial judge approves the request and certifies the point of law for interlocutory appeal, the appeals court still can say, "No," under Fed. R. App. P. 5. This happens less often than a trial judge's actually agreeing to an interlocutory appeal, so once you are over the hurdle of the trial court's certification, the court of appeals part of the process should not cause you to lose too much more sleep.

C. Extraordinary writs – writs of mandamus, writs of prohibition

The most extraordinary way to obtain review of a lower court's determination is to petition the appeals court to issue a prerogative writ quashing or reversing the lower court's action. The writs most commonly requested in general civil practice are the writs of mandamus and writs of prohibition.[1] They are called "extraordinary" because it is an extraor-

---

[1] Other writs are the Writ of Habeas Corpus, demanding the production of some person from captivity or confinement, Writ of Quo Warranto, addressed to quash a continuing exercise of unlawful authority, and Writ of Certiorari, which literally refers to a higher court's order to a lower court to produce a certified copy of the record in a case for review of the proceedings, but has come to refer to any higher court's, but especially the United State's Supreme Court's, exercise of discretionary jurisdiction to review the determinations of a lower court or adjudicatory body.

dinary event when one of these requests is granted. The action of the lower court must be extraordinarily bad, the evidence of the errors and the legal support used to make the challenge must be extraordinarily strong, and the appellate court must be extraordinarily moved by your petition in order to entertain the writ. It is a grave task to chastise the actions of a lower court judge in this way, and the writ will not lightly be granted.

There is no specific time frame in which to bring the request for the writ—you can make the petition "as needed" in a case whenever the court performs an unlawful act or exceeds its powers in an unlawful manner. You should of course resist the temptation to request a writ except when faced with the most egregious mistakes of a judge. The judge you challenge is made aware of your request for the issuance of the writ and may take this challenge to her judicial action as a personal attack on her abilities and good judgment. This perception is unfortunate for at least two reasons: the chilling effect of the desire not to step on the judge's toes probably keeps attorneys from filing a petition for a writ in cases where the issuance of the writ might be warranted, and when an attorney is driven to make the request in good faith, there is a very real possibility that the attorney's future relationship with the judge who was "brought up on a writ" by the attorney may suffer in the instant case or others, whether or not the writ is actually issued.

"Mandamus," which literally can be translated as, "We command," is directed to a judge who has undertaken an illegal action or failed to take a required action, or has taken away rights of a party in an unlawful way. See Black's Law Dictionary 866 (5th ed. 1979); Bryan A. Garner, A Dictionary of Modern Legal Usage 546 (2d ed. 1995); David Mellinkoff, Mellinkoff's Dictionary of American Legal Usage 395-96 (1992). It basically is directed to cure an abuse of judicial power—a refusal to do the right thing for a party, or an insistence on doing the wrong thing. The writ, if granted, commands the inferior judge to restore the rights, perform the required duty, do the right thing, or undo the unlawful act.

"Prohibition" is directed to a judge who has exceeded his or her lawful authority and jurisdiction. Traditionally, it was intended to stop a judge from usurping jurisdiction (i.e., control) over an action or a party or the subject matter of a suit that was beyond the court's jurisdiction. Black's Law Dictionary at 1091; Garner, supra at 700-01; Mellinkoff, supra at 513.

In different jurisdictions, the meaning of the two writs has become blurred, see, e.g., Fed. R. App. P. 21(a)(1); Ill. S. Ct. Rule 381, or it may be more precise to say that the terms sometimes are used as if they were interchangeable. "Prohibition" might be used to cure a number of abuses in one jurisdiction, but in another jurisdiction the same abuses would be cured by "mandamus." Research the law and local practice of your jurisdiction to determine which writ is appropriate. At present, the differences between the two writs largely are academic.

Because the two writs are extraordinary, a litigant needs very good justification for the granting of the writ. You must strive to find the clearest authority that says what the judge did is absolutely wrong *and* reversible error. The best authority to cite is a case from the immediately higher appellate court or the highest court of the applicable jurisdiction that issues a writ of mandamus or prohibition to curb the **same** conduct that the judge did in your case. Next best is an opinion from one of these courts granting the writ in a similar situation. Next best after that is an opinion describing the conduct as reversible error. If you have to go outside your own line of judicial authority for support, generally speaking, the chances that the writ will be issued are much diminished. If you can come up with four or five examples from other appellate courts where the writ was issued to quash the same action when taken by judges in different jurisdictions, you may squeak by with that, but citation to controlling authority is far superior.

In federal court, under the Federal Rules of Appellate Procedure, Rule 21, the writ process involves the following: the aggrieved litigant in the United States District Court petitions the United States Court of Appeals to issue the writ. The legal document it files is called a petition for a writ of mandamus or prohibition. If the Court of Appeals does not believe the petition is meritorious, it will deny the writ, with or without detailed explanation. But if the Court of Appeals believes that the petition has merit, it will order the nominal respondent—the **district court judge**—to respond. While this is the technical form, the true substance is that the opponent of the petitioner responds in the judge's stead and raises the arguments in support of the judge's action that the judge presumably would raise. The district court judge theoretically could file her own response. After this round of briefing, if the appeals court still agrees with the petitioner's charges, it will issue the writ.

If the petitioner fails and the writ is denied at the initial stage or the second stage, you can continue to go up the appellate chain of command until you exhaust all avenues for appeal. For example, in the U.S. Court of Appeals, you can petition the U.S. Supreme Court for a Writ of Certiorari, U.S. S. Ct. Rules 10, 11, or for a Writ of Mandamus, U.S. S. Ct. Rule 20.

Some jurisdictions do not regard these writs with as much disfavor as others. In some states, writs of prohibition and mandamus are sought and granted more often than in the federal courts. The writs still are regarded as *extraordinary* and are rarely granted, but they are not as infrequent as a solar eclipse, which is a fairly accurate description of the frequency of the issuance of writs of mandamus in most United States Courts of Appeals.

III. STANDARDS OF REVIEW

Even before your appeal is pending before a court of appeals, an important concept to consider is the standard of review that the court must exercise when evaluating your various allegations of error and grounds for reversal. The standard of review instructs the court of appeals in how much deference to give the determinations of the court or adjudicatory entity below. The standard may allow for no deference, a great deal of deference, or an incredible amount of deference.

The standard of review can have a tremendous impact on the chances of success of an appeal. The difference between an issue on appeal case that is governed by a *de novo* standard, which is essentially no deference to the court below, as opposed to an issue governed by a clearly erroneous standard, which is a great deal of deference, is the difference between an appeal that may have a decent chance and one that may have a snowball's chance in hell. Thus, the issue of the appropriate standard of review must be examined before you take the appeal, and you should counsel your client about the chances for success based on your evaluation of the proper standard of review.

The standard of review is determined by the type of issue that is being asserted on appeal. In that there may be several issues raised in any given appeal, there may be several applicable standards of review that must be anticipated in evaluating and briefing the arguments on appeal. The standards discussed in this chapter generally apply in many jurisdictions, but you must research the law of your own jurisdiction to be sure, because standards do change from jurisdiction to jurisdiction. The types of issues that might arise on appeal and their corresponding standards of review are as follows:

A. Determinations of law – *"de novo"* standard of review

If you are appealing from the lower court's determination of a pure issue of law—what the law is or what the law means, the elements or legal standards that apply, the actual law that applies under a conflict of laws analysis, and other questions of law—then the standard of review is *de novo*. This is the best standard of review for an appellant, because it means that the court of appeals gets to revisit the issue from start to finish and make its own determination of what the answer should be. In essence, no deference to the lower court's determination is required. *De novo* review means that the court of appeals decides the issue as if the lower court had never even taken it up.

An appellant can make the same legal arguments in favor of its interpretation of the law that were made to and rejected by the lower court. Naturally, if the arguments failed once, you should go back to the research table and satisfy yourself that you are presenting the strongest possible argument on the law. Point out the specific areas where the lower court's reasoning and analysis went astray. It will do no good to remind the appeals court that they get to take a fresh look at the issue if you present the same failed arguments and do nothing to rebut the lower court's reasoning in the matter.

B. Determinations of fact by the jury standard of review

On the opposite end of the scale from *de novo* review is the standard of review that applies to review of the findings of fact made by a jury. The Seventh Amendment of the United States Constitution protects a jury verdict from attack by an appellate court: "no fact tried by a jury shall be otherwise re-examined in any court of the United States, than according to the rules of the common law." U.S. Const. amend. VII. The standard of review requires a showing that the jury's findings are not reasonable and are completely against the evidence when viewed in a light that most favors the jury verdict. See, e.g., Bykowicz v. Pulte Home Corp., 950 F.2d 1046, 1050 (5th Cir. 1992); United States v. Dozal-Bencomo, 952 F.2d 1246, 1250 (10th Cir. 1991). If any reasonable inferences can be drawn from the evidence to support the jury's findings, the jury's decision will be upheld. See Bykowicz, 950 F.2d at 1050; Dozal-Bencomo, 952 F.2d at 1250.

In a real and practical sense, there are good reasons for this standard: if a litigant could readily overturn a jury's findings, it would deny his opponent the right to a trial by jury and replace it with trial by appellate court, in which the litigant would be armed only with a transcript of the testimony of the witnesses and boxes of exhibits. The second reason is that the appellate court cannot sit in the same position as the jury in watching the witnesses and evidence and being able to evaluate their credibility from moment to moment in the course of their testimony. Nothing at the present level of technology and procedures for the creation of the record can duplicate the benefits of actually being at the trial. Thus, the appeals court will rarely if ever substitute their impressions and evaluations of the evidence for the jury's based solely on the appellate court's cold reading of the trial transcript and review of the documents and exhibits, divorced as it is from the actual introduction and use of this evidence at trial. The appellant will almost never succeed in challenging the jury's findings under this legal standard, and an appeal will almost always be a waste of the client's time and money.

C. Determinations of fact by the trial court in a bench trial – "clearly erroneous" standard of review

Nearly as onerous for an appellant is the standard of review of determinations of fact made by the trial court in a bench trial. The standard of review is "clearly erroneous"—the trial court's findings will not be set aside unless they are clearly erroneous, giving due regard to the trial court's opportunity to judge the credibility of witnesses. Fed. R. Civ. P. 52(a); United States v. Oregon State Med. Assoc., 343 U.S. 326, 332 (1952). This, again, is a great deal of deference, and it is warranted because of the inability of the appeals court to revisit the trial and judge the credibility of the witnesses and the impact and value of each piece of evidence as it was introduced and used in the proceedings.

D. Mixed questions of law and fact standards of review

The real trouble comes with mixed questions of law and fact—should they be treated like a determination of law, and given little or no deference under a *de novo* standard, or are they more like a determination of fact, and given a great deal of deference under a clearly erroneous standard? If the issue is a finding of historical fact, such as "Defendant was driving at a rate of 55 miles an hour," it is governed by the clearly erroneous standard. But if there is a fact conclusion and an application of the law to the facts so as to make a legal determination, such as "Defendant's driving at 55 miles per hour was reckless," then the issue is more complicated. The court had to make a legal determination of the applicable legal standard (recklessness), and a factual determination of the defendant's rate of speed (55 m.p.h.), in order to make the ultimate determination of whether the legal standard was satisfied by the facts found by the court (defendant was reckless when he drove at 55 m.p.h.). It is the incorporation of these factual and legal determinations to make the ultimate determination challenged on appeal that creates the controversy.

Courts can be split on what is more factual and what is more legal, so a litigant must research the standards in her own jurisdiction to evaluate the problem and be ready to present arguments to demand a favorable standard. There is room for advocacy in this area. If the courts of appeals in the jurisdiction tend to resolve these issues in favor of a finding that a *de novo* standard of review applies, appellant should strive to draft her issues presented so that they sound like issues of law or mixed issues of law and fact, so that they can enjoy the benefits of a *de novo* standard. But if these mixed law and fact determinations are treated like fact determinations, the appellant must be prepared for an uphill climb and must counsel her client accordingly.

E. Review of trial court's rulings on proceedings before and during the trial – "abuse of discretion" standard of review

A trial court makes a great deal of determinations in the course of a litigation, any one of which might cause discomfort to one side or the other, and might be challenged on appeal. The trial court might have to decide whether an amendment to the pleadings will be allowed, whether one party will receive an extension of time, whether certain types of discovery may be had or whether certain categories of information will be subject to discovery. All such decisions are reviewed under an "abuse of discretion" standard, meaning that unless the trial court abused its discretion in making the determination or failed to exercise its discretion at all, the ruling will stand.

The breadth of the discretion afforded to the trial court will vary from issue to issue, and from jurisdiction to jurisdiction. If the matter is one that clearly relates to the operation and proper administration of the court, such as granting an extension of time or allowing additional pages beyond the page limits for motions imposed by local rules, the matter will not be overturned even if the court of appeals thinks the trial judge's decision was ill advised and erroneous. The trial judge has the right to be wrong on these determinations. On the other hand, if the determination has a more profound impact on the outcome and merits of the case, such as the denial of an amendment to the complaint or the denial of the right to conduct additional discovery after new evidence has been uncovered in a case, then the trial court is afforded less discretion, and the decision will more readily be overturned on appeal.

A trial court's demonstrated ignorance of the applicable legal standards for the decision or of available options for the decision can be interpreted as an abuse of discretion or the failure to exercise discretion, and be overturned. Just because the trial court appeared to exercise discretion in a matter does not mean that the court had any discretion to exercise under the applicable legal standards, and so the purported exercise of discretion in and of itself may be an abuse of discretion. Careful research and analysis of the authorities in the local jurisdiction on the particular issue that is being challenged are required before an appellant can properly define the discretion afforded and determine whether it may have been abused.

F. Trial court's evidentiary determinations – "abuse of discretion" standard but the discretion is more limited

A trial court's determinations regarding the admissibility and exclusion of evidence and witnesses is subject to an abuse of discretion standard, United States v. Abel, 469 U.S. 45, 54-55 (1984), but in light of the fact that these decisions are so closely tied to the litigants' ability to prove their case or establish their defenses, the discretion afforded is scrutinized more carefully by the appeals court and tends to be more limited than other determinations made in the course of a trial. See, e.g., United States v. 68.94 Acres, 918 F.2d 389, 392, 395-96 (3rd Cir. 1990). If the trial court applied the wrong legal evidentiary standard or if the court makes an erroneous application of the proper standard to the evidence in the case, the appeals court may find that the trial court abused its discretion and overturn the decision. See id. The appeals court does not completely second guess the trial court as it might in *de novo* review, but it will substitute its judgment for the trial court on legal and mixed law and fact determinations where "a substantial right of the party" is clearly affected by the determination. Id. at 396.

If the trial court merely excludes evidence or witnesses that were not listed in pretrial materials, or were not disclosed to the opponent at the proper time in the litigation, or are otherwise offered in violation of a local rule or pretrial order, these evidentiary rulings will generally be held to be within the "broad discretion" of the trial court and affirmed. See id. at 396-97; Jansen v. Aaron Process Equip. Co., 149 F.3d 603, 609 (7th Cir. 1998).

IV. THE RECORD ON APPEAL

Part of the appeals process is the compilation and reference to the record of the proceedings in the court below, referred to as the "record on appeal." The record on appeal actually can mean three different things: (1) the district court's record, comprising everything that was filed in the district court, plus the trial transcript and docket entries ("district court record"); (2) the record actually transmitted to the court of appeals, which consists of some but not all of the district court record ("transmitted record"); or (3) a further distilled version of the transmitted record provided by the parties to the court of appeals in the form of a joint appendix or record excerpts ("excerpted record").

The transmitted record is prepared or supervised (monitored) in its preparation by the parties. Primary responsibility lies with the appellant, but either side has an interest in the process. The court of appeals would like the parties to get along enough to compile and submit one joint appendix of the proceedings below. That is not always possible, and either side may feel the need to present its own version of the record or submit additional portions not submitted by the other side. If these portions wind up playing a critical part in the court of appeals' review, it will have to sort out the mess and make a determination of what is the actual record.

A. What is the "real record" on appeal – district court record or transmitted record?

Prior to 1967, there was no question that the transmitted record was the "real" record; nothing else mattered. If you left something out of the transmitted record that you later decided you wanted to use, you were sunk. The support for the argument you wanted to make was lost to you. The Federal Rules of Appellate Procedure, Rule 10, sought to eliminate this trap by providing that the entire district court record constituted the record on appeal regardless of what was transmitted to the court of appeals. In other words, as a matter of law the district court's record now constitutes the record on appeal.

As a matter of reality, however, the court of appeals will rarely look beyond the transmitted record. Unless you properly supplement the transmitted record (see below), it will avail you little to argue that the court of appeals may consider something in the district court record that you forgot to include in the transmitted record. The court of appeals is likely to dismiss such an argument with a terse remark about how a party waives or abandons any argument that it fails to support by including the relevant parts of the district court's record in the transmitted record. As a practical matter, the transmitted record becomes the real record on appeal.

B. Supplementing the transmitted record

However, if a party realizes that it inadvertently omitted something from the transmitted record, it may move to supplement the transmitted record. If the court of appeals has not yet considered the case on its merits, the court is likely to grant such a motion. Thus, the district court record remains a reservoir from which the parties may select items for inclusion in the transmitted record throughout most of the appeal.

C. What the transmitted record contains

The transmitted record on appeal contains three types of materials selected by the parties: (1) the court reporter's transcript of the trial, which includes the parties' statements and oral arguments and objections, the judge's statements and rulings and instructions to the jury, the testimony of the witnesses, and the record of the admission of evidence in the case; (2) the pleadings, motions, and other filings from the clerk's office case file; and (3) the actual exhibits. The district clerk's certified copy of docket entries is also part of the transmitted record, but the district court clerk sends that up as soon as the notice of appeal is filed, so that counsel have nothing further to do with it. The court of appeals may order additions to the district court record for materials that were considered by the district court but not included in its record.

D. Appellant's and appellee's duties regarding the record

Appellant's duty is to "monitor" the preparation of the record; appellee's duty is to make sure nothing is left out that can support the trial court's decision. While the appellant has an incentive to make sure the record gets done on time (i.e., appellant must order the transcript and see to it that the file was sent), the appellant only wants to be sure to get the parts of the record sent up that can support an argument that the trial court erred. Appellee needs all the material that could support the trial court's decision. So, appellee must pay attention to what is being sent up.

Chapter 6

Appellate Briefs

I. THE IMPORTANCE OF ADVOCACY IN WRITING IN THE APPELLATE CONTEXT

The appeals process calls for the highest degree of advocacy in writing. As discussed in the previous chapter, most appeals involve an uphill fight, and in many cases the chances of success are dismal. To have a fighting chance, an advocate must pay close attention to the drafting and editing of her briefs.

Oral argument is a wonderful exercise, and we will devote an entire chapter to the examination of the skills and preparation needed to make the most of your time at the podium. But we must point out that of the many appellate court judges we have talked to or heard speak on this topic, the vast majority of these jurists find the briefs filed by the parties to play a greater role than the oral arguments in helping the judges make up their minds as to who should prevail in an appeal. All judges report that oral arguments are helpful, and occasionally these fifteen to thirty minute sessions of intense discussion and questioning of the issues can turn a judge around or convince a fence-sitter to jump to one side or the other. But no one discounts the critical importance of good appellate briefs.

Appellate courts have to look at cases from two perspectives: the rights and equities of the parties before them on the appeal and the effect that their ruling will have on the body of law in the area and on all future litigants in their jurisdiction. Advocates must be sensitive to these dual pressures and not over-emphasize the individual rights and equities of their clients to the exclusion of the bigger picture and the impact of these same arguments on future parties. Policy arguments play a greater role in advocacy the higher you go up the appellate chain because a court of last resort has the power to make the ultimate determination of the public policy that will be embodied in the case law of the jurisdiction. Appellate courts at any level will inquire into the implications of the arguments raised by the parties at oral argument, but you can set the stage for the argument by briefing these policy issues in your appellate briefs.

II. WHAT BRIEFS ARE ALLOWED?

In an interlocutory appeal or regular appeal pursuant to Fed. R. App. P. 28(a)-(c), the parties to the appeal are allowed the following briefs:

❑ Appellant's brief,[1]
❑ Appellee's brief,[2] and
❑ Appellant's reply brief[3] (optional).

With cross appeals, the party who appealed first is considered the appellant. Fed. R. App. P. 28(h). If both parties appealed on the same day, the plaintiff is treated as the appellant unless the parties otherwise agree or the court otherwise orders. Id. In a cross-appeal, the appellee's brief combines an answer to the first appeal with appellee's opening arguments on the cross appeal. Id. The second section of the brief that asserts appellee's cross appeal should not contain arguments that are properly addressed to the opponent's arguments on its appeal—these arguments should be kept in the answering part of the brief. Otherwise, it confuses the issues. Appellant then combines in one brief its answer to appellee's cross appeal and any reply on appellant's appeal. Id., Rule 28(c). Appellee concludes, if it chooses, with a reply to appellant's answering brief on the cross appeal. Id.

Extraordinary writs require a petition for the writ, and an answer that may be filed by some or all of the respondents, if the court of appeals orders respondents to answer. Fed. R. App. P. 21. Nothing in Rule 21 provides for a reply brief. Id. The petition serves the function of an opening brief by an appellant, although the internal structure is more like a trial level brief, as discussed in the next section.

III. STRUCTURE OF APPELLATE BRIEFS AND APPELLATE WRITS

A. Structure of writs of mandamus and prohibition

A petition for a writ is organized like a trial-level brief, with one critical addition: you must clearly state the grounds for the issuance of the writ up front in the introduction or, better yet, create a brand new section that will precede the introduction called "**Grounds for the Issuance of the Writ.**" Sometimes the general rules of procedure or the local rules of the court require additional sections to be drafted. See Fed. R. App. P. 21(a)(2)(B); Il. S. Ct. R. 381; Mo. S. Ct. R. 94.03.

Do not pull any punches here. You are not going to succeed if you hide the grounds for the issuance of the writ in the argument section. You need to get the court's attention early and show why the writ must be issued, using primary controlling authority. If that kind of authority does not exist, your chances of getting the writ issued are virtually nonexistent, but do your best with what you have to work with.

---

[1] In different jurisdictions, this brief might be called Appellant's Opening Brief, or Petitioner's Brief, or Petitioner's Brief on the Merits.

[2] In different jurisdictions, this might be called Appellant's Answering Brief, or Appellant's Response, or Appellant's Brief in Response, or Respondent's Brief, or Respondent's Brief on the Merits.

[3] In different jurisdictions, this might be called Petitioner's Reply Brief.

B. Structure of interlocutory appellate briefs

Interlocutory appellate briefs are organized the same way as the briefs in a regular appeal after final judgment. Of course, in the statement of the case or proceedings below sections, you should point out that the trial court certified the issue you are appealing for interlocutory appeal. Other than that, the briefs will look the same.

C. Structure of appellate briefs in the U.S. Supreme Court

The local rules of the court in which you are practicing will specify what sections you will need to include in your briefs. As an indicative example of these requirements, we will discuss each of the sections of the brief that are required by the United States Supreme Court Rules in the order required by those rules. Rule 24.1 of the U.S. Supreme Court Rules requires the following sections of a brief and it requires them to be presented in this order:

- ❑ Caption
- ❑ Questions Presented for Review (or Issues Presented, Points of Error, Points Relied On, Points on Review)
- ❑ Parties to the Proceeding
- ❑ Table of Contents
- ❑ Table of Authorities
- ❑ Opinions and Judgments Entered in the Case (or Opinions Below)
- ❑ Statement of Jurisdiction
- ❑ Constitutional, Treaty, Statutory, and Administrative Law Provisions
- ❑ Statement of the Case (or Statement of Facts and Proceedings Below)
- ❑ Summary of the Argument
- ❑ Argument
- ❑ Conclusion
- ❑ Appendices (or Addenda)

The rules of other appellate courts might require you to draft other sections, such as:

- ❑ Standard of Review
- ❑ Statement of Facts (if not included in the Statement of the Case above)

Each of these sections deserves closer attention, as follows:

1. Caption (on the Cover)

Appellate briefs are bound, meaning they have a stiff, card-stock cover and backing. The caption appears on the cover, and it generally takes up the entire cover of each appellate brief. The caption names the court, the docket number, the parties, the party submitting the brief, and the title of the brief. Typically the caption also will identify the court from which the appeal is taken and sometimes the name of the judge below, and the identity of the attorneys that produced the brief.

Drafting a caption should not be too much trouble. If you have never seen what the formatting of this information looks like in your jurisdiction, get your hands on a sample brief from a colleague or go to the court and ask to see some briefs that are on file. Briefs can be found on the Internet in a form that reveals the true appearance of the caption, such as the portable document format (.pdf) produced by Adobe Acrobat®. A typical format is shown in the following example:

IN THE
UNITED STATES COURT OF APPEALS
FOR THE FOURTEENTH CIRCUIT

No. 99-234

BRANCH LOUISIAN OF THE UNITED CHURCH OF
CHRIST THE SAVIOR,

Plaintiff-Appellant,

— *against*—

METROPOLITAN SCHOOL DISTRICT OF GOTHAM,
STATE OF NEW KENT,

Defendant-Appellee.

Appeal from the United States District Court for the Central District of New Kent
Hon. Learned Foot, Judge

BRIEF FOR APPELLANT

Mary Patricia Silverberg
D. Heimlich Maneuver
Large Law Firm LLP
25 Commerce Street
Industry, TX 87878
Counsel for Appellant

2. Questions Presented for Review (or Issues Presented, Points of Error, Points Relied On, Points for Review)

As you can see from our heading here, the terms that are used to identify this section vary greatly from jurisdiction to jurisdiction. The basic idea is to lay out in one section all of the issues or points of error that are asserted by the appellant or petitioner so that the appellate court easily can see all of the issues that will need to be resolved in the appeal. It is important to list every issue or error that will be discussed in the brief because failure to do so may be interpreted as a waiver of the unlisted arguments, and the court may disregard any issue or argument regarding an issue that is not presented in this section.

a. Questions presented in an intermediate level appellate court

There are two basic methods for drafting the questions presented section in an intermediate level appellate court, and the local rules or case law of the court where the appeal lies will instruct you in which method to employ. The first is the "Notice" method, and the second is the "Complete Disclosure" method. The Notice method is most commonly used. It requires a description of the issue or error **in the form of a question** that mentions the specific error of the court below and the legal standards that show why it was an error. The Complete Disclosure method largely is the same, but you must add a summary of every argument regarding this issue or error that you intend to present in the brief. If you fail to summarize each legal theory and argument in a Complete Disclosure jurisdiction, you run the risk of the appellate court's ignoring the arguments you failed to list. Compare the two methods in the following examples:

➢ *Notice method:*   Whether the trial court erred in denying Garcia's motion for summary judgment on liability because the evidence cannot support a finding of recklessness under the <u>Dolan</u> standards?

➢ *Complete Disclosure:*   Whether the trial court erred in denying Garcia's motion for summary judgment on liability because the <u>Dolan</u> standards require proof that Garcia acted with careless disregard for the safety of others and the evidence shows that Garcia undertook the unloading of Fernandez's equipment in a prudent manner, Garcia used the standard methods of unloading approved by the Teamsters' Union and the National Transportation Authority, Garcia postponed the unloading for four hours because Garcia determined that the weather conditions were not safe for unloading, and Garcia undertook to unload the equipment only at the insistence of Fernandez's agent and foreman?

If the Complete Disclosure method looks awkward and over-killed, it is. **Do not use the Complete Disclosure method for your issues presented or questions presented section unless you are compelled to do so by the local rules of the court.**

The phrasing of the questions presented should be neutral, not biased in favor of your client. Do not interject argument and accusations into the issues. An appellate court does not want to read a statement laced with rhetoric that drives the parties apart from a consensus on the issues on appeal. The court would rather see a statement of the issues that both sides can agree upon so that the appellee does not have to draft a competing set of issues for review. See, e.g., Fed. R. Civ. P. 28(b). When appellant and appellee do not agree, this makes the court's job harder because it will have to determine what separate issues are raised that will need to be resolved in the appeal.

As discussed in the previous chapter, if the standard of review is a standard other than *de novo* review, you should weave this into the statement of the issue. For example, using the Complete Disclosure method, if the standard of review for the point of error you are drafting is "abuse of discretion," you might phrase the issue as:

> ➤ Whether the trial court abused its discretion when it denied Nunez the right to amend its petition, because under Fed. R. Civ. P. 15, leave to amend shall be freely granted when justice so requires, the amendment was required because of new facts and evidence produced to plaintiff just five days before it moved to amend the petition, and there would have been no prejudice to defendant if the amendment were to be allowed?

If the point of error is a pure issue of law, you might use the Notice method to state that the court erred as follows:

> ➤ Whether the trial court erred in its determination that New Hampshire law applied to the contract because the parties chose Rhode Island law in a valid, enforceable forum selection clause?

b. Questions presented in a court of last resort

If you are phrasing a question presented for a court of last resort, you should draft the question so that the individual parties' names are obscured and their roles or the class of persons or entities that they represent are presented instead of the individual parties' names. This method brings to the fore the public policy implications of the dispute for the court to resolve, and reminds the court that it is not just the petitioner and the respondent who will be feeling the effects of their ruling, but all persons in similar situations. Courts of last resort are particularly sensitive to public policy concerns because they will be determining the law and establishing policy for the entire jurisdiction to follow. Consider the following examples:

➤ *Example:* I. Whether a public school district violates a religious organization's First Amendment free speech rights by refusing to post information regarding creationism on the school district's web site created to further the educational mission of the school district?

II. Whether a public school district violates the First Amendment's Establishment Clause by sponsoring a religious organization's web page on the school district's web site created to increase the educational opportunities for students on topics within the curriculum?

Not this: I. Whether Metropolitan Kent School District violated Branch Louisian Church's First Amendment free speech rights by refusing to post information regarding creationism on the Metropolitan Kent School District's web site created to further the educational mission of the school district?

II. Whether Metropolitan Kent School District would violate the First Amendment's Establishment Clause by sponsoring Branch Louisian Church's web page on the Metropolitan Kent School District's web site created to increase the educational opportunities for students on topics within the curriculum?

Note that the first two examples are phrased in the present tense. This reinforces the relevance of the issue for the court—it is a current, troublesome issue for people in similar situations as the petitioner and the respondent. The last two examples were forced to be phrased in the past tense and future tense respectively, in the one case because the party already undertook the action from which the suit arises, and in the other case because the party had not taken the action and now seeks to be heard on what would have happened if it had.

3. Parties to the Proceeding

The rules of the U.S. Supreme Court and other courts require a section that lists all parties to the proceedings in the court whose judgment is sought to be reviewed. If all the parties happen to be listed in the caption, i.e., there were few enough parties to list all their names in the caption, then the rules of the Supreme Court state that this section is unnecessary. S. Ct. Rule 24.1(b). Parent companies and non-wholly owned subsidiaries may have to be listed, too, as per S. Ct. Rule 29.1.

4. Table of Contents

You have seen tables of contents before, and there is little that is unusual about a table drafted for an appellate brief. Although each individual entry in the table is single-spaced, the entries are separated from each other by two spaces, as shown in the example below. When you provide page references for the argument section, be sure to list in their entirety each of your major and minor headings and subheadings in the argument section. In this way, your table of contents can be a useful outline of your entire argument for the busy judge to look at before or during oral argument. For example:

5. Table of Authorities

This is a list in **alphabetical order** of each of the authorities you cite in the brief. A typical way to organize the table is to list cases first, then constitutional and statutory provisions, then rules and administrative law, then treatises and other secondary authorities.

You should italicize or underline the case names (whichever form you are using in the rest of your brief) because you are making a citation to a case in a court document. Jump cites (pinpoint cites, pin cites) to the internal pages of the authorities that you will refer to are ***not*** included. As a rule of thumb, if you cite a case on more than four pages of your brief, you may write *passim* instead of writing all of the page numbers where the case is cited (unless the rules of the court require something else). The page numbers are right justified and preceded by a string of periods. In some word processing programs such as Word Perfect this is referred to as "flush right with dot leaders."

The local rules of the appellate court may ask you to separate the authorities you are using into categories; for example: United States Supreme Court Cases; United States Court of Appeals Cases; United States District Court Cases; State Cases; Constitutions, Statutes and Administrative Regulations; Legislative History Documents; Treatises, Books, and Law Review Articles; Other Authorities. **Alphabetize** the entries in each category. A table of authorities that complies with this rule might look like the following:

TABLE OF AUTHORITIES

United States Supreme Court Cases:

Adams v. Baker, 434 U.S. 456 (1976) 13, 15
Attila v. Romans, 671 U.S. 789 (2005) .... *passim*
Rotten v. Vicious, 668 U.S. 123 (2004) 10

United States Court of Appeals Cases:

Able v. Incapable, 786 F.2d 234 (7th Cir. 1989) 23, 24, 27
Farnsworth v. Williston, 678 F.2d 45 (2d Cir. 1972) 6
Goldfarb v. Silverfarb, 333 F.3d 12 (11th Cir. 2005) 6, 8, 22

United States District Court Cases:

Ford v. Chrysler, 155 F. Supp. 2d 246 (E.D.N.Y. 2004) 34
Helena v. Billings, 55 F.R.D. 23 (D. Mont. 1971) 34

State Cases:

Murphy v. O'Brien, No. 96-CIV-2345, 2001 WL 12345 (Mo. Apr. 22, 2001) 35
Uranus v. Mars, 934 N.E.2d 642 (Ill. 1999) 32

Constitutions, Statutes and Administrative Regulations:

U.S. Const. art. I, § 9, cl. 2 20
U.S. Const. amend. XIV, § 2 20
17 U.S.C. § 107 (1999) .... *passim*
18 U.S.C. § 1401 (1999) 22
15 C.F.R. § 17.234 (1989) 23, 24

<u>Legislative History Materials</u>:

H.R. 3055, 94th Cong. § 2 (1976) 11, 12, 14, 33
S. Rep. No. 89-910 (1965) 14

<u>Treatises, Books, and Law Review Articles</u>:

E. Allen Farnsworth, *Contracts* (1988) 22, 25
Martin Scorsese, *Film Making* (1992) 13
Terri L. Crocker, *Under the Blood Red Sky: Women's Health and the 1997
Amendments to FIFRA*, 88 Colum. L. Rev. 22 (1988) 21, 31

<u>Other Authorities</u>:

William Rosenthal, *White House Staff Strips Aid to President*, N.Y. Times,
June 15, 2001, at A1 23

Even in the absence of a local rule, it makes sense to separate your authorities into cases; constitutions, statutes, legislative history, and administrative regulations; treatises, books, and law review articles; and miscellaneous authorities, as depicted in the following:

TABLE OF AUTHORITIES

<u>Cases</u>:

Able v. Incapable, 786 F.2d 234 (7th Cir. 1989) 23, 24, 27
Adams v. Baker, 434 U.S. 456 (1976) 13, 15
Attila v. Romans, 671 U.S. 789 (2005) .... *passim*
Farnsworth v. Williston, 678 F.2d 45 (2d Cir. 1972) 6
Ford v. Chrysler, 155 F. Supp. 2d 246 (E.D.N.Y. 2004) 34
Goldfarb v. Silverfarb, 333 F.3d 12 (11th Cir. 2005) 6, 8, 22
Helena v. Billings, 55 F.R.D. 23 (D. Mont. 1971) 34
Murphy v. O'Brien, No. 96-CIV-2345, 2001 WL 12345 (Mo. Apr. 22, 2001) 35
Rotten v. Vicious, 668 U.S. 123 (2004) 10
Uranus v. Mars, 934 N.E.2d 642 (Ill. 1999) 32

<u>Constitutions, Statutes, Legislative History, and Administrative Regulations</u>:

U.S. Const. art. I, § 9, cl. 2 20
U.S. Const. amend. XIV, § 2 20
17 U.S.C. § 107 (1999) .... *passim*
18 U.S.C. § 1401 (1999) 22
15 C.F.R. § 17.234 (1989) 23, 24
H.R. 3055, 94th Cong. § 2 (1976) 11, 12, 14, 33
S. Rep. No. 89-910 (1965) 14

<u>Treatises, Books, and Law Review Articles</u>:

E. Allen Farnsworth, *Contracts* (1988) 22, 25
Martin Scorsese, *Film Making* (1992) 13

Terri L. Crocker, *Under the Blood Red Sky: Women's Health and the 1997 Amendments to FIFRA*, 88 Colum. L. Rev. 22 (1988) 21, 31

<u>Miscellaneous</u>:
William Rosenthal, *White House Staff Strips Aid to President*, N.Y. Times, June 15, 2001, at A1 23

6. Opinions and Orders Entered in the Case (or Opinions Below)

In the rules of some courts, such as the Rules of the United States Supreme Court, a section is required that lists the citations of the opinions and orders from courts or administrative agencies from which the appeal arises. Not a very complicated section, but it is necessary nonetheless. If you do not have a full citation for the opinion or judgment, cite as much information as the record gives you and follow citation rules for the citation of slip opinions. At a minimum, you should be able to describe the opinion or judgment and cite the names of the parties, the docket number, the court, and the date of the decision. For example:

OPINIONS AND ORDERS ENTERED IN THE CASE

Order granting summary judgment in favor of defendant Jones and against plaintiff Smith. *Smith v. Jones*, No. 04-CIV-245-DNL (E.D. Cal. Jan. 14, 2005).

Opinion reversing the above order, and remanding the case to the district court for trial. *Jones v. Smith*, No. 05-258-EM (9th Cir. Aug. 24, 2005).

---

7. Statement of Jurisdiction

The Statement of Jurisdiction is a brief section explaining the jurisdictional basis for the case being in the court where it is set. For example:

STATEMENT OF JURISDICTION

This Court has jurisdiction over the subject matter of this case because it is an appeal from the final judgment of the trial court entered on January 12, 2005. 28 U.S.C. § 1291; Fed. R. App. P. 4.

---

8. Constitutional, Treaty, Statutory, and Administrative Law Provisions

Some court rules, including the rules of the U.S. Supreme Court, require a section that quotes the applicable constitutional, treaty, statutory, and administrative law provisions that are implicated by the problem. If the text is short—less than two pages—quote each provision verbatim in this section. If they are lengthy, cite the provision, quote the pertinent language, and then set out the full text in an appendix to the brief, as provided in S. Ct. Rule 24.1(f).

9. Statement of the Case (Including Statement of Facts and Proceedings Below)

In many courts, this section is a summary of the proceedings of the case since the time it was filed to the present. You give only the highlights, such as the date of pleadings and amendments to pleadings, major dispositive motions that were granted or denied, and an explanation of how the case got to the appeals court. This section is not intended to be very argumentative, and it should be kept short. Avoid the temptation to take pot shots at the trial court judge when recounting the history of the case—you will have plenty of opportunity to point out errors in other sections of the brief.

You can draft this section so that it supports your argument by highlighting language used in the courts below, and by trying to summarize and hone down the opinions of the lower courts in such a way that you easily can trounce these opinions in the argument section if you are an appellant or petitioner, or buttress these opinions if you are a respondent. Several of the briefs we have included as sample briefs in this book have excerpted the opinion of the lower court. The skill in choosing what language and what items to highlight in this section parallels the skill you must employ in choosing what facts to highlight in the statement of facts.

In the United States Supreme Court, the rules contemplate that the statement of the case section will encompass **both** a **statement of the pertinent facts** of the case and a **statement of the proceedings below** with citations to the record or joint appendix to support the information in both sections. The facts part of this section should be drafted as a statement of facts as described in the next section, and you would draft both parts (**statement of facts and proceedings below**) under the single heading of statement of the case.

10. Statement of Facts

The statement of facts presents a summary of the historical facts of the case that led up to the date that the case was filed. Since the facts are very important in any appeal, you should take the time to draft them in such a way that your client's position looks strong, by using crisp, active language and strong nouns, adjectives, and adverbs, and by giving appropriate detail to facts that support and sustain your arguments, and limiting the discussion of relevant facts that are detrimental to your arguments. Certainly, there is no need to raise and discuss facts that you believe are irrelevant to the issues on appeal from both your client's and your opponent's perspective, unless you are going to take the time in the argument to demonstrate why certain negative facts are irrelevant. The authors of the **sample briefs** at the end of this chapter have attempted to accomplish these goals with varying degrees of success. Read these samples critically, and note our annotations.

a. Persuasive facts vs. argument

Two principles are at war in drafting the statement of facts. First, the court of appeals would like you to state just the relevant facts, with no argument or innuendo. <u>See</u> Fed. R. App. P. 28(a)(4); Local Rules of the U.S. Ct. App. 7th Cir., Rule 28(d)(1); Il. S. Ct. R. 341(e)(6). Indeed, the local rules of the court of appeals may strictly limit the amount of argument or "bias" that you can interject into the facts. <u>E.g.</u>, Local Rules of the U.S. Ct. App. 7th Cir., Rule 28(d)(1); Il. S. Ct. R. 341(e)(6). Even if the local rules do not prohibit argument or comment on the facts, it is advisable to avoid argumentative language and to eliminate any legal conclusions in the facts.

Factual Conclusions: The truck ***was going fast*** when it approached the curve.
The driver had trouble steering ***because*** the truck began to rock and sway.
The trailer became detached from the tractor ***because*** the connector pin was sheared off.

Legal Conclusions: The truck driver was ***reckless*** for driving at that speed.
The truck driver ***caused*** the trailer to become detached by his ***driving too fast*** in the curve.
He ***caused*** the truck to become ***too unstable to control.***
The driver was ***negligent*** in attempting to take the turn at that speed.

However, the second principle is that a good advocate wants a statement of facts that will persuade the judges to rule in the lawyer's favor as soon as they finish reading the facts. Satisfying both ends requires careful attention to accuracy and advocacy.

b. Accuracy

Accuracy is paramount. You cannot win by misstating facts. If your statement sounds persuasive but your opponent identifies errors or pokes holes in what you told the court, your chances of success will be severely damaged. If evidence is contested, do not recite it as if it were a fact. Give a fair account of the testimony and supporting exhibits, and if you can show why other testimony should be believed or not believed, do so, but do not present one side's witnesses as the only story that was told.

One important part of the requirement of accuracy is to draw only the most logical and most reasonable inferences from the facts in the record.

➢ *Example:* If a commission called for a sculpture to be created in two weeks time, and the facts indicate that the artist completed the work in one week, it would be completely safe to point out that the artist did the work "in half the time anticipated by the parties in their contract." It would not necessarily be fair to say that the artist did the work "quickly," and it certainly would not be fair to infer that the artist "rushed" the job. "Rushing" implies a state of mind, and nothing in the facts we have revealed shows the artist's state of mind. Performing a commission in half the allotted time is not automatically rushing; you do not have enough facts to make that inference. Perhaps the artist routinely does these works in a single day, and one week is a luxurious amount of time.

If the work turned out to be unacceptable to the client—the client found it to be "ugly" and "unappealing"—you could state that "the artist only used half of the allotted time to produce the sculpture, and wound up producing a work that was ugly and unappealing to the client." You could not draw the inference that the artist was "sloppy" or "careless" in producing the work, and certainly could not infer that the artist was "negligent" or "reckless" by producing the work in half the allotted time. Aside from the problem that these are legal conclusions, you do not have enough facts about the artist, her state of mind, her expertise, her prior work production methods, and a host of other factual information that would affect that inference. All you can say is that she produced the work in half the allotted time, and the work was unacceptable to the client because the client found it to be ugly and unappealing.

Missing information from the record necessarily will limit the kind of inferences you logically can draw. Do not get caught up in a spirit of advocacy and fill in details that affect the logical limits of the facts in the record.

➤ *Example:*   If the record states that the commission required the sculpture to be 50% titanium, and tests show that it is less than 50% titanium, you could draw the inference that the sculpture produced "does not meet the terms of the contract," or "does not contain the percentage of titanium that the parties specified in the contract." You cannot automatically draw the inference that the artist "breached the contract." Breach, a legal conclusion, depends on a host of factors relating to performance. The artist may have a lawful excuse or justification for his performance. You cannot state that the artist "purposefully" or "intentionally" left titanium out of the sculpture. You simply do not know what the artist's state of mind was. You only can state exactly what the facts state: "The artist produced a sculpture that did not contain the percentage of titanium that was specified in the parties' agreement."

If you find out additional facts, you might be able to draw other inferences. If you discover that the price of titanium doubled the day after the commission was signed, you now can state that "the price of titanium doubled the day after the commission was signed, and one week later, the artist delivered a work that did not contain the percentage of titanium specified by the parties in their contract." You still cannot infer that the artist "breached" or "purposefully" or "intentionally" left titanium out of the sculpture.

c. Highlighting good facts and downplaying bad facts

You can balance the separate duties of accuracy and advocacy with more subtle but still effective methods. The same set of facts can be drafted differently in ways that better support the client's position and hinder the opponent's. Fed. R. App. P. 28 requires that you present the facts relevant to the issues on appeal. That standard offers considerable latitude in choosing *what* to recite. You can report both favorable and unfavorable facts on a given point, while still presenting the facts in the best possible light for your client.

You can highlight facts with the amount of detail you present, the sequence in which you present them, and your own careful choice of words. Instead of using neutral words, slant the facts with language that carries overtones. Avoid the passive tense and use strong engaging verbs and descriptive nouns and adjectives in sections that discuss facts favorable to your client, and do the opposite in sections containing facts unfavorable to your client.

> *Example 1 - Common Facts:* Client Jones was going 60 m.p.h. in a 45 m.p.h. zone on his way to his therapist, a doctor of psychology. He was late. The road was wet. A poodle came out from behind a parked car and moved into the road in front of him. Jones swerved, his car slid out of control, and he hit a parked car owned by plaintiff.
>
> *Appellant's Version:* Defendant was late for an appointment with his psycho-therapist and was speeding at 60 m.p.h. on rain slick pavement in a 45 m.p.h. zone. A poodle walked into the path of Defendant's speeding car, and Defendant swerved and sent his car spinning out of control. Defendant then smashed his car into the back of plaintiff Smith's parked car.
>
> *Appellee's Version:* Mr. Jones was proceeding to an important appointment. A dog jumped out in front of him taking him completely by surprise. In an effort to avoid hitting the dog, he turned the wheel quickly but the car slid on the damp pavement and came into contact with the plaintiff's car.
>
> *Example 2 - Common Facts:* ABC Corp. laid off thirteen workers in a reduction in force (RIF). ABC used a business productivity formula. Six of the workers who were laid off were over the age of 40, four of these were women. Four more who were

laid off were minorities, two of whom were women. Mr. Smith, a white male age 37, made the final decision of whom to lay off.

Appellant's Version: ABC's most recent RIF was spearheaded by Cliff Smith, a white male. Smith targeted women, minorities, and workers whose age was over 40 for ten of his thirteen cuts. When he fired six elderly workers, he made sure four of them were women, and when he singled out four minorities for firing, he made sure half of them were women. Smith used a formula that ensured that these people could be disposed of with the excuse of increasing productivity.

Appellee's Version: ABC was forced by competitive economic factors to lay off thirteen workers. A formula was used based on a worker's years of service, evaluation grades, and amount of contract revenue generated in the last five years. The thirteen lowest performing workers were laid off.

d. Level of detail

Although the level of detail is one way to highlight important and helpful facts, you can go overboard with too much detail. In a fact intensive appeal, it sometimes is hard to mention all the facts in the statement of facts because it would produce a facts section that is the same length as the argument. In general, ask yourself whether every detail in your recital of the facts is needed. Trial lawyers writing or editing briefs on appeal are especially prone to include facts that seemed important at trial but have little or nothing to do with the issues on appeal. Try to get these weeded out before you send it to the court.

> *Good:*   Defendant Jones was late for an appointment with his psycho-therapist and was speeding at 60 m.p.h. on rain slick pavement in a 45 m.p.h. zone. A poodle walked into the path of Defendant's speeding car, and Defendant swerved and sent his car spinning out of control. Defendant then smashed his car into the back of plaintiff Smith's parked car.

> *Not this:*   Defendant Jones was running approximately eight minutes late for his appointment with his psycho-therapist, Dr. Will Shrinker. He went speeding along on his way to Dr. Shrinker's office on Mulberry Lane, a mixed business and residential street with a 45 m.p.h. speed limit. He was traveling at an average speed of 60 m.p.h. as confirmed by a passive police monitoring unit on Mulberry Lane that Jones passed by; his speed also was generally confirmed by two eye witnesses at the scene, Mrs. Vera Stigmatism and Mr. Esau Nothing. At some point soon after passing by the monitoring unit, a poodle walked out into the path of Defendant's speeding car. Defendant took action immediately. He swerved the car to the left, and sent his car spinning out of control. There is no indication that he was able to regain control

of the car. Jones' car spun out of control for more than two seconds, again, as confirmed by Mrs. Stigmatism and Mr. Nothing. Defendant then smashed his car into the back of plaintiff Smith's parked car. No one witnessed the actions of the poodle after Jones swerved away from it, but the poodle was unharmed in the incident.

The details in the second example above may be interesting, but it is unlikely that they will have any effect on the appeal unless this interchange of the car sliding on the wet road and the collision with the parked car is the only incident from which the appeal arises. If this incident is a tiny part of a much bigger case, and if these details are not relevant for the particular purpose of proving a point of error charged to the lower court, then leave them out. They will wear out your reader and squander her attention span.

e. Divide facts with subheadings

When you have a lot of facts that need to be presented, internal subheadings and topical groupings can help to divide up the facts into more manageable and digestible chunks. Subheadings allow you to focus on separate issues in the facts, presenting only the facts that go with that issue. This paragraph should remind you that you need not present the facts in strict chronological order if that order does little to highlight the important facts of your client's case.

f. Citations to the record

Every fact must be referenced by citation to the record. The appeals court is likely to ignore any facts that are not supported by a citation to the record. Rule 24 of the Supreme Court Rules provides for a cite to the joint appendix, e.g., App. 12, or to the record, e.g., Record 12. Some practitioners place the citations inside parentheses but the rules do not require this method.

➤ *Examples:*   The contract was signed on August 13, 2005 (Record 132, ¶ 12).

Jones testified that he called the police at 10:00 a.m., App. 12, but the police dispatcher records indicate that the call from Jones was received at 10:42 a.m. Plaintiff's Ex. 44, App. 14, ¶ 4.

Other appellate court rules may allow you to shorten the citation to the record to (R. pg. #) or (R-pg. #) as in (R.23) or (R-23), and citations to the joint appendix as (J.A. pg. #) or (JA-pg. #) as in (J.A. 133) or (JA-133).

g. Party names

Describe parties consistently throughout the facts. Do not switch from calling your client "the tenant," to "plaintiff," to "Sam Smith Slaughterhouse Company." Fed. R.

App. P. 28(d) and most appellate judges we have talked to discourage the use of such generic labels as "appellant" and "appellee." Some brief writers believe that it is it acceptable to use the designations used in the trial court (plaintiff, defendant), but we do not agree that this practice promotes the necessary clarity and individuality that you are seeking to achieve in your brief. The authors believe that using the actual names of the parties is the best practice: "McMannis," "Allied Widgets," "Governor Black." Next best is to use descriptive terms, such as "the employer," "the driver," "the taxpayer," "the ship," and so forth.

h. Abbreviations and acronyms

Use abbreviations and acronyms cautiously. You and your client may understand an acronym identifying a party, an agency, a group, a set of laws or regulations, or other items described in the facts, but using abbreviations or acronyms that are not self-explanatory to the court is like using a secret code that taxes the ability and patience of the judges. Most judges know that ACLU refers to the American Civil Liberties Union and RICO refers to the Racketeer Influenced and Corrupt Organizations Act, but how many judges know that FIFRA refers to the Federal Insecticide, Fungicide, and Rodenticide Act or COBRA refers to the Comprehensive Omnibus Budget Reconciliation Act? Be kind to your readers and define all abbreviations and acronyms up front and use them consistently throughout your brief.

i. Tell your client's story

The best possible statement of facts tells a story in which your client is a character, the plot is a straight-forward recounting in lay person's terms of what happened to your client and the opponent and other characters, and the conflict and resolution (if any) is one that shows why your client must win. The moral of the story is the theme of your case, and it should be able to be stated in a single sentence no matter how long it takes you to boil the case down to a single sentence theme. As with most good stories, the reader (the court) should be pulled into it so that they care what happens to the main character (your client) and are eager to know what happens next until they get to the end of the story. Critically evaluate the stories told by the authors of the **sample briefs** at the end of this chapter and decide for yourselves what stories seem the most effective.

11. Standard of Review

In some jurisdictions, the court of appeals' local rules require you to draft a short section laying out what you have determined to be the appropriate standard of review for each issue that is raised on appeal, and stating your legal support for that determination. E.g., Alaska R. App. P. 212(c)(1)(h); Haw. R. App. P. 28(b)(5). In other courts, you will state the standard of review for each point after you list the point in the issues presented section or incorporate the discussion into the argument section, see Fed. R. App. P. 28(a)(6);

Ariz. R. Civ. App. P. 13(a)(6); Ga. Ct. App. R. 27(a)(3), 27(b)(2), so there will be no separate standard of review section.

If the standard of review is obvious, limit the discussion to one sentence for each point of error, and cite one or two powerful authorities that conclusively state the standard. If there is some doubt as to the standard (which might be the case with mixed issues of law and fact), present a short argument with citations to relevant and analogous authority to argue in favor of the standard that benefits your client. Even in this latter situation, you should limit the argument to one or two pages except in the most unusual and complicated of circumstances.

12. Summary of Argument

Federal appellate courts, including the United States Supreme Court, require a separate section entitled "Summary of the Argument" that precedes the argument section. Fed. R. App. P. 28(a)(5); S. Ct. Rule 24.1(h). The drafters of the rule have precluded litigants from simply stringing their argument headings together into roughly connected paragraphs, so avoid the temptation. Instead, make a clear and succinct presentation of the points on review and your arguments on these points, with citation only to the most critical authorities that support your arguments.

Even if the local rules do not limit your pages in this section, we would avoid going over three pages because the judges still have to read your argument section, and you do not want to wear them out with unnecessary repetition, redundancy, duplication, saying the same thing over and over again (see what we mean?).

The reader gets to the Summary first, so even if you draft it second, make it powerful and memorable. That which comes first counts more in legal writing. Judges in a hurry may read only the summary of the argument, not the whole argument section. It definitely is not a section to ignore until the day before the brief is due.

13. Argument

We have now worked our way to the argument section. You must craft the argument with careful attention to organization, citation to authority, as well as the substance of the legal arguments you make. This topic is covered at length in section IV below.

14. Conclusion

Fed. R. App. P. 28(a)(7) requires a short conclusion describing the precise relief sought. The usual question is whether the conclusion should include anything else. The answer typically is "no."

Be as specific as possible about the relief you want. Your request may be in the alternative. The court may deny specific relief that you fail to request. Your request for relief may need some explanation in the argument. If, for instance, you are asking for reversal and remand for the limited purpose of entering judgment in a specified amount, you will need to explain why further evidence is not needed on the question of damages. As a general rule, whenever you seek a remand only for limited purposes, you will need to explain the reasons behind your proposed limits. That explanation belongs in the argument section.

Aside from relief requested, brief writers frequently are tempted to conclude with some rhetoric that does not fit into the disciplined analysis of your argument section. Appellate courts will accept this kind of "traditional" conclusion with appropriate summary and reemphasizing of the arguments you raised. The rule does not forbid this, other than to require that the conclusion be short. If you can keep it brief, a zinger at the end does not hurt. Whether it helps is a matter of some doubt. If your brief has not been persuasive, a rhetorical closing obviously will not save it. Most last-minute points worth making are better included in the argument. You need not worry about coming up with a clever closing—if they did not get it before, they probably will not get it now in the conclusion.

15. Appendices

Sometimes the court requires or allows you include an appendix containing a few choice items—key documents, exhibits, testimony, the full text of statutory and constitutional provisions, unpublished opinions (if the local rules allow you to cite them at all), items such as the contract or instrument sued upon, the final judgment, the notice of appeal, and other important or frequently cited materials. You should be careful about putting things other than the required items into an appendix. You do not want to make the brief twice as fat by virtue of an appendix. But a careful selection can be a great aid to the court by placing the most important documents and authorities at the judges' fingertips.

IV. DRAFTING THE ARGUMENT

The TREAT format (discussed in the Appendix to this volume) applies in the argument section, and you should use your questions presented or Points of Error Thesis statements as your major headings, even if the local rules and practices require them to be excessively wordy. Use minor Thesis headings to guide the reader through the sub-issues that require separate TREAT.

A. Use argumentative thesis headings.

Thesis headings should be meaningful so that they can provide a useful summary of your argument to a judge that is skimming your argument section. A good thesis heading not only reveals a conclusion but provides the "because" part—the legal principles and facts that lead up to the conclusion. For example, the following are good argumentative thesis headings:

> Examples of proper thesis headings in the argument
>   A. The trial court erred in its determination that Bolling provoked the dog prior to the attack because Bolling did not directly attack or threaten the dog as required under Illinois law.

B. The trial court erred in holding that Bolling was trespassing because Bolling was acting peacefully in a place where he had a lawful right to be when he walked on a public sidewalk at Alden Hall without causing any noisy disturbance.

C. The trial court erred in holding that provocation bars Bolling's recovery because the dog's attack on Bolling was vicious and disproportionate to the dusting of snow the Dog received from Bolling.

➤ The following are **not** good headings:

A. Lack of Provocation

B. Bolling was acting peacefully in a place where he had a lawful right to be.

C. The dog's attack was disproportionate.

These last three examples do not suggest enough of the facts and principles of the law to make the headings useful, and the first of these three does not even tell the author's conclusion about the topic. Do not waste a heading by writing something like these. Let your headings be a quick summary of your argument if read one right after the other.

B. Policy counts more on appeal, and precedent becomes a two-way street

In the argument, as in many of the other sections discussed above, you must bear in mind that policy plays a greater role in appellate courts' reasoning, especially in the courts of last resort. Appellate courts do not worry just about following precedent, they have to worry about making it. Appellate courts have to consider the here and now of your case plus the effect that their ruling will have on future cases. You should write briefs with that in mind. If you spend too much effort developing the arguments and equities of your client's position, you may neglect to consider the effect what you are arguing will have on future cases. You should take the time in the discussion of each major issue raised on appeal to address public policy and precedential implications of the arguments you are raising. Usually, the page limits afforded on appeals are ample enough to allow for this, and it may help you persuade more judges of the propriety of your positions even prior to oral argument when the court can drill you in the policies affected by your arguments.

In similar fashion, you might discuss how the case fits into the broader stream of relevant decisions. Fit your appeal into a broader framework of the law and the policies behind the law. Appellate judges are more comfortable applying settled principles than deciding issues of first impression. Many appeals raise something new, but it does not benefit appellant to emphasize that. The law is built on precedent. It seeks the simple and established and avoids the unfamiliar. This means that demonstrating at length the novelty or complexity of your position rarely will help. Make the novel proposition seem familiar or, at most, a natural extension of something that is clearly accepted. The more you can fit your case into established principles, the greater your chance of success.

Start at a logical beginning for the arguments you raise. The page limits generally allow you to present a discussion of the stepping stone principles, both historical steps and steps of a logical progression that lead up to the present principles of the law you are asserting. Too many briefs start in the middle of a legal analysis, rather than building from broad general principles to the specific. Do not go back to the first day or even first semester of contracts, but lay a settled backdrop down before you start throwing the colorful paint around. Put your case into a broader, established legal context first so that judges understand where you are starting. From that they will quickly grasp where you are heading.

C. The continuing benefits of explanatory synthesis[4]

Unless you have controlling precedent that exactly matches your client's case, you should emphasize **principles**, not **cases**. This is another way of looking at the benefits of explanatory synthesis. Individual cases may not say everything you need them to say on exactly what you need them to cover. If you find the magic, controlling, "on all fours" case, use it, but if you do not, you still can convince the court that your appeal fits the broader principles of the law that are illustrated by existing authorities. Synthesize the existing decisions to show how they fit this broader principle. Your argument should show that the cases are not the law itself, but simply illustrations of the law.

If your appeal raises a question of statutory construction, your search for broader principles focuses on what you claim is the statute's objective. Use legislative history to illustrate it. Buttress your construction with interpretations or applications by the implementing agency, and look to the commentators in treatises and law review articles. Whatever the issue, this effort is devoted to assuring the judges that you are not trying to sell them some wild new scheme, but simply that your case fits comfortably into the existing law as you have restated it in plain, straight-forward terms.

D. Be assertive rather than critical about the court below and your opponent's arguments, and remember the standard of review

Too many briefs just try to take pot-shots at the trial judge and the opponents. Even if the judge or opposing counsel have made blatant errors, you first should focus your efforts on what legal principles should apply to the case and only second on what the trial judge or your opponent did wrong. The judges on appeal are far more interested in how to reach and justify the right result. In fact, ad hominem attacks easily can turn the court against you.

You must deal fairly but convincingly with unfavorable authority. We previously have discussed the need to distinguish potentially controlling, negative authority and the decision whether (and **where**) to anticipate and handle negative persuasive authority. Add to that discussion the perception that at the appellate court level, very few dead flies in the bowl of appellate soup are going to go unnoticed. If your opponent does not find the bad case, the judges' clerks probably will. Thus, having the first word on a troublesome authority can make you look upright and truthful and gives you the chance to dull the effect of the authority before your opponent runs amok with it. That said, what is truly "adverse" can be a matter of interpretation. You really need to consider whether the authority is controlling (or just persuasive) and whether your facts are in some way distinguishable.

---

[4]   If the term explanatory synthesis is new to you, please <u>see</u> the Appendix to this volume

Finally, remember the standard of review when you are drafting your headings and the rest of the argument section. The standard of review is the keystone to court of appeals decision-making, so you must tailor your argument to it. When the standard is abuse of discretion, for example, it does no good to make arguments that apply only if the court were reviewing a question *de novo*. Define how much discretion is allowed under the law, and argue that the judge exceeded that level using authorities that actually found a violation of the applicable standard.

E. Minimize alternative arguments

Although there is no limit to the number of good arguments you raise (within reason), alternative arguments that simply crowd the brief with imaginative possibilities choke off the best arguments and drown your better arguments in a sea of words. Such scattergun tactics rarely are effective and can dilute your major points. Your time, energy, and space is better spent bolstering your main arguments.

F. As in other litigation documents, limit the use of footnotes, overuse of emphasis, and lengthy quotes

Limit footnotes if you can, and make sure you follow the rules of your jurisdiction. For example, sometimes the court will say that nothing **argumentative** can be in a footnote (<u>i.e.</u>, nothing that presents part of the legal support for one of your arguments, as opposed to additional facts, statistics, or a side note of interest about something). Even if the local rules allow you to put argument in footnotes, you run the risk of the argument going unnoticed. Many judges skip footnotes completely, and others will not consider legal arguments mentioned only in footnotes.

Do not stress (underline, bold, italicize) too much in your text—you will stress out the judges! Stated otherwise: no one likes a lawyer who is constantly shouting. Overdoing your underlining or other emphasis has that same effect. Putting key words in all capitals and using exclamation points are artificial devices. Sparing use of underlining or italicizing is useful to highlight key words, but effective emphasis depends on the content and arrangement of your text.

Shorten your quotes. No one likes long quotes for at least three reasons: (1) long quotes are too boring and many readers skip over them; (2) the reader knows you are going to (and should) explain the significance of the quote anyway; and (3) readers want to hear what *you* have to say. So, distill long quotes down to their essential point and avoid long descriptions of cases.

V. DRAFTING AN ANSWERING BRIEF

The most important point for appellee is to make your affirmative case first before you start attacking appellant's. The same points made in discussing appellant's strategy fits here, too: fit your case into a broader framework. You want to set the playing field rather than accept the one set by your opponent. If you do a better job of that than your opponent, then when you start responding to specific arguments you can do so from a position of strength.

Storytelling in the statement of facts is as important for appellee as it is for appellant, and more so if the appellant has done a good job getting out its side of the story. If your opponent told a good story in her opening brief, acknowledge it, but immediately turn the tables around to your side: "Appellant told a good story about XYZ. Now here is the rest of the story." At best you will pull the court's attention and concern away from your opponent and on to your client. At least you should make sure the court is returned to the middle ground, neutral territory, not swayed by the sympathies of either side. This task will be difficult enough if your opponent was an excellent storyteller.

In developing your analytical framework, it will help if you can synthesize the broad principles in a way that highlights the novelty of appellant's position. As mentioned before, appellate judges generally take more comfort in fitting cases into established principles than in breaking new ground. When you can show that appellant is trying to turn the law on its head, you have an excellent chance of winning.

When you start responding to specific arguments, you have the option to follow the sequence of issues used by appellant but you are not bound to follow this structure. Courts appreciate the simplicity of this structure, but you should consider the possibility that this structure might not be the most effective way to structure your arguments. Appellant's third best point might be your best point, and appellant's best point is likely to be your worst point. It is more important to present your best point first and next best point second than it is to limit your brief to the order picked out by your opponent.

What is most important is to make sure you answer all of appellant's arguments. Even if your opponent has raised an argument that obviously lacks merit, you should explain why. Do not leave the court guessing whether you intended to concede something, or force the court to undertake independent research on why appellant's last two arguments should fail, simply because you failed to address them. In addition:

> ➤ Never assume that appellant has laid the necessary foundation for its arguments. Go through a mental checklist on each argument: Did appellant preserve this point below? Are the grounds appellant is advancing now for overturning an evidentiary ruling the same ones it offered below? Is the legal theory appellant advances now the same one presented below? If not, stress that before you even consider a response on the merits.
> ➤ If the appellant seems to have scored points by showing defects in the trial court's approach, remind the court of appeals that it is reviewing the lower court's result, not its reasoning. It can affirm on any basis supported by the law. If you have focused your brief on what should be the controlling principles, you need not worry about defending the lower court's faulty reasoning.

Appellees have the opportunity to call the court's attention to shortcomings in appellant's brief—an inference stated as a fact, an adverse case ignored, and so forth. The tendency is to overdo these comments as if an appeal were a debate where you are scoring points. Keep these comments to a minimum, and stress only those that are substantial. Your goal is to affirm the district court, not eviscerate your opponent.

In rare instances, appellee may want to skip the jurisdictional statement, statement of the issues presented for review, statement of facts, statement of the case (or proceedings below), and the statement of the standard(s) of review (unless, of course, appellee is dissatisfied with appellant's statements of them). This can pose something of a dilemma, especially with the statements of issues or facts. You may find nothing specifically wrong with appellant's statements except their emphasis and implications. Should you accept them for fear the court of appeals will think you a nit-picker? Should you restate them in their entirety, or simply those parts you especially dislike?

You are not required to prove that appellant's statements are wrong before you can write your own. The rule allows you to rewrite whenever you are dissatisfied with one or more of appellant's statements. In other words, it is entirely up to you. You need not apologize. Whether you submit an entire restatement or portions of one will depend on how much needs restating. If your opponent did a decent job of telling its story in the statement of facts, you really must do your best to tell a better story or at least tell "the rest of the story" to restore equilibrium in the case. If your opponent's facts section was mundane, however, you need not go to great lengths to correct the record, but you should take advantage of the situation and tell your own story. Do not miss out on the chance to get the court to care about your client so that it will be happy to listen to your legal arguments that provide the means to the end of victory for your client.

VI. DRAFTING THE REPLY BRIEF

Appellant's right to reply is a valuable right. Do not squander it by rehashing or repeating arguments already covered in your opening brief. Having the last word, as such, does not necessarily have a tremendous effect on the appeal because the judges are likely to wait until the parties have filed all their briefs and then read them all together. Appellant should use its right of reply to focus the appeal down to its core. You know what you said in your opening brief; you now see what appellee has said in response. Refine the issues in light of both. A reply brief is the best vehicle for narrowing the true issues, so sharpen the focus. Now is your chance to tell the court what this appeal is really all about. If appellee did not answer all the issues raised in your opening brief, make the most of that. The reply is your chance to put the issues in their starkest terms that are favorable to your client.

Sometimes you also must use your reply for damage control. If appellee has hurt your position, you must do what you can to repair it. Whatever you do, do not try to interject new issues in your reply. Not only will the court likely ignore them, the judges also will be irritated that you tried to sneak something in without giving your opponent a chance to respond. If something new (a case, statute, rule, regulation, etc.) has come up that the court should know about, use the procedure for submitting supplemental authorities rather than putting it in your reply brief. That way you do not co-mingle the separate functions of replying and submitting supplemental authorities.

A reply brief is optional. However, it is hard to imagine a situation where appellant would not exercise its right to reply where the local rules permit it.

VII. SAMPLE BRIEF GRADING SHEETS

The following are sample brief grading sheets we have used in advocacy and moot court courses and competitions. The first is a general grading sheet for a moot court brief, while the second is a grading sheet created for a particular assignment. In both samples, you can see the breakdown of items and the relative importance of each. By using these forms as a checklist, you can perform a self-guided edit of your own brief.

MOOT COURT BRIEF GRADING SHEET

Student: _____   Argument Section(s) Drafted: _____

INITIAL SECTIONS (40 points possible):
Cover (3):
    Correct color (1 pt); Proper caption, bound at the left (1 pt)   _____
    Identifies team #, students' names, sections drafted (1 pt)   _____
Questions Presented (3):
    Presented in correct order per U.S. S.Ct. Rules (1st) (1 pt)   _____
    Describes issues in proper Supreme Court style (Chap. 3 and
    lecture) (0-2 pts)   _____
    Notes: _____
Table of Contents (3):
    Presented in correct order per U.S. S.Ct. Rules (2nd) (1 pt)   _____
    Listing for Argument section w/ full headings for subsections (0-2 pts)   _____
    Notes: _____
Table of Authorities (3):
    Presented in correct order per U.S. S.Ct. Rules (3rd) (1 pt)   _____
    Separates Cases, Statutes, Legislative History, Secondary Sources
    (0-2 pts)   _____
    Notes: _____
Opinions Below (3):
    Presented in correct order per U.S. S.Ct. Rules (4th) (1 pt)   _____
    Gives citation (1 pt); References record pages where opinion is found
    (1 pt)   _____
Constitutional and Statutory Sections (3):
    Presented in correct order per U.S. S.Ct. Rules (5th) (1 pt)   _____
    Quotes const. & stat. sections or cites them w/ ref. to full text
    in Appdx. (2 pts)   _____
Statement of the Case (10):
    Presented in correct order per U.S. S.Ct. Rules (6th) (1 pt)   _____
    Properly describes facts, proceedings below w/o legal argument (0-5 pts)   _____

Section is slanted in favor of client, but not outrageously biased (0-4 pts) _____

Notes: _____

Summary of the Argument (10):

Presented in correct order per U.S. S.Ct. Rules (7th) (1 pt) _____

Properly summarizes arguments in concise manner (0-5 pts) _____

Section is strong and punchy, and makes best points clearly and directly (0-4 pts) _____

Notes: _____

Conclusion (2): Appears last (1 pt); requests relief properly (1 pt) _____

SUBTOTAL for INITIAL SECTIONS: _____

ARGUMENT SECTION (60 points possible):

Use of Facts to further arguments (0-10 pts) _____

Use of Cases and Statutory Authorities - each point is well researched and supported with proper authority; demonstrates knowledge of controlling vs. persuasive authority (0-10 pts) _____

Use of Legislative History and secondary interpretive authorities (0-5 pts) _____

Organization - logical, coherent; uses IRAC or TREAT format; proper division of argument into main issues and sub-issues (0-10 pts) _____

Persuasiveness and Advocacy - presents arguments in compelling and convincing manner; best points are emphasized; weak points are explained, defused (0-15 pts) _____

Anticipates Opponent's positions and provides counter-analysis (0-5 pts) _____

Public Policy - identifies and explains how arguments further public policies (0-5 pts) _____

SUBTOTAL for ARGUMENT SECTION: _____

TOTAL for INITIAL SECTIONS +ARGUMENT SECTION: _____

PENALTY DEDUCTIONS:

Citation Errors (-0.5 pts for each error; max -5 pts) _____

Format Errors: 2.0 spacing, 12 pt. font, 1" margins, 25/40 pg limit (-0.5 pts/pg; max -5 pts) _____

Grammar, Spelling Errors, Typos (-0.5 pts for each error; max -3 pts) _____

Late Penalty (-5 pts per 24 hour period late) _____

TOTAL POINTS (out of 100): _____

FINAL GRADE: _____

APPELLATE BRIEF (FINAL) GRADING SHEET

Student _____   Total Points (out of 100):_____

INITIAL SECTIONS (25 points possible):

Cover (2): Correct color (1); Proper caption, bound at the left (1)   _____

Questions Presented (2): Describes two issues (1) Uses broader, public
policy style - e.g., artist, celebrity (1)   _____

Table of Contents (2): Proper style (1) Listing for Argument section
w/ full headings for subsections (1)   _____

Table of Authorities (2): Proper style (1) Separates Cases, Statutes,
Legislative History, Secondary Sources (1)   _____

Statement of Jurisdiction (1)   _____

Standard of Review (1)   _____

Statement of the Case (6): Properly describes facts, proceedings below
w/o legal argument (3)   _____

Section is slanted in favor of client, but not outrageously biased (3)   _____

Summary of the Argument (7): Properly summarizes arguments in
concise manner (3)   _____

Section is strong and punchy, and makes best points clearly and directly (4)   _____

Conclusion (1): requests relief properly   _____

Sections appear in correct order (1)   _____

SUBTOTAL for INITIAL SECTIONS: _____

ORGANIZATION (5 points possible)   _____

Overall organization-two issues: News, Parody (2)   _____

Sections have an obvious difference in focus even if some authorities
are used in both sections (2)   _____

Brief is coherent and makes intelligent use of transitions, roadmaps
or sub-sections (3)   _____

NEWS (30 points possible)   _____

Statutes and Const.(4):   _____

      Quotes § 3344(a)   _____

      Quotes § 3344(d)   _____

      Quotes U.S. Const. amend. I   _____

      Quotes Cal. Const. art. I, § 2   _____

Discusses commercial speech effectively - distinct from selling speech (3)   _____

Use of controlling authorities (5)   _____

Use of other primary persuasive authorities (5)   _____

Use of secondary persuasive authorities (2)   _____

Explanatory Synthesis (5)   _____
Counteranalysis (3)   _____
Weaving of public policy into arguments (3)   _____

PARODY (30 points possible)   _____
Notes and cites authority as to whether parody is defense to right of
publicity (2)   _____
Use of controlling authorities (5)   _____
Use of primary persuasive authorities (5)   _____
Use of secondary persuasive authorities (2)   _____
Explanatory Synthesis (5)   _____
Counteranalysis (3)   _____
Weaving of public policy re: right to criticize public figures and politicians (4) _____
Weaving of public policy re: artistic expression and transformation (4)   _____

ADVOCACY AND RESEARCH (10 points possible)   _____
Theme: attempted to develop theme for the entire brief that furthered
public policies concerning the issues of the case and tied together the
brief as a whole (3)   _____
Advocacy Skills and Persuasiveness: overall demonstration of adversarial
writing skills learned in the course (4)   _____
Evidence of Research (3)   _____

SUBTOTAL 1 (out of 25)   _____
SUBTOTAL 2 (out of 75)   _____

POINTS BEFORE DEDUCTIONS   _____

Proofreading and Other Errors (Deductions):
Citation errors (-0.5 each/max. -5)   _____
Missing citation (-1 each/max. -5)   _____
Typo/spelling (-0.5 each/max. -3)   _____
Formatting: 2.0-sp, 1" marg, page limit, 25 lines/pg; 12 pt courier
font (-2 each/max. -4)   _____
Rules: no name in upper right corner p.1; no page #s (-2 each/max. -4)   _____
Lateness: (-20 each 24hr per/-5 late email)   _____

Total Deductions   _____

TOTAL POINTS   _____

VIII. SAMPLE BRIEFS

The samples that follow are two student briefs from an intramural competition that was patterned after the Association of the Bar of the City of New York's National Moot Court Competition, and two actual practitioners' United States Supreme Court briefs from one of the cases that was central to the problem used in the intramural competition briefs. The last sample brief is a practitioner's petition for a writ of mandamus filed in the United States Court of Appeals for the Eleventh Circuit.

We have annotated the briefs with our comments and criticisms. When we have a comment to make, we have inserted it into the middle of the brief, as seen below:

> Naturally, the briefs did not have these comment boxes in them when they were submitted. Do not be confused by the placement of the comment boxes.

Although these briefs appear in the same font as the rest of this book, most of them would have been submitted in Courier or Courier New font. Remember to check the rules of your court or competition when you chose the font of your briefs. We have spaced the briefs with the same line spacing as the rest of this book, when the actual briefs would have been produced with double spacing. Please note that we have left the briefs in original form with regard to citation forms, wording, and other stylistic choices that may not be completely consistent with the rules and recommendations we have given earlier in this text.

Sample Brief No. 1:

Student Brief of Petitioner
in the moot court case:

Metropolitan School Dist. of Gotham
v.
Branch Louisian of the United Church of
Christ the Savior

> This caption follows the form we discussed earlier in this chapter.

DOCKET NO. 00-100

SUPREME COURT OF THE UNITED STATES

March Term 2000

METROPOLITAN SCHOOL DISTRICT OF GOTHAM,
STATE OF NEW KENT,

Petitioner,

——*against*——

BRANCH LOUISIAN OF THE UNITED CHURCH OF
CHRIST THE SAVIOR,

Respondent.

On Writ of Certiorari to the United States Court of Appeals for the Fourteenth Circuit

---

BRIEF OF PETITIONER

Student 1 and Student 2
1234 Streetname Apt. A
St. Louis, MO 63108
Counsel of Record for Petitioner

These Questions Presented work well. They reflect the fact that the case is pending in a court of last resort (the U.S. Supreme Court) that will set a precedent for all courts applying federal law. The questions do not refer to a single party but to the *categories of party* into which the actual parties fit—a school district and a church. The questions have an appropriate level of detail and they are non-argumentative. They are good examples of the proper way to present the issues.

Questions Presented for Review

I. Whether a public school district violates a religious organization's First Amendment free speech rights by refusing to post information regarding creationism on the school district's web site created to further the educational mission of the school district?

II. Whether a public school district violates the First Amendment's Establishment Clause by sponsoring a religious web page on the district's web site created to increase the educational opportunities for students on topics within the curriculum?

> This Table of Contents is ineffective primarily because it is too short. The Argument section should display each thesis heading and sub-heading of the Argument, with a page reference for each. Then the table of contents becomes a useful outline for the judges. Note that there is no "Opinions and Judgments Entered in the Case" section. This could have been an oversight because some courts require such a section in addition to the summary of the case. Lesson? Check the local rules.

Table of Contents

> This Table of Authorities is nicely formatted, but it should have been broken down into categories of authorities as shown above in this chapter, and the authors should have left out the jump cites (pinpoint cites). They also should have cited the two lower court opinions from the moot court problem.

Table of Authorities

Constitutional Provisions and Statutes

U.S. Const. amend. I:

Congress shall make no law respecting an establishment of religion, or prohibiting the free exercise thereof; or abridging the freedom of speech, or of the press; or the right of the people peaceably to assemble, and to petition the Government for a redress of grievances.

> The students improperly quote Fed. R. Civ. P. 56(c) here. The purpose of the section is to provide the text of substantively controlling constitutional, statutory or regulatory provisions, not procedural rules.

Fed. R. Civ. P. 56(c):

The motion shall be served at least 10 days before the time fixed for the hearing. The adverse party prior to the day of hearing may serve opposing affidavits. The judgment sought shall be rendered forthwith if the pleadings, depositions, answers to interrogatories, and admissions on file, together with the affidavits, if any, show that there is no genuine issue as to any material fact and that the moving party is entitled to a judgment as a matter of law. A summary judgment, interlocutory in character, may be rendered on the same issue of liability alone although there is a genuine issue as to the amount of damages.

Statement of the Case: The first paragraph of this section is done properly, although it does little to advance petitioner's case. To improve the section, zero in on some specifics that the lower courts held, and quote those portions that help your appeal, or at least that box in the lower courts to a position that you can handle. The remaining paragraphs tell a little of the facts. Again, petitioner is holding back a lot. This is a very cautious facts section. You can be more creative in terms of facts to detail and emphasize, and in the way you word the facts so as to paint a picture for the court, and get the court in a frame of mind to agree with your side. Regarding the cites to the record, the U.S. Supreme Court Rules tell you to cite them as Record 3 instead of using the form (R. at 3). Always check Local Rules!

Statement of the Case

Respondent, Branch Louisian of the United Church of Christ the Savior ("Church"), filed a complaint under 42 U.S.C. § 1983 against Petitioner, the Metropolitan School District of Gotham, State of New Kent ("School District"), claiming the School District violated Church's rights under the Free Speech and Establishment clauses of the United States Constitution, Amendment 1, by refusing to allow the Church's religious web pages on the topic of creationism to be displayed on the School District's Internet web site. (R. at 3.) The District Court of New Kent ruled in favor of the School District and denied Church's Motion for Summary Judgment. (R. at 9.) The Church appealed. The United States Court of Appeals for the Fourteenth Circuit reversed the District Court's decision. (R. at 21.) This Court granted certiorari. (R. at 22.)

Petitioner began operating an Internet service provider and managing a web server for the purpose of promoting information about the areas of study currently being taught in the School District. (R. at 11.) The School District invites faculty of the School District and other educational institutions in Gotham to propose web pages for inclusion in the site. (R. at 11.) Any entity seeking access to the web site must submit a proposal to the School District. (R. at 11.) The School District then reviews the proposals and determines whether access should be granted based upon whether the web pages are directly related to a topic currently included in the School District's curriculum guide. (R.. at 11.)

The School District's home page contains an alphabetical listing of all sponsored web sites and pages that have been accepted and linked to the School District's web page. (R. at 12.) Each listing includes a small icon designed by the creator of the sponsored pages, the title of the web site, a short description of the contents of the pages, and a link to the actual "http" address of the pages. (R. at 12.)

Church applied to the School District for permission to post its web site on March 5, 1999. (R. at 13.) The Church described the proposal as a "thorough examination of the doctrine of Creationism from the Book of Genesis in the Bible . . . and a comparison and contrasting . . . with the purportedly scientific doctrines of Evolution and Natural Selection." (R. at 13.) The proposal also included commentary from religious leaders about creationism in text, audio, and video formats and religious depictions of the story of creation in Genesis. (R. at 13.) The School District rejected the proposal because the topic did not directly relate to a subject included in School District's curriculum guide. (R. at 14.)

Summary of the Argument: This section is nicely done. It is punchy, it does not beat around the bush, and it gets a lot of information out in a short space. About the only thing we can point out is that the petitioner did not cite any authority in this section. You may want to consider citing one or two of the major cases or statutes on which your argument is truly based, although not all attorneys follow that practice (in fact, some are strongly against it).

The authors actually disagree with each other on this, and perhaps that underscores a separate point. You will find that no two attorneys you work with will have identical styles, and written work product can never be entirely divorced from personal style. Some attorneys maintain that no cases should be cited in the SOA, while others find it odd if at least the one or two leading authorities are omitted. You will have to use your own best judgment—coupled with the knowledge you can compile about your colleagues (read briefs they have filed in the past) and, of course, a thorough reading of the court's rules.

Summary of the Argument

The Supreme Court should reverse the appellate court's judgment and grant summary judgment to School District because the School District has not infringed on Church's constitutionally protected free speech rights. The web site at issue is a nonpublic forum due to the control the School District maintained over the forum and because the forum was never opened to the general public. Additionally, the School District properly made a content-based, non-viewpoint centered discrimination of the Church's offered statement on creationism because creationism neither relates to any topic in the school district nor does creationism comport to the policy of the School District in teaching evolution. Finally, regardless of the forum or the type of discrimination, the School District's censorship survives strict scrutiny. Both the School District's interest in providing the best education for children and its duty to abide by the Establishment Clause of the Constitution are compelling state interests. The censorship at issue was narrowly tailored to fulfill both of these interests as evidenced by the fact that this has been the only restriction of its kind since the inception of the web site.

The Supreme Court should reverse the appellate court's judgment and grant summary judgment to School District because sponsoring of the Church's religious web pages by the School District amounts to a violation of the Establishment Clause of the First Amendment of the Constitution. The Church's web pages are on creationism, a religious doctrine. The Establishment Clause is violated by the School District's sponsorship of the Church's web pages under any test this Court chooses to apply. Sponsoring of the web pages creates a coercive mechanism in which students are coerced to acknowledge the religious doctrine of the Church. The inclusion of the Church's religious web pages on the School District's home page lead a reasonable person to believe

> The student authors of this brief were not careful about how they referred to the parties. We like the fact that they are not using the confusing terms "petitioner and respondent" or "plaintiff and defendant," but you will see the authors switch from "the School District" to "the District" to "School District," and from "the Church" to "Church" in this brief. Stick to one form of the parties names throughout the brief to preserve your readers' comprehension.

that the District is endorsing the religious doctrine of creationism. The purpose of the web server was to provide educational opportunities for the students. This secular purpose is subverted by inclusion of the Church's religious web pages and creating the effect of endorsement of creationism by the School District. The School District monitoring, reviewing, and surveillance of the sponsored web pages leads to an excessive governmental entanglement with the Church and thus a violation of the Establishment Clause if the School District sponsors the Church's web pages.

Argument

> Argument: The first heading is a mouthful. It is almost a Complete Disclosure type drafting job of the issue, but you may remember that the Questions Presented for Review on the second page of the brief were not drafted in Complete Disclosure form, but in proper Notice form. There is nothing inherently wrong with this heading as a grammatical matter, but it is probably too dense. We can see why the petitioners did not want to list their substantive headings and subheadings in the table of contents.
>
> We do like the thesis stated in the heading—it is forceful and bold. "The school district is allowed to discriminate on the basis of content . . ." This is good, affirmative drafting. Take a stand in your theses; make your point and stick to it. So much the better if the heading were put in the table of contents, where the court might read it up front and get very interested in looking into the argument right away.
>
> The "introduction" subsection here is a reasonable start to the argument, but do not waste the reader's time with a one word heading; write an argumentative thesis heading that summarizes the section, or drop the heading. You do not need a heading that says "Introduction" when everyone expects this section to serve that role.
>
> The first paragraph is useful to set up the rest of the section. In the second paragraph, the reference to *de novo* review is a very good thing (check local rules on where Standard of Review should appear), but the reference to Fed. R. Civ. P. 56 is completely unnecessary. You could strike the whole second sentence in the second paragraph and never miss it.

I. THE UNITED STATES SUPREME COURT SHOULD REVERSE THE APPELLATE COURT'S DECISION GRANTING SUMMARY JUDGMENT TO CHURCH AND GRANT SUMMARY JUDGMENT TO SCHOOL DISTRICT BECAUSE THE SCHOOL DISTRICT'S WEB SITE IS A NONPUBLIC FORUM AND THE SCHOOL DISTRICT IS ALLOWED TO DISCRIMINATE ON THE BASIS OF CONTENT SO LONG AS THE DISCRIMINATION IS REASONABLE AND VIEWPOINT NEUTRAL.

A. Introduction

The First Amendment, applicable to the States via the Fourteenth Amendment, provides protection from unnecessary governmental interference in free speech. <u>Cohen v.</u>

<u>California</u>, 403 U.S. 15, 19 (1971). The First Amendment provides, "Congress shall make no law respecting an establishment of religion, or prohibiting the free exercise thereof; or abridging the freedom of speech, or of the press; or the right of the people peaceably to assemble, and to petition the Government for a redress of grievances." U.S. Const. amend. I. In order to invoke First Amendment jurisprudence, the entity claiming a violation of its Constitutional rights ("speaker") must seek access to a "forum." <u>Cornelius v. NAACP Legal Defense & Educ. Fund, Inc.</u>, 473 U.S. 788, 801 (1985). A forum is either public property or private property dedicated to public use. <u>Id.</u>

When a speaker claims a violation of its First Amendment rights after being denied access to a forum, this Court reviews the facts *de novo*. <u>Edwards v. South Carolina</u>, 372 U.S. 229, 235 (1963). Additionally, summary judgment should only be granted when the pleadings, discovery, and all affidavits, if any, "show that there is no genuine issue as to any material fact and that the moving party is entitled to a judgment as a matter of law." Fed.R.Civ.P. 56(c).

> Here, the authors are trying to get the section moving, but the engine is balking a little. The authors jump into the "forum" argument in the first paragraph, but then the second paragraph steps away from the topic and moves on to the "teach and nurture the children" argument. It doesn't sound that bad, but it could be more focused. We take it that authors probably were trying to write an umbrella or roadmap section for the rest of the subsections under section I.
>
> The discussion of education and the courts' "hands off" policy is a very good point for petitioner, especially to get into right up front. Petitioner may be shaky in some areas of the First Amendment law implicated by this case, but not this area. You should try to lead off with your strong points, as these authors did.

Protection of speech rights varies depending upon the nature of the forum. <u>Perry Educ. Ass'n v. Perry Local Educators' Ass'n</u>, 460 U.S. 37, 44-46 (1983). The Court has consistently recognized that a forum is either public, limited public, or nonpublic depending on the historical or present treatment the government has afforded the property. <u>See id.</u> at 44-46. Whether the government can deny a speaker access to a particular forum depends upon whether the forum is public, limited public, or nonpublic.

> We would break up the following paragraph into at least two paragraphs. There are too many connectors—"additionally," "moreover," "finally"—used here trying to keep it all together. It would be better to lose one or more of the connectors and make it two or three paragraphs.

Furthermore, this Court must give deference to school official's decisions regarding educational matters. <u>Hazelwood Sch. Dist. v. Kuhlmeier</u>, 484 U.S. 260, 273 (1988). This Court has long applied the standard that the education of children is primarily the responsibility of parents, teachers, and state and local school officials, not of federal judges. <u>Id.</u> Additionally, the Court has noted that it is only when the government censors with no valid educational purpose that the First Amendment is "directly and sharply implicated." <u>Id.</u> Moreover, when a party asks the courts to review a genuinely academic decision, the courts should show "great respect for the faculty's professional judgment." <u>Regents of the Univ. of Mich. v. Ewing</u>, 474 U.S. 214, 225 (1985). Educators have the primary freedom to determine who may teach, what may be taught, and how it shall be taught. <u>Sweezy v. New Hampshire</u>, 354 U.S. 234, 263 (1957) (Frankfurter, J., concurring). Finally, the Court has most recently held, "When the government appropriates public funds to promote a particular policy of its own it is entitled to say what it wishes, and it may take legitimate and appropriate steps to ensure that its message is neither garbled nor distorted . . ." <u>Rosenberger v. Rector and Visitors of the Univ. of Va.</u>, 515 U.S. 819, 833 (1995). As a final introductory point, web sites, web pages, and web servers are subject to First Amendment forum analysis even though they are somewhat new areas for discourse. <u>See generally</u> <u>Reno v. ACLU</u>, 521 U.S. 844 (1997); <u>Loving v. Boren</u>, 956 F.Supp. 953 (W.D. Okla. 1997); <u>CompuServe, Inc. v. Cyber Promotions, Inc.</u>, 962 F.Supp. 1015 (S.D. Ohio 1997).

The District's decision to exclude the Church's web page discussing creationism was a proper educational decision to which this Court owes great deference. Further, by creating a nonpublic forum, the School District was allowed to engage in content-based discrimination. There is no question that the School District properly made a content-based, non-viewpoint centered censorship in denying access to the Church. Moreover, even if this Court finds that the School District's web page was a limited public forum, the content-based censorship exercised by the School District passes strict scrutiny analysis as it is narrowly tailored to promote a compelling state interest.

> Section B is omitted.

* * *

> Section C is well-structured as it obviously presents an IRAC (or TREAT) discussion. It shows how one issue in the chain of issues suggested by the problem can be dealt with in a clear and succinct manner using the classic IRAC or TREAT format. On the negative side, the heading is incomplete—it does not have the "because" part containing the facts and principles that support the conclusion stated here.

C. The District's web site is a nonpublic forum.

The first issue involves identifying the nature of the forum. The web site at issue is a nonpublic forum. A non-public forum is created when the government does not open the property to the general public. <u>Perry Educ. Ass'n</u>, 460 U.S. at 46. "The First Amendment does not guarantee access to property simply because it is owned or controlled by the government." <u>Id.</u> (quoting <u>U.S. Postal Serv. v. Greenburgh Civic Ass'n</u>, 453 U.S. 114, 129 (1981)). Moreover, "the State, no less than a private owner of property, has power to preserve the property under its control for the use to which it is lawfully dedicated." <u>Id.</u> (quoting <u>Greenburgh Civic Ass'n</u>, 453 U.S. at 129).

> It is regretful that the authors chose to present an unsynthesized explanation section rather than a synthesized explanation. Why not synthesize <u>Perry</u> and <u>Cornelius</u> with other cases to make a better illustration of what is a nonpublic forum? The unsynthesized explanation forces the authors to apply cases instead of principles to the facts in the application section.

In <u>Perry</u>, the Court held that the internal mail system created by the school district to disseminate information to teachers and staff was a non-public forum because neither the district's intent nor its practice opened the mail system to the general public. <u>See generally id.</u> The Court found as dispositive the fact that the district had to grant permission to any person seeking access to the mail system and the fact that permission had not been granted to all who requested it. <u>Id.</u> at 47. The evidence revealed that some groups other than district employees and administrators had been granted access to the mail system. <u>Id.</u> However, the Court concluded that selective access does not create a public forum. <u>Id.</u> <u>See also</u> <u>Cornelius</u>, 473 U.S. at 788 (holding that government run charity drive for nonprofit organizations was nonpublic forum where government retained the power to exclude non-healthcare or non-welfare nonprofit organizations); <u>Arkansas Educ. Television Comm'n v. Forbes</u>, 118 S.Ct. 1633, 1644 (1998) (holding that political debate operated by public television station was nonpublic forum where participation in debate was contingent on the station's permission).

The Court's analysis in <u>Perry</u> strongly supports a finding that the web site at issue here is a nonpublic forum. First, the School District's implementation of standards relating to the type of information the speaker must contribute to the site in order to gain access shows the forum has never been opened to the general public. (R. at 11.) Requiring any speaker's message to relate to a topic of education in the District shows that the forum was not created for the general public because the average person in the community could not be admitted as most people do not possess information pertaining to primary or secondary education. Further, the standards are actively enforced. (R. at 14.) As in <u>Perry</u>, in order to gain access, the speaker must obtain permission from the School District after tendering a written proposal. (R. at 11.) The School District also performs periodic checks of the site for information that is in violation of the policy. (R. at 11.) Finally, the School District maintains the right to remove any non-conforming information. (R. at 11.) Therefore, the District maintained control over the web site by requiring permission, reserving the right to remove information, and setting standards on whom may enter the forum. This control, like in <u>Perry</u>, exhibits the District's purpose that the forum not be opened to the general public. As such, the web site is a nonpublic forum; and the appellate court's decision should be overturned.

> Section D is another clear IRAC or TREAT discussion although it fails to use explanatory synthesis.[5] Once again, bringing in the education of school children is a great idea for petitioner. Always return to your strengths.

D. <u>The District's refusal to allow Church's information regarding Creationism is reasonable, content-based, non-viewpoint discrimination.</u>

Once it has been determined that the web site is a nonpublic forum, the next question is whether the School District properly refused the Church's proposal. It is clear that in this case, the School District properly refused the Church's proposal because its decision was content-based, reasonable, and made irrespective of the Church's viewpoint.

When the forum is characterized as nonpublic, the speaker forbidden access has no First Amendment or other right to the forum. <u>Perry Educ. Ass'n</u>, 460 U.S. at 54. As such, the censorship does not have to be narrowly tailored, the objective does not have to be compelling, and the most efficient means of fulfilling the state's interest do not have to be used. <u>Id.</u> The School District has acted properly as long as its restriction is reasonable and not based on the speaker's viewpoint on the subject. <u>Id.</u> at 46. Distinctions may be drawn between applicants to the site based on subject matter and speaker identity. <u>Id.</u> Furthermore, the reasonableness required need not be the most reasonable or the only reasonable limitation; the state need only show that it was legitimately justified in its actions. <u>Cornelius</u>, 473 U.S. at 808.

> Subsection 1 is strange in that it promises to discuss "Supreme Court precedent<u>s</u>" and then only discusses <u>Cornelius</u>. Do not make a promise and then not keep it. Just say, "under <u>Cornelius</u>" not "under precedent<u>s</u>."
>
> The thesis heading here is a throw-away; it lacks the "because" information to support the thesis.

1. <u>The District's restriction is reasonable.</u>

Any government restriction on speech in a nonpublic forum must be reasonable. Reasonableness of the restriction on access to a nonpublic forum must be determined in

---

[5] For more information on explanatory synthesis, <u>see</u> the Appendix to this volume.

relation to the government's purpose and surrounding circumstances of the forum. Id. at 809. The School District's censorship of the Church's proposal is reasonable in light of Supreme Court precedents.

After determining that the forum in Cornelius was nonpublic, the Court analyzed the government's reasonableness in refusing to allow legal defense and other nonprofit litigation organizations from receiving proceeds from the charity drive designed to support health and welfare nonprofit entities. Id. The Court found the restriction reasonable. Id.

In relation to speech restrictions in nonpublic fora, the reasonableness test requires only a threshold showing that the government has appropriate purposes in limiting access. See generally id. The Court has stated that the government acts reasonably when it discriminates in order to maintain administrative manageability; access to the public can be obtained by the speaker through some other means; where it has denied access in order to avoid the appearance of favoritism to one political group over another; and where it restricts in order to avoid controversy. Id. at 809-810. Furthermore, the government does not have to resort to other agencies' restrictions or findings in different circumstances to determine reasonableness. Id.

Applying Cornelius to the case at bar clearly shows the School District's actions were reasonable. The School District's policy was implemented to supplement the topics listed in the curriculum; and creationism neither is nor ever has been a part of the curriculum for the past 150 years. (R. at 15.) Secondly, the School District reasonably restricted access to the Church to avoid controversy because deeply rooted disagreements may arise over any association between the School District and any particular religious beliefs. The School District also feared jeopardizing the success of the program. Allowing the Church to post information about creationism would inevitably lead to other groups seeking access to post information completely unrelated to any part of the curriculum. This slippery slope would result in the weakening of the evaluative process and would inevitably result in a *de facto* public forum as proper research and analysis of each applicant would become overly consuming of both time and money. For these reasons, the School District reasonably denied access to the Church.

> The next three paragraphs extend the application section to discuss three additional points The authors are fond of prefatory phrases such as "further," "finally," similarly." These words are throat-clearing expressions that add nothing to the meaning. Each should be deleted.

Further, it is clear that the School District had an appropriate purpose in restricting access to the Church in order to maintain neutrality. Like Cornelius, where the Court held limiting the appearance of political favoritism provided reasonable justification, restricting access here to avoid the appearance of religious favoritism shows the reasonableness of the School District's actions. Allowing the Church to post the information would lead non-religious parents in the community to believe that because of their beliefs, their children will be treated differently than those who favor creationism.

Finally, the School District acted properly here because the Church can spread its message to both students and non-students through other means. Traditionally, churches and other religious organizations have spread their message throughout the world by active missionary work. Similarly, the Church can spread its message of creationism throughout the community by distributing pamphlets, door-to-door confrontation, rallies, and persuading non-Christians to visit its services.

The factors set out in <u>Cornelius</u>, as applied to the case at bar, show the reasonableness of the School District's actions. Not only has the School District met the threshold requirement, it has persuasively demonstrated that proper measures were taken in order to maintain the vitality of its program.

2. <u>The District's restriction is content-based and not viewpoint centered.</u>

The next issue is whether the School District's restriction is impermissibly viewpoint centered or whether it is appropriate content-based discrimination. The appellate court erred in finding that the School District's restriction was based on the Church's viewpoint.

> In this section, petitioner is referencing a large number of facts. Petitioner should have cited the record where these facts appear. Even if you already did this in the statement of the case, by now your reader may actually decide that she wants to look into the facts. You do not want to make her have to backtrack and dig through the entire statement of the case to find where these facts appear. In this brief, however, petitioner never gave cites to these facts earlier in the brief, which would make it doubly important to give cites now.
>
> The structure of the argument in section 2 breaks down from a clear IRAC or TREAT to something less, but we still can follow the argument.

It is clear that the School District's restriction is appropriate content-based discrimination because creationism does not relate to a topic of education as detailed in the curriculum guide and creationism does not fulfill the School District's purpose in teaching evolution because it is not based on the scientific method. Further, the restriction is content based in the case at bar because creationism does not relate to the areas covered in "Social Studies" or "Sociology" as these courses are taught in the School District. Finally, the deference the Court must give to school districts in educational matters, the recent holding of this Court regarding what constitutes viewpoint discrimination, and the fact that the School District has allowed the communities religious leaders to post information that relates to topics of education in the past lead to the conclusion that the appellate court clearly erred and the School District's actions were appropriately content-based.

"Although a speaker may be excluded from a nonpublic forum if he wishes to address a topic not encompassed within the purpose of the forum, or if he is not a member of the class of speakers for whose especial benefit the forum was created, the government violates the First Amendment when it denies access to a speaker solely to suppress the point of view he espouses on an otherwise includible subject." Cornelius, 473 U.S. at 806. "Viewpoint restrictions pose the inherent risk that the government seeks to suppress unpopular ideals or information." Id. On the other hand, content-based discrimination is acceptable in a nonpublic forum. Perry Educ. Ass'n, 460 U.S. at 54. Although the Court has never explicitly defined viewpoint discrimination, this analysis necessarily involves discussion of public policy, viewpoint discrimination jurisprudence, and the content of the Church's offered material.

Recently, the Court has taken a narrow view on what constitutes viewpoint discrimination. See Arkansas Educ. Television Comm'n, 118 S.Ct. at 1633 (1998); National Endowment for the Arts v. Finley, 524 U.S. 569 (1988). The Court's decisions in these cases allow the government to restrict more liberally without judicial intervention. See Erwin Chemerinsky, *Court Takes a Narrow View of Viewpoint Discrimination*, Trial, Mar. 1999, at 90.

For example, the Finley Court upheld a federal statute requiring artists receiving grants from the NEA to produce art that meets "general standards of decency and respect for the diverse beliefs and values of the American public," as viewpoint neutral. Finley, 524 U.S. at 576. This decision allows an evaluator to use subjective standards when determining whether access should be granted to a nonpublic forum. See Chemerinsky, supra. Therefore, Finley supports the great deference the Court has afforded school faculty and administrators in making access decisions.

In order for the School District's restriction to be viewpoint centered, this Court must find that creationism is related to a topic in the curriculum. If no such relationship exists, creationism information is properly excludable as a content-based restriction. As mentioned previously, the School District's mission in creating the forum was to provide information that has a direct relationship to a specific topic of education included in the curriculum. (R. at 11.) The court of appeals held that evolution was not a topic covered in the curriculum. (R. at 19.) However, it did find that the "origin of humankind" was a topic in the curriculum. (R. at 19.) This is clearly erroneous.

"Topic" is defined as, "a heading in an outlined argument or exposition; the subject of discourse or of a section of discourse." Merriam Webster's Collegiate Dictionary 1244 (10th ed. 1995). Based on this definition, the proper topic for our purposes is what the School District used as a heading in its curriculum. The words "origin of humankind" have never been printed in the curriculum; nor has evolution ever been included in the curriculum. (R. at 15.) On the other hand, biology has been a part of the School District's curriculum of secondary education. (R. at 15.) Instead of interposing its own definition of "topic," the court of appeals should have given deference to the literal meaning of the word. The Court should give deference to the School District and find that for our purposes, biology is the topic covered in the curriculum. As such, creationism is not one view of a topic as listed in the educational curriculum; and the restriction on the Church's proposal to post information regarding the topic was properly declined as a content-based restriction.

> This is a strong part of petitioner's argument. The difference between creationism and a biology class has to be driven home, and petitioner does a good job of it. Petitioner also makes good use of the Edwards case.
>
> Note that the School District has chosen not to capitalize creationism. This is subtle, but it works in petitioner's favor. Petitioner downgrades creationism from the lofty position of a learned academic theory to a mundane subject. Of course, petitioner matches this by not capitalizing evolution (and not capitalizing other academic subjects of the School District's curriculum). This is the proper approach; you do not want to antagonize any creationism buffs on the court by failing to capitalize only that word, as an intentional slight to the doctrine and its believers. Petitioner goes on to prove its point by showing that evolution is a scientific theory that calls for critical and analytical thinking and the use of the scientific method, while creationism calls for memorization and faith.

Moreover, the School District made a proper content-based restriction in light of its purposes for teaching evolution. Evolution is only part of the biology class offered through the School District. (R. at 15.) The entire course is offered to strengthen and expand students' analytical skills. Biology teaches students to think analytically by introducing them to the scientific method and showing them how scientists in the past used the method to reach a conclusion. See generally Edwards v. Aguillard, 482 U.S. 578 (1987). In other words, through biology, students learn the process of developing a hypothesis based on inferences and observations, testing the hypothesis, making revisions to the hypothesis and re-testing, and eventually drawing a conclusion based on fact. While evolution is discussed, it is not a primary focus of the class and is used overall to teach students how to think for themselves.

In light of the purpose of teaching evolution, it is obvious that creationism is excluded because it was not developed through the scientific method and teaches the students nothing about critical analysis. Id. at 592. Learning creationism requires memorization and regurgitation of material, while biology and evolution forces one to think for one's self both in the laboratory and the outside world. Therefore, the School District denied access to the Church not only because creationism was not listed in the curriculum, but also because, unlike evolution, creationism does not provide an example of the long-standing scientific method. Accordingly, the Court should give deference to the School District as this is an exclusively educational decision and reverse the appellate court's finding that the restriction was based on the Church's views.

> Oops—the authors have started to capitalize all of the curriculum subjects. Inconsistent! They should have stuck to the first plan.

The record further states that the Church sought access to the forum by asking that the creationism information be included under the curriculum topics of "Social Studies" and "Sociology." (R. at 14.) However, they were denied access to the site once against because none of the subtopics of Social Studies and Sociology relate to creationism. The list of subtopics include history, geography, government national and international relations, institutions and movements of social change, the human condition of peoples in America and the world, human interactions, social psychology, mass behavior, gangs and cults, deviant behavior, and analysis of social statistical data. (R. at 14.) However, as the District pointed out to the Church, none of these areas encompass the topics of Theology, Anthropology, religion, or anything related to creationism. (R. at 14.) While the exact areas studied under these subtopics are not contained in the record, this Court should give deference to the District as this decision involves the educational mission in creating the web site and find that creationism does not relate to any of those topics. Accordingly, the appellate court's decision should be reversed as the restriction was based on the Church's content.

Like <u>Finley</u>, the Court should allow the District to use some subjectivity in making a decision that not only affects a program that it has created, but ultimately affects the impressionable students. Further, giving the District deference in this situation allows the Court to place more weight on the reasonableness factor that encompasses many of the policies behind allowing restrictions in nonpublic fora. Clearly, had the District tried to indirectly place creationism in one of the sub-fields of Sociology and Social Studies, more and more people would seek access, the reviewing body would become overloaded, and the success of the program would be jeopardized. The web site would also be jeopardized because of the animosity the School District may have caused in parents and students in the community by allowing such a blatantly non-secular topic to be discussed in an educational forum.

Additionally, the Court should take notice that all of the other non-faculty parties who were allowed to post information on the web site had information that directly involved a topic listed in the curriculum. American History, Art, and Health are all covered in the School District's curriculum. (R. at 12-13.) While the web sites relating to Art and American History clearly relate to those purported topics, the extent to which the "health" sites relate to health is not so clear. However, as discussed below, the District properly allowed inclusion of all of the health pages on the web site. Although the reasons stated below are not grounded in the record, the Court should give deference here as it does in other areas when it applies rational basis analysis. In those cases, if the Court can find a reasonable basis for government action, they uphold the statute even if the reasonable basis was not the actual purpose that the government had in mind when enacting a statute. Here, the Court should apply that same standard and adopt the following reasons why the School District allowed the "health" sites even though the reasons are not founded in the record.

The American Red Cross posted a site relating to health and discussing blood properties, collection, and distribution. (R. at 12.) This not only concerns student personal health by providing them with information as to the contents of blood and the dangers and diseases associated with blood, it also advises students of the importance of blood drives for the promotion of the public health. Additionally, the information regarding student mediation and dispute resolution covers topics relating to mental health and brings the issue to a personal level for the students by informing them of their alternatives to fighting. This information ultimately not only relates to their mental health but also their physical health. (R. at 13.) Finally, the site written by a pastor in the community relates to health by covering the issues of teen pregnancy, drug addiction, gangs, and suicide. This clearly follows the health curriculum as all of these topics relate to physical health of the students, as well as, their mental health and safety.

Based upon the reasonableness of the School District's decision, the content-based nature of the censorship, the lack of viewpoint discrimination, and the fact that this Court has consistently given deference to the government when its purpose is educational and it takes steps to maintain its policy, the censorship of the Church's message regarding creationism is constitutional and this Court should reverse the appellate court's judgment.

> The second sentence under section E must be a typo. Otherwise, it makes little sense. The public is not welcomed to speak in a nonpublic forum. That is why it is called a nonpublic forum. The first two paragraphs of section E are sketchy on the law and make sweeping legal conclusions. That may be one reason why the statements in these paragraphs are completely unsupported by citation to legal authority. Always cite authority for every legal proposition that you state in the argument section.

E. <u>The appellate court erred in finding that the District's web site was not a nonpublic forum.</u>

The appellate court erred in finding that the District's web site is not a nonpublic forum. The general public is welcomed to speak in any nonpublic and public fora. In its holding, the appellate court found that the web site was opened to those of the general public who have information pertaining to a topic of education in the District. However, members of the general public who have information regarding a topic of education in the curriculum are not the general public for purposes of forum analysis. Setting standards on who is to be admitted is a key factor in concluding that a forum is not limited public or public. As such, the District appropriately set limitations on those who could be heard on the web site by requiring a nexus between the speaker's information and the curriculum. This precludes the finding that the web site was opened to the general public.

Furthermore, no speaker ever has to obtain permission from the government in order to gain access to a limited public or public forum. As such, the District's requirement that each applicant obtain the District's permission further supports the fact that the web site is a nonpublic forum. Clearly, the School District's web site cannot be characterized as a public forum or limited public forum. Accordingly, the appellate court erred and this Court should reverse the erroneous conclusion.

> Subsection 1 under section E recovers well from the poor start to this section. It shows clear organization and good use of authority. Subsection 2 is well organized, too. If only the authors had synthesized their authorities.

1. The District's web site is not a public forum.

Public fora are those that "have immemorially been held in trust for the use of the public, and, time out of mind, have been used for purposes of assembly, communicating thoughts between citizens, and discussing public questions." Perry Educ. Ass'n, 460 U.S. at 45 (citing Hague v. Com. for Indus. Org., 307 U.S. 496, 515 (1939)). Public parks and streets are the quintessential public fora. Id. Any content-based restrictions on communication in public fora must survive strict scrutiny. Therefore, the restriction must be narrowly tailored to necessarily achieve a compelling state interest.

In Hazelwood Sch. Dist., 484 U.S. at 260, the Court held that even though students do not shed all of their First Amendment rights at the schoolhouse gate, public schools do not possess all of the characteristics of parks, streets and other traditional public fora. Id. at 267. Furthermore, public schools are only public fora if the administrators "by policy or by practice" welcome the general public for indiscriminate reasons. Id. (citing Perry Educ. Ass'n, 460 U.S. at 37). The Court declared in that the school newspaper at issue in Hazelwood was not a public forum. Id. The Court focused on the school's long-standing policy of keeping the content of the newspaper tied to the school's educational curriculum and retaining ultimate control of the newspaper's content by appointing a teacher to make final decisions. Id. Further, the school had not transformed the paper into a public forum by nonchalance or inaction because the district had not deviated from its long-standing policy. Id.

Like the newspaper in Hazelwood, the web site developed and maintained by the School District in the case at bar is by its very nature not a public forum. Not only has the web site never been likened to public streets and parks, the new and developing nature of the World Wide Web excludes it from this category because of the lack of historical precedence. Furthermore, the school specifically declared that its purpose in creating the site was to further the educational goals of the School District in relation to topics covered in the curriculum, not to freely allow the Internet community to post whatever information it desired. (R. at 11.) Additionally, there is no evidence that the School District has turned the site into a public forum by passively allowing the general public to be heard. Therefore, the web site was not a public forum at its inception; nor has it become a public forum through the School District's passivity.

2. The District's website is not a limited public forum.

The limited public forum is a somewhat less-protected category than the public forum. Perry Educ. Ass'n, 460 U.S. at 45. Although these are not the traditional areas like parks and streets that have been classified as public fora, they are protected from overly prohibitive restrictions because the government has opened them to the general public as a "place for expressive activity." Id. at 45-46. Time, place, and content restrictions are allowed once the state opens the limited forum. Id. at 46. In Perry, the Court held that restrictions in limited public fora must also survive strict scrutiny. Id. Since then, however, the Court has first applied the nonpublic forum test before subjecting the restrictions to strict scrutiny. Rosenberger, 515 U.S. at 829.

In Lamb's Chapel v. Center Moriches Union Free Sch. Dist., 508 U.S. 384 (1993), the Court found a limited public forum where a school district had opened its doors for after-school activities that had "social, civic, and recreational purposes." Id. at 391. Allowing these after-school activities opened the property to the general public because by the terms of the policy almost any activity was allowed after school hours. Id. Therefore, the Court found unconstitutional the school's refusal to allow a group to display a video discussing teenage pregnancy from a religious perspective because a similar video from a non-religious viewpoint would have been admissible. Id.

Comparing the School District's policy in the case at bar with that of the school district's in Lamb's Chapel, it becomes readily apparent that the web site here is not a limited public forum. In Lamb's Chapel, the school's liberal policy of allowing "social, civic or recreational" activity invited the general public onto the school's property. Conversely, the School District here not only restricted the site's participants to those with an educational message, it specifically required that the information be directly related to a topic of education taught in the School District. (R. at 11.) As a result of its policy, the School District maintained control over the web site and forbade the general public from taking part. Therefore, the web site is not a limited public forum.

The District's web site in the case at bar is not a limited public or public forum because the web site is by nature not a long-standing, traditional public forum like parks and streets. Additionally, the School District has created and maintained a strict policy that does not welcome the general public to enlist in the web site. Furthermore, as mentioned previously, the District requires permission to post information on the web site, which is one of the main characteristics of nonpublic fora. For all of these reasons, this Court should reverse the appellate court's erroneous finding and hold that the District's web site is a nonpublic forum.

> We expected this section F below to be part of the argument on the second major issue—avoidance of an Establishment Clause violation as a compelling state interest sufficient to allow prior restraint of speech. We do not think that it belongs here, legally or logically.
>
> The <u>Rosenberger</u> case is twisted by the petitioner in this section; you almost can tell this just from reading the text. Other cases do a better job of spelling out the principle that avoidance of an Establishment Clause violation is a compelling state interest that will justify a prior restraint of religious speech, and they are better than <u>Rosenberger</u>. This section needs work.

F. <u>If the Court finds that the District's web site is a public or limited public forum, restricting access to the Church in order to maintain separation of church and state as mandated by the Establishment Clause satisfies strict scrutiny analysis.</u>

Should the Court find that the School District's restriction is viewpoint centered and/or that the web site is a limited public forum, the Court should still uphold the restriction because it meets strict scrutiny.

As mentioned earlier, the <u>Rosenberger</u> Court used viewpoint, content-based, and reasonableness requirements in striking down a restriction in a limited public forum. <u>Rosenberger</u>, 515 U.S. at 829. However, the Court did not overrule <u>Perry</u> and its progeny that require the Court to use strict scrutiny analysis to any restrictions in a limited public forum. <u>Id.</u> at 842. In fact, the <u>Rosenberger</u> Court, after finding that the restrictions were viewpoint-based, performed a strict scrutiny analysis. <u>Id.</u> Thus, the School District's restrictions may still withstand constitutional challenge, even if found to be viewpoint centered, if the School District can show that the restriction was narrowly tailored to a compelling state interest. <u>Id.</u>

The Court in <u>Rosenberger</u> found that the government would not violate the Establishment Clause if it was forced to give funding to a student-run, religious publication where the university had opened the subsidy program to virtually any group but religious ones. <u>Id.</u> In so finding, the Court held that preventing a violation of the Establishment Clause was not a compelling state interest. <u>Id.</u> The Court's decision in <u>Rosenberger</u>, however, does not preclude the Court from finding here that Establishment Clause issues are a compelling state interest as the finding is largely based on facts unique to each situation. The compelling nature of the Establishment Clause issues can be seen in the section below. Essentially, if the Court finds that posting the Church's information on the web site would be a violation of the Establishment Clause, any restriction under free speech analysis should be upheld as a narrowly tailored means of fulfilling a compelling state interest.

Moreover, the School District also has a compelling state interest in educating its students. As mentioned previously, this Court has stated that educating children is the primary concern of the state. <u>Hazelwood Sch. Dist.</u>, 484 U.S. at 273. Also mentioned previously, the Court owes great deference to any decision that the School District may make when the decision is purely educational. <u>Id.</u> Educating children so that they become knowledgeable, self-serving, productive citizens is one of the most important tasks the federal government has left for the states. The Framers of the Constitution recognized the importance of such a responsibility and thought best to leave the decisions to the local administrators who could see the results of their decisions first-hand. States, granted with the power given them by the Framers of the Constitution, have a compelling state interest in seeing that their children are properly educated. Therefore, the School District can survive strict scrutiny by narrowly tailoring its policy to achieve the state interest.

Accordingly, the Court must also consider whether the School District's restriction was narrowly tailored to achieve the compelling state interest. Here, the School District's restriction was narrowly tailored to fulfill a compelling state interest because it only restricted information that was violative of its policy and of the Establishment Clause. The School District did not mandate the exclusion of every religious entity or person from the web site. Moreover, the policy was narrowly drawn to only exclude those speakers who had nothing to contribute to the education in the District. The School District evaluated every piece of information that was proposed for inclusion on the web site. Only after determining that the information was violative of its policy and of the Establishment Clause did the School District restrict the Church's information.

> The use of transitional words such as "moreover," "accordingly," or "additionally" can be useful in providing your reader with clear directions and cues for where you are headed and how sentences logically relate. However, you want to be careful not to overuse such words or to use them where, as here, no transitional word or phrase is necessary. These paragraphs would flow nicely without such words or phrases. Do not fall into a pattern of using them as a substitute for a proper transitional sentence at the start of paragraphs if you need to flow the discussion in a new direction.

Additionally, one can find further support for the closely tailored nature of the School District's restriction in the fact that this is the only restriction of its kind and that the School District has allowed other religious leaders in the community to contribute to the web site after finding that the information was not religious in nature and that it pertained to primary or secondary education.

The School District's limited actions at issue, taken only when necessary to fulfill its compelling interest of remaining separated from religion and fulfilling its educational policy, is narrowly tailored and survives strict scrutiny analysis. Therefore, even if the

Court should find a limited public forum and/or viewpoint discrimination, the Court should still uphold the restriction as a constitutionally necessary censorship.

As discussed above, we saw the second issue (Roman II) as whether petitioner would have violated the Establishment Clause by hosting respondent's web pages, because if so, petitioner would have a compelling interest sufficient to allow a prior restraint of respondent's speech. This petitioner split up these two concepts, putting the latter issue first, in the previous section (section F) on the forums and the nature of the discrimination. Altogether, the brief probably covers all of these issues, but we think it would have been easier to understand the argument here if both the potential Establishment Clause violation and its status as a compelling interest were to appear together.

Petitioner treats the Establishment Clause jurisprudence as creating three, disjointed, incoherent, and competing tests—a virtual "Cafeteria plan" of constitutional law. Petitioner's plan is to show that they win under any and all of the three tests. This is a novel idea, and perhaps it is born out by the oftentimes contradictory statements of law in First Amendment cases, but in most cases we would counsel petitioner to try harder to synthesize the authorities and come up with a more coherent rule on the issue and apply that rule.

Petitioner does provide the reader with a new backdrop on which to discuss all three of the tests: the primary educational requirements and goals in public schools. This was an absolutely wonderful idea because it allows a common theme to be used in the analysis of all three tests and common scenarios to analogize and apply under all three. The backdrop used is incredibly favorable to petitioner.

II. THE UNITED STATES SUPREME COURT SHOULD REVERSE THE APPELLATE COURT'S DECISION BECAUSE ALLOWING THE CHURCH TO MAINTAIN A WEB SITE HOSTED BY THE SCHOOL DISTRICT VIOLATES THE ESTABLISHMENT CLAUSE UNDER ANY CRITERIA EVER ADOPTED BY THIS COURT.

Violation of the Establishment Clause is determined by application of three complimentary and overlapping tests. Recent Supreme Court decisions have made it unclear which Establishment Clause test is applicable. Therefore, this brief will apply each of the three tests. The first test is the coercion test. If the activity has a coercive effect on the students then it violates the Constitution under the coercion test. <u>Lee v. Weisman</u>, 505 U.S. 577 (1992). The oldest, most developed test is the three-part <u>Lemon</u> test, under which a school district's practice is unconstitutional if it lacks a secular purpose, if its primary effect either advances or inhibits religion, or if it excessively entangles government with religion. <u>Lemon v. Kurtzman</u>, 403 U.S. 602 (1971). A government action violates the Establishment Clause if it fails to satisfy any of the three prongs of the <u>Lemon</u> test. <u>Edwards v. Aguillard</u>, 482 U.S. 578 (1987). Under the third and final test, the endorsement test, a school district's practice is unconstitutional when it conveys a message that religion is favored, preferred, or promoted over other beliefs. <u>County of Allegheny v. ACLU</u>, 492 U.S. 573 (1989).

The Court has an historic awareness of "the sensitive relationship between government and religion and the education of our children." <u>Grand Rapids v. Ball</u>, 473 U.S. 373, 383 (1985). The importance of maintaining strict neutrality toward religion within the public education system is a thread that weaves together all modern Establishment Clause decisions of this Court addressing the issue of religion and public schools. Any analysis of the constitutionality of the Church's posting a web site hosted by the School District must begin with recognition of the special nature of the public school setting.

The web site is an integral part of the School District's educational mission. Official sponsorship of the Church's religious web pages would entangle the religious belief and the School District's governmental authority, provide the Church with an official platform to proselytize to students, and subvert the secular purpose of the web server. The School District's sponsorship of the Church's web pages creates an impermissible endorsement of a particular religious belief.

A. <u>Sponsorship of the Church's religious web pages by the School District amounts to government coercion to participate and believe in a religious doctrine.</u>

The First Amendment, at a minimum, guarantees that government may not directly or indirectly coerce anyone to support or participate in religious exercises or its beliefs. <u>Lee v. Weisman</u>, 505 U.S. 577 (1992). Even subtle coercive pressure by a governmental body violates the Establishment Clause. <u>Id.</u> at 591.

The Court has recognized that there are heightened concerns with protecting students from subtle coercive pressure in the public school setting. <u>See</u> <u>School Dist. of Abington v. Schempp</u>, 374 U.S. 203 (1963); <u>Edwards v. Aguillard</u>, 482 U.S. 578 (1987); <u>Board of Educ. of Westside Community Sch. v. Mergens</u>, 496 U.S. 226 (1990). In a school context, what might otherwise be a reasonable request that the nonbeliever respect religious practice, may appear to the nonbeliever or dissenter to be an attempt to employ the machinery of the State to enforce a religious orthodoxy. <u>Weisman</u>, 505 U.S. at 592. Public schools should be allowed to prevent activities that might appear to advance religion out of their concern for impressionable youth. <u>Wallace v. Jaffree</u>, 472 U.S. 38, 46 (1985).

The specific question addressed in <u>Weisman</u> was whether the school district's practice of inviting local clergy to offer invocation and benedictions as part of high school graduation ceremonies was a violation of the Establishment Clause. 505 U.S. at 592. Although no student was required to attend the graduation ceremonies, the Court noted that students feel psychological pressure to attend such important events in their lives. <u>Id.</u> The school district's supervision and control of graduation ceremonies places public pressure and peer pressure on attending students to observe the religious portion of the ceremony. <u>Id.</u> at 593. This subtle and indirect pressure amounts to a violation of the Establishment Clause. <u>Id.</u>

Recently a school district attempted to subvert the holding in <u>Weisman</u> by delegating decision-making authority to graduating senior students who would determine if religious messages would be delivered at graduation. <u>Adler v. Duval County Sch. Bd.</u>, 174 F.3d 1236 (11th Cir. 1999). The school board did not succeed in dissociating itself from proselytizing prayer at a school-controlled graduation ceremony. <u>Id.</u> at 1248. Similar to <u>Weisman</u>, the policy coerced objecting students to participate in the religious observation and thus amounted to coerced participation. <u>Id.</u>

In the case at bar, the design and purpose of the School District's web server is coercive. The School District encourages teachers to create their own web pages pertaining to the subject they teach. (R. at 11.) The pages sponsored by the School District are to provide resources and links that provide additional educational material not otherwise available to students pertaining to subjects taught. (R. at 11.) In <u>Weisman</u>, the Court found that subtle psychological pressure by the school district to attend graduation ceremonies was sufficient to fail the coercion test. Here, not only does subtle psychological pressure exist to use the web server, but the School District directly coerces teachers to utilize the web server for educational purposes. Requiring the School District to maintain the Church's religious web pages will force the teachers to refrain from encouraging students to use the web server in order to prevent direct coercion of participation in a particular religious belief.

The School District periodically reviews all web sites accepted for sponsorship to ensure compatibility with the curriculum. (R. at 5.) To be accepted, the applicant must submit a written proposal describing the contents of the proposed web pages for review. (R. at 11.) In <u>Weisman</u> and <u>Adler</u>, it was precisely the schools supervision and control over the ceremonies that created the coercive behavior violative of the Establishment Clause. Here, the School District is also supervising and controlling the web site. Allowing the Church to post its message on the web site would create enough supervision and control over the Church's information to create a violation of the Establishment Clause.

Like the graduation ceremonies in <u>Weisman</u> and <u>Adler</u>, a student may choose not to participate in a particular web site. However, an icon present on the School District's home page creates a subtle coercive pressure that a particular religious belief is being promoted. If a student chooses not to visit the School District's web site altogether because of the church's message, then the student must forsake access to other academic opportunities and information.

The School District's web site was created to promote information about areas of study taught in the schools, and all participating web pages are controlled and supervised by the School District. (R. at 11.) Just as the religious benediction at graduation in <u>Weisman</u> created a subtle coercive pressure, in the case at bar the prominent display of the Church's icon on the home page acts as a coercive mechanism. The various links to other web pages are meant to entice students to partake of the particular learning experience available at each site. This is not only subtle coercive activity, but the very nature of the web site creates direct coercion due to the School District's control over the information therein contained.

The fact that the Church's site is listed on the School District's home page constitutes a coercive pressure that this religious belief is a part of the District's curricula and must be believed or learned. Allowing the Church's religious web pages to be sponsored by the School District creates an impermissible inference that the State is endorsing a particular religious orthodoxy. Therefore, the School District would inevitably violate the Establishment Clause by coercing students to participate in the Church's religious message.

> In section B, we would have liked to have seen a definite IRAC or TREAT here concerning the <u>Lemon</u> test and its three elements. We think it would have improved this section. Instead, we are dropped into the middle of a good discussion of "secular purpose" as if we would know that this is the first element under <u>Lemon</u>. The reader probably can stay afloat in this section, but only through her own efforts, not through careful drafting by the authors.

B. <u>The School District's sponsorship of the Church's religious web pages violates the Establishment Clause because it subverts the secular purpose, creates the primary effect of endorsement, and results in excessive entanglement of the government and religion.</u>

1. <u>Creationism is a religious belief and as such would subvert the secular purpose of the School District's web server.</u>

The theory of creation is a religious belief and is not a scientifically based theory. <u>Edwards</u>, 482 U.S at 593. Local policies and state laws promoting the teaching of creationism in public schools are unconstitutional because they violate the secular purpose requirement of the <u>Lemon</u> test. <u>See Edwards</u>, 482 U.S. at 586; <u>Epperson v. Arkansas</u>, 393 U.S. 97, 106 (1968). The First Amendment does not permit the state to require that teaching and learning be tailored to the dogma of a religious sect. <u>Epperson</u>, 393 U.S. at 106.

In <u>Edwards</u>, a state law requiring that "creation science" be taught in conjunction with evolution was struck down as unconstitutional. 482 U.S. at 594. The Court refused to entertain the argument that creationism is a legitimate scientific theory. <u>Id.</u> at 593. Thus, any attempts by the Church to portray 'creation science' as anything more than a religious belief must be rejected based on Epperson and Edwards.

In a recent California case, a local school board initiated an advertising sponsorship program to benefit the high school baseball team. DiLoreto v. Board of Educ., 87 Cal. Rptr. 2d 791 (Cal. Ct. App. 1999). One of the advertisers sued when the school district refused to allow the advertiser to display the Ten Commandments in his ad. Id. Applying the Lemon test, the court determined the original purpose of the fund-raiser to be secular and concluded that the secular purpose would be subverted if the board of education were to begin accepting signs of a religious nature. Id. at 276.

Like the board of education in DiLoreto, the School District's web server and home page have a secular purpose as required under the Lemon test. The purpose of the web server was to promote information about the areas of study currently being taught throughout the District. (R. at 11.) If sponsored by the School District, the Church's religious web pages would subvert the secular purpose of the web server and Internet provider service, resulting in a violation of the Establishment Clause.

The School District's purpose in establishing the web server is secular. Creationism, the topic of the Church's web pages, is a religious belief. Sponsoring of the Church's web pages by the School District would violate the Establishment Clause because the secular purpose would be subverted.

> Sub-sections 2 and 3 below are drafted as sub-TREATs or sub-IRACs of the elements of the Lemon test, and as such, they are much easier to read and understand. We are not dropped headfirst into the discussion as we were in the previous sub-section. The analogies used in the Application sections of sections 2 and 3 are very strong.

2. Sponsorship of the Church's religious web pages will have the primary effect of improper endorsement of a religious orthodoxy.

The second prong of the Lemon test is whether compelling the School District to sponsor the Church's religious web pages will have the primary effect of either advancing or inhibiting religion. Lemon, 403 U.S. at 612. This is similar to analysis under the endorsement test in which a government practice may not aid a religion or favor one religion over another. County of Allegheny, 492 U.S. at 576. The appellate court erred because a reasonable person would believe the School District is endorsing the Church's religious belief.

Under the endorsement test, the Establishment Clause is violated where government operation of a forum has the effect of endorsing religion. County of Allegheny, 492 U.S. at 577. The test is whether a reasonable observer would be likely to perceive the activity as an endorsement by the government of a particular religious belief. County of Allegheny, 492 U.S. at 631. Even where the government does not intend nor actively encourage the appearance of endorsement, the Establishment Clause is violated if a reasonable person might perceive such.

> Use of a dissenting opinion always is a risky venture. Since Justice O'Connor is such an Establishment Clause maven, it makes more sense to cite one of her dissents than some of the other judges, but it still is weak authority.

Capital Square Review and Advisory Bd. v. Pinette, 515 U.S. 753, 777 (1995) (O'Conner, J., dissenting).

> This section really could use some explanatory synthesis.[6] Not only does it walk the reader through several cases, one after the other, it also applies each case to the facts as if each case were a law unto itself. Lesson: SYNTHESIZE!

In <u>Capital Square</u>, this Court determined that a display of the Ku Klux Klan's cross on public property historically designated an open forum would not lead a reasonable person to believe that the state was endorsing a religious doctrine. <u>Id.</u> at 765. The reasonable person would be aware that the property has been designated as an open forum and thus not conclude that the state was sponsoring the Ku Klux Klan's cross. <u>Id.</u>

In the case at bar, the School District's web site is a new innovation. Established case law regarding the Internet has not been well developed. The Internet has not been historically designated as a public forum. Thus, unlike the historically designated public forum property in <u>Capital Square</u>, the School District's web site is not a public or a limited public forum.

In <u>Lamb's Chapel v. Center Moriches Union Free Sch. Dist.</u>, this Court found that permitting a religious group to use school facilities to show religious films did not constitute a violation of the Establishment Clause. 508 U.S. 384, 395 (1993). The Court found dispositive the fact that the films would not be shown during school hours and were in no way sponsored by the school. <u>Id.</u> at 394. Similarly, in <u>Mergens</u>, allowing a religious student group to form and meet on school property during non-instructional time was found not to be a violation of the Establishment Clause. 496 U.S. at 250. The Court found the following facts dispositive: (1) the school policy strictly forbade school officials' participation in the student groups; (2) meetings had to take place during non-instructional time; and (3) no classroom activities were involved. Thus, the Court concluded that there was no danger that a student might believe the school was endorsing the religious group's belief. <u>Id.</u> at 228.

Applying <u>Lamb's Chapel</u> to the case at bar clearly shows that the reasonable person would conclude that the School District is endorsing a religious belief. Unlike the school facilities in <u>Lamb's Chapel</u>, the Internet and the School District's home page is accessible during instructional time and available for teachers to use in the classrooms as an instructional tool. Also, unlike the religious films in <u>Lamb's Chapel</u>, the School District is spon-

---

[6] <u>See</u> Appendix to this volume.

soring organizations whose links are displayed on the home page. A reasonable person or student would be led to believe that the School District is endorsing the religious doctrine of creationism. In <u>Mergens</u>, allowing religious organizations access to school property was not endorsement only because no school officials participated, meetings were during non-instructional times, and no classroom activity was involved. Unlike <u>Mergens</u>, in the case at bar, the School District is encouraging participation by faculty and the web server is not only accessible during instructional times but involves classroom activities and topics. (R. at 11.) A student could easily believe that the School District is endorsing the Church's religious doctrine.

In <u>Church of Latter Day Saints v. Amos</u>, 483 U.S. 327 (1987), employees filed a religious discrimination suit against the Church of Latter Day Saints for terminating their employment because they were not members of the church. This Court upheld a state law exempting religious organizations from Title VII employment discrimination charges. <u>Id.</u> at 335. The Court held that to be unconstitutional the government entity itself must be advancing religion through its own activities. <u>Id.</u> at 337. The State was merely exempting religious organizations, thus allowing churches to base hiring decisions on the religion of its employees. <u>Id.</u>

In <u>Amos</u>, the government was merely acting passively to prevent its interference or entanglement with religious organizations. Whereas, in the case at bar, the School District's own affirmative activity established the web server and home page. Unlike <u>Amos</u>, the School District would be advancing religion through its own affirmative activity if it sponsors the Church's web pages.

The Internet's accessibility during instructional time, its lack of historical precedent or analogy as a public forum, and the School District's sponsoring of the web pages lead a reasonable person to conclude that the School District is endorsing the Church's religious belief. The School District's affirmative activity of establishing the web server and encouraging faculty involvement and classroom activities through the home page would amount to an improper endorsement of a religious doctrine if the Church's web pages are sponsored by the School District.

3. <u>**Sponsoring of the Church's religious web pages by the School District is an entanglement of government and religion and is a violation of the Establishment Clause.**</u>

* * *

> The Supreme Court is not in the business of awarding summary judgment to litigants, so petitioner's prayer for relief is inappropriate. We simply would ask the Court to reverse the 14th Circuit and order that the order and judgment of the District Court be reinstated.

<u>CONCLUSION</u>

For the reasons stated above, the decision of the United States Court of Appeals for the Fourteenth Circuit should be reversed, and this Court should grant summary judgment to School District as there are no genuine issues as to any material fact and School District is entitled to judgment as a matter of law.

Sample Brief No. 2:

Student Brief of Petitioner
in the moot court case:

Metropolitan School Dist. of Gotham
v.
Branch Louisian of the United Church of
Christ the Savior

IN THE SUPREME COURT OF THE UNITED STATES

March Term 2000

———————————

NO. 00-100

METROPOLITAN SCHOOL DISTRICT OF GOTHAM,
STATE OF NEW KENT

Petitioner,

v.

BRANCH LOUISIAN OF THE UNITED CHURCH OF
CHRIST THE SAVIOR,

Respondent.

On Writ of Certiorari to the United States Court of Appeals for the Fourteenth Circuit

---

BRIEF OF RESPONDENT

Student 1 – Issue 1

Student 2 – Issue 2

These Questions Presented would be acceptable if this brief were drafted for an intermediate level appellate court such as the United States Court of Appeals. The questions are phrased in a very neutral manner and give sufficient information about the case to inform the court of the issues. However, this brief was to be filed in a court of last resort, the United States Supreme Court, so the questions presented should have been drafted as a general issue of federal or constitutional law with broad application to persons in the same class as the petitioner and respondent. Petitioner had the right idea about this in sample brief #1 above. In addition, we do not like the use of the term "Fourteenth Circuit Appellate Court." The appropriate term is "United States Court of Appeals for the Fourteenth Circuit."

QUESTIONS PRESENTED

1. Whether the Fourteenth Circuit Appellate Court erred in holding that Petitioner violated the First Amendment by denying Respondent access to its web site solely on the basis of the religious content of its proposal?

2. Whether the Fourteenth Circuit Appellate Court erred in holding that Petitioner's conduct in initiating a web site, open for general use to all members of the community, created a limited public forum for the purpose of the right to free speech under the First Amendment?

3. Whether the Fourteenth Circuit Appellate Court erred in holding that Petitioner's denial of Respondent's proposal, based upon its religious content, is in violation of the First Amendment regardless of the type of forum because the denial constitutes viewpoint discrimination?

4. Whether the Fourteenth Circuit Appellate Court erred in holding that the hosting of Respondent's creationism web pages on Petitioner's web site did not violate the Establishment Clause?

Underlining all of the entries in the Argument section of the Table of Contents clutters up this section and makes it hard to read. We see no advantage to doing it this way, and a lot of disadvantages. Eliminate the underlining (unless the local rule specifically requires it).

TABLE OF CONTENTS

This is the strangest Table of Authorities we have seen in quite some time. The authors have abandoned the "flush right with dot leaders" way of formatting in favor of this strange design. The authors also failed to separate the table into different categories of authorities, and they failed to cite the opinions of the lower courts in the instant case.

TABLE OF AUTHORITIES

* * *

> This Decisions Below section is adequate. The problem did not give citations for either case, and yet, we are not sure where respondent came up with these versions of the case names. Compare this section with the example we gave in this chapter, above.

DECISIONS BELOW

The decision of the court of appeals finding for the Church is reported as <u>Branch of the United Church of Christ the Savior v. Metropolitan School District of Gotham</u> (14th Cir. 1999).

The decision of the district court finding for the School District is reported as <u>Branch of the United Church of Christ the Savior v. Metropolitan School District of Gotham</u> (C.D.N.K. 1999).

Aside from the title, this Constitutional Provisions section is nicely done. The respondent is quite correct to cite the Fourteenth Amendment—it is what makes the First Amendment apply directly to the states. We quibble with the title because readers would think this means "public policy," and they would be confused because they will expect this section to be about constitutional, statutory, and administrative law, not public policy. The respondent meant to refer to the School District's web site policy, but few readers would pick up on this.

CONSTITUTIONAL PROVISIONS AND POLICY

The First Amendment to the United States Constitution provides as follows:

> Congress shall make no law respecting an establishment of religion, or prohibiting the free exercise thereof; or abridging the freedom of speech, or of the press; or the right of the people peaceably to assemble, and to petition the Government for a redress of grievances.

U.S. Const. amend. I.

The first section of the Fourteenth Amendment to the United States Constitution provides as follows:

> All persons born or naturalized in the United States, and subject to the jurisdiction thereof, are citizens of the United States and of the State wherein they reside. No State shall make or enforce any law which shall abridge the privileges or immunities of citizens of the United States; nor shall any State deprive any person of life, liberty, or property, without due process of law; nor deny to any person within its jurisdiction the equal protection of the laws.

U.S. Const. amend. XIV, § 1.

The policy of the Metropolitan School District pertaining to the hosting of web pages on its web site is set forth in the Record of Transcript, R-11.

> The Statement of the Case is very well done. The most important facts are highlighted and respondent's case is furthered, but it still does not read as argumentative and divisive. This is good drafting. Note that citations to the record should be in the form of Record 3 not (R. at 3).

STATEMENT OF THE CASE

Petitioner School District ("Petitioner") is a political subdivision of the State of New Kent. (Record of Transcript [R.] at 10). For the last 150 years, Petitioner has operated all of the public schools in Gotham, New Kent. (R. at 10-11). Petitioner brings this case to the United States Supreme Court on appeal from a decision of the United States Court of Appeals for the Fourteenth Circuit. This Appellant Court found for Respondent, Branch Louisian of the United Church of Christ the Savior ("Respondent"), a religious organization, registered and operating in the State of New Kent. Respondent, a proponent of Judeo-Christian doctrine of Creationism, conducts religious education and worship services each week in a church located in Gotham, New Kent. (R. at 4, 10).

Petitioner is an Internet service provider and hosts web sites from sources outside of the School District system. (R. at 4). Petitioner began operating as an Internet service provider in June 1998. (R. at 11). Petitioner manages the Internet server and operates a web site for the purpose of hosting other web pages on its site. (R. at 11). The home page site reads:

> This site was created by the [School District] for the purpose of promoting information about the areas of study that are currently being taught in the schools of the [School District]. The pages we hope to sponsor will not only highlight topics of interest in the curriculum of the [School District], but also provide resources and information and links to other sources of information that may not be available in the textbooks and other materials provided to our students in the courses taught in the [School District]. In this spirit of expanding the educational potential of this site, we invite faculty of the [School District] and other educational institutions in Gotham, members of the community, and other organizations to propose web pages for inclusion in the site, as long as the subject matter of each page is tied to topic of education in this [School District]." (R. at 11).

All persons seeking inclusion in the site must submit a written proposal to Petitioner for review describing in detail the title and contents of the proposal. (R. at 11). Petitioner will also review the web site periodically to insure the pages posted on the site meet the requirement being "tied to a topic of education" in the School District's curriculum and are created in such a way "as to uphold the high academic standards of the School District." (R. at 11).

On March 5, 1999, Respondent made a proposal for Petitioner to host its web site on the subject of "Theological Anthropology" the title of which was "Creationism: Past and Present." (R. at 13). The proposal was further described as an examination of the doctrine

> Respondent needs to proofread the word "form" and change it to "from" in several places here. This is one of many examples we could offer of why running a "spell check" in your word processing program is not the same as proofreading. Spell check would not catch the "form" error because that is the correct spelling—albeit of a word other than the one that the author intended.

of Creationism form the Book of Genesis and a comparison and contrasting of the "purportedly scientific" doctrines of Evolution and Natural Selection. (R. at 13). The contents of the proposal were described as a multimedia presentation of commentary form scholars and educators regarding the doctrine of Creationism and five centuries of religious artwork regarding the doctrine of Creationism. (R. at 13). On March 7, 1999, Petitioner denied Respondent's proposal stating that, "its subject matter is not directly related to a topic of education in the district." (R. at 14). On March 11, 1999, Respondent resubmitted its proposal but changed the description of the subject matter to "Social Studies" and "Sociology". (R. at 14) On March 12, 1999, Petitioner once again denied Respondent's proposal on the same grounds as stated before. (R. at 14).

The topics of "Social Studies" and "Sociology" are topics listed under the School District's curriculum guide, however, they do not encompass the topics of Theology, Anthropology, or anything relating to Creationism. (R. at 14). On the other hand, the curriculum guide does include the Darwinian theories of Evolution and Natural Selection, which are currently taught in Biology courses in the School District and have been taught in the District since 1922. (R. at 14-15). Prior to Respondent's proposal, Petitioner had never rejected a proposed web page form a member of the community. (R. at 15). A variety of web pages created by entities having no affiliation with the School District are currently being sponsored on Petitioner's web site. (R. at 12). These entities include, but are not limited to, The Council for Alternative Dispute Resolution with a site on health that features an interview with its founder and director, Reverend Carla Boulevardier, Pastor of St. Peter's AME Church of Gotham, and The Greater Gotham Youth League with a site on health that features an article on suicide written by Fr. John Berrigan, a Roman Catholic Priest of the Gotham Cathedral Church. (R. at 13).

Respondent has made several additional oral requests to have its web pages posted on the Petitioner's web site. Each request was denied. In the hope of exercising it's constitutional right to free speech, Respondent filed this lawsuit against the School District on May 15, 1999.

> The Summary of Argument is very good, but once again, we would like to see a few citations to respondent's best legal authorities. What if the justices only read your summary of the argument before your oral argument? Would you not want them to get in their minds the names of the four or five cases that really hold up your argument? Otherwise, this section is very effective. One note: in the first sentence, we would not say "not so new." This sounds a little too informal. We would say "not new."

SUMMARY OF ARGUMENT

Although the constitutional issues raised pertaining to the right of Free Speech under the First Amendment and the requirement that there be a separation of church and state under the Establishment Clause are not so new, the issue of how these two vital constitutional components are addressed as they pertain to the internet is novel. The judgment of the Fourteenth Circuit Appellate Court should be affirmed because the Metropolitan School District's discriminatory exclusion of the Branch Louisian Church's proposed web pages, solely on the basis of religious content and ideology is in violation of the First Amendment's free speech clause and against public policy. The School District has created a public forum by initiating a web site open to all members of the community and other organizations for the purpose of promoting information regarding current curriculum and providing alternative sources of information that may not be available in the curriculum. Therefore, the School District's conduct in devising the web site for the sole purpose of expressive activities has created a designated public forum. Even if the District's web site is not found to be a pure designated public forum it must qualify as the subset, a limited public forum. Based upon finding the web site a limited public forum, the District's denial of the Respondent's web page solely based upon the religious content therein, constitutes content-based discrimination in violation of the First Amendment's Free Speech Clause. The School District's content-based exclusion of Respondent's web page from its public forum triggers a strict scrutiny analysis. The District offers no compelling state interest to justify content-based discrimination, therefore, the strict scrutiny standard cannot be met. Regardless of the nature of the forum, however, the District's conduct of excluding Respondent's web page based upon Respondent's religious ideology constitutes viewpoint discrimination which is a per se violation of the First Amendment's Free Speech Clause.

The Establishment Clause does not bar the Metropolitan School District from hosting a creationism web page as part of a curriculum focused web site. The inclusion of Respondent's web pages by the Metropolitan School District will be found constitutional because it meets every test articulated by this Court to determine violations of the Establishment Clause. The hosting of Respondent's web pages by the Metropolitan School District respects rather than offends the School District's neutrality towards religion as required by the Establishment Clause. The hosting of Respondent's web pages by the Metropolitan School District comports with the three-pronged <u>Lemon</u> test and, therefore, does not violate the Establishment Clause. The purpose of the District's web site is secular, its primary effect is not the advancement of religion, and the inclusion of the creationism web pages does not create an excessive government entanglement with religion. By including Respondent's web pages on the Metropolitan School District's web site, Petitioners are not intending to endorse nor are they perceived to endorse a particular religious belief. Finally, the District's inclusion in its web site of Respondent's web pages create a policy of religious coercion. Based upon Respondent's arguments, the Appellate Court's ruling should be upheld.

Respondent is in the enviable position of having a United States Court of Appeals agree with it, and it makes the most of that here by wrapping itself in the flag in the third and fourth paragraphs in this section. It is fine to try this once in a while in a brief, but it is even better to leave out the flag waving and let the court salute the flag when they write up the opinion agreeing with your legal position, after you have bowled them over with your argument.

This entire section from Roman I to the first section heading (A) is devoted to setting the mood (the background) for the brief. It is not an IRAC or TREAT of any of the main issues, nor is it a roadmap or "umbrella" section. But we like the mood it creates. The stage is set up nicely for the rest of the argument in this section. The initial issues are dealt with smoothly and concisely in this section. It flows nicely right to the first major contested issue in section A. We also like the thesis heading here. Very good work, respondent.

ARGUMENT

I. THE JUDGMENT OF THE APPELLATE COURT SHOULD BE AFFIRMED BECAUSE PETITIONER'S DISCRIMINATORY EXCLUSION OF RESPONDENT'S PROPOSED WEB PAGES SOLELY ON THE BASIS OF RELIGIOUS CONTENT AND IDEOLOGY IS IN VIOLATION OF THE FIRST AMENDMENT'S FREE SPEECH CLAUSE AND AGAINST PUBLIC POLICY.

The Appellate Court made a proper decision, in support of public policy, holding that Petitioner's denial of Respondent's web pages violates the Free Speech Clause of the First Amendment. (R. at 19). The Appellate Court accurately found that Petitioner created a public forum by opening its web site to any member of the community wishing to be heard on educational topics that are tied to the School District's curriculum. Moreover, Petitioner's denial was solely based upon Respondent's religious viewpoint; an act that is presumed unconstitutional. (R. at 19).

The First Amendment provides, in part, that "Congress shall make no law...abridging the freedom of speech." U.S. Const. amend. I. The First Amendment's guarantee of free speech is applicable to restrictions enacted by state and local governments, including public school boards, by way of the Due Process Clause of the 14th Amendment. East High Gay/Straight Alliance v. Board of Edu. of Salt Lake City Sch. Dist., No.CIV.A.2:98-CV-193J, 1999 WL 1103365, at *1 (D. Utah Oct. 6, 1999).

The guarantee of free speech is a vital fundamental right to citizens of the United States upon which our democratic society is built. In <u>Ferlauto v. Hamsher</u>, 88 Cal.Rptr.2d 843 (Cal. Ct. App. 1999). California court held that the "First Amendment's free speech guarantee safeguards a freedom, which is the matrix, and the indispensable condition of nearly every other form of freedom." <u>Id.</u> at 848.

This enumerated freedom, which is the matrix of our great democracy, has begun a recent evolution with the inception of the Internet and cyberspace. This evolution has crept into the realm of authority of the United States Supreme Court, which has set precedent for how this issue must be resolved. In <u>Reno v. ACLU</u>, 521 U.S. 844 (1997), this Court recently addressed the nature of the Internet and held that it most closely resembles books and newspapers and is therefore deserving of the utmost freedom from content-based restrictions. <u>Id.</u> at 885.

> We like the interjection of the Internet into the discussion. It makes this argument punchier. And look at what case respondent uses to set out the standard of review: <u>New York Times v. Sullivan</u>. Classy! Even though <u>New York Times v. Sullivan</u> is not a religion case, it is effective to use a monumental First Amendment case like this for the standard of review because it reminds the court of the importance of the issues and policies in First Amendment litigation.

In reviewing a constitutional claim, this Court will apply a de novo review of the issue. <u>New York Times Co. v. Sullivan</u>, 376 U.S. 254, 285 (1964). However, when a fundamental right, such as free speech is at issue and the State restriction is content-based, the restriction is subject to strict scrutiny. <u>Widmar v. Vincent</u>, 454 U.S. 263, 263 (1981). Under a strict scrutiny analysis, the restriction is found unconstitutional unless the State can prove that the restriction advances a compelling state interest by the least restrictive means available. <u>Bernal v. Fainter</u>, 467 U.S. 216, 219 (1984). Petitioner is unable to meet this heavy burden.

A private religious expression is entitled to the same protection under the Free Speech Clause as secular private expression. <u>Capitol Square Review and Advisory Board v. Pinette</u>, 515 U.S. 753, 760 (1995). The State may not discriminate against speakers, by denying them the ability to speak based upon their religious viewpoint. Although the State may not endorse or assist religious activities in a way that violates the Establishment Clause, the State is limited by the First Amendment's Freedom of Speech Clause when it denies benefits to, or imposes burdens on religious speakers. <u>Id.</u> at 760. Petitioner's decision to deny Respondent's proposal based upon its religious content and ideology constitutes an egregious form of discrimination in violation of the First Amendment. The Appellate Court carefully reviewed this vital issue and made a fair and proper ruling in support of Respondent's fundamental right of free speech. Therefore, the decision by the Appellate Court should be affirmed.

> Here we see the first use of the IRAC or TREAT format. The first five sentences are definite legal statements, but no citation to authority is given. This is a loose style of which we do not approve. ***Always cite authority for legal propositions.*** Do not reserve your citation(s) until the end of the paragraph, as respondent did here. The reader cannot tell if the single cite (here to <u>Cornelius</u>) is supposed to support all six sentences or just the sixth sentence.

A. <u>Petitioner has created a public forum by initiating a web site open to all members of the community and other organizations for the purpose of promoting information regarding current curriculum and providing alternative sources of information that may not be available in the curriculum.</u>

In analyzing a regulation of speech under the First Amendment, the nature of the forum involved must be determined because the extent to which the State may restrict access depends upon the type of forum. There are two general categories, public and nonpublic forums. Within the public forum category, however, there are subsets, traditional and designated public forums. The designated public forum category also has a subset, limited public forums. Access to a public forum may only be restricted when necessary to serve a compelling state interest and the exclusion is narrowly drawn to achieve that interest. Access to a nonpublic forum may be limited as to subject matter and speaker identity as long as the distinctions drawn are reasonable in light of the purpose served by the forum. <u>Cornelius v. NAACP</u>, 473 U.S. 788, 807 (1985). This Court first recognized and classified three types of forums in <u>Perry Educ. Ass'n v. Perry Local Educators Ass'n</u>, 460 U.S. 37, 45-46 (1983).

The Court in <u>Perry</u> described a traditional public forum as a place that has a history of being devoted to assembly, debate, and communication between citizens. <u>Id.</u> at 45. Parks, sidewalks, plazas, and streets define a traditional public forum. The rights of the State to limit expressive activity in this type of forum are sharply circumscribed and subject to strict scrutiny. Further, content-based discrimination is only allowed when the State can prove that the regulation is necessary to serve a compelling state interest and the regulation is narrowly drawn to achieve that interest. <u>Id</u>.

> We said this was the first attempt at IRAC or TREAT, and the attempt was short-lived. Perhaps this is a long, extended Rule section.

The second type of public forum described in <u>Perry</u> is a designated public forum which is public property not traditionally open to assembly and debate, but which the State has intentionally designated for the purpose of expressive activity. <u>Id</u>. The State is bound by the same standards as a traditional public forum, and strict scrutiny will be applied in reviewing a State regulation. <u>Id.</u> at 46. Therefore, content-based discrimination is prohibited except when it is necessary to serve a compelling state interest and the regulation is narrowly drawn to achieve that end. 460 U.S. at 46. Unlike a traditional forum, however, the State is not required to keep this forum open indefinitely.

A designated public forum may be created for a limited purpose, such as use by certain groups, <u>e.g.</u>, <u>Widmar v. Vincent</u>, 454 U.S. 263 (1981) or for the discussion of certain subjects, <u>e.g.</u>, <u>Madison Joint Sch. Dist. v. Wisconsin Pub. Employment Relations Comm'n</u> 429 U.S. 167 (1976). This subset of a designated public forum is categorized as a "limited public forum". Within a limited public forum, the State must still show that the restriction is "narrowly drawn to effectuate a compelling state interest". <u>Perry</u>, 460 U.S. at 46. However, the State may also confine the forum's use to the limited purposes for which it is created as long as the regulation is reasonable and not an effort to suppress a speaker's viewpoint. <u>Rosenberger v. Rector of Univ. of Virginia</u> 515 U.S. 819, 829 (1995).

The third type of forum described in <u>Perry</u> is a non-public forum, which is public property that is not by tradition or designation a forum for public communication. 460 U.S. at 46. The State may preserve this forum for its intended purpose, expressive activities, or otherwise, as long as the regulation on speech is reasonable and not an effort to suppress a speaker's viewpoint. 460 U.S. at 46. However, the State has the right to make restrictions to access based upon subject matter and speaker's identity. <u>Id.</u>

> Sub-section 1 appears to be an Explanation and Application section if you view section A as one long Rule section. This appears to be what respondent intended. After considering this structure, we can see that these sections show a decent amount of organization, and respondent just had a complicated Rule to get through.
>
> Sub-section 1 is nicely drafted. We especially like the last paragraph of this sub-section that analogizes the Internet to a traditional public forum—the quintessential public forum—in the words carefully chosen by respondent. Strong stuff.

1. <u>Petitioner's conduct in devising the web site for the sole purpose of expressive activities created a designated public forum.</u>

As stated earlier, the court in <u>Perry</u> addressed the distinctions between the three forums. While the Court did not offer a precise test to determine between a designated public forum and a nonpublic forum, the Court did define the designated public forum as being created by the State for the allocated purpose of expressive activity. 460 U.S. at 45. The nonpublic forum has no such allocation. In <u>Perry</u>, the school district's internal mail system was placed in the third category, nonpublic forum. 460 U.S. at 46. This Court found that the intended function of the mail system was only to facilitate internal communication of school matters and therefore not open to the general public. <u>Id.</u> at 46. This

Court further surmised that if the school district's policy was to open the mail system for indiscriminate use by the general public, then it could be considered a designated public forum of the second category. Id.

Petitioner's open access policy clearly meets this "indiscriminate use by the general public" set out in Perry, 460 U.S. at 47. Petitioner created the web site for the sole purpose of sharing ideas related to the curriculum among members in the community. The web site is open to faculty, other educational institutions, members of the community, and other organizations who wish to be heard. This policy is far from the restricted policy of the internal mail system in Perry, which provides a paradigm of a nonpublic forum. Unlike Perry, Petitioner opened its web site to "members of the community, and other organizations" who wished to be heard. (R. at 11). This policy of open access more closely resembles the forum created in Widmar, where a state university made its facilities generally available to all registered student groups. This court held that the university, having opened the forum for use by all registered student groups, created a public forum. 454 U.S. at 263. The forum in the instant case is even more expansive, as it is not open only for use by students or school employees but also for all members of the community, other educational institutions in the community, and other organizations.

Further, this Court held that public school facilities become designated public forums when "school authorities have, by policy or practice, opened those facilities for indiscriminate use by the general public, or by some segment of the public, such as student organizations." Hazelwood Sch. Dist. v. Kuhlmeier, 484 U.S. 260, 267 (1988). In the instant case, both "policy and practice" compel the conclusion that the web site is a designated public forum. Petitioner states that its policy invites "faculty of the School district, any other educational institution in Gotham, members of the community, and other organizations" to propose web pages for inclusion in the site. (R. at 11). Through its policy, Petitioner has created a forum "generally open to the public" as stated in Hazelwood Sch.Dist. Id. at 267. It is difficult to imagine a more expansive use policy than one explicitly open to "members of the community and other organizations" as expounded in the instant case.

It has been the consistent practice of Petitioner to allow a wide diversity of groups access to the web site. Numerous organizations from the League of Women Voters' to the American Red Cross, to articles written from heads' of churches for the Council for Alternative Dispute Resolution and The Greater Gotham Youth League, have been allowed to post web pages on Petitioner's web site. (R. at 12-13). In fact, no other web pages have been previously denied. (R. at 15). This is a classic example of "indiscriminate use by the general public" as this court called for in Perry and Hazelwood School Dist. 460 U.S. at 47; 484 U.S. at 267.

The very nature of the forum as a web site argues in favor of defining it as a public forum. While the Internet's modernistic nature precludes it from being a traditional public forum it does share many of the same characteristics. Similar to traditional forums, the Internet is devoted to assembly, debate, and expressive communication. Arguably, the Internet is even more dedicated to expressive activities than traditional forums. Traditional forums, such as parks and plazas were not created solely for the purpose of public discourse. One may visit a park for the purpose of relaxing, recreation, or simply to observe and enjoy the serene setting. The Internet, on the other hand, was created for the sole purpose of communication. The "information super-highway" is slowly replacing traditional public forums as an outlet for citizens to express and exchange ideas. As this medium of expression evolves so must our legal definitions.

> Subsection 2 is a good alternative argument. It clearly is secondary to the first position, but it is strongly supported by authority and convincing in its own right. We think this section would be vastly superior and much more readable if the respondent had drafted it in an IRAC or TREAT format. This free flow of legal principles and application of same is a little confusing and hard to puzzle through. It needs some paragraph breaks, at the very least.

2. <u>Even if Petitioner's web site is not found to be a pure designated public forum it must qualify as the subset, a limited public forum.</u>

The Appellate Court found Petitioner's web site to be a limited public forum as defined in <u>Rosenberger</u> and <u>Perry</u>. (R. at 18). The Court stated that the web site is far from a limited forum where only certain groups or certain subjects may be accommodated to preserve the essential purpose of the forum. Rather, this Court found it to be a limited public forum in that it is open to anyone wishing to be heard as long as the material has some relation to the subjects found in the School Districts curriculum. (R. at 18). It may be argued that the web site is not a "pure" public forum, but rather a "limited" public forum. It is limited in that the material presented on the proposed web pages must be "tied to a topic of education in the School District". (R. at 11). Under a limited public forum, reasonable exclusions made in order to preserve the forum's purpose may be allowed. <u>Perry</u>, 460 U.S. at 46. Petitioner claims that Respondent's web pages were rejected because they were not related to a subject found in the School District's curriculum. (R at 14). Therefore, Respondent is not being discriminated against but being rightfully barred based on the purpose of the forum. However, Petitioner's claim is erroneous. The School District's curriculum includes the creation of humankind as viewed through Darwin's theory of evolution and natural selection. (R. at 15). Respondent's web pages are clearly "tied to a topic of education in the school district" as required by Petitioner's policy. Creationism is merely another theory of the origin of humankind.

Furthermore, Petitioner states the exclusion was necessary to preserve the purpose of the forum it created. Petitioner's purpose explicitly set out on its home web page, states:

> [T]his site was created for the purpose of promoting information about the areas of study currently being taught in the schools. The pages we hope to sponsor will not only highlight topics of interest in the curriculum, but also provide resources and

information and links to other sources of information that may not be available in the textbooks and other materials provided to our students in the courses taught. (R. at 11).

Respondent's web pages clearly further the web site's purpose by providing readers with an alternative theory of the creation of humankind, which is not found within the materials taught. Consequently, Petitioner's claim that Respondent's web pages are rightfully barred based on the restrictions of the forum is meritless because the web pages are directly "tied to" theories of the origin of humankind which is included in the District's curriculum and the web pages clearly further the purpose for which the web site was created.

> Section B repeats the abuse of IRAC and TREAT. We suppose section B might be interpreted as one long Rule section, but there is an Application section right in the middle, so respondent is not building an IRAC or TREAT structure. We understand the points that are being made here, but we attribute that to our familiarity with the law. An IRAC or TREAT structure would help even the uninformed reader to keep up with the issues.

B. Petitioner's denial of Respondent's web pages solely based upon the religious content therein, constitutes content-based discrimination in violation of the First Amendment's Free Speech Clause.

By creating a public forum open to all members of the community, Petitioner is barred by the First Amendment from refusing to accommodate Respondent based upon the content of speech. Rosenberger, 515 U.S. at 819. Content-based discrimination is based upon the ideas or information contained in speech. If a restriction occurs because the State objects to the communicative impact of the expression, the State is not being content-neutral. This type of content-based regulation directly suppresses the communicative impact of the speech and therefore must be analyzed under the rigid review of strict scrutiny. Id.

In the instant case, Petitioner's refusal to allow Respondent access to its web site was obvious content discrimination based upon Respondent's religious ideology of creationism. Petitioner has created a public forum by opening up its web site to all members of the community, or organizations who wish to be heard on educational topics that have a connection to the subjects taught in the School District. Concerned with endorsing the separation of church and state, Petitioner objected to the communicative impact of Respondent's web pages because they were based on the religious theory of creationism.

If Respondent wished to address the same topic, the origin of humankind, with the focus on the scientific theory of evolution rather than the religious theory of creationism, then Petitioner would probably have no objection to Respondent's web pages. However, because the web pages include a religious content, Petitioner has denied Respondent's proposal. This is blatant and unconstitutional State content-discrimination of private religious speech.

> Now, in sub-section 1, we see a return to a true IRAC or TREAT structure, and this section absolutely shines with clarity.

1. Petitioner's content-based exclusion of Respondent's web pages from its public forum triggers a strict scrutiny test, which Petitioner cannot meet.

When a fundamental right, such as free speech is at issue and the State restriction is content-based, this Court has subjected the regulation to strict scrutiny. <u>Widmar</u>, 454 U.S. at 276. Under a strict scrutiny analysis, the restriction is found unconstitutional unless the State can prove (1) its regulation is necessary to serve a compelling state interest, and (2) that it is narrowly drawn to achieve that interest. <u>Bernal</u>, 467 U.S. at 219. With a fundamental right at issue, such as free speech, few regulations can meet this stringent test.

The strict scrutiny analysis applied to content-based discrimination is based upon policy which was expounded by Justice Holmes in <u>Abrams v. United States</u>, 250 U.S. 616 (1919). Justice Holmes stated that there must be "free trade in ideas" and truth will become accepted through the "competition of the market." <u>Id.</u> at 630.

The instant case is analogous to <u>Widmar</u>, where members of a registered religious student organization brought a First Amendment action challenging their exclusion from using university facilities. This Court held that the state university created a public forum by making its facilities available to all registered student organizations, and having done so the university could not discriminate among student groups on the basis of religious content. 454 U.S. at 263. This Court applied the strict scrutiny test and found that the university's discrimination violated the First Amendment. <u>Id.</u> at 268.

Respondent can be analogized to the religious student organization in <u>Widmar</u>. Both Respondent and the student organization are within a class for which the public forum was generally available. Here, the forum is open to all members of the community, and other organizations. In <u>Widmar</u> the forum was open to all registered student organizations. Both Respondent and <u>Widmar</u> were denied access to a public forum based upon religious content of their speech. In accordance with <u>Widmar</u>, this Court should apply strict scrutiny, a constitutional standard that Petitioner cannot satisfy, and find that Petitioner's denial of access to Respondent based on religious content of the proposed web pages constitutes content discrimination which is unconstitutional under the First Amendment's Free Speech Clause.

> Sub-section 2 is another true IRAC or TREAT, and it is powerful and persuasive as a result.

2. <u>Petitioner offers no compelling state interest to justify content-discrimination; hence, Petitioner fails to satisfy strict scrutiny.</u>

A State may exclude a speaker from a public forum without violating the First Amendment when the exclusion is necessary to serve a compelling state interest and is narrowly drawn to achieve that interest. <u>Arkansas Educ. Television Communication v. Forbes</u>, 523 U.S. 666 (1998). Petitioner has offered no legitimate compelling state interest for excluding Respondent. Petitioner merely argues that the exclusion was necessary to preserve the separation of church and state. While separation of church and state is a compelling state interest on its face, it is ensured under the Establishment Clause and is not violated in the instant case.

The university in <u>Widmar</u> also claimed separation of church and state as a compelling interest allowing content-based discrimination. This Court addressed the claim and held that the State's interest in achieving greater separation of church than is already ensured under the Establishment Clause and is limited by the Free Speech Clause is not sufficiently "compelling" to justify content-based discrimination against religious speech. <u>Widmar,</u> 454 U.S. at 277. Furthermore, this Court found that the forum created by the State was open to a broad spectrum of groups and would provide only an incidental benefit to religion. <u>Id.</u> at 274. In accordance with its prior finding, this Court held that "an open forum in a public university does not confer any imprimatur of state approval on religious sects or practices." <u>Id.</u> Therefore, separation of church cannot be a compelling state interest justifying content-based discrimination.

> We have not been dwelling on respondent's failure to use explanatory synthesis[7] in these explanation sections. We hope you are starting to notice this for yourself. If respondent synthesized <u>Lamb's Chapel</u> and <u>Widmar</u>, Respondent could derive principles from these two cases concerning how the rule is to be interpreted and applied, and apply these principles to the facts in the application section. Instead, it must apply the cases to the facts as if the cases themselves were rules.

In <u>Lamb's Chapel v. Center Moriches Union Free School District</u>, 508 U.S. 384 (1993), this Court also rejected the Establishment Clause defense as a compelling state interest. This Court reasoned that the school property, although found to be a nonpublic forum, was open to a wide variety of uses. Moreover, this Court stated that the school district was not directly sponsoring the religious group's activities, and "any benefit to the church would have been no more than incidental." <u>Id.</u> at 395.

---

[7] Explanatory synthesis is discussed in the Appendix to this volume.

Quite obviously, the factors considered by this Court in <u>Lamb's Chapel</u> and <u>Widmar</u> exist here. Petitioner created a public forum open to all members in the community for the purpose of expressing alternative ideas and avenues of materials related to current school curriculum. Petitioner would not be endorsing Respondent's religious ideology on the creation of humankind, it merely would be providing an open public forum allowing alternative viewpoints, whether the viewpoints be religious or secular. Under these circumstances, as in <u>Widmar</u> and <u>Lamb's Chapel</u>, there would be no realistic danger that viewers of the web site would think that Petitioner is endorsing Respondent's religious ideology. Permitting Respondent's web page onto the public web site is not an establishment of religion under any of the Establishment Clause tests articulated by this Court and further illustrated in section two of this argument.

Petitioner offers no compelling state interest to trump the content-based discrimination it imposed on Respondent, therefore, there is no need to look into whether the regulation was narrowly draw to achieve that interest. Unable to prove a compelling state interest, Petitioner has violated Respondent's First Amendment constitutional right to Free Speech.

> Section C flip-flops the explanation and application sections, but it otherwise is nicely drafted.

C. <u>Regardless of the nature of the forum, Petitioner's conduct of excluding Respondent's web pages based upon Respondent's religious ideology constitutes viewpoint discrimination which is a per se violation of the First Amendment's Free Speech Clause.</u>

Regardless of the type of forum, restrictions that seek to suppress a speaker's viewpoint are per se unconstitutional in violation of the First Amendment's Free Speech Clause. <u>Arkansas Educ. Television Comm'n</u>, 523 U.S. at 676, <u>Rosenberger</u>, 523 U.S. at 827. Viewpoint discrimination is an egregious subset of content-based discrimination. <u>Id.</u> at 827. While content-based discrimination may be justified by a compelling state interest narrowly drawn to achieve its ends, viewpoint discrimination can never be justified.

As previously stated, Petitioner claims that its web site is a nonpublic forum and the restriction is based not on the content of the web pages or on Respondent's viewpoint, but rather on the religious subject matter of the web pages and this type of subject-matter discrimination is reasonable in light of a nonpublic forum. (R. at 6). Even if the web site is found to be a nonpublic forum, Petitioner's defense of subject-matter discrimination is not supported by the facts because Petitioner has authorized other web pages that contain religious subject matter. For instance, The Council for Alternative Dispute Resolution has posted a site on "health" which includes an article with founder, Reverend Carla Boulevardier, Pastor of St. Peter's AME Church of Gotham. The Greater Gotham Youth League and North Gotham General Hospital also has a site on "health" including an article written by Fr. John Berrigan, Roman Catholic priest of Gotham Cathedral Church.

(R. at 13). Petitioner cannot successfully claim that Respondent is being denied access based on the religious subject matter of the web pages when Petitioner has granted access to web sites that focus on articles written by heads of church.

Moreover, Respondent's perspective on creationism provides a specific premise, a perspective, and a standpoint from which the subject of the origin of humankind may be discussed and considered. The prohibited perspective, creationism, not the general subject matter, origin of humankind, resulted in the refusal to allow Respondent access to Petitioner's public web site, because the subject of the proposed web pages was within the approved category of subjects taught in the School District's curriculum. In arguing subject matter discrimination, Petitioner is merely providing a façade for viewpoint discrimination. Petitioner is not placing the entire topic of the origin of humankind off-limits as it is covered in the School District's curriculum. Instead Petitioner is rejecting Respondent's web pages based upon Respondent's religious ideology of the origin of humankind.

In Lamb's Chapel, this Court found the school district's denial of a church's request to exhibit a film dealing with family and child-rearing issues, to constitute viewpoint discrimination. 508 U.S. at 393. Moreover, this Court found that while opening the school facilities for after school use created a non-public forum, the restriction placed on the church's film was not viewpoint neutral and therefore a violation of the First Amendment. Id. at 393. Furthermore, this Court rationalized its holding by finding that the subject matter of child rearing would ordinarily be permitted; however, it was not permitted in this instance because it was presented from a religious perspective. Id. This rationale was in accordance with this Court's previous finding in Cornelius which held that:

> [A]lthough a speaker may be excluded form a nonpublic forum if he wishes to address topics not encompassed within the purpose of the forum or if he is a member of a class of speakers for whose benefit the forum was created, the government violates the First Amendment when it denies access to speaker solely to suppress point of view he espouses on otherwise includible subject.

473 U.S. at 805.

As established herein, Respondent's proposal encompasses a topic within the purpose of the forum, Respondent is a member of the class of speakers for which the forum was created, and Petitioner has not designated religion as an impermissible subject matter. Therefore, Petitioner's conduct in excluding Respondent's proposal constitutes viewpoint-discrimination, which blatantly violates the First Amendment's Free Speech Clause.

> Respondent starts off issue II with another big background and introduction section. This one sounds a little more like an umbrella or roadmap section. It is a good section, and worth doing if you have the space. Because respondent knows that it is drafting an introduction and background section, it left out a lot of the citations to legal authority. Once again, we do not approve of this tactic. You certainly do not have to explain each case you cite, but *always* give a cite to support your sweeping legal statements.

II. THE JUDGMENT OF THE APPELLATE COURT OF THE FOURTEENTH CIRCUIT SHOULD BE AFFIRMED BECAUSE THE INCLUSION OF RESPONDENT'S WEB PAGES IN THE METROPOLITAN SCHOOL DISTRICT'S WEB SITE DOES NOT VIOLATE THE ESTABLISHMENT CLAUSE.

The Metropolitan School District claims that hosting the Branch Louisian's creationism web pages violates the Establishment Clause. Creationism is defined as "a doctrine or theory holding that matter, the various forms of life, and the world were created by God out of nothing and usually in the way described in Genesis."[8] There is no constitutional provision that prohibits a public school from exposing its students to religion. The Establishment Clause was intended to protect against "sponsorship, financial support, and active involvement of the sovereign in religious activity." Lemon v. Kurtzman, 403 U.S. 602, 612 (1971). Chief Justice Burger stated in writing the opinion for this Court in Lynch v. Donnelly, that the Constitution does not "require complete separation of church and state; it affirmatively mandates accommodation, not merely tolerance, of all religions, and forbids hostility toward any." Lynch v. Donnelly, 465 U.S. 668, 673 (1984). It is upon this foundation that the argument for the inclusion of Respondent's web pages is made. The School District cannot claim to violate the Establishment Clause solely on the basis that creationism is tied to religion. The web site, sponsored by the School District, is comparable to a school's library. Both contain educational materials to enhance the students' appreciation and interest in the areas taught at the schools. The inclusion of religious materials in a school library, in and of itself, has never been found by this Court to violate the Establishment Clause. Neither can a web page with religious content hosted by a public school on its web site, one among many other web pages pertaining to the school's curriculum, be found in violation of the Establishment Clause.

---

[8] Merriam-Webster Dictionary, Inc. (2000).

> Perhaps respondent still thinks it is in an introduction mode, but it is killing the reader with these endless paragraphs. Break them up—please! It also needs to adopt an IRAC or TREAT structure. It is easier for the uninformed reader to follow that kind of rule-based logical syllogism than this "stream of legal principles" format, followed by intermittent application of the principles.
>
> Compared to the sample brief above, it is much more apparent in this brief that respondent has switched authors from the first major issue to the second; one student did Section I and a different student did Section II. Just the length of the paragraphs tells us this much. It should not be so obvious. Moot Court teams should take the time to edit and meld separately authored work together so that the final product is seamless. There is no question that respondent #2 is a good legal writer, but he or she can improve things if he or she constantly tries to employ IRAC or TREAT, and breaks up these monster paragraphs into proper chunks.

The hosting of Respondent's web pages by the Metropolitan School District will be found constitutional because it meets every test used by this Court to determine violations of the Establishment Clause. First, the hosting of the creationism web page by the School District does not offend the requirement that the school remain neutral with regards to religion. Neutrality towards religion is not synonymous with exclusion or absence of religion. Second, the hosting of the creationism web page meets the three-prong test articulated by this Court in Lemon, 403 U.S. at 612-613. The purpose, primary effect, and entanglement issues all support the finding that including Respondent's web pages in the School District's web site would not violate the Establishment Clause. Lemon has its critics, however, and other tests have been recommended by this Court to determine whether the Establishment Clause has been violated.[9] Finally, it will be argued, therefore, that the endorsement and the coercion tests both support a finding that a violation of the Establishment Clause would not occur with the inclusion of a creationism web page on the School District's web site. The hosting of a creationism web page on a School District's web site presents unique issues regarding the Establishment Clause and because of that this case cannot solely be determined by the decisions in other Establishment Clause cases. Chief Justice Burger stated that the line of separation between church and state "is a blurred, indistinct, and variable barrier depending on all the circumstances of a particular

---

[9] See Justice Scalia's concurring opinion in Lamb's Chapel when criticizing the Court's usage of the Lemon test in deciding the case, he states that Lemon is "like some ghoul in a late-night horror movie that repeatedly sits up in its grave and shuffles abroad, after being repeatedly killed and buried." Lamb's Chapel v. Center Moriches Union Free School District, 508 U.S. 384, 398 (1993).

relationship." <u>Lemon</u>, 403 U.S. at 614. The circumstances of the this particular relation-ship support a finding that the School District would not violate the Establishment Clause by including Respondent's web pages on its web site.

A. The hosting of Respondent's web pages by the Metropolitan School District respects rather than offends the School District's neutrality towards religion.

"Neutrality, in both form and effect, is one hallmark of the Establishment Clause." <u>Rosenberger</u>, 515 U.S. at 846 (O'Connor concurring). The inclusion of Respondent's web pages ensures a policy of neutrality toward religion. The School District, however, has chosen to exclude the creationism web page under the guise that it would create an imper-missible relationship between church and state in violation of the Establishment Clause. The web page pertaining to creationism is directly related to the topic of the origin of humankind. The fact that the School District has opened its web site to others and has shut its door to Respondent's web pages "demonstrates not neutrality but hostility toward religion." <u>Board of Educ. of Westside Community Sch. (Dist.566) v. Mergens</u>, 496 U.S. 226, 248 (1990). The School District's contention that the inclusion of the creationism web page would violate their web site policy is warrantless. Like <u>Lamb's Chapel</u>, the basis for the exclusion is due to this particular religious belief. They have opened up a forum under a policy that states that for a web site to be hosted it must "directly relate to a topic" taught in the schools. Evolution is a scientific theory regarding the origin of humankind. Creationism is a theory with a religious foundation regarding the origin of humankind. The fact that Darwin's theory of evolution is taught and has been taught for over 70 years in the School District supports the inclusion of a creationism web page. The School District's policy is focused on curriculum based and enhancing web pages. This policy as stated, therefore, is neutral towards religious web pages which are related to an area in the District's curriculum. The Bible, when integrated into a public school's curriculum, may be consti-tutionally used as an appropriate study of history, civilization, ethics, or comparative reli-gion. <u>Stone v. Graham</u>, 449 U.S. 39, 42 (1980). Creationism is related to an area covered in the curriculum, the origin of humankind, whether that topic is taught under biology or anthropology. "A significant factor in upholding government programs in the face of at-tack under the establishment of religion clause is such programs' neutrality towards reli-gion." <u>Rosenberger</u>, 515 U.S. at 839. Because the School District's policy maintains its neutrality even when hosting a creationism web page, refusing the web pages in order to prevent a violation of the Establishment Clause is an invalid argument.

The School District's web site is neutral in design. As in <u>Rosenberger</u>, there is no sug-gestion that the School District created its web site with the intention of advancing reli-gion or that they "adopted some ingenious device with the purpose of aiding a religious cause." <u>Id.</u> at 840. A government program that is neutral in design cannot use the Estab-lishment Clause to justify "a refusal to extend free speech rights to religious speakers." <u>Id.</u> at 839. The Establishment Clause was intended to protect against "sponsorship, financial support, and active involvement of the sovereign in religious activity." <u>Lemon</u>, 403 US at 612. In the present case, the School District's inclusion of the creationism web pages does not offend any of those objectives. The Branch Louisian Church sponsors the web pages. Any cost to the School District of hosting the web pages is incidental to the Church because the Church is already paying for the web pages and the School District is solely supplying a link to those pages. The School District has little involvement with the web pages it hosts with the exception of creating the link and following their own written policy. The School District would not be actively involved in any manner in the Branch Louisian web pages any more than the District is involved with the other web pages it hosts. The District policy is a neutral curriculum based policy. The sponsorship by the Branch Louisian Church, the lack of financial support, and the limited involvement in the creationism web pages all support the argument that the inclusion of the creationism web pages would maintain the District's neutrality towards religion and would, therefore, not violate the Establishment Clause.

> Sections B(1) and (2) are trying to get into IRAC or TREAT form but ultimately cannot because there is no break in the paragraphs. The semblance of a Rule and Explanation is present, and a little Application here and there. It is just plain difficult to get through these sections because you do not know when to come up for air. IRAC or TREAT structures are much easier to read and comprehend.

B. <u>The hosting of Respondent's web pages by the Metropolitan School District comports with the three-pronged Lemon test and, therefore, does not violate the Establishment Clause.</u>

1. <u>The purpose of the Metropolitan School District's web site is secular.</u>

Under the <u>Lemon</u> test if one prong fails, the statute or policy will be found to be in violation of the Establishment Clause. The first prong of the <u>Lemon</u> test looks at the government's purpose in implementing the policy under question. In order for a policy to be found constitutional, the government's purpose for implementing the policy must be found to have been secular rather than religious. The purpose of the School District's web site, as stated on the home page, was to both promote and supplement those areas of study currently being taught in the District's primary and secondary schools. (R-11). The purpose, therefore, is secular in nature. The purpose prong, however, has been the most effective in finding statutes requiring the exclusion of the teaching of evolution or the inclusion of creationism in violation of the Establishment Clause. Two cases pertaining to the teaching of creationism in public schools have gone before this Court, and both were found to violate the Establishment Clause. <u>Epperson v. Arkansas</u>, 393 U.S. 97 (1968); <u>Edwards v. Aguillar</u>, 482 U.S. 578 (1987). In both <u>Epperson</u> and <u>Edwards</u> this Court found a lack of secular purpose in the enacted statutes. This Court found in <u>Epperson</u> that the purpose of the Arkansas statute was to prevent evolution from being taught in the schools because it was contrary to creationism. "It is clear that fundamentalist sectarian conviction was and is the law's reason for existence." <u>Id.</u> at 108. In <u>Edwards</u>, Justice Brennan stated that the Court would not defer to a State's articulated secular purpose when it obviously does not have such a purpose and in fact is really a "sham". Both cases, however, are easily distinguishable from the present creationism case due to the fact that the statutes enacted did not have a secular purpose. The School District in the present case had only a secular purpose when it implemented its web site. Justice Fortas wrote in <u>Epperson</u> that "while [the] study of religions and of the Bible from a literary and historic viewpoint, presented objectively as part of a secular program of education, need not collide with the First Amendment's prohibition, the State may not adopt programs or practices in its public schools or colleges which 'aid or oppose' any religion." <u>Epperson</u>, 393 U.S. at 104. <u>Epperson</u> and <u>Edwards</u> do not purport to prohibit the teaching of creationism in public schools. It is only when creationism has been required to be taught or evolution prohibited from being taught for religious reasons that the First Amendment is violated. It is the actions and intentions of the government, not the church, that the Establishment Clause restricts. In the case at hand, the School District's policy is secular, and the inclusion of a creationism web pages does not change that purpose from a secular one to a religious one.

2. <u>The primary effect of including the creationism web pages is not the advancement of religion.</u>

The second prong of the Lemon test looks at whether the questioned policy has a primary effect of advancing religion. The primary effect of the School District hosting a creationism web page on its web site is to achieve its secular purpose of enhancing and supplementing the District's curriculum, not the advancement of religion. The study of creationism can certainly be part of a secular curriculum without having the primary effect of advancing a religious ideology. Requiring the teaching of creationism would almost certainly be found to violate the Establishment Clause, however, allowing a greater understanding of the origin of humankind through an exposure to evolution, creationism, and other theories is a valid secular purpose without the effect of advancing any particular belief. It is certainly possible to present information that contains religious content in a public school as an objective part of a secular education program and not violate the Establishment Clause. <u>School Dist. of Abington Township v. Schempp</u>, 374 US 203, 225 (1963). In fact, this Court stated that, "it might well be said that one's education is not complete without a study of comparative religion or the history of religion and its relationship to the advancement of civilization. . ." <u>Id.</u> The inclusion of a creationism web page as part of the School District's web site does not have the effect of advancing religion but rather has the effect of enhancing an objective secular educational program.

> Did we mention that these paragraphs are too long? To save you from the abuse of these paragraphs, we are going to skip to the Conclusion.

* * *

CONCLUSION

> A long winded Conclusion almost never is seen in trial court and appellate briefs. By the time a judge lurches to the conclusion at the end of a 30+ page brief, she is ready to be done, and does not want to read two more pages of a clever rehash of the same arguments she has been pouring over for the last hour or two. Especially if the two pages of conclusion are one long paragraph. Instead, state your prayer for relief and sign off.

As Chief Justice Burger stated in Lynch v. Donnelly, "in our modern, complex society, whose traditions and constitutional underpinnings rest on and encourage diversity and pluralism in all areas, an absolutist approach in applying the Establishment Clause is simplistic and has been uniformly rejected by the Court." Lynch, 465 U.S. at 678. This case and questions involved cannot be dealt with simplistically. In the case before us, the School District elected to sponsor a web site for the purpose of hosting web pages that would "highlight topics of interest in the curriculum" and provide "information that may not be available in the textbooks" (R-11). Petitioner chose to initiate this web site for the purpose of expressive activities and to promote alternative information tied to the School District's curriculum. By opening this web site to all members of the community, Petitioner created a designated public forum. In doing so, Petitioner must abide by the rules of free speech in accordance with this type of forum. While Petitioner chooses to keep this forum open for general use to all members of the community, it must not discriminate against Respondent's religious viewpoint or the religious content of the proposed web pages. This type of content-based discrimination clearly violates Respondent's First Amendment right to free speech. Ergo, the Appellate Court correctly found that Petitioner's discriminatory behavior in denying Respondent's proposed web pages, violated Respondent's constitutional right to Free Speech.

The School District attempts to justify this First Amendment discriminatory behavior by arguing that it was compelled to do so in order to avoid violating the Establishment Clause. However, the Establishment Clause is not implicated in this case. Every Establishment Clause test articulated by this Court finds the separation of church and state well in place. Allowing the School District to prohibit the Branch Louisian's web pages only does an injustice to the children attending the District's schools. "The classroom is peculiarly the marketplace of ideas. The Nation's future depends upon leaders trained through wide exposure to that robust exchange of ideas which discovers truth out of a multitude of tongues, [rather] than through any kind of authoritative selection." Keyishian v. Board of Regents, 385 U.S. 589, 603 (1967). The School District is failing the children, education, and the Constitution by refusing to host Respondent's web pages and casting a "pall of orthodoxy over the classrooms." Id. The School District's argument loses on both issues. Respondent, therefore, requests that this Court affirm the Appellate Court's decision.

Sample Brief No. 3:

Brief of Petitioners in the
U.S. Supreme Court case:

Capitol Square Review and Advisory Board
v.
Pinette

515 U.S. 753 (1995)

Docket No. 94-780

SUPREME COURT OF THE UNITED STATES

October Term, 1994

CAPITOL SQUARE REVIEW AND ADVISORY BOARD, RONALD T. KELLER, DANIEL SHELLENBARGER, AND OHIO SENATOR RICHARD T. FINAN,

Petitioners,

— *against*—

VINCENT J. PINETTE, DONNIE A. CARR, AND KNIGHTS OF THE KU KLUX KLAN,

Respondents.

ON WRIT OF CERTIORARI TO THE UNITED STATES COURT OF APPEALS FOR THE SIXTH CIRCUIT

BRIEF OF PETITIONERS

Question Presented: The question here is adequate, but somewhat densely-worded. It does not flow very well. We would drop the references to the Latin cross and the Ohio statehouse—they are too case-specific for a Supreme Court QP. We also do not like the "such as a . . ." phrasing. Our version would read:

Whether the unattended display on government property of a purely religious symbol, directly in front of a seat of government, violates the establishment clause, even if such display is sponsored by a private group in a public forum?

We understand the desire to get your facts up front as soon as possible, but the bare rendition of the legal issue seems engaging enough to get the reader to look further.

QUESTION PRESENTED FOR REVIEW

Whether the unattended display on government property of a purely religious symbol, such as a large, Latin cross, directly in front of a seat of government, such as the Ohio statehouse, violates the establishment clause, even if such display is sponsored by a private group in a public forum?

> We cut out the **TABLE OF CONTENTS** and **TABLE OF AUTHORITIES** to save space. You have seen enough examples of these by now. What follows is the "Opinions Below" section. It is a necessary section in some briefs (check local rules), and this one is adequate.

OPINIONS BELOW

The opinion of the Court of Appeals for the Sixth Circuit is reported at 30 F.3d 676 (6th Cir. 1994) and is reprinted in the Appendix to the Petition for Writ of Certiorari ("App.") at A1-A12. The Sixth Circuit's opinion affirmed the December 21, 1993 Order and Opinion of the United States District Court for the Southern District of Ohio. The District court's opinion is reported at 844 F. Supp. 1182 (S.D. Ohio 1993) and is reprinted at App. A13-A26. The Report and Recommendation of the Administrative Hearing Examiner, adopted in full by the Capitol Square Review and Advisory Board, is reprinted at App. A27-A37.

The unreported opinion of the Sixth Circuit denying Petitioners' request for an emergency stay of the district court's injunction pending appeal is reprinted at App. A40-A42. The in-chambers opinion of Justice Stevens, sitting as Circuit Justice, denying Petitioners' request for an emergency stay of the district court's injunction pending appeal is reported at 114 S. Ct. 626 (Stevens, Circuit Justice 1993) and is reprinted at App. A38-A39.

> The Statement of Jurisdiction is another required section. This one is adequate.

STATEMENT OF JURISDICTION OF THE COURT

The decision of the Court of Appeals for the Sixth Circuit was entered on July 25, 1994. See App. A1. The petition for writ of certiorari was filed on October 24, 1994, and was granted on January 13, 1995. This Court has jurisdiction pursuant to 28 U.S.C. § 1254(1).

> This Constitutional Provisions section is fine. Note that none of these required sections should be argumentative. The Question Presented in this brief was a little too argumentative, but these other required sections are properly neutral.

CONSTITUTIONAL PROVISIONS INVOLVED

Constitution of the United States, Amendment I.

Congress shall make no law respecting an establishment of religion, or prohibiting the free exercise thereof; or abridging the freedom of speech, or of the press, or the right of the people peaceably to assemble, and to petition the Government for a redress of grievances.

Constitution of the United States, Amendment XIV, Section 1.

All persons born or naturalized in the United States and subject to the jurisdiction thereof, are citizens of the United States and of the State wherein they reside. No State shall make or enforce any law which shall abridge the privileges or immunities of citizens of the United States; nor shall any State deprive any person of life, liberty, or property, without due process of law; nor deny to any person within its jurisdiction the equal protection of the laws.

In the Statement of the Case, the brief writers take the opportunity to bolster their case in an otherwise non-argumentative section by using compelling language and by the selection of the facts they choose to emphasize. They quickly bring out in section 1 the respondents' overtly religious message that is intended to go along with the cross. The petitioners continually refer to the cross as "large," even though we have not yet heard the actual dimensions of the cross. This is a neat trick, because it allows the readers to envision whatever they might come up with when they hear "large cross"—the readers might get a mental picture of a fifty foot high, shining white cross with spotlights on it. Allowing the readers' minds to run amok helps the petitioners in this instance.

This section shows the proper Supreme Court combination of a statement of facts and proceedings below section, all under the single heading of "Statement of the Case." This statement of the case is a great deal longer than that of any of the preceding briefs. We would venture to say that it is far too long to keep the readers' attention, but it is well drafted.

STATEMENT OF THE CASE

1. Respondents in this action, the Knights of the Ku Klux Klan (Ohio Realm) and two of their officers, brought this suit originally against the Capitol Square Review and Advisory Board, its executive director, spokesperson, and chairperson. Joint Appendix (J.A. 22-23). The lawsuit sought in effect to compel the State of Ohio to allow Respondents to erect a large, unattended Latin cross directly in front of the Ohio Statehouse during the Christmas season, between December 8, 1993 and December 24, 1993. (J.A. 26). Respondents openly acknowledged that their purpose in seeking to erect the display at this location was to erect "a symbol for our Lord, Jesus Christ" (J.A. 173) in furtherance of their more general purpose to "establish a Christian government in America." (J.A. 144-147).

Section 2 of the statement of the case does a nice job of setting out how visible the state house is – details here paint a clear and compelling picture of the scene. Petitioners downplay the other religious items they have allowed to be displayed in the square; there is no point in dwelling on these bad facts.

2. The Capitol Square is owned by the State of Ohio and located in downtown Columbus. It is the site of Ohio's state capitol building, also known as the Ohio Statehouse, which is a large rectangular building that centers the Capitol Square. The Ohio Statehouse, which is a distinctive example of Greek Doric architecture, is topped by a large rotunda. For well over a century, it has housed both chambers of the Ohio General Assembly as well as the offices of the Ohio Governor and other statewide officeholders. (J.A. 96-97). The Ohio Statehouse is the dominant feature of the Capitol Square, and it is plainly and unavoidably visible from every vantage point on the Capitol Square. See App. A43 (photograph). The District Court held in this case that the Capitol Square is a public forum. See App. A18.

For the past several years, the State of Ohio has allowed certain holiday seasonal displays to be placed on the Capitol Square for limited periods during the month of December. (J.A. 98). The State's traditional policy is to allow a broad range of speakers and other gatherings of people to conduct events on the Capitol Square. (J.A. 98). These displays are generally an exception to that policy because they are unattended structures. The holiday seasonal displays permitted by the State in the past have included a Christmas tree and a menorah. (J.A. 98).

On November 18, 1993, the Capitol Square Review and Advisory Board, which is authorized by law to regulate the uses of the Capitol Square, voted not to permit unattended displays on the Capitol Square during December of 1993. (J.A. 98). That vote was later declared invalid, and on November 23, 1993, the Board voted to approve displays of a Christmas tree and menorah. (J.A. 98-99). The State displayed its own Christmas tree, and a permit application to erect a menorah on the Capitol Square from December 8-16, 1993, which was explicitly stated to be a "seasonal display," was granted. (J.A. 99).

> Section 3 – okay, *now* we find out the cross is only ten feet high and six feet across.
>
> The footnote that appears on the next page is appropriate in this section, but in general, you should limit footnotes to nonessential matters. Footnotes should not contain information that is important to the analysis of the case. Footnotes are for additional facts or minor legal issues that pop up in the discussion, but have no bearing on the main argument you are making. If the material in the footnote does have a bearing on the main argument, put the material in the text where it will not be missed.

3. On November 29, 1993, Respondents applied for a permit to display a cross on the Capitol Square from December 8-24, 1993. (J.A. 99). The application described the type of event as being to "erect a cross for Christmas." (J.A. 99). Executive Director Keller denied the application on December 3, 1993, "upon the advice of counsel, in a good faith attempt to comply with the Ohio and United States Constitutions, as they have been interpreted in relevant decisions by the Federal and State Courts." (J.A. 99). Respondents

later clarified that they sought to erect a cross in the style of a Latin cross,[10] about ten feet high and six feet across and accompanied by a suggested disclaimer open to negotiation. (J.A. 100).

On December 9, 1993, Respondents filed an administrative appeal of this action to the full Board; the appeal was perfected on December 13, 1993. (J.A. 100-101). On December 17, 1993, a state administrative appeal was conducted by a hearing examiner who took evidence and heard argument from both sides. On December 21, 1993, the administrative hearing examiner issued a report and recommendation which found that the initial denial of a permit to Respondents was proper. App. A27. The hearing examiner held, among other things, that whereas holiday seasonal symbols have by virtue of that association taken on "cultural significance extending well beyond the religious sphere," the Latin cross "is generally regarded as having a purely sectarian purpose (i.e., to advance or endorse the Christian religion)." App. A34-A35. For that reason, the display of a Latin cross directly in front of the Ohio Statehouse, unlike the display of a Christmas tree or a menorah, was held to violate the Establishment Clause. App. A36. The Board unanimously adopted this report and recommendation as its own final ruling later that day. App. A16.

> Sections 4, 5, 6, and 7 of the Statement of the Case really drive home some important points by focusing on the language used by the lower courts when they rejected petitioners' arguments. This sets the scene nicely for petitioners' attempt to get a reversal by reasserting the same arguments that failed below. Hopefully, they will reassert them with new emphasis and stronger support. But petitioners need to confine the opinions below to a more manageable—and refutable—size. They do this by quoting the court's language and passing off these excerpts as the holding of the cases below.
>
> Note the language used here. Strong action verbs, adverbs, and adjectives are used—such as "immediately"—to connote a sense of rush to the proceedings below. A sense of urgency is also communicated by the fact that these hearings took place right in the middle of the holiday season. "Rushing around" is not an admirable description when you are considering weighty legal questions. If petitioners can

---

[10] "Latin cross" is the proper term for any "cross whose base stem is longer than the other three arms." American Civil Liberties Union v. City of St. Charles, 794 F.2d 265, 271, cert. denied, 479 U.S. 961 (1986) (affirming preliminary injunction against display of lighted Latin cross on top of city fire department building during Christmas season because it would violate the Establishment Clause).

suggest to the Supreme Court that the courts below rushed their decisions, it may be easier to convince the Court that these decisions are wrong. Never mind that the petitioners probably wanted the proceedings to go as quickly as possible below; you take the cards dealt to you and play them to your advantage.

We like that the sense of urgency here is more implicit than explicit. If petitioners had come out and said, "The proceedings below were rushed because of the holiday season," then respondents undoubtedly would respond with something like, "Respondents will not sit by and let petitioners impugn the decisions of a United States District Judge, three judges of the United States Court of Appeals for the Sixth Circuit, and Justice Stevens of this Court. The proceedings were not rushed. Careful deliberation and explanation of the decisions were undertaken. In any event, whatever need to proceed forthwith was procured by petitioners' own timing of their decision to refuse to display respondents' cross."

Mentioning in section 6 the vandalism of the first cross erected by the Ku Klux Klan is a tactical move, most likely thrown in to remind the high court of the widespread popular sentiment against the Klan. There really is no other reason to mention it here. But we think it was a great idea.

Having photos to refer to is a great advantage here because, visually, the scene described must have been quite a compelling one. Petitioners' reference to it serves two purposes: first, to remind the Supreme Court of the sentiment against the Klan, and second, to remind the Court that separation of church and state symbols is a good idea; otherwise, you get chaotic scenes like this one. Nice work, petitioners.

4. In the meantime, on December 15, 1993, Respondents filed this lawsuit in District court, asserting that the denial of their application for permit to erect a cross violated their constitutional right of free speech. (J.A. 27). The court set the matter for hearing on December 20, 1993, and consolidated the hearing on Respondents' motion for a preliminary injunction with a trial on the merits. At the close of this hearing, the court deferred its ruling pending the outcome of the state administrative appeal process. Once that process was completed on December 21, 1993, the court granted a permanent injunction requiring Petitioners to approve a permit for Respondents to display a cross on the Capitol Square through December 24, 1993. App. A26.

> Note: we will not comment on the citation forms, spacing, or other formatting of the brief. The text we were able to obtain was not formatted and did not have standard Bluebook citations, so do not rely on the forms and formatting depicted here.

In its ruling, the District Court considered whether Respondents' display of a large, unattended Latin cross directly in front of the Ohio Statehouse would constitute an impermissible "endorsement" of religion under Lemon v. Kurtzman, 403 U.S. 602 (1971), as subsequently interpreted and applied in such "holiday seasonal display" cases as Lynch v. Donnelly, 465 U.S. 668 (1984), and County of Allegheny v. American Civil Liberties Union, 492 U.S. 573 (1989). On the basis of a recent en banc decision by the Sixth Circuit Court of Appeals that addressed essentially the same issue, Americans United for Separation of Church & State v. Grand Rapids, 980 F.2d 1538 (6th Cir. 1993) (en banc), the District Court held that the unattended religious display in this case would not constitute an impermissible endorsement of religion so as to violate the Establishment Clause. App. A7-A8.

5. Immediately after the District Court issued its ruling, Petitioners moved for a stay pending appeal, which the court denied. Petitioners filed a Notice of Appeal to the Sixth Circuit on the same day — December 21, 1993 — and filed a motion for an emergency stay of the injunction pending appeal, which the Sixth Circuit denied on December 22, 1993. App. A40. Petitioners then filed an emergency application for a stay of injunction with Circuit Justice Stevens, which was denied on December 23, 1993. App. A38.

6. Respondents erected a cross on the Capitol Square sometime during the night of December 21, 1993, and it was displayed there the following day until it was apparently vandalized. The cross was displayed by itself in the middle of the lawn directly in front of the Ohio Statehouse, see App. A43 (photograph), located at some distance from the Christmas tree.[11] On December 22, 1993, Petitioners received yet another application from a group of Christian ministers, who sought to erect twenty more Latin crosses in front of the Ohio Statehouse. Petitioners believed themselves obligated, by the force of the District Court's ruling, to grant this further application, and thereafter numerous other crosses were erected and displayed in the same vicinity on December 23-24, 1993. (J.A. 60) (Appendix to Brief In Opposition To Writ Of Certiorari p. RA 31 ("Opp. App.")).

7. On appeal, the Sixth Circuit affirmed the District Court's ruling. App. A1. The Sixth Circuit adhered to its recent en banc decision in Americans United, which "held that a private organization's unattended display of a religious symbol in a public forum does not violate the Establishment Clause." App. A8. The court focused in particular on the nature of the display and the nature of the forum. It essentially held that because this display was privately sponsored, it did not matter what was contained in the display — for

---

[11] The menorah had been removed almost a week earlier, when that permit expired on December 16, 1993.

example, a Latin cross in this case as opposed to a menorah in cases like Americans United and County of Allegheny. Because this display was to be located in a public forum, moreover, it did not matter what kind of location was to exhibit the display — for example, the Ohio Statehouse in this case as opposed to a public park

> The Sixth Circuit is made to look foolish by the wording of the court's holding (that a big Latin cross sitting right in front of the Ohio statehouse would not suggest any approval of or endorsement of Christianity). The point is a good one, but this section is phrased too strongly—it is an insult to the Sixth Circuit, not a neutral report of its findings. It should have been toned down for equal legal effect, but less insult.

in cases like Americans United and Lynch. The Sixth Circuit thus determined that a reasonable observer could not conclude that the State of Ohio endorsed Christianity after viewing a large, unattended Latin cross standing directly in front of the Ohio Statehouse because "truly private religious expression in a truly public forum cannot be seen as endorsement by a reasonable observer." App. A9 (quoting Americans United, 980 F.2d at 1553) (emphasis in original). On this ground, the Sixth Circuit held that Respondents' display of a Latin cross directly in front of the Ohio Statehouse did not constitute an impermissible endorsement of religion under the Establishment Clause.

The Summary of Argument is a critical section. Never shortchange this section by writing it at the last minute, when you are exhausted and could care less what goes in there. This section is *definitely* going to be read by even the busiest judge or justice. They may tire of your actual argument section, but they most likely will read your entire summary of argument. So give it your best shot. Write it *after* you have completed the argument, and take the same care in drafting—and especially in editing and revising—the section as you do with the full argument.

Petitioners have done a good job with this section. They make their points clearly and concisely. You should never beat around the bush in this section. Notice how short the paragraphs are—two or three sentences each, in most cases. This makes it easy to read and drives home the points quickly and smoothly. The most important authorities are cited in this section, *not all* of the authorities, which improves readability.

On the other hand, we do not think this section is perfect. We seriously question the suggestion that the free speech clause should not trump the establishment clause because the establishment clause is listed first in the First Amendment. This sounds flaky, and it is phrased almost as a rhetorical question. You should avoid such flippant remarks in something as grave as a Supreme Court brief.

SUMMARY OF ARGUMENT

Displays of purely religious symbols at the seat of government, such as the large solitary and unattended Latin cross placed directly in front of the Ohio Statehouse in this case, violate the Establishment Clause of the First Amendment.

A purely religious symbol, such as a Latin cross, the ultimate sectarian symbol of Christianity, conveys a clear message of religion. See American Civil Liberties Union v. City of St. Charles, 794 F. 2d 265 (7th Cir.), cert. denied, 479 U.S. 961 (1986). At the same time, the symbol of the seat of government, in this case the Ohio Statehouse, conveys a clear message of government authority. Kaplan v. City of Burlington, 891 F. 2d 1024 (2nd Cir. 1989), cert. denied, 496 U.S. 926 (1990). The conjunction of the two communicates powerfully to an observer that the message conveyed by each symbol comes from the same source — the government. Id.

In most circumstances, an observer can easily identify those responsible for speech: the speaker at the microphone, the group chanting a slogan, the person holding a sign or passing out brochures. But when speech is conveyed by an unattended display, the author of the speech is not readily ascertainable and usually is perceived by most reasonable observers to be the owner of the property on which the display stands.

The Establishment Clause protects against religious messages bearing the government's imprimatur. Widmar v. Vincent, 454 U.S. 263 (1981). The juncture of the cross and the government building in an unattended setting creates the danger against which the Establishment Clause guards.

The Court has not addressed whether a union of church and state is legally permissible if it occurs in a public forum. The Sixth Circuit adopted a per se rule that, because a display is privately sponsored in a public forum, there can never be a misperception of the message. But nothing in the Court's precedents removes, for Establishment Clause purposes, the obligation of a court to determine the nature of the message being sent and received. The fact that the message is delivered in a public forum does not give the government the right to advocate religion. Nor may it permit a private party to proffer speech which is likely to be perceived as government speech endorsing religion. Public forum or no public forum, government may not throw its weight behind sectarian evangelism, nor may it permit a private party to create the impression that government supports religion. But just such an impression is created when an unattended, purely religious symbol, such as the Latin cross, is positioned with the state capitol as its backdrop.

The court below incorrectly held that one part of the First Amendment — the free speech clause — always trumps another part of the First Amendment — the Establishment Clause — when speech is uttered in a public forum. Under such rationale, no inquiry ever need be made whether, under the circumstances of the case, the speaker in the public forum appears to be the government and the speech appears to be endorsement of religion. If the Framers had intended such power of the Free Speech Clause, one would think that they would at least have placed it before the Establishment Clause.

The Court's cases dealing with holiday seasonal displays offer two tests for evaluating the issues in the instant case. See County of Allegheny v. American Civil Liberties Union, 492 U.S. 573 (1989). Each test attempts to strike a proper balance so that government neither advances nor inhibits religion. See Lemon v. Kurtzman, 403 U.S. 602 (1971). This includes not preferring the religious practices of one group at the expense of other groups, or even religious non-adherents. County of Allegheny.

The union of an isolated and unattended religious icon and the seat of government upsets this constitutional balance. Kaplan; Smith v. County of Albemarle, Va., 895 F. 2d 953 (4th Cir.), cert. denied, ___U.S.___, 111 S. Ct. 74 (1990). There is a significant risk that observers of the message conveyed by this union will perceive it as emanating from the government. For that reason, the unattended display in this case violates either test previously established by the Court.

Neither the Court's opinions nor reasoning in its "equal access" line of cases alters this conclusion. The equal access cases dealt with whether the message conveyed by government when allowing or denying access to government property communicates government preference for or intolerance to religion. Widmar; Board of Education of Westside Community Schools v. Mergens, 492 U.S. 226 (1990); Lamb's Chapel v. Center Moriches

Union Free School Dist.,___ U.S.___, 113 S. Ct. 2141 (1993). The Court concluded in the context of those cases that equal access was necessary to convey government neutrality toward religion. Although in those cases the Court found no significant risk of misperception of the message conveyed by government, the inquiry was directed toward the perception of the listener or observer under each set of circumstances. See generally id.

In stark contrast, the Sixth Circuit's analysis in this case ceased once the court established that speech was uttered in a public forum by a private non-governmental party. The court below incorrectly limited its analysis to a factual determination of who spoke, rather than, in the circumstances presented, who a "reasonable observer" might rationally conclude spoke.

Government may make distinctions in speech if compelling interests exist for doing so. Lamb's Chapel. Here government has a compelling interest to avoid violating the Establishment Clause. A complete prohibition on purely religious symbols at the seat of government is the only, and, therefore, the most narrowly tailored way to accomplish that goal. Disclaimers are entirely ineffectual and themselves create the risk of government entanglement with religion.

The petitioners take quite a risk by opening their Argument section with **criticisms** of the Supreme Court (e.g., that it engages in the "jurisprudence of minutiae" in establishment clause cases). There does not seem to be any purpose for this kind of commentary, and it is best to avoid openly criticizing the Court from which you are seeking relief. Petitioners do go on to say in effect, that "you won't have to do that in our case," but the sting nevertheless remains.

Beyond that, we think the "symbols" discussion petitioners lead off with is a good topic, but we question the argument petitioners have drafted. The talk of "symbolism" is a little esoteric. We wouldn't lead off with this kind of argument if we had lost twice in the courts below. We would have led with a simpler, more direct, and absolutely well supported argument.

ARGUMENT

I. A PURELY RELIGIOUS SYMBOL, SUCH AS A LARGE UNATTENDED LATIN CROSS, CLOSELY ASSOCIATED WITH THE SEAT OF GOVERNMENT, CONVEYS AN UNMISTAKABLE MESSAGE OF GOVERNMENT IMPRIMATUR OF RELIGION.

In the Court's line of seasonal holiday display cases, the Court has confronted the fact-specific nature of each case. That inquiry has been criticized as dealing with "jurisprudence of minutiae". County of Allegheny v. American Civil Liberties Union, 492 U.S. 573, 674 (1989) (Kennedy, J., concurring in the judgment in part and dissenting in part). The Court need not engage in the same analysis in this case. Any isolated, unattended display of a purely religious symbol at the seat of government violates the Establishment Clause. The combination of symbols representing church and state conveys too powerful a message that can easily be misunderstood, especially in a context where an observer has no readily identifiable source to which to attribute the message, other than government itself.

Symbols elicit direct and immediate emotions due to their strong and enduring meaning. A religious, especially sectarian, symbol, no matter what the particular physical setting may be, conveys the unmistakable message of that symbol's religious doctrine. The Latin Cross is a powerful example of just such a symbol: ". . . the cross is a symbol par excellence of Christianity itself as well as of Christ its head. . . . [T]he cross is endowed with transcendent significance." Anderson Affidavit PP 8 and 11 (J.A. 131-132). No ambiguity about the symbolic meaning of the Latin cross exists.

Similarly, a seat of government such as the Ohio Statehouse stands inexorably as a symbolic "metaphor for government." American Jewish Congress v. City of Chicago, 827

F.2d 120, 128 (7th Cir. 1987). When the universal symbol of Christianity is placed directly in front of the Ohio Statehouse, it is inseverably linked to the symbolic center of government. In West Virginia State Board of Education v. Barnette, 319 U.S. 624, 632 (1943), the Court recognized the inescapable association between various symbols:

> Symbolism is a primitive but effective way of communicating ideas. The use of an emblem or flag to symbolize some system, idea, institution, or personality is a short cut from mind to mind. Causes and nations, political parties, lodges and ecclesiastical groups seek to knit the loyalty of their followings to a flag or banner, a color or design. The State announces rank, function, and authority through crowns and maces, uniforms and black robes, the church speaks through the Cross, the Crucifix, the altar and shrine, and clerical raiment. Symbols of State often convey political ideas just as religious symbols come to convey theological ones. (emphasis added).

The meaning of a symbol must be viewed in the overall context of its setting. "The context in which a symbol is used for purposes of expression is important, for the context may give meaning to the symbol." Spence v. Washington, 418 U.S. 405, 410 (1974). Scholars have observed that "people's responses to a symbol will be contingent upon their assessments of the circumstances of its usage." C. Elder & R. Cobb, The Political Uses of Symbols 57 (1983). This is especially true if the symbol is visually linked to other symbols. "When a particular symbol is used in conjunction with several other symbols, they may all become linked in the eyes of the general public." Id. at 77.

Respondents in the instant case were permitted, based upon the lower courts' decisions, to erect a Latin cross at the seat of secular government. Just as the Latin cross conveys a powerful message of religion, the Ohio Statehouse conveys a powerful message of governmental authority. See American Jewish Congress, 827 F.2d at 128 (discussing the symbol of city hall); Kaplan v. City of Burlington, 891 F.2d 1024, 1029-30 (2nd Cir. 1989), cert. denied, 496 U.S. 926 (1990) ("the park involved is not any city park, but rather City Hall park. This Park is bounded on the east by City Hall, the seat and the official symbol of Burlington city government. . . ."). And, just as the Latin cross is the most recognizable symbol of Christianity, the Ohio Statehouse is the single most visible and recognizable symbol of government in the State of Ohio. Any association of the two threatens to blur the distinction between church and state because the observer will view it as government's sponsorship of religion.[12]

---

[12] The Latin cross was not erected as part of a holiday seasonal display but stood majestically by itself in the middle of the front lawn of the Capitol Square. App. A43. Respondents' application specifically requested this location which was apart from and a distance away from where the Christmas tree and menorah were located. (J.A. 43).

The Establishment Clause protects against "any imprimatur of state approval of religious sects or practices." Widmar v. Vincent, 454 U.S. 263, 274 (1981). The combination of the cross and government, in a context where the latter is perceived to support the former, creates this danger.

It has long been recognized that speech may take many forms, including such nonverbal forms as symbolic displays. Not all forms of speech, however, have equivalent impact. Sometimes, such as in this case, speech must be evaluated not only on the basis of its content, but also as to the identity of the speaker. A determination of authorship often is directly determinable from the columnist, the television commentator, the rally speaker, the sign holder. All can be noted directly by the reader or the listener. But in the case of an unattended display, the source of the communication must be inferred. In the absence of clear and direct information to the contrary, an observer reasonably perceives the message conveyed by an unattended display as the message of the landowner.

The grounds of the Ohio Statehouse, in addition to being a public forum, as observed by the Sixth Circuit, are home to statues of historical figures important to Ohio and Columbus. As the record reflects, these grounds have previously housed only two other temporary, unattended displays — a secular and pluralistic seasonal display and a chart showing the progress of the community's United Way campaign. Observers of these unattended displays correctly will perceive the message conveyed by these symbols as messages supported and approved by the State of Ohio.

The Sixth Circuit declared that since the unattended display of the Latin cross was presented in a public forum, only a "hypothetical dolt" would not realize this message came from private citizens, not the government. Because government can and does convey symbolic unattended messages from the very grounds upon which private speech rallies frequently occur, however, the mere fact that private speech is permitted does not remove the inference that an unattended display on government property is government endorsed.

> Starting here, we find the first, clear, powerful, and concise argument that petitioners have made so far: No federal case has ever found the display of a Latin cross on public land by a state or state subdivision to be constitutional. We would have led with this argument, first thing out of the gate. Arguing that the Supreme Court has to make new law to force a state to put a KKK cross up on the state's front lawn will give the justices pause.

A battery of cases has held that the display of a cross on government property "dramatically conveys a message of governmental support for Christianity, whatever the intentions of those responsible for the display may be." American Civil Liberties Union v. City of St. Charles, 794 F.2d 265, 271 (7th Cir. 1986), cert. denied, 479 U.S. 961 (1986). See Gonzales v. North Township of Lake County, 4 F.3d 1412, 1423 (7th Cir. 1993) (court held that the cross "does not bear secular trappings sufficient to neutralize its religious message," and indeed "does not convey any secular message, whether remote, indirect, or incidental").

For this reason, courts regularly and persistently have granted injunctions and other proper relief when an Establishment Clause challenge is raised against an attempt by anyone to display a Latin cross on government property. See, e.g., Mendelson v. City of St. Cloud, 719 F. Supp. 1065, 1069 (M.D. Fla. 1989) ("no federal case has ever found the display of a Latin cross on public land by a state or state subdivision to be constitutional"); American Civil Liberties Union v. Mississippi General Services Admin., 652 F. Supp. 380, 384-85 & n.2 (S.D. Miss. 1987) ("in no other federal case either before or since Lynch v. Donnelly has the public display of a cross by a state or subdivision thereof been found to be constitutional").

This judicial result has been the same whether the Latin cross on government property is large, see, e.g., Jewish War Veterans v. United States, 695 F. Supp. 3, 5 (D.D.C. 1988) (65' illuminated cross serving as war memorial on Marine Corps base; permanent injunction granted); Mendelson, 719 F. Supp. at 1066 (12' cross on city water tower; injunction granted), medium-sized, see, e.g., Libin v. Town of Greenwich, 625 F. Supp. 393, 394 (D. Conn. 1985) (3' X 5' illuminated cross on firehouse; preliminary injunction granted), or quite small, see, e.g., Harris v. City of Zion, 927 F.2d 1401, 1402-04 (7th Cir. 1991), cert. denied, ___U.S.___, 112 S.Ct. 3054 (1992) (Latin cross appeared in one quadrant of municipal corporate seals; permanent injunction granted); Friedman v. Board of County Commissioners, 781 F.2d 777, 779 (10th Cir. 1985) (en banc), cert. denied, 476 U.S. 1169 (1986) (Latin cross appeared on county seal; injunction granted).

In addition, this has been true even when the display of the Latin cross on government property has existed for many years, see, e.g., American Civil Liberties Union v. Rabun County Chamber of Commerce, 698 F.2d 1098, 1101 (11th Cir. 1983) (cross in state park originally dated back almost 30 years; permanent injunction granted); Jewish War Veterans, 695 F. Supp. at 5 (cross on Marine Corps base more than 22 years; permanent injunction granted), and even where it was privately sponsored. See Gonzales, 4 F.3d at 1422-23 (crucifix in public park for more than 40 years; permanent injunction granted). It is this judicial recognition of the inability of an observer to separate the state from the message of the Latin cross that undermines the decision below.

> Petitioners are too loose in their citation usage. They occasionally make a sweeping statement about the law without citation to legal authority. You can attribute some of these unsupported statements to their placement in "umbrella" or "road map" paragraphs, but we recommend a more "religious" use of citations. *Whenever* you make a statement about the law, a legal conclusion, or a statement about a legal rule (or element thereof), you should include a citation to authority. Unsupported rhetoric in appellate briefs is not going to win you very many appeals. Find a source that comes close to what you are saying and cite it.

II. THE ESTABLISHMENT CLAUSE MAY REQUIRE A FINDING OF THE UNCONSTITUTIONALITY OF AN UNATTENDED RELIGIOUS DISPLAY, EVEN IF SUCH DISPLAY STANDS IN A PUBLIC FORUM

The decision of the court below is sweeping in scope, creating a per se rule obviating the need to examine how the message is perceived by a reasonable observer. The lower court focused not on the risk that the government's message will be misperceived, but only on the public nature of the forum in which the message is relayed.

The nature of a public forum guarantees broad communication. The Court first recognized the concept of the public forum in Hague v. CIO, 307 U.S. 496 (1939). The Court observed that streets and parks in this country universally have been considered public forums:

> Wherever the title of streets and parks may rest, they have immemorially been held in trust for the use of the public and, time out of mind, have been used for purposes of assembly, communicating thought between citizens, and discussing public questions. Such use of the streets and public places has, from ancient times, been a part of the privileges, immunities, rights, and liberties of citizens.

Id. at 515. See also Lamb's Chapel v. Center Moriches Union Free School District, ___U.S. ___, 113 S. Ct 2131, 2146 (1993) ("parks and sidewalks are traditional public fora"); International Soc'y for Krishna Consciousness v. Lee, ___ U.S. ___, 112 S. Ct. 2711, 2717 (1992) (Kennedy, J., concurring) ("types of property that we have recognized as the quintessential public forums are streets, parks, and sidewalks").

In these traditional public forums, as well as in so-called "designated" or "limited" public forums, the government may not prohibit all communication. Cornelius v. NAACP Legal Defense and Education Fund, Inc., 473 U.S. 788 (1985); Perry Educ. Assn. v. Perry Local Educators' Assn., 470 U.S. 37, 45 (1983) ("[I]n places which by long tradition or by government fiat have been devoted to assembly and debate, the rights of the State to limit expressive activity are sharply circumscribed.") (emphasis added).

The public forum doctrine by itself, however, does not require the State of Ohio to permit the erection of any symbol upon government property characterized as a public forum. Just as "[t]he principle that government accommodation of the free exercise of religion does not supersede the fundamental limitations imposed by the Establishment Clause", Lee v. Weisman, ___U.S.___, 112 S.Ct. 2649, 2655 (1992), the public forum doctrine should not be permitted to "swallow up" the Establishment Clause. Kaplan, 891 F.2d at 1029. That a message is delivered in a public forum does not give government the right to advocate religion. Nor may it permit a private party to proffer speech that is likely to be perceived as government speech endorsing religion. Public forum or not, government may not lend its support to a particular religious message or allow private parties to manipulate government for that purpose.

In Burson v. Freeman, ___U.S.___, 112 S.Ct. 1846 (1992), Justice Kennedy squarely recognized the inherent clash between competing constitutional doctrines:

The same use of the compelling interest test is adopted today, not to justify or condemn a category of suppression but to determine the accuracy of the justification the State gives for its law. There is a narrow area in which the First Amendment permits freedom of expression to yield to the extent necessary for an accommodation of another constitutional right.

Id., 112 S.Ct. at 1859 (Kennedy, J., concurring). And just as competing doctrines were balanced in that case, they must be balanced here. The Sixth Circuit's holding does not balance competing doctrines. It allows one to trump the other.

> We are skipping to the Conclusion.

* * *

> This is the typical kind of Conclusion you will see at the end of a long brief. Pray for relief and end it.

CONCLUSION

For the reasons set forth, this Court should reverse the decision of the court below.

Respectfully submitted,

BETTY D. MONTGOMERY, Ohio Attorney General
MICHAEL J. RENNER, Chief Counsel, Counsel of Record
CHRISTOPHER S. COOK
ANDREW S. BERGMAN
SIMON B. KARAS
ANDREW I. SUTTER
Assistant Attorneys General,
State Office Tower
30 East Broad St.,17th Fl.
Columbus, Ohio 43215-3428
(614) 466-5026
Attorneys for Petitioners

Sample Brief No. 4:

Brief of Respondents in the
U.S. Supreme Court case:

Capitol Square Review and Advisory Board
v.
Pinette

515 U.S. 753 (1995)

Docket No. 94-780

SUPREME COURT OF THE UNITED STATES

October Term, 1994

CAPITOL SQUARE REVIEW AND ADVISORY BOARD, RONALD T. KELLER, DANIEL SHELLENBARGER, AND OHIO SENATOR RICHARD T. FINAN,

Petitioners,

— against—

VINCENT J. PINETTE, DONNIE A. CARR, AND KNIGHTS OF THE KU KLUX KLAN,

Respondents.

ON WRIT OF CERTIORARI TO THE UNITED STATES COURT OF APPEALS FOR THE SIXTH CIRCUIT

BRIEF OF RESPONDENTS

> Question Presented: It is interesting to note that respon-
> dents chose to call the item in question a "Ku Klux Klan
> cross." This may be accurate, but it is a loaded term that
> easily could distract the court away from the pure legal issue
> on which the respondents twice have prevailed in the courts
> below. It would have been more neutral to call the item a
> "Latin cross" or simply a "cross." Otherwise, this question is
> appropriate because it is drafted broadly to encompass more
> of the public policy at stake in a brief directed to a court of
> last resort.

QUESTION PRESENTED FOR REVIEW

Whether the temporary, unattended display of a Ku Klux Klan cross on a public forum open to all other political and religious expression violates the Establishment Clause solely because the public forum is in proximity to the seat of government.

The Respondents respectfully urge this Court to affirm the judgment of the United States Court of Appeals for the Sixth Circuit in this proceeding.

Once again, we cut out the **TABLE OF CONTENTS** and **TABLE OF AUTHORITIES** to save space. What follows is an "Introduction" section. It is not required by the rules. In general, we like introductions, and this one turns the tables on the petitioners.

INTRODUCTION

The State asserts that the primary issue in this case is whether the Establishment Clause creates a flat ban on the private, unattended display of a Klan cross on a public forum open to all other political and religious communication where the forum is near the seat of government. The State's assertion is wrong. The record in this case makes clear that the State's reliance on the Establishment Clause is pretextual. The State's objection to the Ku Klux Klan cross had much less to do with the cross than with the Ku Klux Klan itself. The discriminatory denial of access to a public forum under these circumstances is clearly prohibited by the First Amendment.

> Proceedings Below: Pure housekeeping. This section is adequate.

PROCEEDINGS BELOW

Following the filing of the complaint in this case, the District Court sua sponte divided its proceedings into two segments. An Opinion and Order was entered for each segment. Both shared a common nucleus of operative facts. The District Court opinion directly resulting in the Petition for Certiorari is reported at 844 F. Supp. 1182 (S.D. Ohio 1993). It is also appended to the Petition at A13-A26;[13] n1 the other opinion and order is reported on Westlaw at 1994 WL 749489 and is included in the Respondents' Appendix at RA1-RA10.[14] The December 20 and 21 hearings focused on injunctive relief regarding the cross which the District Court granted on December 21, 1993. A26. The January 3 hearing focused mainly on discriminatory treatment, injunctive relief related to the rally, and a claim for damages; the Court issued the injunction permitting the rally and denied damages. RA10, Pinette v. Capitol Square Review and Advisory Board, Case No. C2-93-1162, U.S.D.C. S.D. Ohio, Opinion and Order of January 4, 1994, (1994 WL 749489). The subject of the Petition before this Court is the injunction ordering the Petitioners to grant the permit to erect the Klan's cross; the State did not appeal the injunction ordering the State to grant a permit for the rally. The record of both hearings constitutes the record on appeal, together with a supplemental record from the District Court.

The opinion of the United States Court of Appeals for the Sixth Circuit is reported at 30 F.3d 675 (6th Cir. 1994) and is appended to the Petition for Certiorari at A1-A12.

---

[13] References to the Appendices contained in the Petition are identified herein as A1, A2, etc. References to the Respondents' Appendices contained in the Brief in Opposition to a Writ of Certiorari are identified herein as RA1, RA2, etc. References to the Appendices included in this Brief of Respondents are identified as 1a, 2a, and 3a.

[14] The Respondents' Complaint and Amended Complaint raised two issues: one was related to erection of the Klan's cross on the same forum as the menorah; the other related to the denial of a permit to the Klan to hold a rally on Capitol Square in January 1994. Two hearings were set: one was primarily devoted to the cross issue, and the other was primarily devoted to the rally. References herein to the record include R. 9: TR I (record of hearing of December 20 and 21, 1993), and R. 23: TR II (record of the morning portion of the hearing of January 3, 1994) and R. 23: TR III (record of the hearing of the afternoon of January 3, 1994).

> Statement of the Case: Look at the rest of the story here, the parts petitioners left out (and with good reason). Bringing these facts to light will help in small part to mollify respondents' negative public persona.
>
> But this section is too long (seven pages when double spaced). Starting in section (b) of the Statement of the Case, respondents include too much detail and minutiae. We are not certain that the court needs to hear all of these facts. Some of the "This is unfair" innuendo also is a little forced and not at all compelling when uttered by respondents. The discussion of the "Klan cross" as "a symbol of freedom to rally men against political oppression and tyranny" also sounds like a stretch. Nevertheless, this is respondents' position.

STATEMENT OF THE CASE

The Knights of the Ku Klux Klan filed this case on December 15, 1993, to challenge, inter alia, the discriminatory refusal of the Capitol Square Review and Advisory Board[15] to grant a permit allowing display of a Ku Klux Klan cross on the public forum on the west side of the Capitol Building in Columbus, Ohio. Hearings to consider the Plaintiffs' requests for injunctive relief were held on December 20-21, 1993 and on January 3, 1994. The order that is the subject of the Petition was entered on December 21, 1993.

a. Background

On October 29, 1993, prior to initiating this case, the Knights of the Ku Klux Klan had applied for a permit to hold a public assembly in the Capitol Square forum. The purpose of the public assembly, which the Klan planned to hold the following January 15, 1994, was to express the organization's political views.

On November 18, 1993, while the application for the January 15th rally was still under consideration, the members of the Capitol Square Review Board met in executive session and discussed the issue of Ku Klux Klan access to the same forum during the holiday season. They feared that the Knights of the Ku Klux Klan might follow the example of another Klan group in Cincinnati by seeking to put up a Ku Klux Klan cross during the Christmas season. RA14, RA18; RA19-RA21. As a result of its discussion in executive session, the Board reconvened in public and voted sua sponte to bar display of both the State Christmas tree and the private display of the Lubavitch sect's menorah from Capitol Square during December 1993. A14. At the time, the Lubavitch Sect had

---

[15] The Capitol Square Review and Advisory Board is alternatively referred to as the "Board" or the "State" in this brief.

not yet applied for its 1993 permit nor had the Klan yet sought a permit to erect a cross in Capitol Square. Nevertheless, the Petitioners decided to bar the Christmas tree and the anticipated Lubavitch display of its menorah solely to foreclose any claim to equal access that the Klan might present. RA12 (Plaintiffs' Exhibit 33, Broadcast No. 5).

The decision of the State to bar the tree and menorah resulted in a great public uproar. A statement was released by the Office of the Governor objecting to imposition of a ban on all symbols as a means to prevent display of a Klan cross. According to the statement, the "[p]eople of this great State think that we ought to have a Christmas tree and think that we ought to have a menorah at the Statehouse and so do we. We've had a Christmas tree at the Statehouse for tens of years, and you can't let a single group or groups of people dictate to the people of Ohio what they are and aren't going to do." RA14 (Plaintiffs' Exhibit 33, Broadcast No. 6, Statement of Mike Dawson, Press Secretary to the Governor.) Newspaper accounts described the Governor as "disappointed and upset." RA20 (Defendants' Exhibit D, The Columbus Dispatch, November 20, 1993, front page). The Governor was also quoted as saying: "The Board's initial decision was a mistake. I trust this matter will be resolved quickly." Id.

Consistent with these public statements, the Governor and the other State officials who appoint the members of the Board[16] signed and delivered to the Board a letter calling upon the Board to permit the tree and menorah. Id.; RA14; RA19-RA20; JA 167-168, TR I 94. The Board met in special session on November 23, 1993, and resolved into executive session. Immediately following the executive session, the Board reconvened in public to formally declare its earlier vote invalid. In addition, it approved the State display of its Christmas tree and the private display of a menorah by a nine-to-zero vote. A15; JA 167-168, TR I 94. The vote to approve both the Christmas tree and the menorah was made even though no permit applications for displays on the Capitol Square had been filed. The reason for the change in vote was explained by Board Chairperson Richard Finan (a Petitioner herein): "I've been in politics for twenty-one years. When you get a letter from the Governor, the Speaker, and the President of the Senate, you do respond," he said. RA16 (Plaintiffs' Exhibit 33, Broadcast No. 8).

b. Capitol Square Public Forum

The public forum in question is a large park-like area, a block wide, on one side of the State Capitol building in Columbus.[17] Temporary, unattended[18] displays have been per-

---

[16] Ohio Revised Code Section 123.022.

[17] The forum area at issue in this case is one city block wide and approximately 240 feet deep, JA 96-97 (Stipulations, P12), about 3 1/2 acres. The entire Capitol Square block consists of ten acres, some 435,600 square feet. REDI REALTY ATLAS, City Map Volume I (22nd ed. 1991) p. 397. Views of the public forum are included at Brief of Petitioners, Appendix, at 1a (Plaintiffs' Supplemental Exhibit 104), 3a, (Plaintiffs' Supplemental Exhibit 106), JA 64 (Defendants' Supplemental Exhibit 109), and JA 65 (Defendants' Supplemental Exhibit 110).

[18] As used in this brief, "unattended" means that the given display has been permitted to remain at least overnight without accompanying personnel or ongoing ceremonies.

mitted in the public forum for many years. For example, the State of Ohio has erected a Christmas tree annually and has hung a "Seasons Greetings" banner from two of the Statehouse's pillars. 2a. The Lubavitch sect has been granted annual permits to display a large Chanukah menorah in Capitol Square. A14. And, permission has been granted for secular displays, such as United Fund campaign "thermometers" and arts festivals exhibits and booths. JA 159-160. There is no rule or regulation that confines unattended displays to any particular time of year, and they have in fact been present at various times over the years. A16.

In addition to these unattended displays, Capitol Square has been the site of numerous speech activities including gay rights demonstrations, anti-war demonstrations, and religious rallies and marches. A18. It is undisputed that Capitol Square has "been used from time immemorial for all manner of public gatherings and demonstrations by groups of all kinds, including political parties, charitable and religious groups, labor unions, civil rights groups, and the proponents and opponents of all manner of social and political issues." RA6. As the District Court summarized the record, the Capitol Square "grounds have been made available for speeches and public gatherings by various groups advocating various causes both secular and religious." A14.

c. Administration of the Capitol Square Forum

The Capitol Square Review and Advisory Board is authorized by law to regulate the uses of Capitol Square. Ohio Revised Code Section 123.022. According to Section 128-4-02 of the Ohio Administrative Code, "Capitol buildings and grounds are available for use by the public . . . for free discussion of public questions" if the applicant adheres to a stated procedure for requesting such use, and if the proposed use:

(1) Does not interfere with the primary use of the capitol buildings or grounds;
(2) Is appropriate to the physical context of the capitol buildings or grounds;
(3) Does not unduly burden the managing authority;
(4) Is not a hazard to the safety of the public or state employees; and
(5) Does not expose the state to the likelihood of expenses and/or damages which cannot be recovered.A32 (Report and Recommendation of Hearing Examiner, Conclusions of Law, P2).

Ronald Keller, Executive Director of the Board, is responsible for management of the Capitol Square complex. In this capacity, he grants and denies permits for the use of Capitol Square. TR I 84-85; JA 97, Stipulations, P19. Persons desiring to use Capitol Square submit their requests on the Board's form, "Application For Permit to Use Statehouse Grounds." JA 99, (Stipulations, P27-28); JA 103-111 (Exh. 3,4).

d. Display of the Menorah and the Tree

On November 29, 1993, Rabbi Chaim Capland submitted an official application for the display — previously approved by the Board — of a menorah on Capitol Square from

December 8 through December 16, 1993, to coincide with the days of Chanukah. Keller issued Capland's permit on November 29, 1993, the same day the application was submitted. A15, JA 168-169, TR I 97-98. The menorah was erected at the Capitol Square on December 8, 1993.

The State Christmas tree was erected on December 7, 1993. A16.

e. Denial of a Permit to Display the Ku Klux Klan Cross

The Klan's application for a permit to display its cross on the Capitol Square forum from December 8 through December 24 was also submitted on November 29, 1993. A15. The period covered by the application overlapped the period during which the menorah would be displayed. Executive Director Keller denied the Klan's application by letter of December 3, 1993. Id. Mr. Keller wrote that:

> [The denial] . . . was made upon the advice of counsel, in a good faith attempt to comply with the Ohio and United States Constitutions, as they have been interpreted in relevant decisions by the Federal and State Courts. We would direct your attention in particular to controlling decisions recently rendered by the United States Supreme Court under the First Amendment to the United States ·Constitution.JA 91-93 (Plaintiffs' Exhibit 5); A15 (District Court Findings of Fact, P9).

The Klan filed an administrative appeal of the permit denial. Although the administrative appeal was denied on December 21, 1993, the hearing examiner concluded that:

> The evidence adduced at the [administrative] hearing in this matter does not offer a complete explanation of the process or basis for the Board's denial of the Appellant's request. Board Executive Director Keller did, however, advise the Appellant that the Board denied its request on advice of counsel, who had raised constitutional objections to the request. . . .A33 (Report and Recommendation of Hearing Examiner, Conclusions of Law, P4).

Respondents had filed the instant action prior to the issuance of the hearing examiner's report. On December 21, 1993, following the report, the District Court issued a permanent injunction ordering the State to grant a permit which would allow the Klan to display its cross through December 24. Pursuant to that injunction, the cross was set in place in the early morning hours of December 22, 1993. RA24-RA30 (Plaintiffs' Supplemental Exhibits 102, The Columbus Dispatch, December 23, 1993, front page, and 103, The [Akron] Beacon Journal, December 23, 1993, page B5). It was vandalized a short time later. RA28-RA29, RA31. Meanwhile, on December 22 the Board granted permits to several religious groups that applied to display crosses around the Klan Cross; the purpose of those crosses was to protest the presence of the Klan cross.

f. The Menorah as a Religious Symbol

At the hearing before the District Court, Cantor Jack Chomsky of Tifereth Israel Congregation in Columbus, Ohio, testified that the menorah permitted by the State of Ohio, like other Chanukah menorahs, "is a religious symbol. It is used in conjunction with fulfilling the obligations incumbent upon a Jew for the celebration of the festival of Chanukah." JA 152, TR I 70. Cantor Chomsky explained that Jews have an obligation to "put candles in it as appropriate, as prescribed by our tradition, and they recite blessings which state as part of the blessings that we were commanded to perform this act. Blessings such as this make this into very much a ritual act." JA 155, 75-76. Rabbi Harold Berman also stated that the menorah "is a religious symbol. . . ." JA 53.

g. The Klan Cross

Plaintiff Carr testified that he applied for a permit to display the Klan cross because he had heard that the State was going to permit a tree and a menorah but not a Klan cross. JA 134-137, TR I 42-44. Mr. Carr said that his motivation for filing the request was that "since we were being excluded by the city or the state, the Capitol Square Review and Advisory Board, that we would attempt to obtain a permit to erect a cross for the Christmas season." Id. Mr. Carr also testified that while the cross communicates a religious message, it also conveys a political message: "To us, it is a sacred symbol, but it is also a symbol of going against tyranny, a symbol of freedom." JA 142, TR I 51. He noted that the "Klan's use of the cross originated from the early Scottish clans in Scotland in the 1300's which used the cross as symbol to rally the clans together to fight against their English oppressors." JA 143. And Mr. Carr observed "the cross was also incorporated in the Confederate battle flag. . . ." JA 150.

In addition, counsel for the Klan informed the State that accompanying the cross would be a disclaimer stating that "this cross was erected by private individuals without government support for the purpose of expressing respect for the holiday season and to assert the right of all religious views to be expressed on an equal basis on public property." A15-16.[19]

h. The Opinion of the District Court

In granting the injunction, the District Court found that the area in question was a traditional public forum, A18, that there was no policy against free-standing displays in Capitol Square, and that for many years a variety of unattended displays have been permitted on Capitol Square for limited periods, including, during December, a free-standing Christmas tree and a free-standing menorah. A16.

---

[19] Counsel for the Klan also invited State suggestions concerning the content of the disclaimer. Id.

The Court observed that one of the Board's reasons for denying the Klan's application — the purported failure of the Klan to post a bond — was "not a proper ground for the denial of the permit . . ." and that the State "does not contend that the erection of a cross poses a security risk of any kind." A16. The Court concluded, based on all of the facts, that "the State of Ohio is in no way associating itself with the Klan's display," that there was no appearance of endorsement of religion, and that "the reasonable observer should conclude that the government is expressing its toleration of religious and secular pluralism" in the public forum. The Court then held that "freedom of speech would be meaningless if it did not apply to all groups, popular and unpopular alike." A26.

i. The Opinion of the Sixth Circuit

The Sixth Circuit affirmed the District Court on Free Speech, Free Exercise, and Equal Protection grounds. A6-A7, A11-A12. It rejected the Petitioners' claim that there was any endorsement of religion by the State in this case. Instead, it held that a reasonable observer could not conclude that the display of the Ku Klux Klan cross on Capitol Square was a state endorsement of religion. It also concluded that religious groups and groups communicating controversial or offensive messages could not be selectively denied access to a public forum in the name of the Establishment Clause. A11-A12.

> Summary of Argument: This section is well-drafted. However, respondents share the belief of the student authors that no legal citation should be used in the Summary of Argument.
>
> As stated in the comment on the Summary of Argument in sample brief #1, the authors actually disagree with each other on this. Some attorneys maintain that no cases should be cited in the SOA, while others find it odd if you fail to cite one or two of the most important authorities that support your argument.

SUMMARY OF ARGUMENT

The Free Speech and Free Exercise Clauses of the First Amendment and the Equal Protection Clause of the Fourteenth Amendment require a state to permit the temporary unattended display of a Ku Klux Klan cross in a traditional public forum that is open to other political and religious symbols — even if that forum is near the seat of government — absent any special indicia of endorsement.

1. The State's discriminatory refusal to permit the display of the Ku Klux Klan cross in a traditional public forum where the State has permitted other secular and religious symbols violates the Free Speech and Free Exercise Clauses of the First Amendment.

In this case, the State has singled out the Ku Klux Klan and has refused to permit the Klan to display its cross in the Capitol Square forum. The cross is symbolic of the Klan's view about politics and religion.

The record establishes that the denial was based upon the controversial communication of a controversial speaker. On that record, the State clearly discriminated among political and religious symbols. Moreover, the discrimination was unlawfully accomplished by means of standardless procedures permitting the exercise of unbridled discretion.

The State's only response to the claim of discrimination is that the Board relied upon the Establishment Clause; however, this explanation rings hollow given the State's tolerance of other religious symbols at the same site.

2. Given the facts of this case, both courts below correctly held that no reasonable observer could conclude that the Ku Klux Klan display of its cross on the Capitol Square public forum constituted an endorsement or appearance of endorsement of religion.

The State erroneously insists that, because of the inherent power of an unattended cross as a symbol, the Establishment Clause automatically bans from the Capitol Square forum the unattended display of the Klan cross at any location at any time under any circumstances. This flat ban is wrong as a matter of law precisely because it forecloses consideration of all relevant facts and circumstances.

The State's contention that the Establishment Clause flatly bans all symbols alleged to be "purely religious" precludes the application of the "reasonable observer" standard set forth by this Court in County of Allegheny v. Greater Pittsburgh ACLU, 492 U.S. 573

(1989) and followed by the courts below. While the State claims that banning the Klan cross is necessary to serve its interest in obeying the Establishment Clause, it ignores its parallel obligation to fulfill the requirements of the Free Speech and Free Exercise Clauses. These interests must be reconciled on a case-by-case basis by use of the "reasonable observer" standard.

The State fails to acknowledge that providing a public forum is not an endorsement of the speech thereon. It also ignores the distinction, recognized in Allegheny, between private religious expression in a public forum and government religious expression.

3. Privately sponsored displays of religious symbols cannot be excluded from a quintessential public forum even at the seat of government, absent some indicia of state endorsement. Indeed, the defining characteristic of a public forum is that the state may not discriminate against speech on the basis of content.

Respondents do not quarrel with the endorsement test under the Establishment Clause as it has been developed by this Court. But, endorsement cannot be presumed from the mere fact of private speech in a public forum. Yet, without this inference, there is no plausible claim of endorsement on the facts of this case, as both lower courts found. The judgment below should therefore be affirmed.

> Argument: Respondents begin their argument by reciting the facts again. We do not like this decision. Get your rule and explanation out there, and then do the application to the facts. Moreover—where is the IRAC or TREAT structure? It is not clear to us that it is present anywhere in the first section of their argument. We hear a lot of facts, and then get some rule (or is it explanation?) material at the end of the section. This is not our recommended drafting style.

ARGUMENT

I. THE STATE'S DISCRIMINATORY REFUSAL TO PERMIT DISPLAY OF THE KU KLUX KLAN CROSS IN A TRADITIONAL PUBLIC FORUM VIOLATES THE FREE SPEECH AND FREE EXERCISE CLAUSES OF THE FIRST AMENDMENT AND THE EQUAL PROTECTION CLAUSE OF THE FOURTEENTH AMENDMENT

The record in this case clearly establishes that officials of the Capitol Square Review and Advisory Board persistently engaged in a series of discriminatory actions to prevent the Ku Klux Klan from displaying the Klan cross in the public forum at Capitol Square. The maneuvering began after the Ku Klux Klan filed an application to hold a rally at Capitol Square on the birthday of Martin Luther King, Jr. On October 29, 1993, the Board received, but did not act upon, the Klan's permit request. Then, on November 18, 1993, Board Chairman Richard Finan conceded that there was no legal basis to prevent the Klan from holding its rally. RA11.[20] The Board's attention shifted to efforts to forestall the possibility that the Klan might obtain a permit to erect a Klan cross in Capitol Square, because similar applications had been filed in Cincinnati by another Klan group. RA12.

The Capitol Square Review and Advisory Board announced its strategy to forestall possible display of the Klan cross on November 18, 1993. On that date, Board officials stated that the traditional state Christmas tree would not be erected in the Capitol Square during the 1993 Christmas season. They also stated that the Board would not allow the Lubavitch sect to display a menorah that had been permitted in previous years.

The Board's initial strategy crumbled on November 23, 1993, after vigorous public protests and after strong political pressure from the Governor and legislative leaders who appointed the members of the Board. In response to this pressure, the Board suddenly changed course and agreed to permit the menorah and to display the tree. A15; JA 167-

---

[20] The Board did not issue a permit for the Klan rally until ordered to do so by the District Court on January 4, 1994. RA1.

168. A few days later, Rabbi Capland applied for a permit to erect the Lubavitch menorah. His permit was granted the same day. A15.

The Board's change of position, which was reported in detail by the press, caused Donnie Carr to file a permit application to display the Klan cross. According to Carr, the permit application was filed to protest the Board's gratuitous policy of denying Klan access to Capitol Square while granting access to the Lubavitch sect. During his testimony at the hearing below he explained that "since we were being excluded by the City or the State, the Capitol Square Review and Advisory Board, that we would attempt to obtain a permit to erect a cross for the Christmas season." JA 136-137.

A. The Constitution prohibits discrimination based on political or religious viewpoint.

It was against this record detailing the State's plan to bar the Klan cross that the Court of Appeals for the Sixth Circuit concluded, in a gross understatement, that "there was no indication that Ohio treated the Klan or its display favorably." A10. Indeed, as the Circuit made clear, this case has much less to do with endorsement of the Klan's speech than with discrimination against it. Thus, it commented: "Zealots have First Amendment rights too. Some speech may be distasteful, unpopular and outright offensive, but as Thurgood Marshall so persuasively wrote, the protection found in the First Amendment does not depend on popular opinion[.]" A11. The Sixth Circuit underscored its point by quoting Justice Marshall's statement in Police Department of Chicago v. Mosley, 408 U.S. 92 (1972):

Necessarily then, under the Equal Protection Clause, not to mention the First Amendment itself, government may not grant the use of a forum to people whose views it finds acceptable, but deny use to those wishing to express less favored or more controversial views. And it may not select which issues are worth discussing or debating in public facilities. There is an "equality of status in the field of ideas," and government must afford all points of view an equal opportunity to be heard. Once a forum is opened up to assembly or speaking by some groups, government may not prohibit others from assembling or speaking on the basis of what they intend to say. Selective exclusions from a public forum may not be based on content alone, and may not be justified by reference to content alone. A11-A12 (30 F.3d at 680), 408 U.S. at 96 (footnote omitted by the Circuit).

This Court has consistently restated this principle in cases decided since Mosley. For example, in Carey v. Brown, 447 U.S. 455, (1980), this Court stated that "[a]ny restriction on expressive activity because of its content would completely undercut the 'profound national commitment to the principle that debate on public issues should be uninhibited, robust, and wide open.'" Id. at 462-63, quoting New York Times v. Sullivan, 376 U.S. 254, 270 (1964). Similarly in R.A.V. v. St. Paul, U.S., 112 S. Ct. 2538 (1992), this Court stated, "The First Amendment generally prevents government from proscribing speech, see, e.g., Cantwell v. Connecticut, 310 U.S. 296, 309-311 (1940), or even expressive conduct, see e.g. Texas v. Johnson, 491 U.S. 397, 406 (1989), because of disapproval of the ideas expressed. Content based regulations are presumptively invalid." R.A.V.,

112 S. Ct. at 2542. According to FCC v. Pacifica Foundation, 438 U.S. 726 (1978)," . . . the fact that society may find speech offensive is not a sufficient reason for suppressing it. Indeed, if it is the speaker's opinion that gives offense, that consequence is a reason for according it constitutional protection." Id. at 745-46.

> We are all the way to section I(B), and we see no sign of the IRAC or TREAT paradigm. Legal points are argued, but they appear in a form that we would call "legal narrative reasoning." We do not believe that a presumption of victory—even if you are 99.9% certain the court will go your way—trumps the need to organize your arguments in a clear, concise, and convincing manner. Some form and structure would make this a much stronger section—and, remember, most cases are won or lost on the briefs.
>
> If you were to read on to the end, you would see that there is no attempt to use a traditional legal writing structure for this Argument. Ultimately, this is more like a legal essay than anything else.
>
> Finally—this brief clearly is written in response to petitioners' brief. Many of the headings used directly address points raised in petitioners' brief. This limits its usefulness as a model for moot court briefing, but as a model for appellees' and respondents' briefs, it is a decent example.

B. The State's Establishment Clause claim is a pretext for discrimination.

Faced with this overwhelming authority, the State fails to address whether its efforts to prevent display of the Klan cross were motivated by the unpopularity of the Ku Klux Klan and its symbol. Instead, the State prefers to argue that its efforts to prevent display of the Klan cross were motivated solely by a desire to avoid an Establishment Clause violation. According to the State's brief, display of the Klan cross at Capitol Square conveys the "message of government imprimatur of religion" because it is a Latin Cross which, in turn is the symbol of Christianity. Pet. Br. 12-17.

The disingenuousness of the State's Establishment Clause claim is patently apparent. First, contrary to the State's assertion, the Klan itself clearly regards the cross as both a political symbol and a religious symbol. Second, even if it is assumed that the Klan cross is a purely religious symbol, the State may still not discriminate against it nor engage in "maneuvers to bring about a legal ascendancy of one sect over another." Thomas Jefferson, Letter to Elbridge Gerry, January 26, 1799, reprinted in SAUL K. PADOVER, A JEFFERSON PROFILE (1956) 112. Yet, the evidence of discrimination on this record is undeniable. When the menorah was erected in December of 1993, the governor participated in the lighting ceremony. RA23 (The Columbus Dispatch, December 9, 1993). In addition, the menorah has been displayed without state objection for several years. Unlike the permit application for the Klan cross, the application for the menorah was approved in advance of the day it was filed.

Under this Court's well-established precedents, the State may not permit the menorah and bar the cross by selectively invoking the Establishment Clause. For example, in Niemotko v. Maryland, 340 U.S. 268 (1951), the Court unanimously struck down the discriminatory refusal of government officials to allow a Jehovah's Witness group from holding a bible meeting in a public park. Similarly, in Fowler v. Rhode Island, 345 U.S. 67 (1953), this Court found that the First Amendment was violated when a Jehovah's Witness religious service was treated differently than those of Catholics or Protestants. Id. at 69-70.

In Larson v. Valente, 456 U.S. 228 (1982), this Court underscored the constitutional prohibition against discrimination among religions. "The clearest command of the Establishment Clause is that one religious denomination cannot be officially preferred over another." Id. at 244. And, as this Court stated in Allegheny, "[w]hatever else the Establishment Clause may mean . . ., it certainly means that at the very least that government may not demonstrate a preference for one particular sect or creed. . . ." 492 U.S. at 605.

The State's discriminatory motives were highlighted by the Capitol Square Review and Advisory Board's use of ad hoc procedures designed to obstruct Klan access to the Capitol Square. The Board's vacillation over whether to impose a flat ban on all unattended displays at Capitol Square during the Christmas holidays was justified by no published rule or regulation. Nor was any rule or regulation cited as a basis for the anticipatory denial of a permit for the display of the Klan cross.

The ad hoc quality of the Board's permit denial in this case was noted in the findings of the Board's administrative hearing officer. According to these findings:

The evidence adduced at the [administrative] hearing in this matter does not offer a complete explanation of the process or basis for the Board's denial of the Appellant's request. Board Executive Director Keller did, however, advise the Appellant that the Board denied its request on advice of counsel, who had raised constitutional objections to the request. The record does not establish whether other objections were raised by the Board's counsel. A33, P4. The standards applied to the Klan are thus unpublished and unknown. The use of such ad hoc procedures to facilitate discrimination against disfavored speakers is forbidden by the First Amendment. Forsyth County, Ga. v. Nationalist Movement, U.S. , 112 S. Ct. 2395 (1992); Lakewood v. Plain Dealer Publishing Co., 486 U.S. 750 (1988).

The rule against discrimination is thoroughly consistent with the command of this Court, more than fifty years ago, that no public official "can prescribe what shall be orthodox in politics [or] religion . . .," West Virginia Board of Education v. Barnette, 319 U.S. 624, 642 (1943). The decisions of the District Court and the Court of Appeals were based on this command and therefore should be affirmed.

> Sections II and III of the argument are omitted.

* * *

An appropriately short Conclusion that simply asks for
the relief sought.

CONCLUSION

For the foregoing reasons, the Respondents respectfully urge this Court to affirm the
decision of the United States Court of Appeals for the Sixth Circuit.

Respectfully submitted,

BENSON A. WOLMAN, Counsel of Record, MOOTS, COPE & STANTON, 3600
Olentangy River Road, Building 501, Columbus, Ohio 43214-3913, (614) 459-4140

DAVID GOLDBERGER, c/o The Ohio State Univ. College of Law, 55 West Twelfth
Avenue, Columbus, Ohio 43210, (614) 292-6821

BARBARA P. O'TOOLE, Roger Baldwin Foundation of ACLU, 203 N. LaSalle Street,
Chicago, IL 60601, (312) 201-9740

STEVEN R. SHAPIRO, American Civil Liberties Union Foundation, 132 West 43rd
Street, New York, NY 10036, (212) 944-9800, Attorneys for Respondents

Of Counsel

PETER JOY, Case Western Reserve Univ. College of Law, 11075 East Boulevard,
Cleveland, Ohio 44106, (216) 368-2766

KEVIN FRANCIS O'NEILL, American Civil Liberties Union of Ohio Foundation,
1223 West Sixth Street, Cleveland, Ohio 44113, (216) 781-1078

Sample Brief No. 5:

Petition for a
Writ of Mandamus

IN THE
UNITED STATES COURT OF APPEALS
FOR THE ELEVENTH CIRCUIT

No. 12345

In re ABC CAROLINAS, INC.,
ABC SOUTHEAST, INC., and
ABC SOUTHWEST, INC.,

Petitioners.

PETITION FOR WRIT OF MANDAMUS

I.M. Madashell
Big Law Firm LLP
One Address Square, Suite 123
St. Charles, Missouri 64102
Phone: (555) 555-2000
Fax: (555) 555-2001

[We have eliminated the required sections on Interested Persons and Corporate Relationships, the Table of Contents and the Table of Authorities]

> The first section here is the most important. You must grab the court of appeals' attention right away and convince them that a grave injustice has occurred and action needs to be taken. Fortunately for the author here, he had the authorities to back up this claim.

SUMMARY OF THE ARGUMENT AND REASONS WHY MANDAMUS SHOULD ISSUE

This petition for writ of mandamus presents two issues that have been conclusively determined by binding precedent of this circuit: *first*, that the district court clearly abused its discretion by failing to enforce a valid contractual forum selection clause requiring the dismissal or transfer of the underlying lawsuit. In re Fireman's Fund Insurance Companies, 588 F.2d 93, 95 (5th Cir. 1979) (forum selection clause preempts statutory venue provision); In re Ricoh Corp., 870 F.2d 570, 572-74 (11th Cir. 1989) (district court clearly abused its discretion in failing to enforce forum selection clause), petition for writ after remand from Stewart Org., Inc. v. Ricoh Corp., 487 U.S. 22 (1988); and *second*, that mandamus should issue to correct this manifest error. Ricoh, 870 F.2d at 571-72 (writ of mandamus is to be issued to correct district court's failure to enforce forum selection clause).

This lawsuit arises from a dispute among partners concerning the proper disposition of approximately $23 million in proceeds from the sale of partnership properties in three related partnerships. The partnership agreements contain a forum selection clause calling for any partnership disputes to be brought either in Delaware, the state in which the partnerships are organized, or one of the venues where the partnership properties are located. No properties are located in Florida. Nevertheless, the general partner filed an interpleader action in the U.S. District Court for the Southern District of Florida. The general partner claimed that it was an innocent stakeholder of the disputed proceeds as between the two limited partners, Petitioners and a sister company of the general partner. Plaintiff invoked 28 U.S.C. § 1397, which provides that venue for statutory interpleader actions is appropriate wherever any claimant resides. Both the general partner and its affiliate/limited partner are based in southern Florida.

Petitioners moved pursuant to Fed. R. Civ. P. 12(b)(3) and 28 U.S.C. § 1406 for the case to be dismissed for improper venue because Florida was not one of the contractually agreed-to venues. Alternatively, Petitioners sought transfer to the District of Delaware where a separate action, filed by Petitioners, is pending. The Honorable William J. Zloch, United States District Judge, Southern District of Florida (Respondent), issued two opinions on Petitioners motion. In his initial opinion, he found that:

- The forum selection clause was valid and applicable to this controversy.
- The forum selection clause did <u>not</u> permit venue in Florida.
- The forum selection clause was not preempted by 28 U.S.C. § 1397 because even exclusive statutory venue provisions can be waived by contractual agreement of the parties.

After requesting further briefing on the issue of whether 28 U.S.C. § 1404(a) or § 1406 was the proper vehicle to effectuate transfer or dismissal of the case, Judge Zloch issued a second opinion. Without altering any of his initial conclusions, Judge Zloch held that <u>neither</u> § 1404(a) <u>nor</u> § 1406 authorized dismissal or transfer of the case. Judge Zloch held that venue in Florida was not improper as that term is used in 28 U.S.C. § 1406 because venue in Florida was available under the interpleader venue statute, 28 U.S.C. § 1397; therefore, he could neither dismiss nor transfer the action pursuant to § 1406. Judge Zloch also refused to transfer the case pursuant to 28 U.S.C. § 1404(a), holding that § 1404(a) was inapplicable because the case could not originally have been brought in the District of Delaware under 28 U.S.C. § 1397. Judge Zloch refused to reconsider his ruling and refused to certify it for interlocutory appeal.

Although mandamus is an extraordinary remedy, it is appropriate where there has been a clear abuse of discretion. Here, Judge Zloch clearly abused his discretion by refusing to enforce the contractual forum selection clause between the parties. The applicable precedent leaves no doubt that the parties contractual selection of venue should be honored even if other venues are specified by statute. <u>Fireman's Fund</u>, 588 F.2d at 95. Indeed, Judge Zloch so found in his initial opinion. His subsequent decision not to give effect to the forum selection clause because of the venue provisions of § 1397 simply cannot be reconciled with his original holding. Nor can it be reconciled with the law.

Petitioners have no other adequate alternative remedy. The option of seeking reversal on venue grounds only after being forced to endure full discovery, litigation, and trial in southern Florida is not only inadequate but is terribly wasteful. This Court has determined that mandamus is appropriate to correct a district court's refusal to enforce a forum selection clause. <u>Ricoh</u>, 870 F.2d at 571-72. This remedy should be granted here.

STATEMENT OF THE ISSUE PRESENTED AND RELIEF SOUGHT

Whether the venue provisions of 28 U.S.C. § 1397 are subject to contractual waiver through a forum selection clause and, if so, whether an action filed in violation of the forum selection clause should be dismissed or transferred to a contractually agreed forum pursuant to either 28 U.S.C. § 1406 or 28 U.S.C. § 1404(a). The district court's opinion denying dismissal or transfer of this case is directly contrary to the following controlling authorities:

<u>In re Fireman's Fund Insurance Companies</u>, 588 F.2d 93 (5th Cir. 1979).

<u>In re Ricoh</u>, 870 F.2d 570 (11th Cir. 1989), <u>petition for writ after remand from</u> <u>Stewart Org. v. Ricoh</u>, 487 U.S. 22 (1988).

The Bremen v. Zapata Off-Shore Co., 407 U.S. 1 (1972).

Carnival Cruise Lines, Inc. v. Shute, 499 U.S. 585 (1991).

Petitioners request this Court to issue a writ of mandamus ordering the district court to dismiss this action for lack of proper venue or, alternatively, to transfer the action to the United States District Court for the District of Delaware pursuant to the forum selection clause applicable to this matter, and to order such further and other relief as the Court deems appropriate in the circumstances.

[We have eliminated the statement of facts and proceedings below sections]

> The argument uses the words "clear" and "clearly" a lot, which normally would make a reader cringe, but in this case, the trial judge really did make an obvious mistake. Arguably, "clear" errors are the *only* kind that ever warrant the issuance of a writ of mandamus. Nevertheless, we would limit or omit the use of these words.

ARGUMENT

I. MANDAMUS IS AN APPROPRIATE REMEDY TO CORRECT RESPONDENT'S CLEAR ABUSE OF DISCRETION

Mandamus is a proper remedy where the trial court fails to enforce a forum selection clause that requires the dismissal or transfer of an action. In re Ricoh, 870 F.2d 570, 571-72 (11th Cir. 1989), petition for writ after remand from Stewart Org. v. Ricoh, 487 U.S. 22 (1988). It is particularly appropriate for the Court of Appeals to issue the writ when the district court has failed to certify the issue for interlocutory appeal. Id. at 572 n. 4.

> The author makes heavy use of Ricoh because it was an 11th Circuit case that granted a writ in the exact same circumstances as the instant case. It does not get much better than that.

The district court clearly abused its discretion when it failed to enforce a valid forum selection clause. In Ricoh, this Court was explicit about the necessity to enforce forum selection clauses by transfer under 28 U.S.C. § 1404(a):

> In considering Ricoh's motion under section 1404(a) to transfer this action to the Southern District of New York, the district court . . . clearly abused its discretion . . .

. . . [The district court's] deference to the filing forum would only encourage parties to violate their contractual obligations, the integrity of which are vital to our judicial system. See Stewart, [487 U.S. at 33], 108 S.Ct. at 2246 ([E]nforcement of valid forum selection clauses, bargained for by the parties, protects their legitimate expectations and furthers vital interests of the justice system.) (Kennedy, J., concurring); see also Stewart, 810 F.2d 1066, 1075 (11th Cir. 1987) (en banc) (Where, as here, the non-movant has not shown that it would be unjust to honor a forum selection clause that it has freely given, the interest of justice requires that the non-movant be held to its promise.) (Tjoflat, J., concurring). We conclude that when a motion under section 1404(a) seeks to enforce a valid, reasonable choice of forum clause, the opponent bears the burden of persuading the court that the contractual forum is sufficiently inconvenient to justify retention of the dispute.

In so concluding, we adhere to the reasoning advanced by the Supreme Court in its opinion in this case. See Stewart, [487 U.S. 22] , 108 S.Ct. 2239, 101 L.Ed.2d 22 (1988). . . . [T]he clear import of the Court's opinion is that the venue mandated by a choice of forum clause rarely will be outweighed by other 1404(a) factors.

Ricoh, 870 F.2d at 572-73. The facts of Ricoh parallel the instant case:

Looking to the specific facts of this case, we note that the instant contract was freely and fairly negotiated by experienced business professionals. . . . Stewart has neither alleged nor shown the presence of fraud, duress, misrepresentation, or other misconduct that would bar the clause's enforcement. Nor has Stewart demonstrated that because of intervening and unexpected occurrences between the contract's formation and the filing of the suit, the contract's purpose would be frustrated if we were to mandate the transfer of this case to a Manhattan forum. This suit, therefore, does not present the type of exceptional situation in which judicial enforcement of a contractual choice of forum clause would be improper. See Stewart, [487 U.S. at 33], 108 S.Ct. at 2246 (Kennedy, J., concurring). The district court clearly abused its discretion in concluding otherwise.

Ricoh, 870 F.2d at 573-74.

In these circumstances, Petitioners have no other adequate alternative remedy. The only conceivable alternative remedy, "inevitable reversal by this court after the defendants have been forced to endure full discovery, full litigation, and a full trial is scarcely . . . adequate." In re Cooper, 971 F.2d 640, 641 (11th Cir. 1992) (citing In re Watkins, 271 F.2d 771, 775 (5th Cir. 1959)). Therefore, this Court should issue a writ of mandamus to order the Respondent to dismiss or transfer the underlying action.

II. RESPONDENT CLEARLY ABUSED ITS DISCRETION BY DENYING THE MOTION TO DISMISS OR TRANSFER

There is an unbroken line of controlling authorities that require the enforcement of contractual forum selection clauses. The Bremen v. Zapata Off-Shore Co., 407 U.S. 1 (1972); Carnival Cruise Lines, Inc. v. Shute, 499 U.S. 585 (1991); Stewart Organization v. Ricoh, 487 U.S. 22 (1988); Ricoh, 870 F.2d 570; In re Fireman's Fund Insurance Companies, 588 F.2d 93 (5th Cir. 1979). This point is not disputed by the parties. Judge Zloch concluded, however, that neither § 1406 nor § 1404(a) empowered him to dismiss or transfer the action. This conclusion was clearly in error.

Judge Zloch determined that 28 U.S.C. § 1404(a), rather than § 1406, applied to the motion to dismiss or transfer. Judge Zloch followed what Petitioners believe is a minority opinion among the courts that was triggered by a footnote in the Stewart case, 487 U.S. at 28 n. 8. See, e.g., Jumara v. State Farm Ins. Co., 55 F.3d 873, 878-79 (3d Cir. 1995). This position holds that cases are not subject to dismissal under Rule 12(b)(3) or 28 U.S.C. § 1406 on the basis of a forum selection clause because the venue where the case is filed is not made improper by operation of the forum selection clause. Id. Instead, these courts apply 28 U.S.C. § 1404(a) to determine whether the case is to be transferred. Id.

Judge Zloch concluded, however, that § 1404(a) was inapplicable because this case could not have been brought in Delaware under the interpleader venue provision, 28 U.S.C. § 1397. This conclusion is directly contrary to the established law of this circuit, In re Fireman's Fund Ins. Co., 588 F.2d 93, 95 (5th Cir. 1979).

In Fireman's Fund, this Court held that the specific, exclusive venue provision of the Miller Act, 40 U.S.C. § 270b(b), mandating that [e]very suit instituted under this section shall be brought . . . in the United States District Court for any district in which the contract was to be performed and executed and not elsewhere, was nonetheless subject to a forum selection clause between the parties which called for a transfer to a forum where the contract was not to be performed or executed. 588 F.2d at 95. The Court noted that a motion to transfer under 28 U.S.C. § 1404(a) applies to any civil action. Id. Furthermore, the Court noted that even an exclusive venue provision containing the phrase, and not elsewhere, was still subject to alteration by the parties forum selection clause, because venue may be varied by contract. Id.

The Miller Act's exclusive venue provision is worded much stronger than 28 U.S.C. § 1397, yet this circuit recognized that a party's power to contract into another forum is even stronger. This opinion is buttressed by numerous other cases cited by Judge Zloch in the 10/22/96 Order (at pp. 6-7) holding that forum selection clauses preempt the operation of venue statutes, including exclusive venue provisions. B & D Mechanical, 70 F.3d at 1117; FGS Constructors, Inc. v. Carlow, 64 F.3d 1230, 1233 (8th Cir. 1995); Pittsburgh Tank, 62 F.3d at 36; Bense v. Interstate Battery System of America, 683 F.2d 718 (2d Cir. 1982).

Judge Zloch initially followed these authorities in the 10/22/96 Order, specifically holding that section 1397 . . . is a venue provision and thus subject to contractual waiver. 10/22/96 Order at 7. But he then ignored these authorities in the 12/5/96 Order, concluding that a contractually designated forum that would not be an appropriate venue for the action under the interpleader venue statue, section 1397, is not a court where the action might have been brought under section 1404(a). 12/5/96 Order at 8.

Judge Zloch cited <u>Hoffman v. Blaski</u>, 363 U.S. 335 (1960), as his sole authority for this proposition. 12/5/96 Order at 8. However, this case is inapposite to the issue because it has nothing whatsoever to do with a forum selection clause or the parties right to make a prior selection of venue by consent or agreement. In <u>Hoffman</u>, the defendants moved under section 1404(a) for transfer to a forum where the defendants had not been amenable to service of process and had no contacts, and where venue was obviously improper at the initiation of the action by plaintiffs. 363 U.S. at 336-37 and n. 2, 338-39 and n. 5. Defendants' motion stated that defendants were willing to submit themselves to the jurisdiction and venue of the alternative forum, if the court would consider the transfer on the basis of convenience to the parties and witnesses. <u>Id.</u> The forum to which defendants sought to be transferred was clearly one in which the case could <u>not</u> have been brought by the plaintiffs when the suit was filed. <u>Id.</u> In these circumstances, the court determined that a transfer to the forum under section 1404(a) was not proper. 363 U.S. at 342-43.

<u>Hoffman</u> is inapposite because in the instant case, plaintiff had every right to bring this action in the forum selected by the Agreements forum selection clause. The controlling authorities hold that forum selection clauses must be enforced unless the opponents of the motion prove that there are exceptional circumstances that render the enforcement of the clause unreasonable and improper. <u>Ricoh</u>, 870 F.2d at 572-74; <u>Stewart</u>, 487 U.S. at 33 (Kennedy, J., concurring). Respondent ignored these authorities, and made a clearly erroneous determination of Petitioner's motion to dismiss or transfer that flies in the face of these authorities and even contradicts Respondent's prior order in the instant case. Therefore, the Court should issue a writ of mandamus to remedy Respondent's clear abuse of discretion and usurpation of judicial power.

CONCLUSION

WHEREFORE, Petitioners respectfully request this Court to issue a writ of mandamus ordering the district court to dismiss this case for lack of proper venue, or to transfer this action to the United States District Court for the District of Delaware pursuant to the forum selection clause applicable to this matter, and to order such further and other relief as the Court deems appropriate in the circumstances.

Chapter 7

Oral Advocacy at Pretrial, Trial and Appellate Stages

We have concentrated on the use of writing for communication in the practice of law. It is true, however, that any lawyer will have at least as many and sometimes more occasions to use oral communication in the practice of law:

> ➤ to provide advice to a client or other attorneys in the lawyer's office
> ➤ to discuss matters or negotiate with other attorneys
> ➤ to orally communicate and argue motions, requests, objections, and other legal arguments to a decision maker such as a judge

If we were to compare the amount of time we have spent on the telephone and talking on our feet as an attorney to the amount of time hunched before a keyboard drafting documents, we are sure we would find that the former balances out and sometimes even outweighs the latter.

Clear and effective communication skills in person and over the phone are a great asset for any attorney. Many times your clients or your superiors who vote on your future in the law office will only have these types of encounters with you—they never will have read a single thing you have written, and the only impression they will have of you as an attorney is from your oral communication skills. This should be a great incentive to try to refine your skills. Talk in complete sentences. Avoid excessive slang, and fillers such as "ya know," "uhhhhh," "like," and others. Be concise in speaking—an economy of words and a depth of meaning should be your goal.

This chapter focuses on the more particular skills required in litigation settings. Unlike most legal method and legal writing texts, we will discuss argument in the trenches of the trial level courts before going to the mountaintop of appellate level oral argument. The skills needed in the former type of forum are slightly different and somewhat more crude than the skills needed in the latter.

I. BACKGROUND PRINCIPLES OF THE PRACTICE OF ORAL ARGUMENT

Lawyers often puzzle over the true meaning of oral argument. As with writing, we think it is prudent to look at oral argument from the perspective of the audience, the trial or appellate court judge. Judges have several ends that are achieved by oral argument:

A. It is an efficient use of the court's time and resources.

At the trial court level, complicated motions can be summarized and reported orally in capsule form to the court, who, after hearing the argument, might have an immediate answer for the parties on the merits of the motion. If the court is one in which the judge has an abundance of cases and no law clerks, oral argument enables the court to process a great number of cases in the shortest possible time. Even if the judge is forced to take a motion "under advisement" after the oral argument, the argument still may have served its purpose to educate the court enough to allow it to proceed rapidly through the briefs and memoranda filed on the motion, and ultimately lead to a quicker decision.

On appeal, the judges generally have law clerks who can summarize the legal briefs for the judges in the form of a bench memo, but appellate court judges often will take the time to personally consult the parties' briefs before the oral argument. In these instances, oral argument still can assist the court to make sense of complicated issues and provides the judges with a forum to question the litigants, as discussed in the section below, which can assist the court in reaching its decision in a shorter period of time.

B. It allows a judge to question the two sides about the motion or appeal.

If a judge did read and digest the motion or appellate briefs ahead of time, or her clerks did, and they summarized the case for the judge, the judge still may have questions that need to be answered before she can rule. Oral argument is just the place for this. Many advocates think of oral argument as "their time" to present their arguments, but judges quite properly think of argument as the court's time to clarify and explore the issues.

An advocate may spend days preparing a wonderful fifteen minute oral argument just to show up and have the court use up thirteen of the fifteen minutes with questions. This is not a failure, it is exactly what the advocate should expect and even welcome. The days spent working on and thinking hard about the case will enable the advocate properly to address those thirteen minutes of questions, and the judges will leave this argument with a much better understanding of those aspects of the case that troubled them the most.

C. It can assist a judge in making up her mind.

Trial court judges often have no idea that a motion was filed in your case until you step up to the podium and address the court on the motion. The only time you will have the judge's undivided attention on your motion is during these brief periods of argument. If the judge cannot devote long periods of time to the briefs filed by the parties and has no law clerks to help her, the oral argument is the most important time for the judge to make up her mind about the merits of the motion.

Of the appellate court judges we have heard on this issue, most have reported that they make up their minds based on the briefs of the parties. The arguments serve as a chance to reconfirm this initial opinion or perhaps to have one or two questions answered that might push the judge a little farther in one direction or the other. These judges do allow for the possibility that from time to time the parties might explain their case orally in such a way that the judges actually will change their minds solely because of the oral arguments. This should be enough incentive for you to take the argument process seriously.

II. ORAL ARGUMENT IN TRIAL LEVEL COURTS PRIOR TO TRIAL

An oral argument in the pretrial stage can happen several ways. The ways will depend on the local rules and local practices of the jurisdiction and occasionally on the individual judge to which your case is assigned.

A. "No oral argument" jurisdictions

You may find yourself practicing in a jurisdiction that does not allow oral argument on motions except when it is specifically ordered by the court. This is what we characterize as a "no oral argument" jurisdiction, because the rule commonly is interpreted to mean that oral argument will be extremely rare on motions, and reserved only for the most complicated motions where the parties and the court think it will be of benefit.

The parties might request oral argument because they think it will lead to an earlier ruling on the motion. They also might think that the court will benefit from having the parties run through the motion in person, so that they can address any problems that the court might have with the facts, or the law, or the positions of the parties.

The court might go along with the request or, even more rarely, *sua sponte* order oral argument on a motion for the same reasons as stated above. Different judges have different opinions about the benefits and costs of oral argument. Some judges love to see and hear the attorneys in the case, others started their judicial career in a court where oral arguments were routinely heard, and they think of the process as a great way to clear their docket of a number of motions in a short period of time. Other judges would rather reserve their court time for trials and hearings and will not be bothered to hear motions argued.

B. "Motion Day" or "Law Day" jurisdictions

In some courts, one or two days a month or sometimes one or two days a week are set aside for motions to be heard on oral argument pursuant to local rules. E.g., Ala. R. Civ. P. 78; Ariz. R. Civ. P. 78; Ark. R. Civ. P. 78; Colo. R. Civ. P. 78; Haw. R. Civ. P. 78. These days are called "motion days" or sometimes "law days." The movant generally will have to schedule a place on the motion docket with the court, and then give notice of the date and time to all parties and the court. Occasionally, a court will allow any and all parties with pending motions simply to show up and sign up on the motion day, without prior scheduling or notice to the court. It will be necessary to notify your opponents that you are going, because if you show up by yourself, the court is unlikely to entertain an *ex parte* argument on the motion.

C. "Open Court" Jurisdictions

Occasionally, a court will hear oral arguments on motions any day that the court is in session. A simple call to the court to confirm that they are in session on the chosen day, perhaps to sign up on the docket, too, and notice given in writing to all parties and to the court will secure your oral argument whenever it is convenient for you and the other parties.

D. Informal matters and "show up" jurisdictions

Courts sometimes will set aside a short period of time, usually in the morning when the court first opens for business, for the hearing of informal matters and motions, and any party with such a request or motion simply can show up and present their request to the court. Prior notice to the court is not required, although it will be necessary to contact the other parties to let them know what you are up to. These sessions usually are reserved for smaller, often uncontested motions, such as requests for extensions of time to answer or to respond to discovery or to file an amended complaint, requests to file a brief with additional pages over the local page limit, for attorney admission to the court, for a minor amendment to pleadings, or other fairly simple requests. Discovery motions, such as motions to quash or motions to compel might be brought here, especially if the timing of the discovery (a deposition, for example) demands expedited attention from the court. Substantial requests, such as dispositive motions to dismiss or for summary judgment, motions for preliminary injunctions, and complicated discovery motions or motions in limine generally will not be entertained in informal matters, and the court may get angry at you for trying to bring up a complicated, contested motion in these sessions.

E. The necessity to "notice up" motions

In many courts, other than those in category A above, the parties must call for oral argument by "noticing up a hearing" on a motion because that is the only way their motions are going to get ruled on. Notice of a hearing on a motion alerts the other parties that if they have not filed an opposition to the motion yet, do it now or before the hearing. Notice also puts the court file in the judge's hands on the day of the hearing, and gives him a strong incentive to deal with the motion then and there, rather than hear the oral argument, let the motion go under advisement, and forget about it.

F. Style of oral argument in trial courts in the pretrial period

Oral argument at the pretrial stage differs from the appellate level oral argument in several ways: usually, you do not get a fixed period of time to talk. You talk until the judge shuts you up, or your opponent interrupts you and cuts you off, or until you run out of things to say, or until the judge walks out and they turn the lights off in the court. You do not get just one chance to argue your position; you can go back and forth several times arguing your side then listening to your opponent argue hers, then interrupting her and trying to command the judge's attention, until she cuts you off or the judge calls it quits.

In the best instances, the judge will control the argument and demand an orderly presentation so that each side gets a chance to say what it wants to say. The best judges will not tolerate counsel interrupting each other and will quash such rudeness quickly. The judge may question each side so as to explore the strengths and weaknesses of their positions. The judge, not the parties, decides when she has heard enough on the motion.

At its worst, the court will not regulate the argument, and will sit by while counsel interrupt and cut each other off, and bluster and rage so as to command the most attention. In these situations, it matters much less whether or not you have a structured and logical outline, and a start and finish to the argument worked out on a pretrial motion; rather, what is important is the ability to divert the judge's attention away from your opponent and capture it long enough to say your two or three points any way that you can. Being quick of tongue, loud, blustery, and ready and willing to interrupt and cut off your opponent will help in these dismal situations.

III. ORAL ARGUMENT DURING A TRIAL

Aside from the opening statement and the closing argument, which are directed to the jury of laypersons, not to the court, and which have nothing to do with our topic here, oral arguments to the court are not regularly scheduled during trials. However, in our experience, we have more often than not been called on to make miniature oral arguments during a trial to argue evidentiary points, to argue motions made during the trial, and to argue or defend motions for directed verdict or for judgment as a matter of law.

These arguments usually are conducted like the pretrial motions described above—you do not get a set amount of time and you get to go back and forth several times, but far fewer of the same "style" advantages carry over to this setting because a sense of decorum prevails during a trial that is absent in the average pretrial hearing. As a result, the arguments generally are cleaner with fewer interruptions. Nevertheless, the content of the arguments typically are no more organized, detailed, or thought-provoking than the average pretrial argument.

IV. APPELLATE ORAL ARGUMENT

The rest of this chapter focuses on the more particular skills required in appellate court and moot court settings. The paradigm of oral argument for law students is appellate level oral argument. This is the model followed by most law schools in first year oral arguments and in the moot court programs and competitions in the second and third year.

Compared to oral arguments in the trial courts, appellate level argument is a "mountaintop" experience, because you get a certain amount of time to speak, no one interrupts you (except the panel), and getting out your full argument does not depend on your ability and willingness to interrupt and cut off the other side.

The standard procedures for oral argument are remarkably similar from place to place and competition to competition: usually there is more than one judge on the panel. Each side (appellant - appellee, or petitioner - respondent) gets a specific period of time in which to speak. It can be as little as ten minutes or as long as the court wants to give you, although most courts will not give each side more than forty-five minutes or an hour for any argument. No one except the panel can interrupt the oralist. No counsel can yell, "Objection," or "She's misstating the facts!" during their opponent's argument. A bailiff or clerk keeps time, and periodically will hold up a card, light up a small light in front of you, or rap a gavel to let you know how many minutes you have left. Each oralist makes her arguments and answers the panel's questions and sits down.

Generally, the appellant or petitioner oralists speak first and the appellee or respondent oralists speak second. The appellant usually can reserve a few minutes for one oralist to do rebuttal, and once in a great while the rules of the court or the moot court competition will allow the appellee to reserve time for an oralist to do surrebuttal. If you have a partner or associate with you, your side will have to pre-determine how to split the time between the two oralists. Most of the time, an even split is the best idea. You do not want to deny the panel the opportunity to have a good look at both oralists.

Where there is more than one issue at stake in the appeal, some courts allow an appellant or petitioner to argue issue one followed by the appellee or respondent's argument on issue one, followed by the appellant or petitioner's argument on issue two, followed by the appellee or respondent's argument on issue two, and so on. Some moot court competitions follow this procedure, too.

The classic and expected practice is for the judges to interrupt your argument with questions. Panels will vary from how **active** they are (lots of questions), how **hostile** they are (how much they show their dislike for one or both sides' arguments), or how "**hot**" they are ("hot" means they read the parties' briefs or the bench briefs carefully, and are prepared to question you on the issues and authorities; "cold" means they did not read anything before hand, and will just give you a cold indifferent stare when you start). A good panel for almost any oral argumentative is an active, hot, but not hostile panel.

V. HOW TO PREPARE FOR ORAL ARGUMENT

Appellate oral argument follows the briefing of the case in which the appellant or petitioner files its opening brief, the appellee or respondent files its answering brief or opposition brief, and the appellant or petitioner files its reply brief. An argument date is set by the court. A panel of judges from the court is selected unless the matter is to be heard by the court *en banc*. As the day of the argument approaches, counsel should be doing the following things to prepare themselves for the argument:

A. Know every case and legal authority inside and out.

You probably will be nervous before your first two or three oral arguments, but use this energy to drive you through the preparation. Channel your nervous energy into reviewing the points you will make and the points raised by your opponent in her brief. Read all of your cases and authorities again for facts, holding, rationale, and policies. Key Cite or shepardize them one more time. Now do the same for your opponent's cases: find her bad cases.

If you have one or more partners, you should spend some time discussing all of the good and bad cases as a team when you are preparing for oral argument. Everyone on the team should have a working knowledge of the issues and the authorities in the case, both good authorities and bad. It is common in oral arguments to hear an oralist beg off a question by disclaiming "That is a question that my co-counsel will address," or worse yet, "That issue has been discussed in my co-counsel's part of the argument, and I am not able to discuss it." The only time you should be uttering these words in oral argument is if you are completely stumped by a question thrown at you by the panel, **and** it happens to be an issue that your co-counsel, who is going next, will address. If you are well up to speed on the case, you should not have to beg off. Some judges are looking to see how up to speed on the whole case you really are, and if you handle an "off your position" question well, they will be very impressed.

B. Write an outline, not a script.

Draft an **outline** of what you want to say. You do not want to write out things word for word because if you then read from a prepared text, this will not sound conversational, sincere, and from the heart. Good oral arguments sound more conversational than speeches delivered from a podium. You also are supposed to make eye contact with everyone on the panel, and you cannot do that if you are looking down at your notes. Oral arguments have the illusion of being an impromptu discussion from someone who knows and cares, and thus are more persuasive than the average lecture. If you write out your entire argument, you will have too much paper up there with you at the podium, and in trying to follow it, you may get distracted by a question and lose your place.

Your outline does not have to follow the exact order of arguments that you put in your brief. Think about ways to get to the best argument quickly and work on a transition from that to the next best argument and so on. The judges have your brief, and they can read the whole story of your case if they want to. Oral argument is the place for you to drive home your best points and make them stick in the judges' minds, so that when the judges retire to the conference that follows the arguments, they will remember these points and be more inclined to vote in your favor.

C. Prepare an introduction.

The only exception to the rule against scripting that we encourage you to follow is for you to script the first forty-five seconds or so of your oral argument and to commit this portion to memory. The start of the argument has certain formal requirements expected of counsel in most jurisdictions:

➤ Most oralists will start their argument with the phrase, "May it please the court." This is a convention, not a rule in most jurisdictions, but it is a convention followed by the vast majority of oralists. If you decide to buck the convention, you should be aware that from time to time you will encounter a judge who will view your free-spirited thinking as rebellion. You will not necessarily win points for originality; instead, judges will think you started the argument incorrectly. Many oralists soften the formality by adding, "Good morning, your honors" or other greeting appropriate for the time of day. Oralists at the United States Supreme Court begin by stating, "Mr. Chief Justice, may it please the court."

➤ Personal introductions come next. Introduce yourself and your co-counsel, and the party you represent. Remind the court of the reason for your argument and your prayer for relief. Explain the breakdown of the points you and your co-counsel will be addressing.

Example: May it please the court. Good afternoon, your honors. My name is Walter Scott and I, together with my co-counsel, Edith Wharton, represent petitioner George Elliot. Mr. Elliot asks the court to reverse the order granting summary judgment in favor of respondent Twain issued by the United States District Court for the Western District of Tennessee. I will be addressing the issues of news reporting and political speech. My co-counsel will address the issues of parody and the right to comment on and criticize political figures under the First Amendment.

➤ The next portion should be an introduction to your argument and your theme. Most counsel draft a short statement of the two or three major bullet points of their argument, followed by a statement of the theme of the case from your client's perspective.

Example: {**introduction**} Mr. Elliot requests that you reverse the lower court for three reasons: first, that the First Amendment protects and encourages political commentary to such a degree that respondent Twain's publicity rights must give way to Mr. Elliot's commentary. Second, that the Tennessee Personal Rights Protection Act specifically provides an exception for "news reporting" and commentary on "public affairs," and Mr. Elliot meets the requirements of this exception. Third, that Mr. Elliot's commentary is not commercial speech. {**theme**} Your honors, the protection of the right of political commentary is the core value protected by the First Amendment. The preservation of all other topics of expression is secondary to the goal of preserving an open and robust dialogue on politics in a democracy.

Some counsel will flip the theme and the introduction:

Example: {**theme**} Your honors, the protection of the right of political commentary is the core value protected by the First Amendment. The preservation of all other topics of expression is secondary to the goal of preserving an open and robust dialogue on politics in a democracy. {**introduction**} Mr. Elliot requests that you reverse the lower court for three reasons: first, that the First Amendment protects and encourages political commentary to such a degree that respondent Twain's publicity rights must give way to Mr. Elliot's commentary. Second, that the Tennessee Personal Rights Protection Act specifically provides an exception for "news reporting" and commentary on "public affairs," and Mr. Elliot meets the requirements of this exception. Third, that Mr. Elliot's commentary is not commercial speech.

Still others will combine the theme and the introduction in one statement of the case:

{**thematic introduction**} Mr. Elliot requests that you reverse the lower court for three reasons: first, that the First Amendment protects and encourages political commentary to such a degree that respondent Twain's publicity rights must give way to Mr. Elliot's commentary. Indeed, this is the core value protected by the First Amendment, which outweighs the protection of all other topics of speech. Second, that the Tennessee Personal Rights Protection Act specifically provides an exception for "news reporting" and commentary on "public affairs" so as to ensure an open and robust dialogue on matters of public interest in a democracy. Mr. Elliot meets the requirements of this exception. Third, that Mr. Elliot's commentary is not commercial speech and thus deserves the full protection that the First Amendment affords to political commentary.

A bullet point introduction of the two or three main points of your argument notifies the court of what you think are your most important points. The judges will appreciate the outline if it is short and manageable. An outline of five or six major points is excessive. Rarely would even the most skilled oralist be able to cover six points adequately in fifteen minutes even if the judges withheld all of their questions. The judges will be discouraged if you ask them to try to keep that many major points straight in their heads as you make the effort to cover them. It is much better to distill your argument down to two or three points. Telling the judges your two or three best points up front also allows them to direct you to address whichever of the points the judges are the most interested in, which most likely will be the points that the judges are having the most trouble with. You might be disappointed that the judges do not want to hear point one, your best point, but if they already have resolved that point in their minds, argument over this point would be a waste of your time and theirs.

Do not be misled into thinking that our recommendation of scripting your opening means that you might plan on reading from the script. Nothing could be further from the truth. The script is there for you to memorize well before you step up to the podium. After memorizing your opening, practice it several times each day leading up to the argument. Memorization and practice allows two things to happen simultaneously in your argument: first, you will be assured that you have command of the first forty-five seconds of your argument. If you are tense or nervous about the argument process, at least you will know that you can speak confidently without stumbling or getting tongue tied for the first forty-five seconds. This allows you precious time to get comfortable with the process and get into the flow of a conversation. Second, memorization allows you to make eye contact with the entire panel and to establish rapport during the opening seconds. A smooth opening relaxes the panel and draws them in. They will be happy to be listening to a competent oralist who can begin smoothly and who invites them to join the conversation by making eye contact with each member of the panel. That is why reading from your script is a cardinal sin.

If you have not had much experience memorizing passages of this length, here are two tips:

> ➤ Copy over your script by hand at least three times. The exercise of copying engages the mind in several activities at once—considering the words individually, considering how they flow one to the other, and directing your hand to write them down correctly. Actors use this technique to memorize their scripts, and on average they have a lot more lines to commit to memory than you will have.
> ➤ Practice your opening several times a day. If you stumble, go back and copy over your script three more times. Repeat this process until you have the opening committed to memory.

If you still are uncomfortable with the thought of forgetting your opening, do not bring your script to the podium. Instead, outline your opening on an index card:

(1) May it please the court
(2) Introduce yourself and your co-counsel–what are each of you arguing
(3) Ask the court to reverse
(4) Give your outline:
       point one: political speech
       point two: statutory exception
       point three: not commercial speech
(5) Give theme: political speech and First Amendment

At least then you will have a crutch, but you will not be encouraged to read off of the card.

D. Themes are not just for briefs.

As mentioned in the section above, you should work on a theme for your argument that fits with your facts and the majority of your written arguments. Hopefully, you already had a good theme in your brief, but if not, there still is time to come up with one. A good sound bite that sums up your arguments, that you can return to frequently in your argument and in answers to questions, can drive home your arguments faster than a long winded explanation. Try to find the best (and safest) analogy for your situation, and use it whenever you want to remind the court of the equities or legal realities that drive your arguments to their conclusions. Short and vivid themes are the best. Paint a small picture—or come up with a one panel editorial cartoon with a one line zinger that sums up you case, and build the argument around that. Do not get too wordy or complicated—think advertising copy, not a treatise discussion.

E. Try to anticipate likely questions, and work out good answers to them.

Try to think up questions your panel of judges might ask, and work out answers that are good, complete responses to the questions and which can segue you back to the points you want to raise.[1] Judges will ask about the strengths of your case and your opponent's case, and explore the weaknesses of both sides. Judges will ask about the public policy and precedential implications of the arguments you are making. They will ask questions about specific cases and authorities—What were the facts of that case? Who was the plaintiff? Did that case have anything to do with [XYZ topic]? When was that statute enacted? When did that regulation go into effect? Do not neglect your opponent's authorities and the major points of your opponent's argument; you must be prepared to discuss these, too. You can put these questions and the outline of your sample answers on a flip stack of 3X5 cards to include with the materials you will bring to the podium.

F. Organize your materials for easy access.

Ideally, your outline should fit on one or two pages. Try pasting it or stapling it to the inside of a legal size manila folder. With a manila folder, you can add a flip stack of 3X5 cards with all your important cases and authorities, your rebuttal points, and perhaps some details of the areas of law you will be discussing summarized on the cards, and a flip stack of question and answer cards described in the section above. If you think of additional points or questions, you still can stick Post-it™ notes on to the pages all the way up

---

[1] See also section IX infra, "Questions from the panel."

to the argument. We also have used three ring binders with well marked tabs leading you to your outline, your questions and answers, your rebuttal points, and your authorities information pages.

Put tabs on your brief and the opponent's brief, in case you need to look up something in these documents. If you think you might use the record, go through and tab the parts that you think might come up.

What you bring up to the podium matters less than your ability to use what you have brought quickly, quietly, and neatly. In most cases we will bring one binder or a legal size manila folder for our outline and our question-answer cards and authority cards, the briefs of the two sides, and whatever parts of the record we think we might absolutely have to use. We will expect to look at only ten percent of what we bring to the podium— usually only the outline. Your preparation for the argument should have instilled in your brain the information needed to answer the panel's questions and to make your argument without reference to the note cards and briefs.

At the very least, do not be the person who drags up several bulging file folders, full of papers sticking out this way and that, who takes five minutes to get set up before he can begin, and another six minutes to clean up after he is finished, while the judges stare at him with mixed feelings of ire and pity. You are trying to make an impression on the court that will cause them to vote in your favor. You do not want to lose points for sloppiness, of all things.

G. Go and do some field research – see how this is done.

Go watch real life oral arguments and moot court arguments. Get a feeling for what goes on, and pay attention to the kinds of questions that are asked and how they are answered. Note the tone of the oralists. Very few of them will be shouting. Theatrics probably will not be evident. It will probably sound like a conversation, one in which the oralist dominates but the judges can join at any time.

If you cannot leave home or cannot pry yourself away from the law library, you still can take advantage of the work of Prof. Jerry Goldman at Northwestern University Law School, who has prepared Real Audio® files of hundreds of oral arguments of U.S. Supreme Court cases that you can access and listen to at the Oyez Project web site, www.oyez.org (last visited April 11, 2005). The U.S. Supreme Court typically is a very active and hot panel, so you can listen to how the oralists handle intense questioning in their arguments. Court TV's site, www.courttv.com/video/ (last visited April 11, 2005), allows you to browse for video clips of trial level arguments (particularly opening statements and closing arguments).

H. How do you get to the Supreme Court? – practice, practice, practice.

Practice arguing in front of a camcorder or mirror; then practice in front of your friends and teammates. You do not necessarily have to give a legal argument in order to get the feeling of standing at a podium; present any kind of argument for some position, and answer questions from your "judges." Whatever topic you choose, take the process seriously, because you will not learn much from a session that breaks down into kidding and laughing. Just getting the feeling of talking and answering questions on your feet can make you more comfortable with the process.

After this, hold regular moot court practice sessions with your classmates or teammates—at least two or three a week in the weeks that precede the arguments. You and your teammates should grill each other as best as you can on the weaknesses and trouble spots of the case. It may seem foolish and tiresome the fourth or fifth time you do it, but practice rounds of oral argument are like batting practice or shooting free throws: the more you drill yourself to respond cooly and competently to hard questions, the more likely it will be that you will respond cooly and competently to these same questions when you are at your oral argument and the pressure is on. Have someone videotape these practice sessions. Watching yourself on tape will reveal all kinds of amazing things you never imagined yourself doing.

VI. MOOT COURT JUDGES

Whether you are facing an oral argument as part of your first year curriculum or you are facing it in the context of an upper division moot court competition, you are likely to face the same kinds of judges. The common pool for intramural and interscholastic competitions are alumnae of the school where the competition is being held, whether they be private practitioners, government lawyers, public defenders and prosecutors, in-house counsel, or actual judges. Even a regional moot court competition is going to be housed by local lawyers and judges.

The sponsors of a national competition may draw in a number of judges from out of town (the Jessup International Law Moot Court competition coordinates their international final rounds with the yearly convention of the American Society of International Law, so they have a bunch of conventioneers to choose from). You are more likely to get high powered judges who are actually judges at a regional or national competition finals.

Almost all judges you will face had a strong interest in moot court in law school, and most will have had several years of experience in litigation and oral advocacy. Most will know that they should ask questions, and many of them even will know how to ask short, cogent questions without droning on for a minute or more. (Just kidding, judges!). Judges will try to test your arguments with worst case scenarios, parades of horrors, and the edge of the slippery slope.[2] They may try to test your composure by interrupting you frequently and trying to quarrel with you about the law or the facts. Do not take the bait; they are testing you to see if you will get angry and fire back at them, but they are expecting you not to.

Actual judges are not necessarily the best oral argument judges. Actual members of the judiciary have a habit of listening to arguments rather than spicing them up with a lot of

---

[2] See also section IX infra, "Questions from the panel."

questions. This carries over from actual courtroom practices. Something about wearing a black choir robe every day makes a person more dignified and ready to listen, rather than fostering a desire to stir things up and test the knowledge and abilities of the advocates before them. Do not expect real judges to behave like television's "Judge Judy" and give you a good tongue lashing. A panel of actual judges can get all riled up in moot court as well as in real court, but in our experience, practitioners ask more and harder questions on average than actual judges.

VII. DECORUM, APPEARANCE, AND DELIVERY

Strict rules of decorum apply in appellate level oral argument. You must show respect for the panel at every turn. You always should address a judge as "Your honor," or two judges as "Your honors," and the whole panel as "the Court."

Disagree with a judge or judges gracefully and respectfully. When you want to say "no" to a judge, say "I respectfully disagree" or "Your honor, the answer is not [XYZ]" or "With all due respect, your Honor, the cases in [PDQ jurisdiction] do not support the argument that . . ." Avoid saying "No" or "No, your honor" directly to a judge unless the judge asked you a "yes-no" question that demands a "yes-no" answer. This is a matter of decorum and politeness, not substance. The judges expect you to disagree with them when they try to undo part of your case, but you should explain your disagreement with grace and respect.

Polite attention and eye contact is expected and is effective in oral argument. Staring or glaring at a judge for minutes at a time is not. Grinning, laughing, or otherwise goofing or joking at oral argument is not acceptable. If a judge makes a joke, you should politely laugh (not bust a gut and slap your knee), and smile and move on with your answer or with your argument. Resist the temptation to make a follow-up joke. Oral argument is serious business, not open-mike night at the local comedy club.

There is no "backstage" in the courtroom, so behave yourself at the counsel table. Sit patiently and listen attentively and respectfully or quietly take notes during your opponent's oral argument. Do not roll your eyes or snort or slam your pen down; these theatrics cost you much more than they will ever gain you. If you have a partner, pay close attention to the back of her head and give her focus in this way when she is arguing. Resist the urge to nod vigorously or pump your fist in the air when she makes a good point. You do not want to draw focus away from her and to yourself by nodding, fidgeting, picking your fingernails, slouching on the table, leaning way back in your chair, spinning your chair back and forth, or other such distracting conduct. Do not try these things on your opponents, either; it is very unprofessional and detrimental to the judges' opinion of you. Beaming happily at the back of your partner's head is permitted.

In every oral argument, whether it be in a real appellate court or in moot court, your appearance must be professional and appropriate. Wear your best job interview suit for an interview at a stodgy law firm. Wear your hair in a conservative lawyerly way. Jewelry and accessories (men's ties, women's scarves, chains, and earrings) should be somewhat subdued and preferably conservative. Do not wear a watch or jewelry that is loose and clunky that you might bang the podium with in the middle of your argument.

You should stand fairly still at the podium with your hands gently placed on the edge near you or gently intertwined at your stomach; the latter is especially good if you have no podium and have to argue in front of a table or desk. The reason for this is to keep your hands where you need them and not where you do not want them—it gives your hands something to hold on to in a tidy way. Often the panel will not be able to see your hands in these positions because of the podium. In these positions, your hands can rise up to make a gesture of emphasis, or flip pages, or lift a note card smoothly, quickly, and quietly.

If you can stand and comfortably deliver your argument with your hands at your sides, that can look very impressive. The trouble is that few people can do this for a long enough period of time, and wind up letting their hands go somewhere they do not want them to go; they snake into a pocket, or one or both hands wind up on your hips, or your hands start swinging back and forth, which are inappropriate places for them to be during the argument.

Do not sway back and forth or from side to side at the podium. You will make the panel seasick. Do not wander from your spot—this is not a closing argument before a jury where you may want to walk the rail and make eye contact with all of the jurors. Do not grip the podium like a dying man or lean your full weight on it or slouch with your elbows on it as if you are exhausted or lazy.

Arms crossed are hostile. Arms forced behind the back or nailed to your sides will look peculiar and should be avoided unless you were in the military or other occupation where you were asked to stand in a rigid, formal posture and you are the most comfortable standing that way. Putting one or both hands in your pockets looks cavalier or disrespectful; it is too casual for this situation. Hands on the hips look impatient or disapproving .

Small gestures used sparingly for emphasis can be effective, but do not point or shake a finger directly at a judge or take any other subliminally hostile action. Arm waving or fist shaking is beyond the pale. Any arm gesture that puts your hands above the level of your shoulders is suspect. Think friendly counselor, not fire-and-brimstone preacher. Never pound the pulpit no matter how worked up you get. It is too comical and theatrical for a serious situation like oral argument.

A conversational tone may come naturally to you, or you may have to work at it. Tape yourself and listen to what you sound like. Ask your friends and associates to listen to you and evaluate your tone. Does it sound like a normal tone of voice for speaking? Does it sound like the start of a conversation that a person would feel comfortable joining? Or does it sound like preaching, shouting, addressing a large crowd from a stage, or other public speaking style that no one would characterize as conversational.

High speed is your enemy. It is hard enough to be understood when explaining something orally, speeding up just a little can lose your audience a lot. If your normal conversational tone is rushed, consciously slow yourself down a little bit. But — do — not — talk — abnormally — slowly — because — this — does — not — allow — your — argument — to — sound — conversational. Ask your co-counsel to evaluate how well you are doing.

Above all, try to consciously eliminate verbal fillers such as "uhhh," "ahhh," "ummm," and lackluster vernacular phrases such as "uh-huh," "ya-know," "like" (as in "It's like so illegal," or "The Constitution like bans this conduct."). These phrases are distracting and can make a judge tune you out. Worse yet, the judge might start a score card with how many "uhhh's" and "ummm's" you say in the argument; take it from us—that judge is not paying proper attention to the substance of your argument any more.

VIII. CONSTRUCTING THE ARGUMENT

As mentioned above, you do not have to rigidly follow your brief. Truly consider what is your best argument, and find a way to get to that argument quickly and logically. Then plan the transition to the next best argument and so on.

Certainly do not plan to argue using just the table of contents from your brief as your outline. Presume that the judges have read that much. Instead, focus on planning a route to your best issue so that you have a shot of getting that out before the questions start firing.

It is customary in some courts for the first person who argues to ask if the court requires a recitation of the facts (note that this is not expected of the second, third, or fourth person to argue in the session). If you are lucky, they will turn you down and not waste five to ten minutes of your allotted time on background facts. Of course, if you want to talk about the facts, just launch into them; this applies whether you are arguing first or last in the session. If the judges really do not want to hear about the facts, they will tell you to move on. If you absolutely do not want to present a summary of the facts, ask the court for permission to **dispense with a recitation of the facts**. State: "With the court's permission, may I dispense with a recitation of the facts?" This should help to remind the panel that you do not have enough time to dwell on facts.

As mentioned above, you should write a theme for your argument and interject it whenever the point you are arguing or the question you are answering touches on the theme. It helps you drive home points and tie things together in a memorable way. Your theme must fit the case and your facts, of course.

Be prepared to be interrupted and distracted with questions from the panel, so make sure you have in mind the few points you absolutely want to make in the argument, so that you can fight to return to them each time you are sidetracked.

IX. QUESTIONS FROM THE PANEL

Aside from showing up and being respectful in your argument, the most important part of oral argument is effectively dealing with and responding to the questions from the panel. These questions are your friends—in real life and in moot court. In real life, they represent the issues that the court is sticking on and needs to be resolved by you before they are willing to vote for your side. This is information you want them to have, so you should be happy to get questions. In moot court, the ability to answer questions well and still transition back to your argument and make points along the way is what you are being graded on. At the very least, questions indicate that the judges are listening to your argument. Welcome the questions; pray that your argument does not end without a single question being asked.

You must never show annoyance or frustration over being interrupted by a question. Do not ever snort or roll your eyes or fume when you are repeatedly interrupted. It is much more important to answer all the panel's questions than it is to get through your outline.

Decorum and respect require you to stop talking the instant a judge on the panel starts talking. Literally stop in mid-sentence—in mid-syllable if necessary.

If your time runs out during a question or during your answer to a question, the proper thing to do is to politely point out to the panel that your time is up and ask permission to complete your answer to the question. 99% of the time permission will be granted, but do not take this as an opportunity to drone on for five more minutes. Answer the question completely and correctly, but as succinctly as you can. Never bring up a new argument or issue in this "grace" period.

There is great value in answering questions quickly and succinctly, but do not leave out important information in the process. Complete answers are better than quick answers. Impress the judges with your candor.

If you can, during your answer (thinking on your feet, remember), try to plan a **transition** from the answer you are giving back to a point of your own that you want to make. For example:

> ➤ Question: What about the appellee's Internet cases? Do they answer this issue and go against you?
>
> Answer: Your Honor, the Internet cases relied on by my opponent do not cover the situation of transaction of business via the Internet. This is an issue of first impression in this jurisdiction and, I might add, in this country, and there is no controlling authority on this point. However, the analogous area of law covered in the controlling law of this jurisdiction is business conducted over telephone wires and electronically by facsimile and telephone and email. The cases on this point, including <u>Scullin</u>, definitively support my argument, because they hold . . .

Try once, and perhaps twice not to concede an important point even if it is clear that the judges are not buying your argument. It is especially important not to concede the ultimate issue of the case (are we liable or not, for instance)—never give in on the ultimate issue. But if one section of your argument definitely annoys the panel and you cannot convince them that you are right the first two times, **and** you have alternative arguments to rely on if you give in on that sticking point, then concede the point and move on. Do not keep beating the dead horse three and four times. If you do not concede, the panel may tell you to move on, and at that point you had better do what they tell you.

Oral argument judges tend to gravitate to certain types of questions, so we have prepared a chart of the most common questions and what you should try to do when answering them:

Form of Question	Why are they Asking it?	What you should do to Answer it
The Information Seeking Question - What is the holding of that case? When did that statute go into effect? Did your client telephone the authorities that night or not?	These are fairly mundane questions designed to illicit information about the record or the authorities. Usually, the court is seeking the information for a simple reason: they want to know the answer. Occasionally, a judge will ask this type of question to test your knowledge of the record or the authorities.	Be prepared to discuss the facts from the record and the authorities on the law. Re-read your own authorities and your opponent's authorities. Study the most important documents and testimony from the record. Make sure when you do your practice rounds that your "judges" quiz you on details such as these so that you will not be thrown when you get your first question of this kind.
The Slippery Slope Question - Aren't you opening the floodgates to ...? Aren't you asking the Court to set a dangerous precedent for ...? Aren't you asking the Court to plunge into uncharted and dangerous territory?	Appellate courts in general, and courts of last resort in particular, must be cognizant of the fact that they are not just deciding the single case before them but also are setting a rule and precedent for all future cases in that jurisdiction. They do not want to issue an overly broad opinion. They do not want to create a rule that might work fine in the case before them, but it might be applied to other situations to produce unintended negative results.	Be aware of the impact of your arguments on future cases. Take a long view and a broad view when you are drafting your brief and preparing for oral argument. Think of the ways your arguments might affect future cases, related and analogous areas of the law, and other kinds of parties (plaintiffs and defendants) than are in the case at hand. Be prepared to discuss how your arguments can and should be limited to the parties in the case at hand and other future parties just like them. Show how the impact of your arguments is limited to the case at hand, and only will control future situations just like the one at hand. Alternatively, if you think a broader precedent should be set, be prepared to discuss the parameters of the new rule you would have the court set and the public policies that are furthered by the new rule.

Form of Question	Why are they Asking it?	What you should do to Answer it
The Drawing the Line Question - How do we draw the line? Where do we need to draw the line?	Related to the above type, drawing the line here does not refer to an aggressive act to defy someone (<u>i.e.</u>, drawing a line in the sand), but rather to finding the place where the strength and logic of the arguments you are making ends. The court wants to know where your arguments should be cut off so that they can articulate reasons in their opinion why the precedent they will create will be limited to certain types of situations, such as the situation involving the parties in the case before them, and not to other situations. The court is searching for a way to write a more limited rule and precedent.	Once again, you should be prepared to discuss the reasonable, logical, and lawful boundaries of your arguments. How and why should your arguments be limited to the parties in the case at hand and other future parties just like them? Show how the impact of your public policy arguments is limited to the case at hand, and why the precedent to be set by the court need only control future situations just like the one at hand. Show how the logic of your arguments easily answers the issues in the case at hand but does not need to be extended further. Try to articulate standards for drawing the line that you have derived from the authorities, rather than simply describing individual factual situations from cases that are "good" and cutting off the situations of cases that are "bad." Alternatively, if you think a broader precedent should be set, be prepared to discuss the parameters of the new rule you would have the court set and the public policies that are furthered by the new rule.
The Roving Hypothetical - What if the plaintiff were a ...? What if a defendant came along and tried to ...? What if the next case involves a ...?	Law students probably are familiar with this kind of question because it is part and parcel of the Socratic method. Yet, sometimes they are surprised to find Socrates wearing a black robe and bearing down on them in an oral argument. The purpose of these questions is twofold:	Because the purpose of these questions is to try to test your ability to think on your feet, you might think it is hard to prepare for them. But, as with the categories of questions discussed above, you should prepare ahead of time by thinking through the impact of your arguments on future cases. Think of the ways

Form of Question	Why are they Asking it?	What you should do to Answer it
	first, the judges are testing you to see how well you are able to think on your feet; second, they may indeed be trying to find the limits of your argument—the future situations you think will be controlled by their decision and which will not be— which relates to the category of questions discussed above.	your arguments might affect future cases, related and analogous areas of the law, and other kinds of parties (plaintiffs and defendants) than are in the case at hand.

The first answer to these questions should not be, "Well, your honor, that is not our case." After wrestling with a hypothetical or two, you may wind up having to bring the court back to the case at hand somewhat more skillfully—"Your honor, that might be true if the plaintiff were to . . . but in our case, plaintiff did not do X-Y-Z and so . . ." Do not get lost in a sea of hypotheticals. If the court is marching into stranger and stranger territory, calmly bring them back to reality and drive home that your arguments easily answer the issues raised by the case at hand.

As with all of these question types, when you hold your practice sessions, have your "judges" drill you on hypotheticals. Have them force you to think on your feet so that you can become comfortable addressing strange and troubling hypotheticals while standing at the podium. |
| The "If we do X-Y-Z, do you lose?" Question - If we do not buy your argument that . . . do you lose? If we do not | This question is testing you on your knowledge of the law and your knowledge of the issues of the case and the arguments needed to answer them. The judges are looking | In order to address this type of question, you must be well versed in the law and the necessary steps in the pathway to victory. Very often there are multiple pathways to victory, but some paths are |

Form of Question	Why are they Asking it?	What you should do to Answer it
accept your position on . . ., can you still win? If we rule against you on this claim, is your case finished?	to see if you have the ability to recognize alternative arguments that are alternative pathways to victory; or they want to see if you understand that in order to prevail, you must convince the court of at least some parts of your argument. This type of question also is used as a test to see how strongly you feel about some of the alternative arguments you are raising, and whether you are willing or able to abandon some claim or alternative argument you are raising.	harder to get through than others. Most of this book is devoted to getting you to think through your strongest arguments and present them first and foremost in your brief and oral argument. In preparing for oral argument, you must be certain of the necessary steps that the court must pass on in order for you to win. As for the alternative steps, you should be aware of those that can be abandoned with little or no impact on the rest of your arguments, and those whose abandonment might have a negative impact on your legal or public policy arguments elsewhere in the case. Do not concede an argument just because you have others—if you have raised it in your brief or oral argument, the judges will expect you to be able to defend it as far as it goes—but you must know the distance you are willing to go on alternative arguments, and do not dig in your heels past the necessary and logical end of your arguments when the panel is trying hard to knock you off your position. Defending your positions is expected, but being flexible about the pathway to victory when you can be flexible also is a virtue. Of course, you never should concede a necessary step on the pathway to victory.

Form of Question	Why are they Asking it?	What you should do to Answer it
The "What would you have this Court do?" Question - What would you like our opinion to say? What precedent would you have this court set? What is the rule of law that you think we should write on this issue? What cases are you arguing that we should overrule? What relief are you seeking here?	This type of question is asking you to clarify what you want the court to do. As an aid to drafting their opinion, the court may want to know what you think their opinion should hold, what prior cases should the court reconsider or overturn, and what new law should the court write as a precedent for future cases. At a minimum, the court is testing you to see if you understand the relief you are seeking, but more often, the court is testing you to see if you really understand what the court needs to do in order to rule in your favor.	Strangely enough, this type of question can be a real stumper in moot court. Having been alerted to it, you should prepare for oral argument by writing a page or an index card that lays out exactly what you would like the court to do. Do not just focus on the obvious—e.g., please reverse the decision of the court of appeals—but also lay out the essentials of the opinion you think the court should write, and the precedent to be set, which discusses the factual situations that should be covered by the rule that you are stating should be applied, and the cases and other authorities that should be clarified or overruled by the court's decision. This type of inquiry really is not intended to be a trick question, and it will not be one if you have prepared for it ahead of time. Your response to the question may prompt the court to inquire further—why do you think the Smith case should be overruled?—but that is true of any solid response to a question.

X. OTHER CONSIDERATIONS

A. Winning points

You win points by proper argument and proper answers to questions. It is proper and customary to address points raised by your opponent in her brief, and to respond to things she said in her oral argument if you are going second. Do so in a professional way, countering the legal or factual points of your opponent's position. You do not win points by beating up and ridiculing your opponent or your opponent's brief or her argument, or by beating up the lower court.

B. Candor toward the court

Do not pretend to know things you do not really know. If you are asked about a case or a law review article that you never have heard of, confess that you are not familiar with it and ask for more details. If it is a major case that you should have found, you may be marked down for failing to uncover it in you research, but you cannot take the chance of being shown to be a liar and a cheat as well as a poor researcher by pretending that you are familiar with the case and that you are ready to discuss it.

If the panel asks about facts and details that are not in the record, it is appropriate to state that they are not in the record. If you are wrong, so much the worse for your score, but in most cases, the judge is trying to see if you know the limits of the facts that are in the record. Often a judge will not be as up to speed on the facts as she needs to be, and your job is not to assume that the judge knows something about the facts that you have forgotten.

If the question really is addressed to an inference from the facts, and you think it is a proper and logical inference, go ahead and address it as an inference—you actually might say, "That is logical to infer from the facts"—but be prepared to stop and remind the panel that the record does not expressly indicate that a fact exists. Inserting facts into the record is fraught with peril. The panel might call you on it, and your opponent might beat you up about it when they get up to argue second or on rebuttal. In most instances, the court will know when the record is silent on a certain topic, and they will expect you to respect this situation.

C. Finishing your argument

If you finish your outline and still have a minute or two left in your allotted time, the safest practice in moot court and even in real court is to simply conclude by reciting the relief you request (e.g., "For these reasons, appellant respectfully requests the court to reverse the decision of the district court and remand this case for a new trial"). Then say, "Thank you, your honors," and move to sit down. If the panel is not through with you, they will jump in with more questions. They might do this even if your time has expired. Asking the panel if they have any additional questions before you sit down is a risky business. This invitation usually prompts a mean old question or two, usually the ones the judges were holding onto for a while, just waiting for a chance to dump them on you.

D. Pay attention to the stop sign.

As discussed above, if you still are talking when time runs out, ask for permission to finish your sentence or the point you were making (e.g., "I see that my time is up. May I finish what I was saying?"), or simply ask for permission to conclude, which generally means stating your request for relief, as shown in the example in the paragraph above. If you were in the middle of answering a question, ask permission to finish your answer. Do not ignore the stop sign, and never use the permission granted by the court as an opportunity to continue your argument for a minute or more. It is especially bad to try to use the grace period to make a new point. The panel may decide to cut you off altogether, and that can be embarrassing.

E.   Wait and listen to the whole question.

Wait and listen to the whole question that is being asked. Do not start answering before the judge gets the whole question out just because you are sure you know where the question is going. Judges can give amazingly long and rambling questions, and sometimes they change their minds midstream and the question takes a turn at the end that you were not expecting. If at the end of the question you realize you have no idea what the judge wants you to answer, do not just launch into something; explain that you do not understand and politely ask the judge if he might clarify or restate the question.

F.   Give a direct "yes-no" answer to a "yes-no" question; then explain.

Give a direct answer to a "yes-no" question first (i.e., answer "Yes" or "No"), then immediately proceed to explain your answer. Above all, do not attempt to dodge the substance of the question because you are uncomfortable with it or because you are not quite sure what answer the judge wants you to give. If you try to avoid answering, the judge simply will point out that you did not answer her question, and she will ask it again.

G.   Unexpected events

Do not be worried if you sneeze or cough or if you lose your train of thought in midsentence. The judges know you are human. Pick up where you can and move on. If you completely lose your entire train of thought, take a moment to try to get back on track, but if the thought is gone forever, simply confess to the court: "I'm sorry, I have completely forgotten what I was about to say." If you think a question was asked, but you do not remember what it was, ask: "Is there a question pending?" or "May I hear the question again?" or if you simply do not know what end is up, say "May I proceed with my next point?", and jump back into the argument wherever you can. A charley-horse of the brain sometimes happens, and these are appropriate ways to massage it out.

If a cellular phone or pager goes off in the room, it is best to ignore it. Let the judges comment on it if they choose. Your own cellular phone or pager never will go off because you **never** should have an activated telephone or pager with you in any courtroom or moot court room.

H.   Poker face

A good poker face is an asset for an oralist. If your opponent makes a great point, do not blanch and furiously start looking up things in your materials in a panic. Stare forward as if nothing has happened. If you realize that your argument is coming apart at the seams during questioning, keep a stiff upper lip and remain calm. Judges may not immediately know that your opponent has made a great point or that the panel has hit on the lynch pin of your case which, if removed, will pull the whole thing apart. But if your face reveals it, they will know it immediately.

Chapter 8

Strategies for Moot Court and Beyond

I. MOOT COURT COMPETITIONS

A. A taste of practice

Moot Court competitions simulate appellate practice in particular and all types of adversarial practice in general. By briefing your side and arguing it in person, you learn important skills in advocacy that will carry on into your practice if you do any kind of litigation or contested matter practice.

Moot court may be your first foray into a simulated litigation experience. Some law schools allow you the chance to experience this in your first year. Most law schools run intramural competitions and sponsor interscholastic moot court teams for second and third year students.

Moot court is a lot like the situation in real life of taking on an appeal, particularly if you are an appellate specialist in your firm or law office. Appellate specialists take on a case after it has been tried and someone has won and someone has lost. Most general practice litigators have the privilege of living with the case for a couple of years, then trying it, then losing it, before they get to take the appeal.

Certainly, the simulation does not exactly duplicate actual practice. For one thing, the record in moot court typically is extremely limited. An actual practitioner probably will get a large record to plow through. This record likely will consist of the entire court file with all of the pre-trial motions and orders in it, all the documents and things produced in discovery, deposition transcripts, trial preparation materials, a complete trial transcript along with all the exhibits entered into evidence and any that were refused, and any post-trial motions. Although some moot court directors tell us that they have at times gone so far as to buddy up with a prosecutorial appellate department, and from them they have obtained actual appellate files with complete "records" in criminal cases for their students to use in moot court classes—including, for example, little glassine pouches containing the actual bullets that killed the actual person whose homicide prompted the prosecution— most moot court records consist of only a few documents. You might get a stipulation of facts, an exhibit or two, and the orders and opinions of the lower courts.

Moot court forces you to engage in a process of in depth review of a client's case, to research and analyze that case as thoroughly as possible with no holds barred. You must write a significant document laying out your arguments, and stand on your feet and defend your client's position against an onslaught of questions. Rarely in law school do you get to work up a single case as thoroughly as you will in moot court. You will know your client's facts and the law that governs the case intimately. In the several months that you will work on your moot court problem, you will become an expert on the particular issues implicated by this client's case. This is what litigation practice is like.

If you wind up working on an appeal when you get out of law school, it will feel very much like your moot court experience. But moot court is not just a good experience for future appellate litigators. Much of your time in practice will involve researching and writing your analysis of legal issues, explaining your analysis orally, and defending it before your colleagues, clients, and the courts. Your first "oral arguments" in practice will not be in front of an appellate panel, but rather in an armchair in front of your boss's desk, as you explain your research to her, and she probes the strengths, weaknesses, and troubling spots of your analysis with questions. Corporate attorneys, banking and real estate attorneys, even trusts and estates attorneys all have to face this kind of probing and explain themselves to senior colleagues in their office when these colleagues want to explore their research and legal conclusions. Being able to calmly and competently think on your feet—even if you actually are sitting in an armchair—and address your colleagues' concerns will further your professional career at the firm.

Some of your toughest audiences will be your clients. One of the authors recalls that his toughest, most unpleasant oral arguments were before an in-house counsel at one of his firm's clients. She would drag him back and forth on his findings and recommendations, working him over like an old punching bag. He would welcome a chance to be vetted by the state supreme court before going back to her "court" again. Then, there were the oral arguments with clients over legal bills. Try explaining why it cost $10,000 to produce a 10 page research memorandum to an irate client some time. You will long for the patient attention of a moot court panel after going through that exercise once or twice. An experience in moot court will help you prepare for these and other real practice encounters.

B. Devil's advocacy skills

There are some twists in moot court that do not appear in real practice. You may be called upon to switch sides and argue "off brief"—argue the position you did not brief—during one or more of the oral argument rounds. This requirement will force you to look at the case as a whole, to evaluate the strengths and weaknesses of your brief position and the opposite side's position, and to make a convincing argument for either side.

Once again, this is not just a trick invented by law professors to amuse themselves and befuddle their students. We are not perpetuating a joke about lawyers who can talk out of both sides of their mouth, or trying to teach you that there is no such thing as truth or right and wrong in representing a client. The skill we are promoting is objectivity about your client's case. Objectivity is an asset to any litigator. Too often lawyers get caught up in their client's cases and fail to see the weaknesses and shortcomings until their opponents shove them in their faces at some critical juncture in the case. Being a good devil's advocate is an excellent skill to develop, and moot court often forces you to work on that skill.

If you are confident and skilled enough to present a coherent and credible argument for either side of the case, then you will have excellent skills for law practice. It takes a lot of thought, an in depth examination of all of the issues and all of the authorities, and sufficient attention to the policies and themes of the area of law to pull off this task in a coherent and credible manner. If you can be this objective in each of your cases, then you will be much sought after as a lawyer, even if the devil never pays you a retainer.

II. IDEAL TRAITS FOR A MOOT COURT PARTNER

The model for moot court success presented in this chapter relies on a team effort. The power of a good team effort can make a huge difference in moot court. Try to imagine the Lone Ranger without a Tonto; Batman without a Robin; George W. Bush without a Dick Cheney.

A moot court partner should not be a silent partner in this business. Both partners, or as many partners as are on the team, should plan to take on the same amount of work and the same amount of responsibility. It will do no good if one person on the team winds up doing 90% of the work. This will require careful selection of your teammates. It will not help you to figure out that you made a bad choice when you are several weeks into the drafting of the brief.

An ideal teammate should have the following traits:

A. Dedicated and hardworking

Find teammates who are as driven and devoted to excellence as you are. Your drinking buddies and best friends are not necessarily good candidates. Your boyfriend, girlfriend or significant other may or may not be a great candidate; you will have to decide.

Ask the following questions about any prospective partner: Have you and your prospective partner ever worked or studied well together on legal matters? Does she study as much as you do, or is she always several rounds ahead of you when you run into her at the local hangout after the library has closed?

Even a hard worker may not be a good match. Ask whether your work styles are compatible—do you like late nights and weekends and she likes early days and ruthless scheduling between classes? Is he an exercise fanatic?—"I can't work on the brief this weekend because I am in an Iron Man competition." Is she single and you are married with significant childcare responsibilities. All of this can affect your ability to work together.

B. Available

The hardest working student in the law school still is not an ideal partner if she never is available to sit down with you and discuss the brief or do a practice oral argument. Many of the best students are over-committed. If you are equally over-committed, and will have to carve out the time to edit and revise the brief through ruthless time management, then a workaholic partner may be ideal for you. But consider the downside if you have put moot court as your number one priority for the semester, and your partner is on a journal and has a part-time job and has several other high priority time commitments.

Note well that being on a journal and doing moot court and carrying a full load of classes is not an impossible task for an upper division law student. Do not shy away from an otherwise perfect match just because she wants to squeeze the most out of her second or third year of law school. The point is to pick a partner who you can work with. So, if you plan to spend twenty hours each week working on moot court, and there is no way your prospective partner can do that in her schedule, face up to that fact, discuss it, and figure out whether you can work with it. It is the unspoken resentment building up over time that destroys most moot court partnerships.

C. Balanced

Moot court competitions grade heavily on both brief writing and oral argument. Neither skill can be counted out of the equation when forming your team. If you have the luxury of having three or more team members, and only two need to argue at the competition, then you can cherry pick a team with a brief writing specialist and two oral argument specialists. Add to that an editing and proofreading specialist, and you will have a juggernaut that cannot be stopped. But in most intramural competitions and some interscholastic competitions, you only will have two members on the team, so each one must be adept at brief writing, editing, proofreading, and oral argument. A team with one good brief writer may do fine in the brief judging portion of the competition, but oral argument scores always are based on the scores of both oralists, so you will trip up in that portion of the competition if your team lacks two strong oralists.

You may be attracted to a partner because you have seen his dazzling oral argument skills. Some people's gifts in that area are obvious. It is harder to evaluate someone's writing and editing skills. Experience on a journal or law review may indicate something, as will disclosure of someone's first year legal writing grade. But the most important thing to do is ask: "Are you comfortable at brief writing, editing, and proof-reading?" "Have you had success doing these things in law school?" You may be a great brief writer, editor and proofreader, but unless you plan to carry the bulk of the writing load, and the responsibility for that part of the grade, be wary of persons who disclaim that they really are only in it for the oral argument experience.

Not everyone is able effectively to criticize legal writing, but it is hard to test this skill except under actual practice. Certainly, a partner who is or was a law journal editor or a legal writing teaching assistant has the resume credentials to do a better job at this task. It would be of great interest to us to see how a potential partner would edit our own work— and not just a trashy throw-away piece of work, but something with real effort put into it. Exchanging writing for mutual editing is a lot to ask a potential partner, but you would learn valuable things about your partner in the process. And having a process to learn these things is better than never knowing them at all.

D. Good match for your strengths and weaknesses

A good partner should complement your team, not throw it out of kilter. If you are a better oralist than a brief writer, you should try to find someone who is a great brief writer, and at least a decent oralist. Two great oralists with no brief writing and editing skills will look good at the arguments, but rarely can progress to the advanced rounds. The same goes for two excellent brief writers and editors who cannot stand up and do a decent oral argument. You may win the best brief award, but you will be going home from the competition on Friday afternoon instead of late Saturday night or Sunday morning.

There is room for different styles of oral argument. You can match two oralists who have very different argument styles, as long as each style is effective and will score well based on the criteria laid out in this book in the chapter on oral argument. But two brief writers with very different writing styles may be a problem. If you are a flamboyant writer and your partner is low key, you may have to decide whose style will give way when you get around to the editing process and are striving to make a single coherent document out of the two parts of the brief each of you has drafted. Are you willing to go toe to toe over whether that paragraph will remain in section II(B) on page 18 of the brief and still walk away friends?

Having someone on the team who is a meticulous editor, proofreader, Bluebook checker, and grammarian will be a great asset to a moot court team—as long as everyone knows their work will be ruthlessly edited and corrected. Being able to take criticism is a must in this process. As a potential partner on a moot court, you must ask yourself whether you can you give and receive constructive criticism on writing and oral argument in a way that will not drive you and your partners apart forever. Our advice is to drop your ego at the door. This is a team effort to produce a team brief and to maximize the team's oral argument performance. It is not about you, it is about the team, and there is no "I" and no "U" in the word "Team."

III. INTERPRETING MOOT COURT RULES

More than a few tears of frustration are shed trying to figure out some of the rules that arise in intramural and interscholastic moot court competitions. The following is our take on some of the more common and troublesome rules we have seen. Be aware that this is *only* our personal interpretation—the final arbiter of any competition's rules is the organization or committee that sponsors and runs the competition and writes the rules. Our interpretation is based on our own experience in reading rules, trying to comply with rules, and seeing the kinds of penalties that are handed down for non-compliance. It certainly is possible that we may be wrong on some of these rules, but we believe our reading would be better than average.

A. Read the rules

The first advice we can give you is to read the rules. In fact, do not just read them, parse them. Pour over them. Outline and summarize them, and discuss them as a team.

There is a hidden educational aspect of moot court competitions: they can teach you the importance of reading and interpreting rules. Litigation in the real world is full of rules—local rules, administrative orders of the court, rules of procedure, standing orders, and more. Failing to follow these rules will quicky cause your case to be jammed up, and this will embarrass you in front of your opponent, the court, and your client. Failing to follow moot court rules will cause you to incur penalties, and when you lose points that way, you really are taking yourself out of contention in the competition. As recently as November 2000, the last time one of the author's law school hosted the regional of the Association of the Bar of the City of New York's National Moot Court competition, he observed that a Best Brief contender was edged out of the title by a competitor who scored lower on the substance of the brief, but had less penalty points than the contender. We are sure that this happens frequently in competitions across the country each year.

B. United States Supreme Court rules

It is very popular for competitions to adopt the Rules of the Supreme Court of the United States regarding briefs. If your competition has adopted these rules, pay attention to the following:

1. Rules on typesetting and printing

The Supreme Court rules require briefs to follow strict typesetting and printing rules, to be permanently and professionally bound, and to use a reduced paper size of 6 X 9¼ inches (more like a "Monarch" sized stationery page than a standard 8½ X 11 inch page). See U.S. Supreme Court Rule 33.1(a, d). Most competitions have recognized the impracticality of these rules, and have opted out of them. But if your competition has adopted the Supreme Court rules and has not seen fit to opt out of the printing rules, you should immediately write to the sponsors to request clarification of the rule. Otherwise, you may find yourself looking for a commercial printer to produce your multiple copies of the brief at great expense to you or your law school.

2. Brief covers

The brief cover rules for the U.S. Supreme Court are complicated only because there are a lot of colors to choose from. To make things simple, you are looking for the brief color for a brief on the merits, and you want the color for the petitioner or the respondent. Petitioner's brief on the merits is light blue, and respondent's brief on the merits is red. See U.S. Supreme Court Rule 33.3(e, f). The rules say "light red," but we do not know what a light red is, and neither will the guy at Kinkos®. We know the Supreme Court does not mean pink, and we assume you will not interpret "red" to mean maroon or deep crimson.

3. Brief length

Look at the page limits in U.S. Supreme Court Rule 33.3(e, f): if your brief is commercially printed, it can be 50 pages long! If it is typed and double-spaced, it can be 110 pages long!! That is why competitions invariably will write their own page limitation rules.

C. Page limits and typeface rules

There are a number of ways to express page limitations. The idea is to make sure everyone has a level playing field and turns in a brief with no more than a certain number of words. You can imagine the chaos if everyone could decide their line spacing, text size, characters per inch, and so on.

If page limits are used, they usually are straightforward. There most often will be a limit on the number of pages you can devote to the argument section, and sometimes a limit on the number of pages for the other parts of the brief, or a limit on the total length of the brief.

The trickier parts are the rules that prevent you from cramming fifty pages of material into the allotted thirty pages of argument. You may see a "characters per inch" rule, such as "type at no more than 12 characters per inch," or "type size not capable of producing more than 12 characters per inch." Competitors that trip up on this rule usually do so because they use a non-uniformly spaced font. Here is a word to the wise: Courier is a uniformly spaced font; Times Roman and CG Times are not. What this means is that in Courier font, every character and space between characters is the same width. If you set the type size of 10 or 12, you can measure how many characters you will get per inch on your printout. In Times Roman and CG Times, certain characters are narrower than others; t's and f's and i's and l's are especially narrow. (Get out a ruler and compare the length of this word in both fonts if you do not believe us: Illustration (Courier) and Illustration (Times Roman)). If you use Times Roman or CG Times, you will not know how many characters per inch you will get when you use 12 point font. More particularly, under the language of the rule, 12 point font size in Times Roman or CG Times is capable of producing more than 12 characters per inch. Brief graders are attuned to this fact, and they probably will assess a penalty if they see Times Roman or CG Times anywhere in your document, even if you increase the font size to try to compensate for the uneven spacing. If the rules of your competition have a limit on the characters per inch your font can generate, use Courier to be on the safe side, not Times Roman or CG Times.

Some competitions avoid all of this font measuring by setting a limit on the number of words that can be in the Argument section. You will have to use a spell checker or some other word processor function to do the counting unless you want to go word by word and count them yourself. We suspect that the brief graders will not sit and count each word either, so you probably will have to turn in a copy of your brief on a floppy disk or by email attachment so that the graders can run it through a program that counts the words.

Line spacing also is regulated. Many competitions use double spacing as the rule; others use a limit of so many lines of text per vertical inch, or so many lines of text per page, which usually comes out to mean double-spacing. We can tell you from experience in grading papers that when you cheat and try to use 1.9 or 1.8 spacing or anything less than 2.0 spacing, it is painfully obvious to the grader, and you will get penalized for it.

The "shrink to fit" function on many word processing programs—used to "shrink to fit" your argument into the 30 pages allocated for such—merely compresses the line spacing, font size, and kerning (spacing between characters) so that the text will fit the number of pages you tell it to fit. All of this tweaking stands out like a sore thumb when the brief grader reads several correctly formatted briefs in a row, and then gets to the "shrunken to fit" brief. You will be penalized for this.

D. Binding

Binding of briefs usually is covered in the rules of the competition because no one wants to go through the requirements of the U.S. Supreme Court rules. Sometimes a specific binding is identified, such as "three staples on the left margin." Other times, it will be more cryptic, such as "bound in a volume." We read "bound in a volume" to mean some kind of nonremovable binding that creates a booklet, such as tape binding. Velo-binding might satisfy this requirement. We do not think it necessarily includes spiral binding or comb binding, but a lot of people disagree with us on this. In any event, if there is a certain kind of binding that is identified as acceptable in the rules, go with that kind of binding rather than taking a chance of being wrong, even if that means using three staples.

E. Outside assistance

The rules of moot court competitions typically limit the kind of help you can get when writing the brief, and sometimes even when preparing for oral argument. There are at least three ways of going about this: first is the absolute prohibition on assistance; second is the prohibition of "direct" or "specific" assistance; and third is the allowance of assistance on specific topics, such as allowing assistance on issues, organization, and strategy, but prohibiting assistance on research, brief writing, editing and proofreading.

In the absence of a rule limiting outside assistance, presumably, you can talk to anyone about anything, and use any material you find, as long as you do not plagiarize. We never have seen an interscholastic competition that did not put some limit on outside assistance. Some intramural competitions may allow open, unabated assistance, but we doubt it.

An absolute prohibition is easy to understand—do not look for assistance from anyone, and do not take any.

We take "no direct assistance" or "no specific assistance" to mean direct or specific assistance in researching, writing, editing, and proofreading the brief, and direct assistance in answering or organizing a response to the very issues presented by the problem. You cannot have a faculty member review your draft of the brief and offer advice on how to revise it, nor can you ask them how to complete your research to pump up your brief with better authorities. But this rule should not prohibit general questions about the subject matter of the problem, or questions about the area of law in which the problem arises, or general advice and assistance about brief writing in the area of law in which the problem arises. This does allow a significant gray area to tread in, and it might be easy to stray from the gray into the black (or red, as it were).

> ➤ *Example:*   If the problem involved the effect of the 1999 OPRAH amendments to ERISA (we made up these amendments—do not get excited) regarding Medicare disclosure requirements for home health care workers who follow the teachings of television's Dr. Phil, we would find it a violation of the "no specific assistance" rule to approach an ERISA expert (faculty member or practitioner) and ask, "In general, in what ways are home health care workers affected by the new Medicare disclosure requirements in the 1999 OPRAH amendments to ERISA." We would find it acceptable to ask about the OPRAH amendments in general, or the process of Medicare disclosure in general, but not the process as currently applied to home health care workers.

Other competitions liberally allow outside assistance. For example, the Jessup International Law Moot Court Competition states in its rules:

> All research, writing and editing must be solely the product of Team members. However, faculty members, coaches, librarians and other research professionals, and other Team advisors may provide advice to a Team. Such advice shall be limited to: general discussions of the issues; suggestions as to research sources; consultations regarding oral advocacy technique; the location of legal sources; general legal research methods; general commentary on argument organization and structure, the flow of arguments, and format; and advice during Competition elimination rounds as to pleading option or similar strategy.

Philip C. Jessup International Law Moot Court Competition, 2005 Official Rules, Rule 2.4.

No one can draft and edit your brief (the "memorial," as it is called in Jessup) for you, or tell you how they would answer the problem, but they can help you with almost anything else.

Some competitions, such as the National Health Law Moot Court Competition, have a rule that states, "No participants shall procure a copy of any pleadings or papers actually filed in any trial or appeal of any case upon which the record is founded. Contact with the actual litigants or their attorneys is prohibited." 2004-2005 National Health Law Moot

Court Competition, Official Rules, Rule 8(a). This would seem to us to be a dead give-away that the sponsors of the competition use an actual lawsuit as the basis of their problem. The rule creates an interesting "Catch 22" situation—the rule does not prohibit the procurement of materials from a case that the problem is not based on, but how do you know if the materials you procured from an actual case are from the actual case the problem is based on unless you procure the materials and read them? We do not know how to answer that one. We suppose the sponsors could come right out and tell you, this case is based on *Jones v. Smith*, 234 F.3d 123 (9th Cir. 2001), but we do not think they do this. In any event, the rule reminds you to look beyond case reporters and treatises in the preparation of your case.

IV. ANALYZING A MOOT COURT PROBLEM

A. Careful reading

The best advice we can give you about your moot court problem is to read it carefully. Yes, this should go without saying, but we have read enough briefs and seen enough oral arguments to know that students do not always get the facts right, whether they be the historical facts that led up to the lawsuit, or procedural facts about how the case wound its way through the court system to get to the court where the problem is set.

Some people like to read through a problem and highlight parts that interest them, much like they are reading a case for class. We like to take notes as we read and re-read the problem, and then write up a summary of the entire case—historical facts and procedural facts—before moving on to the next step. Summarizing and synthesizing the facts should force you to come to grips with them, and the process of writing often reveals gaps or areas that you glossed over on your earlier readings. All of this is time well spent in the process of getting ready to research and analyze the problem.

B. Handling the facts

Once you have read through the problem a few times, it is time to get serious with the facts. The facts determine what you can argue, how you can argue it, and the strength of the various arguments you can make. Facts dictate the law that determines the case—is it a contracts problem, a torts problem, a tax problem, or a combination of several areas?—the way the law is going to be applied to the case, and the play of the public policies around the area of law you are briefing. In order to succeed at moot court, you must be adept at organizing and marshaling the facts that support your client, and at explaining, defusing, and otherwise handling the facts that hurt your client.

1. Put the facts in chronological order.

In order to start the process of mastering the facts of the problem, you first should put all of the facts in chronological order. The problem may not present the facts in this kind of sequence. As lawyers, we often look at facts in chronological order, and getting the facts down in date sequence probably will help you make sense of the case.

The significance of certain facts may jump out at you more readily when you put them next to other facts that happened at the same time. Gaps in the factual information provided to you may become obvious when you lay out the facts in date sequence. At the very least, putting the facts in chronological order will produce an orderly version of the facts to refer to in later stages of the process.

2. Separate good facts from bad facts.

The next step is to separate the good facts from the bad. You may not be able to complete this task your first time through because your research and analysis into the law will often reveal that certain facts are indeed bad, and others are good. You can start with your gut feeling about the facts, and then return to the facts again and again as you are researching the law to make sure you have the good and the bad facts straight.

The point of this exercise is to compile those facts that you will want to emphasize in the statement of the facts and throughout the brief, and those that you will want to downplay or put your best spin on. Moot court writing is adversarial writing, and you should never be satisfied with a complete chronological approach to the facts in your writing and argument unless you are in that rarest of situations where all the facts seem to go your client's way.

3. Make reasonable and logical inferences from the facts.

It is appropriate to draw reasonable and logical inferences from known facts. What you must avoid is drawing inferences that are too extreme and are unsupported by the facts. This is the equivalent of inventing facts that are not in the record. The judges certainly will mark you down for inventing facts, and your standing similarly will be discounted if you try to stretch the facts to the breaking point.

Be conservative and draw only the most reasonable and logical inferences from the facts:

> *Example:*   If the facts indicate that the Maryland Board of Healing Arts describes two hours as the average time for a surgical procedure, and a certain doctor did the procedure in one hour, it would be a logical inference to state that the doctor operated "quickly." It is completely safe (and obvious) to point out that the doctor did the procedure "in half the time provided by the Maryland Board of Healing Arts."

What would not be reasonable is to infer that the doctor "rushed" the procedure. "Rushing" implies a state of mind, and nothing in the facts we have revealed shows the doctor's state of mind. Performing the procedure in half the time is not automatically rushing; you do not have enough facts to make that inference. Perhaps the doctor is the most skilled surgeon in the state, and twenty experts would testify that she ought to take half as much time to do the procedure because of her expertise.

You also cannot draw the inference that the doctor was "negligent" or "reckless." Aside from the problem that these are legal conclusions, you do not have enough facts about the doctor, her state of mind, her expertise, and a host of other factual information that would affect that inference. All you can say is that she performed the operation "quickly" and "in half the time provided by the Maryland Board of Healing Arts."

Missing information from the record necessarily will limit the kind of inferences you logically can draw. As stated above, in moot court, your record will be more limited than in a typical real life litigation. Do not get caught up in a spirit of advocacy and fill in details that affect the logical limits of the facts in the record.

➤ *Example:*   If the record states that the defendant had five alcoholic drinks in a two hour period, you should not automatically draw the inference that the defendant became intoxicated. Intoxication depends on a host of factors (such as the defendant's weight, percentage of fatty tissue to lean tissue in the body, whether the alcohol was consumed with other food or beverages that might limit its rate of absorption into the body). The concept of intoxication also depends on the context; do you mean too intoxicated to drive, or too intoxicated to sit in a chair and watch television? You can state exactly what the facts state: "the defendant drank five alcoholic drinks in two hours."

If you know the blood alcohol content of the defendant, you then can combine this with other facts to make further inferences. For example, if the record indicates that the defendant had a blood alcohol content of 0.12, you can perform research that might indicate that "defendant's blood alcohol level was above the legal limit for operating a motor vehicle in all fifty states of the United States."

4. Group the facts by topic and subject matter and look for themes.

The next step is to group the facts by topic and subject matter so that you can evaluate what the potential themes of the case will be. The theme of the case is different from the legal issues raised by a case and the subject matter of the applicable law that governs these legal issues. Themes are a rhetorical device, designed to reinforce your arguments and persuade the reader to accept your position and vote for your client. A theme is used in the brief and in oral argument as a focal point to tie together the facts of the case, the legal arguments you will make, and the policy issues you will argue. Thus, you cannot have a theme that lacks one of the essential elements of facts, law, and public policy. The facts you are studying will reveal potential, viable themes. You cannot superimpose a popular theme onto your case if the facts will not support the theme.

> ➤ *Example:*   One potential theme in a business dispute over the performance of a contract is that the larger company took advantage of the smaller company, and exerted improper pressure and used abusive tactics rather than performing the contract in good faith. When you begin to group the facts by topic, you notice that the two companies had a long working relationship, and the relationship was punctuated by fairness and equity at every point discussed in the record. Your theme is doomed—there is no point to asserting a factually unsupportable theme to the case, because sooner or later your theme is going to be shot down by your opponent, and the brief grader and oral argument judges will mark you down for this.
>
> On the other hand, if the problem throws you some bones that make it look like your company was trying to do business with a Microsoft-type giant or other functional monopolizer, it would behoove you to pursue a theme that the reason the court should accept your legal interpretation of the contract and your argument that the contract was breached is because your opponent is an arrogant giant that uses its superior size and market position to wrest improper demands from its contractual partners. This argument uses the facts to bring the public policy against monopolizers and unfair competitors into view, and thus to cast a favorable light on your legal arguments regarding the contract and its performance.

Themes are the sunshine and pleasant breeze of legal rhetoric that make the brief graders and oral argument judges want to hang out in the backyard of your argument. Cheap window dressing that is not held up by solid facts in the record will crash down on your head, and cause these same brief graders and judges to walk out on your party early, leaving low scores behind. Thus, a careful review of the facts that are available for various topics and themes is essential.

5. Return to the facts again and again.

You will need to return to the facts at every stage of the moot court process: spotting the issues, researching the issues, analyzing the case, drafting and revising the brief, and preparing for oral argument. The facts determine the issues, and if you think that an issue might be present, you must confirm that the facts exist to create an appropriate question for appellate review, as discussed further in the section that follows. At the research and analysis stage, certain facts that you reviewed at the initial run through will take on new meaning and new importance to your case. At the drafting stage, you must return to the facts again and again for the drafting of the statement of facts or statement of the case, and to confirm and provide citations to details that your are using in your argument section. At the oral argument stage, you must determine which facts and themes you will present first and will return to in answers to questions and transitions from answering questions back to your argument.

All of this means that your initial review of the facts is only an initial review. The facts are too important to the moot court process to allow you to visit them once and learn them wrong. You should be reciting the facts in your sleep before the moot court competition is over.

C. Issue spotting

Issue spotting is the next important task in the moot court process. In some competitions, it can be a relatively straightforward process. The problem might set out the issues as "questions presented" as part of the packet. In other competitions, the notice of appeal or petition for certiorari in the packet might set out the issues in clear and straightforward language. In these instances, there is no guesswork involved.

The authors of moot court problems for intramural or interscholastic competitions often do not want you to guess at the issues either, so they too will take great pains to write a problem that makes the issues obvious. When we say obvious, we mean they will write one or two lower court opinions for the record that state two issues as Roman numerals one and two in the lower court opinions, and they will attempt to create documents and other factual sources for the record that only can lead to those two issues. If you miss those two issues, you are done for, and there will be little hope for you.

On occasion—and perhaps too often for comfort's sake—the author intentionally or unintentionally obscures the issues, or intentionally or unintentionally allows issues into the record that can be spotted and briefed. The record may leave the door open for a jurisdictional argument, or a preservation of issues argument, or reveal a constitutional defect in the proceedings. The material that follows will help you to spot these issues and to determine whether and to what extent they present questions that should be briefed and argued on review.

1. Harmless error, appealable error, preservation, and clear error

Not every error or mistake that occurred in the trial court presents a proper issue for review. No one is guaranteed a perfect trial or perfect handling of their case in the trial court. The doctrine of **harmless error** provides that if an error caused no harm to your client, you cannot raise it on appeal. If a jury instruction was requested and not given, the instruction that was given in its place must be more favorable to the party that prevailed on that issue; if the instruction given was less favorable, or your client actually prevailed on this particular claim or defense, you cannot appeal from this error. If a witness was barred from testifying, but the substance of the witness's testimony presented in an offer of proof obviously duplicates testimony from other witnesses that were allowed to testify, then the barring of this one witness may be harmless error.

In general, an issue must have been raised and preserved in order for it to be an **appealable error**. If you never asked the trial court to do something, and the court winds up not doing it, you cannot later raise the court's failure to do that thing as an error. Thus, if you did not request a continuance to allow a witness to appear, or did not ask for leave to amend a petition to insert a new claim, you cannot later complain on appeal that a continuance was not granted to you and the witness did not appear, or that your additional claim was not heard. In general, an issue must have been raised and the trial court must have had the opportunity to address the issue and correct the mistake in order for the error to be raised on appeal.

Preservation is a trickier concept. Some errors require a formal procedure to preserve the issue, such as a defect in venue or personal jurisdiction, which must be raised through the timely assertion of a motion to dismiss, and not later abandoned by a general appearance in the case without preserving the error in the pleadings. Evidentiary issues raised in motions in limine or during trial generally must be preserved by the aggrieved party through a formal statement on the record and sometimes with an offer of proof that is received into the record but not presented to the jury. In many jurisdictions, the rules of procedure require a litigant to raise all points of error in a post-trial motion for new trial in order for them to be preserved for appeal.

If the record presented in your moot court problem is complete enough to make a determination whether the issues have been preserved or not, you should use the record to prove that each issue you will argue was properly raised and preserved. However, your moot court problem may prevent you from resolving these questions because it may not give you any indication whether or not an issue was properly preserved at or before trial. Some moot court problems consist of a trial level opinion and an appellate level opinion, with nothing before or in between. One or both of the opinions may make a catch all saving phrase to the effect that "This issue was properly raised at trial and preserved for appeal," in which case the author of the problem wants you to forget about objection and preservation as issues in the case. But the problem might be silent. Unless the issue is one of venue or personal jurisdiction (discussed in the next section), if the issue is discussed by both courts, you most likely are to presume that the issue is preserved for review even if there are no facts in the problem that expressly spell this out.

An exception to the objection and preservation requirements is the doctrine of **clear error** or **plain error**. If an error is so egregious that it should have been taken up by the court *sua sponte* and a mistrial ordered, the fact that no party raised the issue in the trial court does not bar it from being raised on appeal for the first time. A potential clear error is not subtle. It should leap out at you from the record, and cry out for justice. Even if you think you have found one, research the applicable law of your jurisdiction to make sure that this type of error has been identified as clear error or plain error before. Appellate court judges and moot court judges will not readily accept an issue as clear error or plain error if you do not have the goods to prove to them that it is one.

2. Jurisdictional errors in the trial court

You should always review the jurisdiction and venue of the trial court over the subject matter of the action and the parties to the action, because improper jurisdiction can present an appealable issue. You will recall from legal research and writing and civil procedure that a court must have three kinds of power in a case:

- subject matter jurisdiction over the claims raised in the action;
- personal jurisdiction over the parties to the action effectuated by proper service of process; and
- venue over the place where the action occurred or arose, or over the parties or the subject matter of (the *res* or property involved in) the suit.

A clever author of a moot court problem may sneak a jurisdictional issue into the problem. A not so clever author might let one in without knowing it. It will most likely be a problem with the subject matter jurisdiction of the trial court, because questions regarding personal jurisdiction and venue must be raised and properly preserved or they are waived, and if the author has gone to the trouble of putting enough information into the record to indicate that a personal jurisdiction or venue issue is preserved, then it should be obvious to you that the issue is present and appealable.

3. Appellate court jurisdictional issues

You also should verify that the appellate courts that heard the case had proper jurisdiction over the case. Appellate courts can only take jurisdiction over an action by three means:

- extraordinary writ,
- interlocutory appeal, or
- appeal after final judgment.

A petition for an extraordinary writ may be filed at any time, and if the record indicates that an extraordinary writ was issued and the lower court was required to answer, then there is little else to stick up the works in the form of appellate procedural error. Your moot court problem may or may not include the petition for a writ, the response of the opponent, and any orders requiring an answer or issuing a preliminary writ. The problem may simply state that the petition for a writ is granted, in which case there is little to question in the way of appellate jurisdiction.

Interlocutory appeals also may be filed at any time. In federal court, 28 U.S.C. § 1292(b) provides that the trial court may certify one or more issues for immediate review, and the appellate court may accept review of the certified issues under Fed. R. App. P. 5. This is a popular way for the author of a moot court problem to get two discreet issues of law sent up for review.

If your problem involves an interlocutory appeal, you should look to see that the requirements of 28 U.S.C. § 1292(b) and Fed. R. App. P. 5 have been met. At a minimum, the district court opinion should have stated that the court's "order involves a controlling question of law as to which there is substantial ground for difference of opinion and that an immediate appeal from the order may materially advance the ultimate termination of the litigation." 28 U.S.C. § 1292(b). However, the author of the moot court problem may not have given you enough information to resolve the question. If the problem indicates that an intermediate level appellate court took up and resolved an issue arising from an interlocutory order of the trial court, it probably is safe to presume that the requirements of the rule and statute were met.

An appeal after final judgment must be initiated by a timely filed notice of appeal, as per the requirements of Fed. R. App. P. 3 and 4, or their state rule equivalents. The author of your moot court problem may inadvertently have allowed an untimely appeal to have been filed by not being careful with the dates in the record. This almost assuredly was unintentional, because the issue of timeliness is jurisdictional, and if the appeal is untimely, there is nothing the appellate court can do to help the parties out. Your moot court argument would end right then and there. If you figure out that the dates in the problem indicate that an appeal was not timely, contact the sponsor of the moot court program and request a clarification of the dates. You most likely will get a clarification.

A shrewd author might allow an issue as to whether a judgment was final or not when the notice of appeal was filed. If this was inadvertent, then the record probably will be corrected rather than allowing this defect to destroy the entire appeal. If you suspect that a claim or defense of a party was not resolved by the order and judgment of the trial court, you should request clarification, and if none is given, you should research the definition of finality in your jurisdiction to see if your author has created a dispositive issue for briefing and argument.

In addition, check the record to see that the steps required for the filing and docketing of the appeal appear to have been followed in the case, but do not be surprised if the record is silent on these facts. Authors of moot court problems rarely attempt to confound law students by inserting an issue regarding the filing or docketing of the appeal, so if the record says nothing, assume that this means the problem intends no issue regarding filing or docketing. Only worry about these factors if the author inserts facts into the record that affirmatively indicate that a filing or docketing was botched.

There may be a subject matter jurisdiction issue in the appellate court. An appellate court's subject matter jurisdiction is governed by the applicable constitution, statutes, or court rules of the jurisdiction. An example of this is the rule set out in 28 U.S.C. § 1295 that provides that all appeals from patent cases litigated in the U.S. District Courts are to be heard by the U.S. Court of Appeals for the Federal Circuit, rather than the court of appeals that would normally entertain appeals from the district court in question. If you stumble on an appeal from a patent case that is filed in the U.S. Court of Appeals for the

Eighth Circuit, you have a bona fide appellate court subject matter issue to research and brief.

The courts of last resort most often have limited jurisdiction whereby parties seeking to have a case heard in these courts must **request a transfer** to the court or **petition** the court for the issuance of a **writ of certiorari**, or **writ of mandamus**, or other writ, to allow the case to be heard by the court. If the record does not indicate that one of these procedures was used to get to the court, but the problem indicates that the current appeal is pending in the court of last resort, it is probably attributable to poor attention to detail on the part of the writer of the problem. You can point it out in your brief and oral argument, but the record probably will not contain enough information to actually argue the effect of the omission.

4. Constitutional defects of justiciability

There are several constitutional law doctrines regarding the justiciability of actions:

Case or Controversy: In federal court, Article III of the U.S. Constitution provides that the courts shall only hear cases or controversies, which means that if a party has yet to be injured by the conduct of the opponent, the case should not be heard. Federal courts are not to issue advisory opinions. There are some kinds of cases that present a clear enough picture of the type and amount of injury that will occur that they can be heard prior to the actual injury's occurrence, such as an imminent breach of a contract or licensing agreement, and there are some procedures, such as temporary restraining orders and preliminary injunctions, that might stop the impending injury in its tracks. But if someone has jumped the gun and gone to court before an injury has taken place, it is worth researching the issue to see if a case or controversy is present. The same defense might apply in a state court, but you should research the constitutional and procedural law of the jurisdiction to be certain (if the problem identified an actual state, as opposed to the "State of Apex" or other fictional jurisdiction).

Ripeness: Ripeness is related to the concept of case or controversy. If the injury complained of in the action is speculative, and has not occurred and may not occur, a ripeness issue may exist.

Mootness: Although moot court is the name of the game, if the cause of action and the injury, and the position of the parties in the underlying action cannot be affected or resolved by the order of the court, then the problem is moot and should not be litigated. There are some exceptions, such as an injury that is capable of repetition yet evading review. See Roe v. Wade, 410 U.S. 113 (1973). If it looks like the court's handling of the case might be futile no matter who prevails in the case, then you should research the mootness issue for possible inclusion in your brief and argument.

Standing: The standing of the plaintiff to bring the action has got to be the sleeper issue of the century for moot court oral argument judges. No competitor ever thinks it is an issue, because those old Supreme Court cases on standing—Baker v. Carr, 369 U.S. 186, 204 (1962); Flast v. Cohen, 392 U.S. 83, 101 (1968); Sierra Club v. Morton, 405

U.S. 727, 732 (1972); and others—do not make any impact on you when you cover them in two or three class periods in your first year civil procedure or constitutional law courses. Nevertheless, in real life, judges get very agitated when they suspect that someone is trying to stand as a private attorney general, or assert the rights of others by assignment or by some other actual or implied legal relationship, or is trying to sue as a third party beneficiary of an agreement. You should spend some time thinking about standing, and if there is any indication in the problem that the plaintiff was not the person directly and personally harmed by the action of the defendant, you should research and resolve the issue in your brief and oral argument.

D. Appellant's determination of which issues to raise

After the issue spotting and research is done, students briefing the appellant's or petitioner's or applicant's position still might want to weed out their issues before they start to draft the brief. This is particularly necessary if you think you have found five or more main issues to argue. Moot court is supposed to simulate actual appellate practice, and in actual appellate practice, when you are evaluating the possible errors committed by the lower court, quality is far more important than quantity.

The authors of moot court problems typically intend to present two significant issues to brief—often identified by upper-case Roman numerals I and II in the court opinions found in the record—and most authors probably hope that there are no other issues suggested by the facts. Although two main issues is the norm, occasionally, a moot court problem will present three or more main issues. We discussed above how an author may intentionally or inadvertently insert a jurisdictional or constitutional issue into the problem. When additional issues are suggested by the facts of the problem that are not part of or related to the issues that were discussed in the problem in the sections under the big Roman numerals, then you will have to decide if these side issues are worth briefing. If you have undertaken the analysis described in this chapter, and you have determined that the issue is an appealable error (e.g., it was raised and preserved), and is not harmless error, then the issue should be briefed.

If, however, you are in a situation where it appears obvious that the author only intended for there to be two issues, and you are stuck on a third, an appellant safely can jettison a side issue as long as it has absolutely no bearing on the main issues that are presented in the problem. We can say this, because every appellate court judge and every worthy appellate practitioner will tell an appellant that less is more. It is better not to go fishing for issues or sub-issues to write about. In moot court, as in actual appellate practice, you will do much better if you find and argue the two horrible, unforgivable errors that are set out in the record, rather than "finding" and briefing a dozen somewhat troublesome errors that arguably might be raised. In real life, certain litigators will throw up as many assertions of error as they can think of, hoping that one will stick and cause the case to be overturned. This is a tactic of desperation, not of effective advocacy. Moot court judges are sensitive to this tactic, and they will not want you to develop such bad habits, so they will punish you on your score if you let a quantity of "also ran" errors drown out the effectiveness of your arguments on the main issues of the case.

However, appellants should make sure that the "side issue" you are thinking about discarding does not have an impact on the analysis of the other, main issues in the case. The validity of a signature on a contract in a licensing case, or inconsistent testimony about the road conditions in a car accident case may not stand alone as separately appealable issues, but they might have an impact on the main issues of liability and defenses to liability in the case. If the side issue has a direct bearing on the "main" issues, it should not be discarded, but instead you should brief it. You may wind up briefing it as a sub-issue or threshold issue that leads up to one or more of the ultimate issues in the case. Err on the side of briefing an issue that has a direct bearing on the main issues if you are in doubt.

If you find three or more issues, and the problem does not clue you in on how to split them up, you may have to figure out how to divide them up with your partner. There is no magic to this, and the decision is not so critical under our plan for drafting and revising the argument section because all teammates will wind up looking at the brief as a whole when the first complete draft of the brief is written.

E. Appellee's determination of which issues to rebut

An appellee or respondent must analyze the problem in a similar way as the appellant in order to anticipate what issues the appellant is likely to raise. One of the serious limitations in moot court as it is practiced today is that the appellee does not have the opportunity to see and respond directly to the appellant's brief and the issues the appellant chooses to raise. Appellees most likely will be required to turn in their brief at the same time as appellants. Most moot court problems fail even to provide the notice of appeal filed by the appellant, which also would give a strong indication what the questions presented will be. (This is intentional, and it has more to do with testing the appellants to see if they can spot appealable issues than with punishing appellees by not giving them enough information.) Unfortunately, you may have to make an educated guess as to what issues are going to be raised by your opponent.

As discussed above, authors of moot court problems usually do not want you or the appellant to have to guess about the issues. These authors often will go to great lengths to point out that there are two main issues that they want both sides to address. But sometimes your review of the record will uncover a potential appealable issue that is not one of the two main "Roman numeral" issues presented by the problem. You may have identified an issue regarding the subject matter jurisdiction of the trial court or the appellate court, or one regarding ripeness or mootness, or the standing of the plaintiff—who might be you—to have brought the action in the first place. Appellees do not have as much discretion to jettison issues as appellants have. Even if you think an issue is tenuous, not likely to produce a reversal, and easily refuted, it will be in your best interest to raise it and rebut it as quickly and competently as you can. Spend a page or less on a straightforward issue that is resolved by controlling authority; spend more time on a more complicated error that requires analysis of the facts, controlling and persuasive authority, and public policy.

You will not be penalized for discussing actual appealable issues found outside the main "Roman numeral" issues. In fact, it may separate your brief from the pack and boost your score if your keen analysis reveals a thorn that almost everyone else overlooked. On the other hand, chasing after hobgoblins that are not reversible errors, or raising straw men issues just so you can tear them down in your brief, will not be a credit to your analytical skills. You also must be cognizant of not spending too much time and too many pages on tertiary issues that crowd out more important analysis and discussion of the main issues. Being able to budget your space is one of the skills on which you will be graded in moot court.

V. THE COLLABORATIVE WRITING PROCESS

Moot court may be your first foray into the collaborative process of legal writing, the style of writing which is used most often in actual legal practice. Through this process, each team member edits, comments on, and redrafts the work of the other member or members of the team to produce the best possible final product. You should take advantage of this opportunity, not only to get a very accurate taste of what real law practice is all about, but also to employ the premise that two or three heads are better than one. If done properly, following the advice given below, your moot court brief will be a much better product than if you follow the lazy and undemanding method of splitting your writing between team members who do not comment on each other's work, and merely agree to meet the evening before the brief is due to try to cram the individual work of each team member into one somewhat coherent brief.

The advice below is hard, demanding, and time-consuming, and it will sound extraordinary in comparison to what you have done for other writing assignments in law school and elsewhere. That is the great thing about advice—you can take it or leave it. If you cannot devote the time to do it all, do as much as you can.

A. Write a complete first draft of the brief as early as you can

The first advice we have is to write a complete first draft of the brief as early as you can, preferably three to four weeks before the final brief is due. Note that we said a *complete* first draft—we mean everything but the table of contents and table of authorities. Draft the questions presented, statement of jurisdiction, statement of the case or statement of facts, and summary of the argument, as well as a complete draft of the argument section.

The purpose of this is to allow yourself the time properly to review the problem and evaluate the brief. You should leave yourself the time to make mistakes, to change your mind, to add new issues and to drop others. You must leave the time for your teammates to edit and critique the brief. This amount of time is generous, but not overly generous when you think about how busy you will be in the middle of a semester with your other classes and responsibilities.

If you have a teaching assistant or advisor who, under the rules of the competition, can comment on the drafting of the brief itself, producing a complete product for them to look at and evaluate is much better than an outline and a few notes about things you promise to fill in. No one knows what to say about notes you write in the draft such as: "Add section on preemption," "Find cases," or "Here I'm going to argue that the award is unconstitutional under <u>Perry</u>."

B. Write multiple drafts

Do not just do one complete draft and then the final. Take advantage of the time you saved and write a draft every two or three days. You should know from experience that the first two or three drafts take a lot of time to write and revise, but the next two or three will take a lot less time, and each draft after that will take even less time to turn around. When you get to the level of fine tuning each sentence and paragraph, you may be able to turn around drafts in a matter of one or two hours.

C. Meet frequently with your teammates and let them comment on each draft

We mentioned choosing people who can give constructive criticism on legal writing, and that you should leave your ego at the door on a team project such as this. The sessions you spend hashing over the brief and discussing its contents will be some of the most valuable time you will spend in your legal education if you have top notch teammates who all can contribute to the effort. Rarely in private practice did we ever get to sit down for an hour or two and hash through a brief that we were working on with several other lawyers; you simply do not get the time to do it, or the client will not pay for these consultation sessions. When this did occur on major projects, we savored the experience. We invite you to have a taste of it while you still are in law school.

Do not cut yourself short in these sessions. Anything less than two hours is a rush. Schedule four two-hour sessions a week—three meetings on weekdays and one on the weekend. If you are on a vacation or break, meet every day. If you have a teaching assistant, try to get them involved two or three times a week.

D. Talk about each section the first week, each paragraph the second and third weeks, and each sentence and word the last week

Start big in your evaluations of the brief by looking hard at each major section of the brief and the Argument section. Ask yourself: Is this section coherent? Is there enough authority here? Does this argument ring true? Are these facts sufficient, or are they too detailed? Is this Summary of the Argument strong and punchy enough? Does the whole section flow easily and read quickly without having to go back and reread it one or more times? Am I transitioning to the next section adequately?

Next, look at each paragraph: Does it have a good topic sentence? Is the idea stated in the paragraph clear enough? Is it coherent? Is it short enough, or is it too wordy? Does it flow easily? Can you easily understand it without having to read it two or three times?

Remember that three sentences can be an excellent paragraph, and even two sentences will work when you want to be extremely direct and punchy. We have not met any brief judge who will bust you for having a paragraph that is too short, but many will comment on a paragraph that is too long. Readers will get lost in a long paragraph, and will start to ask themselves questions—"Why did I get into this discussion? How did this start? Are we still talking about the same topic?" Our rule of thumb is that no paragraph should be more then five sentences or more than one third of a page in length. Use the editing process to cut every paragraph down to size.

The last effort is word-smithing; going sentence by sentence and word by word, and making the language as tight and convincing as possible. Do we need this word? Why do we say "immediately" instead of "quickly"? Let's rephrase this sentence and make it shorter.

This part of the process usually is where we get into the most trouble with our cohorts—we like a certain word or phrase, and they do not. Try to get along, but remember, your ego should not matter and the end result should be a team effort. If you have three or more people, vote on final changes if you need to.

E. Thoroughly discuss each authority

When you are working through each draft, discuss each authority that you citing: Why are we citing this case? What does it mean? What are the facts? Does this authority stand for this exact proposition? Can we rephrase the sentence so that we do not have to say *See* or *See also* or *Cf.* when we cite the authority? Isn't there a stronger case for this point? Are there any negatives associated with using this case? Are we opening ourselves up to a counterattack because we are using this case?

The value of this exercise to your brief should be apparent, but you also will be doing yourself a favor when it comes time for oral argument. All this discussion and review will help you learn everything you need to know about the authorities for oral argument. You will be a walking, talking expert on this little area of the law before you are through, and that will make you a deadly force in oral argument.

F. Use another team or persons briefing the opposite position if the rules allow it

If you are in a situation where the rules of the competition allow you to consult with another team or persons that are briefing the opposite position on the problem (usually a team from the same school), take the opportunity to consult with them. If you can, use this opportunity. You will learn a lot from the fresh and contrary perspective of an opponent. They can try to poke holes in your argument, question your sources, present their take on the issues, and discuss how the authorities support or do not support certain positions. Of course, you can help them with their brief, too.

G.   Use all the outside help the rules allow

Outside assistance typically is limited by the moot court competition's rules. Where it is permitted, you should plan to take advantage of it, and scheduling a date and time with one or more faculty members and practitioners will help you to stay on track and get your act together before these meeting dates arrive. Unless you really are struggling with the issues or the research, you should wait until your research is fairly complete and your brief is well on the way to completion before inviting a law professor or practitioner to comment on it. Every legal professional values her time, and law professors are no exception. Law professors also tend to be a very critical audience, so you should strive to have a strong product in place before you fly it past them. We never felt comfortable in law school dogging our professors to ask them advice on moot court briefs until we were good and prepared on the law, and had specific questions to ask.

Remember, too, that even if you ask for help, you may not get very good outside assistance regarding a moot court problem because the issues chosen for moot court treatment usually are cutting edge issues for which people do not have a good answer. You can get direction, and a sense of what track is right and which tracks are wrong, but the answer will be up to you and your team. At the end of the process, your team will be better experts on this narrowly focused area of the law than anyone else who has not handled an actual case with the same issues. That is what actual litigation practice in the real world is like, too.

Appendix

Organization of Legal Writing

This appendix presents the organizational format that will be used for analyzing a legal issue and reporting your conclusions in legal writing. The format discussed herein addresses the discussion of a single issue—it will be duplicated one or more times in each piece of writing to address each individual issue you are analyzing.[1] The format is derived from the rule-based reasoning syllogism[2] and it instructs you to introduce your <u>T</u>hesis on the issue in the form of a heading, provide the <u>R</u>ule or rules that address the issue, <u>E</u>xplain each rule and instruct the reader about how the rules are to be interpreted and applied, <u>A</u>pply the rules to your client's situation, and restate your <u>T</u>hesis as a conclusion. Thus, the format is referred to as **TREAT**.[3]

I. THESIS HEADING

The TREAT method begins when you have done all of the research and analysis of an issue and are ready to report your conclusions. Your discussion of an issue will begin with your position on the issue, called your thesis. The thesis almost always is written in one sentence, and it states what the issue is and how the issue should come out based on your analysis of the issue. In legal writing, you will start off your discussion of the issue by putting your thesis in a heading.

Presenting your thesis on the issue first brings to the front the most important part of the discussion: your answer to the legal question posed by the issue. Your readers will appreciate not having to wait for your answer. Putting your thesis on the issue in a heading that precedes the analysis and discussion of the issue further highlights this critical information for the benefit of the reader. When you consider that most of the writing you will do will discuss a number of issues in the same document, you can begin to understand that separating and highlighting your conclusions by use of thesis headings will help even

---

[1] Recall the definition of an "issue": An individual legal question implicated by a problem (a set of facts) that needs to be answered in order to render advice concerning the problem.

[2] Rule-Based Reasoning Syllogism: The answer is X because the authorities establish the rule that governs this situation, and the rule requires certain facts to be present, and these facts are present, so the application of the rule to the facts produces X result.

[3] TREAT is a refinement of the organizational scheme known as IRAC. <u>See</u> section VI of this appendix.

the busiest reader to pick up the most important parts of your discussion quickly and efficiently.

Consider the situation of a client who owned a Doberman pinscher. Your client's dog encountered a girl as she was selling Girl Scout cookies, and the dog became agitated when the girl swung her bag of cookies at the dog's head. The dog apparently thought the girl was threatening it and it reacted by clamping its jaws onto her arm. Unfortunately, the girl and her mother got into it with the dog, and in the skirmish, the girl received several deep cuts on her arm. For the purposes of this appendix, we will present the law as if you had done the research in Texas.

After completing your research and finding the rule that addresses the issue in Texas, and after analyzing your client's situation under the Texas rule, your conclusion is that your client, the dog owner, will be liable for the injuries inflicted on the woman's arm by the dog. When you write up your analysis, your thesis will be, "The dog owner will be liable for plaintiff's injuries."

When drafting the discussion of an issue, the thesis is stated as the heading of a section, and the paragraph that follows the heading will state the rule, as in the following example:

THESIS HEADING AND RULE SECTION:

1. <u>The dog owner will be liable for plaintiff's dog bite injuries</u>.

In Texas, a dog owner is liable for all injuries caused by his dog unless the dog is provoked by the victim. <u>Smithy v. Jonesy</u>, 123 S.W.2d 345, 347 (Tex. 1965); <u>Johnson v. Anderson</u>, 789 S.W.2d 234, 237 (Tex. App. 1989). The elements of a cause of action for dog-bite liability are therefore: (1) defendant's ownership of the dog, (2) injuries caused by the dog, and (3) lack of provocation of the dog by the plaintiff. <u>See</u> <u>Smithy</u>, 123 S.W.2d at 347.

Many practitioners, judges, or professors would prefer that you repeat or rephrase your thesis as the first sentence of the text in the section. This practice is particularly helpful if your thesis heading was a brief recitation of the points that are covered in the section rather than a more detailed summary of your conclusions. Restating your thesis as the first sentence of the section will benefit those readers who routinely skip reading the headings in a document. For example:

THESIS HEADING AND RULE SECTION:

1. <u>The dog owner will be liable for plaintiff's dog bite injuries</u>.

Defendant Jones, the dog owner, will be liable for all injuries caused to plaintiff by his dog because plaintiff did not provoke the dog. In Texas, a dog owner is liable for all injuries caused by his dog unless the dog is provoked by the victim. <u>Smithy v. Jonesy</u>, 123 S.W.2d 345, 347 (Tex. 1965); <u>Johnson v. Anderson</u>, 789 S.W.2d 234, 237 (Tex. App. 1989). The elements of a cause of action for dog-bite liability are therefore: (1) defendant's ownership of the dog, (2) injuries caused by the dog, and (3) lack of provocation of the dog by the plaintiff. <u>See</u> <u>Smithy</u>, 123 S.W.2d at 347.

II. RULE SECTION

A. Statement of legal principles and requirements that govern the issue

The rule section follows the thesis, and states the rule or rules that govern the legal issue. You will recall that a rule of law is a statement of the legal principles and requirements that govern the analysis of the legal issue at hand. Sometimes there is one rule that is followed by all the authorities in your jurisdiction. However, in other instances there will be authorities that state the rule in a slightly different way, or add a sentence or two describing the rule, or illuminate various nuances of the rule, or that add a new element or factor to the rule. In the previous two chapters, we discussed at length the process of finding and analyzing the authorities that define the rule of law that governs the legal issue at hand. We also discussed the process of synthesizing the various accounts of the rule into one coherent presentation of the rule.

The following chart should refresh your recollection about how to go about putting together the rule from multiple authorities and performing a "rule synthesis."

FORMULATING THE RULE (RULE SYNTHESIS)	
❶ Start with the highest and most recent controlling authority	◆ If you have a statute (or regulation), start with the statute ◆ If you have a watershed case that is controlling, start with that ◆ If your best authority is from the court of last resort, take the most recent opinion from that court, and start with that ◆ If these first three criteria do not apply, start with the most recent actual controlling authority that is on point ◆ Only if none of the above applies would you consider turning to non-controlling authority—primary or secondary ◆ Don't expect to use all of your authorities

❷ Reconcile differing statements or phrasings of the rule from controlling authorities, and attempt to synthesize the material into one coherent statement of the legal principles that govern the issue

◆ DON'T change the wording of or paraphrase rules from statutes, administrative rules and regs, and watershed cases

◆ Unless a processed applied rule can be written smoothly and effectively in one sentence or phrase, write the rule first with modifications second

❸ Write the rule first, interpretative rules second, and exceptions to the rule third

◆ Write interpretive sub-rules on elements of the rule in the section or sub-section of the discussion that discusses that element of the rule. Write exceptions to the sub-rules after you lay out the sub-rules themselves

❹ Do not write a rule with inherent contradictions

◆ Check for ambiguity in the terms you have used to formulate the rule (even if some of these terms came from the authorities)

❺ Do accept the <u>remote</u> possibility that two competing rules on the same issue might exist in the same jurisdiction

◆ When this happens, you may have to analyze the facts under both competing sets of rules

Your findings now have to be reported in the rule section. Occasionally, your rule section might be as small as one paragraph long, but frequently, you will wind up with two or more paragraphs if you have several accounts of the rule or more than one rule to present on the issue. The format of the rule section does not change whether you are talking about an elemental rule (a rule with required elements) or a rule with factors that must be evaluated or balanced.

B. Interpretative rules

The rule section also will present interpretive rules from primary and secondary authorities. Interpretive rules are actual statements from legal authorities that instruct lawyers and judges how to interpret or apply the rule on the issue at hand. They are not elements or factors of the rule, and they are not the same as the principles of interpretation and application that you will derive from a synthesis of the authorities presented in the explanation section, which are discussed in section III below. Instead, these are individual statements phrased in rule language that you will lift from the authorities that have discussed and applied the rule.

For example, in the hypothetical problem we have been working with, a case from your jurisdiction might characterize the rule on the claim for dog bite liability as a "disfavored cause of action," and state that "in order to prove liability for an animal bite, the plaintiff must prove each element of the claim with clear and convincing evidence." A secondary authority, such as a treatise on tort law, might explain that dog bite liability has moved from a point where "every dog was entitled to one unprovoked bite," to a point where "each attack by a dog, even the first, may give rise to a valid claim against the dog owner." These interpretative rules belong in the same section as the actual statement of the rule and its elements or factors, but you should state interpretive rules in one or more paragraphs after you have laid out the elements of the actual rule.

In our example, the rule on liability for dog attacks in Texas was stated the same way with the same three elements in each of the authorities you found in Texas, as quoted in the text box above. Adding interpretive rules for this rule would produce the following rule section:

THESIS HEADING AND RULE SECTION:

1. <u>The dog owner will be liable for plaintiff's dog bite injuries</u>.

In Texas, a dog owner is liable for all injuries caused by his dog unless the dog is provoked by the victim. <u>Smithy v. Jonesy</u>, 123 S.W.2d 345, 347 (Tex. 1965); <u>Johnson v. Anderson</u>, 789 S.W.2d 234, 237 (Tex. App. 1989). The elements of a cause of action for dog-bite liability are therefore: (1) defendant's ownership of the dog, (2) injuries caused by the dog, and (3) lack of provocation of the dog by the plaintiff. <u>See</u> <u>Smithy</u>, 123 S.W.2d at 347. The rule on dog bite liability has moved from a point where "every dog was entitled to one unprovoked bite," to a point where "each attack by a dog, even the first, may give rise to a valid claim against the dog owner." <u>Id.</u> A claim seeking to impose liability for a dog bite is a "disfavored cause of action," and "in order to prove liability, the plaintiff must prove each element of the claim with clear and convincing evidence." <u>Roberts v. Thomas</u>, 676 S.W.2d 34, 37 (Tex. 1979).

III. EXPLANATION SECTION AND EXPLANATORY SYNTHESIS

A. Purpose of the explanation section

In the explanation section, you will use some or all of the legal authorities you have found in your research to explain the rule and to show how the rule operates in various situations. This is the section that employs analogical reasoning. The goal of this section is to teach the reader the principles learned from earlier authorities that tell lawyers how to interpret and apply the rule. You will spell out the legal standards that govern the issue in the rule section. A law-trained reader can review the rules you lay out in the rule section and make an educated guess as to how these rules should work in actual situations, but this only will be a guess. Your job as the author of a piece of legal writing is to confirm or rebut that guess by explaining how the rules work in actual situations, which in most instances will require you to refer to the cases that have applied those rules to produce a real outcome. Consider the following:

THE GOAL OF THE EXPLANATION SECTION

The goal is to illustrate how the rule is to be interpreted and applied based on how the authorities have applied it in actual concrete factual settings, and on how commentators have interpreted the rule

Case-by-case presentations make the reader do most of the work and they are wasteful of space and time (<u>i.e.</u>, the reader's attention span)

◆ You are going beyond what the courts already have said about the rule in interpretive rules found in cases
◆ You are presenting principles of interpretation that are supported by a careful reading of the cases
◆ You are doing the work of digesting and synthesizing the cases so the reader doesn't have to
◆ Avoid case-by-case presentations even though they are easy to write, and sometimes fun to write
◆ Avoid them even though courts use them
◆ The only time to resort to a case-by-case presentation is when you have one or two cases that are so close to the facts that you want to cover them in great detail, or if you want to distinguish one or two troublesome cases in enough detail to make your point

---

The explanation section does not exist simply to provide titillating details from a number of cases to entertain the reader, and it does not exist to fill up the space from the end of your rule or sub-rule section to the beginning of your application section. Details from cases can be exciting, but the facts and details themselves do not teach the reader how the rule actually works. The explanation section exists to present principles of interpretation derived from cases and secondary authorities that will show the reader how a rule or sub-rule works in actual situations.

Lawyers and judges have a number of ways to go about this task. The common **unsynthesized** way used by many if not most lawyers and judges is to write a series of sentences and paragraphs describing the facts and holding of several cases. Typically, the author discusses one case at a time, devoting an entire paragraph to each case. At the end of it, the author hopes the reader has learned something from this list of factual details and holdings. What is learned often is up to the reader, because the typical author fails to continue on and write a paragraph or two summarizing what the cases teach us about how the rule works and drawing connections between cases that otherwise are factually different. In effect, the typical author simply is saying to the reader: "Here are a number of cases where the rule was applied and here is the outcome of those cases. You make sense out of it."

A case-by-case presentation is effective when you want to fully illustrate one or more cases that are exactly on point—they present the same facts and issues as your own case—to show how completely they should control your client's situation. Remember that American courts follow the common law system of precedent and stare decisis, so a prior case from a proper court that presents the exact same facts and issues as your case ought to control the outcome of your case. A detailed discussion of the facts and holdings of these key cases may be necessary and prudent for your analysis.

The second instance where a case-by-case presentation may be necessary is when you need to fully distinguish a potentially controlling authority that goes against your thesis. The process of distinguishing certain authorities may require a detailed discussion of the facts, issues, and holdings of the cases in order to separate them from your case.

In most instances, however, you will not have any positive or negative case that is on all fours with your case. You will have a number of helpful cases to which you can analogize your client's situation, and some that are not helpful, but none that is completely on all points with your case. In these situations, a synthesis of the authorities will aid the reader more than a recitation of one case after another.

In these circumstances, the case-by-case presentation method will fail you because your research does not uncover more than one or two cases on an element or factor of a rule. If you write an unsynthesized explanation section that only discusses one case, the reader will have very little chance of figuring out how the rule works in real life situations. For example, how do you know what "breaking" (an element of burglary) means? Well, you might have found one case in which a defendant broke a window and the court found that this was a breaking. Your explanation of this element might then lead the reader to believe that breaking means breaking a window. This conclusion is logical, but absolutely inaccurate.

B. Explanatory synthesis

THE PROCESS OF EXPLANATORY SYNTHESIS

❶ Read cases and look for common facts and common outcomes

❷ Review the groups to find the factors or public policies that make the difference in the outcome

◆ Group cases by facts
◆ Divide groups of cases by outcome

◆ Reconcile cases that have different outcomes; what policy or theme or factor determined the outcome in these cases
◆ Reconcile cases that have the same outcome on different facts; what common policy or theme or factors brought about the same outcome on different facts

---

---

❸ Write principles of interpretation that explain your findings

◆ Phrase your principles of interpretation in language that mimics interpretive rules
◆ Often you can use interpretive rules as principles that tie together multiple authorities; there is no requirement that you always have to come up with brand new principles

❹ Cite the cases that support your principles of interpretation with parentheticals that provide facts or other information about each case

◆ Parentheticals should contain enough information to illustrate how the individual case supports the general principle you have laid out
◆ Use shorthands and abbreviated phrases to save space

❺ When you draft the Application section, apply the principles of interpretation to your own facts; as a general rule, do not apply individual cases to your facts

◆ Applying principles to facts will make your analysis more convincing; you have spelled out the connections to be made between the authorities and then followed through and showed how the principles learned from a study of the authorities determines the outcome of the case at hand
◆ The exception to this rule is when you have one or two fabulous cases that are worthy of individual attention in the Explanation section; these should be discussed individually in the Application section, whether as support or to distinguish them

---

Explanatory synthesis takes the relevant authorities (those that have applied the rule in actual situations) and derives from them one or more principles of interpretation and application of the rule. These principles are derived from common factual elements, policies, or themes found in the cases and other authorities that are relevant to the interpretation of the rule. In its simplest form, explanatory synthesis requires you to try to identify a common element of earlier cases that is compared to the facts of your case to make the point that your case should enjoy the same outcome because your case shares this common element with the others, or that your case should have a different outcome, because it does not share this common element and thus is distinguishable.

For example, if all the prior dog bite cases in your jurisdiction in which the plaintiffs failed to recover involved adult victims who provoked the dog by striking it, and you have a client who is a dog injury victim but is a small child who accidentally fell against a dog, you could synthesize the earlier cases where plaintiffs did not prevail as "adult provoker" cases, and distinguish your own case because it involves a child who accidentally made contact with the dog, and a child should not be held to the same standard of care as an adult. This principle must be supported by the holdings of the cases, or by appropriate use of dicta from the cases. If the cases themselves anticipate the possibility that the provoker might be a small child who acts inadvertently and unintentionally, and the cases state that this would not have any bearing on the outcome, then your synthesis is unsupported by the authorities and you cannot assert it.

Optimally, however, you should strive to identify a policy or theme that underlies the earlier authorities and that resonates with and defines the applicable rule and the particular area of law in which the rule is found.

> A principle of interpretation that is derived from the central meaning, common ground, public policy, or theme behind a group of earlier cases where the rule was applied is probative of how the rule properly is to be interpreted and applied in cases in the present and future, such as your own. Furthermore, when you apply this principle to the facts of your client's case in the application section, the results will be more reliable than if you simply were to compare one earlier case at a time to the facts of the client's case.

> For example, if all the dog injury cases in your jurisdiction can be tied together with the theme that "the law provides a remedy for injuries suffered when the victim is acting peaceably and the dog is not," then use this as your explanation of the rule, followed by indicative reference to examples of how this theme is played out in the earlier authorities. This technique tells the reader how the rule has worked in your jurisdiction in the past, and how it should work again in the future. This is much more useful to the reader than simply writing a paragraph on each case, and concluding each paragraph with, "Once again, plaintiff recovered because the victim was acting peaceably, and the dog was not."

It is this kind of digested analysis of the cases that is missing from the average lawyer's explanation section, yet this is what is important to an understanding of how the rule works. Secondary authorities may state principles of interpretation and application directly—the authors of treatises, hornbooks, restatements, and law reviews go to great lengths to digest and make sense of the law for the reader—but judicial opinions often do not. The factual details and holdings from a group of individual cases do not in and of themselves define the category of situations that will satisfy the standards of the rule or a particular element or factor of the rule and what categories of situations will not. The factual details of cases often are exciting to write about, but your readers would just as soon have you cut to the chase and tell them the reasons why certain kinds of cases have satisfied the rule in the past and will again in the future, while others did not and will not.

The goal of the explanation section is to explain how the law works in several relevant indicative situations without making it appear that each case you discuss is a law unto itself. A line of precedents should not look like an obstacle course to get through before victory can be won. The cases to use in the explanation section are those that are most indicative of how the courts have applied the rule to facts that are relevant to the case at hand. The questions to ask yourself when drafting this section are, "Does this case add something new to my explanation of the rule?" and "Will my explanation be weaker if the reader does not know about this case?" If the answer to both questions is "no," leave the case out. Later chapters in this book will help you make the determination of which are the most important cases to discuss.

Where the individual facts of the authorities you are using are important, parentheticals can be used to guide the reader through some of the particulars of the facts, and you may be able to make use of the "<u>compare</u> . . . <u>and</u> . . . <u>with</u> . . . <u>and</u>" format of citation to make the kind of connections you need to make to further reinforce how the rule or sub-rule works in various situations. When you explain how the rule works in the various situations represented by your cases, you should bring out the facts and circumstances that make the **positive cases** (the cases where the result is the same as what you predict your client's result will be in your thesis) sound more like your client's case than the **negative cases** (the cases where the result goes the other way from what you predict in your thesis). This technique is called analogizing to the good cases and distinguishing the bad cases. Synthesis aids this process because you can link together a number of positive authorities that stand for a proposition that supports your thesis, and you also can link together a number of negative authorities that do not support your thesis and show a common reason (facts, law, or policy) why each of them should not control the outcome of the instant case. If you do a good job of it, the reader is more likely to agree with your thesis.

C. Comparing unsynthesized and synthesized explanation sections

You might already know what *unsynthesized* explanation sections look like, because you can find them in many of the legal opinions you are reading in the case books for your other courses. An unsynthesized explanation section takes the reader on a historical walking tour of the cases that have interpreted the rule. We will attempt to show the difference between an unsynthesized explanation section and a synthesized section in the following examples.

Example 1:

An element of adverse possession is "exclusive possession" of the disputed land. The following cases explain how this element has been interpreted in Tennessee:

UNSYNTHESIZED EXPLANATION

In <u>Flowers</u>, the claimant cleared a road and cut down trees and used the land for his own purposes for ten years. He even built a fence, but the neighbors who owned the land pulled down the fence. The court held that the possession was exclusive anyway because the neighbors did not move back onto the land to use it after taking down the fence. <u>Flowers</u>, 979 S.W.2d at 470.

In <u>Conaway</u>, the claimant had no fence. He used the disputed land to build a shed and a horseshoe pit, and he put a little fountain on the land. He cut the grass and maintained the land and the improvement he had put on the land. His neighbor, who actually owned the land, came over and pitched horseshoes from time to time, and may have cut the grass once or twice in ten years, but these visits were sporadic. The claimant was the only one to make use of the land for ten years. The court held this to be exclusive. <u>Conaway</u>, 972 S.W.2d at 445.

In <u>Witt</u>, the claimant had a fence around the disputed land. Although the true owner of the land testified that he thought he could use the disputed land any time he wanted, the evidence revealed that the claimant was the only person who used the land. <u>Witt</u>, 845 S.W.2d at 667. Therefore, the claimant proved that his possession was "exclusive." <u>Id</u>.

This is how you could explain how this element has been interpreted and applied using a **synthesized** explanation section:

SYNTHESIZED EXPLANATION

Exclusive possession in Tennessee refers to the claimant being the exclusive user of the land rather than to the actions of the claimant in excluding people from coming on the land. <u>See</u> <u>Flowers</u>, 979 S.W.2d at 470 (claimants were the only ones to use the land for the ten year period); <u>Witt</u>, 845 S.W.2d at 667 (same); <u>Conaway</u>, 972 S.W.2d at 445 (claimants were the principal users of the land, because the true owner only made sporadic visits). Exclusive is used as an adjective to mean that the claimant is the only user, rather than as a verb meaning to exclude. <u>See generally</u> <u>Flowers</u>, 979 S.W.2d at 470; <u>Witt</u>, 845 S.W.2d at 667; <u>Conaway</u>, 972 S.W.2d at 445. Actions that might exclude others, such as fence building, do not determine whether a possession is exclusive. <u>Compare</u> <u>Witt</u>, 845 S.W.2d at 667 (claimant had a fence), <u>with</u> <u>Conaway</u>, 972 S.W.2d at 445 (claimant had no fence), <u>and</u> <u>Flowers</u>, 979 S.W.2d at 470 (claimant built a fence, but the owners tore it down). Total exclusion is not necessary, because the true owner can make sporadic visits to the land and still not defeat claimant's adverse possession claim. <u>See</u> <u>Conaway</u>, 972 S.W.2d at 445 (sporadic visits by the true owner to play horseshoes and cut the grass did not defeat the exclusive possession of claimant); <u>Flowers</u>, 979 S.W.2d at 470 (the owners' tearing down of claimant's fence did not defeat exclusive possession because the true owners still did not take over the parcel for their own use).

The difference between the two methods is that in the unsynthesized explanation section, the reader learns a lot of interesting details from the cases, but never hears about the underlying principles of interpretation of this element of the adverse possession rule that would help the law-trained reader apply this element to all future situations. The focus of the unsynthesized explanation section is on the cases, not on the principles or themes of interpretation that the cases support. A devoted law-trained reader may be able to ponder your history of the cases, and draw her own conclusions about the categories of situations that will satisfy the rule, and those that will not, but most readers would prefer you to take the time to think this through and present a complete analysis of how this element of the rule works.

The synthesized explanation section focuses on the principles of interpretation and application that can be discerned from the cases. This section resembles a small scale treatise on this particular element of the adverse possession rule. Factual details are presented when they are necessary to draw connections between cases and to distinguish positive cases from negative cases. A law-trained reader that reads this section will not have to wonder about the categories of situations that satisfy this element of the rule.

Example 2:

In Connecticut, the elements of money had and received are: (1) Receipt of money; (2) by mistake; (3) under circumstances that render the retention of the money unjust. The following cases explain the third element—whether retention of the money was unjust:

UNSYNTHESIZED EXPLANATION

In First Federal Bank, 678 N.E.2d at 237, defendant Stevens received an unexpected wire transfer from the plaintiff Bank. The court granted summary judgment to defendant Stevens allowing him to retain the funds because Stevens was entitled to the mistakenly transferred sum as an offset of a judgment Stevens had obtained against the Bank in an earlier lawsuit. The court held that the prior debt gave just cause for defendant to retain the funds. Id.

In ATI, 778 N.E.2d at 44-45, defendant Adam's had a potential claim against ATI, but no action had been filed and no judgment entered. Through a fortuitous mistake, Adam's received a wire transfer from ATI that was intended for Adam's replacement on a construction project. ATI immediately informed Adam's of the mistake, but Adam's refused to relinquish the funds. The court held that there was no justification for Adam's retention of the funds. Id.

Blue Cross, 688 N.E.2d at 566-68, shows the effect of time and laches on the unjust enrichment evaluation. Defendant Carson was a regular beneficiary of payments from Blue Cross for medical expenses. The case arose from a mistaken quarterly payment by Blue Cross of three *years* of benefits to Carson instead of three months. Blue Cross did not notice the mistake until a year later; by then, Carson had spent the money on his medical care and nursing home expenses. The court refused to order Carson to reimburse Blue Cross, because Carson had a valid expectation of indefinite quarterly payments from Blue Cross, and had changed his position drastically in reliance on his good faith belief that he was entitled to whatever payments he received from Blue Cross, no matter if they may have been larger or smaller than the average quarterly payment.

A **synthesized** approach to this explanation section would look like the following:

SYNTHESIZED EXPLANATION

Connecticut case law has demonstrated the importance of a present obligation from the transferor to the transferee in determining whether the transferee's retention of the funds is unjust. <u>See</u> <u>First Federal Bank</u>, 678 N.E.2d at 237 (finding no unjust enrichment because bank was under present obligation to pay transferree monetary award from earlier judgment); <u>ATI</u>, 778 N.E.2d at 44-45 (finding unjust enrichment where transferree had only a potential claim against transferor and transferor thus lacked actual, present oblication); <u>Blue Cross</u>, 688 N.E.2d at 566-68 (finding no unjust enrichment in situation interpreted to constitute present obligation). If there is an outstanding debt that is due between the transferor and the transferee, the fact that the transferor did not intend to pay the debt at the time of the transfer does not prevent the transferee from justly retaining the funds it fortuitously received. <u>See</u> <u>First Federal Bank</u>, 678 N.E.2d at 237 (permitting transferree to retain mistakenly transferred funds where separate court action already obligated bank to pay monetary award to transferree); <u>ATI</u>, 778 N.E.2d at 44-45 (finding transferree's retention of mistakenly transferred funds unjust because transferor had no actual obligation to transferree). Even if the funds were not all due at the time of transfer, the expectation of receipt of funds through an existing account or payment scheme can render the retention just. <u>See</u> <u>Blue Cross</u>, 688 N.E.2d at 566-67 (transferor's laches and transferree's good faith reliance that amount of transferred funds was accurate buttressed finding of no unjust enrichment).

As in example 1 above, the unsynthesized explanation section focuses on the cases themselves while the synthesized explanation section focuses on the principles of interpretation and application that can be derived from the cases. Note well that many of the individual facts from the cases are left out of the synthesized explanation section. Facts such as the horseshoe pit and shed in one adverse possession case and the wire transfers in two of the money had and received cases are only relevant if they tell the reader something about how the rule properly is applied and how the facts affected the outcome produced by the application. Since these facts did not affect the application of the rule and the outcome of this application, these facts were left out of the synthesized account. The facts about fences in the three adverse possession cases and the facts about debts and current obligations in the three money had and received cases were relevant to an understanding of how the rule works, so these facts were included in parentheticals in the synthesized version.

A synthesized method is shorter in terms of using up fewer pages out of your page limit than the unsynthesized method. But this result only is one reason to use explanatory synthesis, not the best reason. It is not just a time and space-saving device; it makes the reader's comprehension of the situation clearer and your analysis and conclusions stronger.

Explanatory synthesis also has a positive effect on the application section, discussed in section IV below. If the facts and policies of the cases are synthesized in this way, it makes it easier to compare the client's situation to the category of prior situations that satisfy the rule that are defined by the authorities. You will not write an application section that says, "As in <u>Flowers</u>, our claimant had a partial fence . . . Unlike in <u>Witt</u>, the fence did not go all the way around the disputed parcel . . .," which make it seem like the cases are the rule, rather than the cases standing as individual examples of situations where the rule was applied to produce a certain outcome. Your application section instead might state that, "Claimant and her predecessor in interest were the only persons to use the disputed parcel for fourteen years. Therefore, they will satisfy the exclusive possession requirement." Using the above example on money had and received, it would be simple to write an application section that states, "In our case, there was no outstanding debt or payment scheme to justify the defendant's retention of the funds," and thus to apply the rule to the client's facts in a short, straightforward manner.

D. Use of secondary authorities

The explanation section also may include discussion of secondary authorities—scholarly works that interpret or explain the law. These authorities cannot control the outcome of your case, but they can be used to help persuade the reader that you are on the right track with your thesis. Secondary authorities can be used as support for a principle that you are deriving from the cases in your jurisdiction. If you are joined by one or more scholars in drawing the conclusion that there is a relevant underlying theme that ties together most if not all of the prior cases, then reference to the work of these scholars will make your explanation section more persuasive than if you were to write your own personal thoughts on the same topic and present these thoughts by themselves.

An example of the use of secondary sources to explain a rule is shown in the following paragraph:

> The underlying public policy behind the Texas rule is that persons "attacked by a domesticated animal when the person is acting peaceably and not directly threatening the animal" shall recover from the owner of the animals. See Chester A. Arthur, Texas Animal Laws 234 (1953). Although Professor Arthur was referring to the Roaming Livestock Damage Act, Tex. Agric. Code Ann. § 222.1234 (Vernon 1944), there is no practical difference between livestock that are roaming loose on the property and domestic animals, such as dogs, that are encountered on the property. See Arthur, supra, at 235. The law provides a remedy for injuries suffered when "the victim is acting peaceably and the dog is not." Mary M. McDermott, When a Best Friend Bites: Dog Bite Liability in Texas, 45 Tex. L. Rev. 122-23 (1979).

This paragraph discusses the policies at work in the situation that mitigate in favor of your thesis. We made a point of using secondary authorities that discuss these policies rather than just spinning them out of our own mind and recollection. It is important to support every statement about the law by referring to authority, even if you are talking about public policy.

Given the priority of primary controlling authority in legal analysis, in legal writing, you should discuss the cases from the applicable jurisdiction in your explanation section before you present secondary authorities that further support the principles of interpretation you have derived from these cases. The secondary authorities should be used to buttress the principles found in the controlling case law, not to supersede them.

E. Explanation of rules not found in cases

We have been focusing on rules that were found in cases, but you also will be writing about legal rules that come from constitutions, statutes, and administrative rules and regulations. The same process applies, because to explain the rule that is found in a constitution or statute or regulation, you still will use cases as examples of specific situations where that rule was applied and secondary authorities that explain how the rule should be interpreted. If the statute or regulation is fairly new and there are no reported cases where that statute or regulation was applied and no secondary sources explaining the rule, you will use the principles of statutory interpretation and your own powers of legal rhetoric.

Consider the following two examples dealing with the fictional 1999 Nevada Pit Bull Control Law and its effect on your client's case. Assume that your client does own a pit bull terrier, but this dog was not the dog that caused the injury to the woman (you will recall that client's Doberman pinscher was involved in the incident). The statute provides in pertinent part:

Pit bull terriers pose a significantly greater risk of danger to the public than other dogs. . . . There is no way to insure the safety of persons coming into contact with a pit bull whether or not the person provokes the dog. Therefore, an owner of a pit bull shall be strictly liable for all personal injuries caused to humans by his dog(s) regardless of whether the victim provoked the dog(s) or not.

In the absence of interpretive authorities, you might write a rule, explanation, and application section that would look like something like this:

Rule, explanation and application sections when there are no authorities interpreting the statute	In 1999, the Nevada Legislature passed the Pit Bull Control Law, Nev. Rev. Stat. § 222.5678 (1999), which provides in pertinent part that: Pit bull terriers pose a significantly greater risk of danger to the public than other dogs. . . . There is no way to insure the safety of persons coming into contact with a pit bull whether or not the person provokes the dog. Therefore, an owner of a pit bull shall be strictly liable for all personal injuries caused to humans by his dog(s) regardless of whether the victim provoked the dog(s) or not. No case or commentator has interpreted this section, and nothing in the legislative history sheds light on the meaning of this section of the statute. Although on its face, this section contains an ambiguity as to whether the owner of a pit bull is strictly liable for injuries caused by any of his dogs, pit bulls or others,

> the statute otherwise is clear that the purpose of the provision is to protect the public from the special dangers presented by pit bulls. It defies the internal consistency of the statute to assert that the provision imposes strict liability on a dog owner simply because he owns a pit bull who had nothing to do with the injuries inflicted in the case at hand. Because plaintiff was injured by defendant's Doberman, not his pit bull, this statute will have no effect on this case and will not cause defendant to be strictly liable for plaintiff's injuries.

If there are authorities that have addressed the interpretation and application of the statute in ways that are relevant to your analysis, you would discuss these authorities in the following manner:

Rule, explanation and application sections when there are authorities interpreting the statute	In 1999, the Nevada Legislature passed the Pit Bull Control Law, Nev. Rev. Stat. § 222.5678 (1999), which provides in pertinent part that:

> Pit bull terriers pose a significantly greater risk of danger to the public than other dogs. . . . There is no way to insure the safety of persons coming into contact with a pit bull whether or not the person provokes the dog. Therefore, an owner of a pit bull shall be strictly liable for all personal injuries caused to humans by his dog(s) regardless of whether the victim provoked the dog(s) or not.

Although on its face, the statute contains an ambiguity as to whether the owner of a pit bull is strictly liable for injuries caused by any of his dogs, pit bulls or others, the statute has been limited to attacks by pit bulls on humans. <u>Chuy v. Taylor</u>, 887 P.2d 246, 248 (Nev. 2000). A dog owner will not be strictly liable for an attack by one of his other dogs, a non-pit bull, simply because he owns a pit bull who had nothing to do with the injuries inflicted in the case at hand. <u>See id.</u>; Carlos R. Rivera, <u>Current Developments in Nevada Law</u>, 66 UNLV L. Rev. 322-23 (2000). Therefore, this statute will have no effect on this case and will not cause defendant to be strictly liable for plaintiff's injuries.

IV. APPLICATION SECTION

Application is the section where you apply the rule to your client's facts and show how the rule will work in your client's situation. If you are writing an informative objective work such as an office memorandum, you will explain how you think the client will fare based on your analysis of the law. If you are writing a partisan advocate's brief, you will use this section to argue exactly why your client wins when the law is applied to the facts.

In the application section, you must make the connection between your client's situation and the situations in the authorities you are relying on in support of your thesis. This section presents the second half of the analogical reasoning process that you began in the explanation section. The application section continues the practice of distinguishing bad cases from good cases so as to drive home your thesis. You must show that the negative authorities you discussed in the explanation section are different from your client's situation. If you relied on policy arguments, you must show how the client's situation furthers the policies you discussed in support of your thesis.

A typical, *unsynthesized* explanation section will produce an application section that looks like this:

APPLICATION SECTION FOLLOWING AN *UNSYNTHESIZED* EXPLANATION SECTION

In the instant case, there is no dispute that the defendant's dog attacked and caused injury to plaintiff, his neighbor, when she walked out of her apartment and bumped into the dog with her shopping bag. Thus, the first two elements of this cause of action are established. In reference to the third element, lack of provocation, plaintiff did nothing to present a serious threat to the dog, let alone strike the dog, in contrast to the plaintiff in <u>Smithy</u>. Plaintiff may have swung her shopping bag near the dog in a careless manner, but this is a far cry from the beating that the <u>Smithy</u> dog received before it attacked the victim in that case. Like the plaintiff in <u>Johnson</u>, the Scout was using a public hallway that led to the front door of the apartment building. According to <u>Johnson</u>, walking in a hallway is not a provocative action, and it certainly is no more provocative than mistakenly opening the wrong door of an apartment where the dog is found, as was the case in <u>Russell</u>.

Although the postman in <u>Johnson</u> was acting in the ordinary course of his daily employment duties, and plaintiff here was doing something outside of her ordinary employment activities, this should not be viewed as a legally significant difference precluding plaintiff from recovery. Recovery by plaintiff furthers the policy of allowing recovery where the victim was acting peaceably and the dog was not.

If you used explanatory synthesis to combine authorities in the explanation section, the application section will apply the principles of interpretation derived from the common facts or common theme of the earlier cases, rather than simply comparing the facts of the instant case first to one earlier case, then the next, then the next, and so on. You will explain how the common underlying theme is furthered by your interpretation of how the rule will apply in your case, or you will distinguish the earlier cases because of their common facts or policies that are not present in the instant case. Consider the following modified application section that follows a *synthesized* explanation section:

APPLICATION SECTION FOLLOWING A *SYNTHESIZED* EXPLANATION SECTION

In the instant case, there is no dispute that defendant's dog attacked and caused injury to plaintiff, his neighbor, when she walked out of her apartment and bumped into the dog with her shopping bag. Thus, the first two elements of this cause of action are established.

In reference to the third element, lack of provocation, the underlying theme of the Texas cases is that a plaintiff who is peaceably going about her business and is attacked by an aggressive dog will recover, while a plaintiff who picked a fight with the dog and caused injury to the dog first will not recover. Plaintiff did not pick a fight with defendant's dog. She did nothing to present a serious threat to the dog, let alone intentionally strike the dog. Plaintiff may have been careless in swinging her shopping bag near the dog, but that is a far cry from beating the dog. Recovery by the plaintiff furthers the policy of allowing recovery where the victim was acting peaceably and the dog was not.

This explanatory synthesis and application of synthesized principles only works if it is fair to link all of the prior cases together under the theme of "a plaintiff recovers when the plaintiff was acting peaceably and the dog was not." You cannot invent a common theme that is not present in the earlier cases, nor can you assume common facts that are not discussed in the cases. However, if you can discern a common set of facts and theme or policy that is important to the understanding of how the rule should work, it is helpful to your reader to point this out.

V. THESIS RESTATED AS A CONCLUSION

You should finish your discussion of an issue by restating your thesis as a conclusion. This is not the most critical part of the discussion, but we find that it makes a difference to the reader of legal writing to have that one sentence at the end that brings closure to the discussion.

The conclusion you make can be one sentence, and it can come at the end of the last paragraph of your application section. As an example, the thesis as conclusion line of the example we have been working with might be:

> Therefore, defendant will be required to compensate plaintiff for her injuries in this case.

We do not intend to imply that the thesis restated as conclusion has to be a throwaway. It often is a single sentence, simply there to say this section is completed. But you can spend more time with a conclusion and use it to advance your argument one more step, or to make a smooth transition to the next topic. You only are limited by your own creativity.

VI. OTHER STRUCTURAL FORMATS

You may encounter in your studies a legal writing method of organization know as IRAC, pronounced "eye-rack," which stands for <u>I</u>ssue - <u>R</u>ule - <u>A</u>pplication - <u>C</u>onclusion.

IRAC terminology		TREAT terminology	
<u>I</u>ssue	Identifies the issue for the reader	<u>T</u>hesis	Identifies the issue for the reader and states your conclusion on the issue
<u>R</u>ule	States the legal principles that govern the issue	<u>R</u>ule	States the legal principles that govern the issue
	A good IRAC writer also will explain and illustrate how the rule works in actual situations	<u>E</u>xplanation	Explains and illustrates how the rule works in actual situations
<u>A</u>pplication	Applies the rule to the facts of the case at hand	<u>A</u>pplication	Applies the rule to the facts of the case at hand
<u>C</u>onclusion	States your conclusion on the issue	<u>T</u>hesis restated as conclusion	Restates your conclusion on the issue

IRAC is taught in many legal writing courses, and there is nothing inherently wrong with the method as long as you are clear that the "Issue" item should state your position on the issue, which we call your thesis, and the "Rule" item should not only state the rules but explain them, and provide principles of how the rules should work in various situations based on a synthesis of earlier authorities. Some legal writing authors change the IRAC designation to IREAC for this reason.[4] If you do all of the above using IRAC or IREAC, you are essentially doing the same thing as we are telling you to do in the TREAT

---

[4] Another version of this format is <u>CRAC</u>, pronounced "see-rack" not "crack," which stands for <u>C</u>onclusion - <u>R</u>ule - <u>A</u>pplication - <u>C</u>onclusion. <u>See</u> Alan L. Dworsky, <u>The Little Book of Legal Writing</u> 105 (1992). This is even closer to the TREAT structure, because the <u>C</u>onclusion stated up front is supposed to be your thesis on the legal issue at hand. However, like IRAC, the CRAC form needs to be expanded so that it is clear that the concepts of explanation of the rule and how it works in various situations are part of your discussion.

format. We simply believe it is easier to remember to do all those things if they have their own reference letters.

VII. IDENTIFYING MULTIPLE ISSUES

We have been discussing the treatment of an individual issue within your client's case. The dog bite example with which we have been working boils down to one issue—whether the plaintiff provoked the dog. We mentioned in the application section the other two elements, but only so far as to point out that they are not in dispute, so there is no need to have a separate discussion of each element. We did not ignore them, because you must include in your writing some discussion of each required element or factor of the rule that applies to the case. But a single sentence is all the treatment these elements required.

In real life, this is an unusual position in which to be. More often than not, you will have more than one issue to write about. In the real world, a "client" (as defined earlier in this book to include the person or entity you are working for, which may include your more senior colleagues in the same law office) will come into your office with a problem, and you will have to identify what issues are implicated by the facts of the situation the client is in. Each problem that reaches your desk probably will raise more than one issue, and each issue will have at least one rule that applies to it. Each rule that applies can and often will have multiple elements or factors, each of which can present additional issues. An element or factor of a rule can have a sub-rule that has elements or factors, some of which will require separate treatment. It can get fairly complicated, but the TREAT format is flexible enough to accommodate that much complexity.

In order to determine the number of issues you have to treat, consider:

A. What are the separate legal questions you have to answer?

Most problems your client will bring to you will present more than one legal question to answer. If the client literally asks two questions, or one question that will involve the discussion of two unrelated legal issues—such as what separate causes of action might the plaintiff bring against the client based on the facts—then each question presents a major issue in your discussion. In an outline, the answers (theses) to these questions will appear as the major headings because you will state a thesis concerning each major issue as the heading of the discussion on that issue.

In the single issue discussion above, the major issue was, "Is the dog owner liable for plaintiff's injuries?" which was translated into the thesis heading, "The dog owner will be liable for plaintiff's dog bite injuries." If there were two or more possible claims that the plaintiff might bring against your client, your writing would have two or more major issues and major theses on these issues. For example, Roman I might be, "The dog owner will be liable to plaintiff under common law dog bite liability standards," Roman II might be, "The dog owner will be liable to plaintiff under a theory of negligence," and Roman III might be, "The dog owner will not be strictly liable to plaintiff under the Nevada Pit Bull Control Law." Each major issue must be handled in a separate TREAT discussion.

B. Which elements or factors of the rules and sub-rules of the rules are at issue?

A separate TREAT discussion is required to address each separate legal question, meaning each part of the problem that is in dispute and thus "at issue." If the rule that governs the issue at hand has one basic requirement, and thus one element, it may be handled in a single discussion of Thesis, Rule, Explanation, Application and Thesis as conclusion. If the rule has multiple elements or factors, but only one is in dispute, you also may discuss the entire rule in one TREAT discussion, as in our dog bite example above, where provocation was the only element of the rule that was in dispute. But if the rule itself presents multiple legal questions to answer, it will require more than one TREAT discussion. If the separate questions that must be answered are all based on elements or sub-parts of a single rule, we will refer to the treatments of those questions as sub-TREATs.

For example, if there was a serious question whether or not the defendant "owned" this Doberman pinscher within the meaning of the law—maybe it was a stray, and the defendant had just been feeding it each day out of the kindness of his heart—you would have a separate issue that would have to be answered in a separate sub-TREAT discussion, which would then be followed by the sub-TREAT discussion that addresses the issue of whether the plaintiff provoked the dog or not.

We emphasize that you must cover every element or factor of a rule in your discussion, but if the element or factor is established without question in your case because you are told that by the person assigning the project or because your opponent specifically admits it, the discussion of that element or factor does not require a full-blown TREAT format. A thesis or sub-thesis heading and one sentence can convey the required information:

---

1. Defendant is the owner of the dog.

Defendant concedes that he is the owner of the dog that injured the plaintiff on August 12, 2005.

When multiple elements of a rule are in dispute and present a separate issue for sub-treatment, you should research cases and other authorities discussing that one element and show how that element works in various situations. That is how a sub-TREAT discussion is developed. In addition, a single element of a rule can present multiple issues for discussion, because the element may have a sub-rule that explains what that element means and how that element is to be applied, and the sub-rule itself may have multiple elements, each of which might be in dispute and require an answer. Since the questions suggested by the elements or sub-parts of a sub-rule are all based on the same sub-rule, we will refer to the treatments of these questions as sub-sub-TREATs. The same process occurs with a multi-factor rule that has at least one factor that has multiple sub-parts all of which raise separate issues to address.

VIII. STRUCTURING THE DISCUSSION OF MULTIPLE ISSUES

If you have multiple elements or factors at issue and sub-rules that present multiple issues to answer, you must organize your writing so that each part of the major rule or sub-rule is discussed in the TREAT format. In the case of a rule with multiple elements, a sub-TREAT on a single element will contain your <u>T</u>hesis on how that element will work in your client's case, any sub-<u>R</u>ule of law concerning that element, an <u>E</u>xplanation of what that element means and how that element works in various situations, an <u>A</u>pplication of that element or the rule concerning that element to your client's situation, and your <u>T</u>hesis on that element restated as a conclusion.

Consider the following chart: if the rule on your major issue has multiple elements, and there is a sub-rule on each element of the rule on the major issue, and a sub-sub-rule on each element of the sub-rules on each element of the rule on the major issue, and all of these elements of the rule, sub-rules, and sub-sub-rules are in dispute and thus require discussion, you must layer your TREAT format to cover all the issues. The outline of the discussion of this major issue would take the following form:

I. THESIS on the Major Issue
  RULE on the Major Issue has two elements: A, B

  A. SUB-THESIS on Element A of the rule on the Major Issue
      SUB-RULE on Element A has two elements: 1, 2

      1. SUB-SUB-THESIS on Element 1 of the sub-rule on Element A
          SUB-SUB-RULE on Element 1 of the sub-rule on Element A
          EXPLANATION of sub-sub-rule on Element 1 of the sub-rule on Element A
          APPLICATION of sub-sub-rule on Element 1 of the sub-rule on Element A
          THESIS RESTATED as Conclusion on Element 1 of the sub-rule on Element A

      2. SUB-SUB-THESIS on Element 2 of the sub-rule on Element A
          SUB-SUB-RULE on Element 2 of the sub-rule on Element A
          EXPLANATION of sub-sub-rule on Element 2 of the sub-rule on Element A
          APPLICATION of sub-sub-rule on Element 2 of the sub-rule on Element A
          THESIS RESTATED as Conclusion on Element 2 of the sub-rule on Element A

      APPLICATION of the sub-rule on Element A
      THESIS RESTATED as Conclusion on Element A

  B. SUB-THESIS on Element B of the rule on the Major Issue
      SUB-RULE on Element B: Elements 1, 2, 3

      1. SUB-SUB-THESIS on Element 1 of the sub-rule on Element B
          SUB-SUB-RULE on Element 1 of the sub-rule on Element B
          EXPLANATION of sub-sub-rule on Element 1 of the sub-rule on Element B

        APPLICATION of sub-sub-rule on Element 1 of the sub-rule on Element B
        THESIS RESTATED as Conclusion on Element 1 of the sub-rule on Element B

  2. SUB-SUB-THESIS on Element 2 of the sub-rule on Element B
      SUB-SUB-RULE on Element 2 of the sub-rule on Element B
      EXPLANATION of sub-sub-rule on Element 2 of the sub-rule on Element B
      APPLICATION of sub-sub-rule on Element 2 of the sub-rule on Element B
      THESIS RESTATED as Conclusion on Element 2 of the sub-rule on Element B

  3. SUB-SUB-THESIS on Element 3 of the sub-rule on Element B
      SUB-SUB-RULE on Element 3 of the sub-rule on Element B
      EXPLANATION of sub-sub-rule on Element 3 of the sub-rule on Element B
      APPLICATION of sub-sub-rule on Element 3 of the sub-rule on Element B
      THESIS RESTATED as Conclusion on Element 3 of the sub-rule on Element B

    APPLICATION of the sub-rule on Element B
    THESIS restated as Conclusion on Element B

APPLICATION of the rule on the Major Issue
THESIS restated as Conclusion on the Major Issue

You will note that when a rule presents multiple issues, the sub-treatment of those issues takes the place of the explanation section of the rule. The same goes for a sub-sub-treatment of a sub-rule on an element of a major rule. You write the sub-sub-treatment as the explanation of the sub-rule and return to the sub-rule's treatment in the application section.

INDEX

References are to pages

---

†